Narra

235-302

MW01029912

7-73

74-149

150 -188

189-234

Narrative of the Incas

by

JUAN DE BETANZOS

Translated and edited by

Roland Hamilton and Dana Buchanan

from the Palma de Mallorca manuscript

UNIVERSITY OF TEXAS PRESS

Austin

LIBRARY OF CONGRESS CATALOGING-IN-PUBLICATION DATA

Betanzos, Juan de, d.1576.
  [Suma y narración de los incas. English]
  Narrative of the Incas / by Juan de Betanzos ; translated and edited by Roland Hamilton and Dana Buchanan from the Palma de Mallorca manuscript.
    p.   cm.
  Includes bibliographical references and index.
  ISBN 0-292-75560-0 (cloth). — ISBN 0-292-75559-7 (paper)
    1. Incas—History.   2. Peru—History—Conquest, 1532–1548.   3. Indians of South America—Andes Region—History.   I. Hamilton, Roland, 1936– .
II. Buchanan, Dana, 1939– .   III. Title.
F3429.B5413   1996
985'.02—dc20
                                         95-42695

CONTENTS

PART TWO

MAPS

FIGURES

The following illustrations were taken from the chronicle of Felipe Guaman Poma de Ayala, Nueva coronica y buen gobierno.

INTRODUCTION
Juan de Betanzos and Inca Traditions

Juan de Betanzos was born in Spain but spent his adult life in the Viceroyalty of Peru. By far the most important source of information about him comes from his only remaining work, originally entitled *Suma y narración de los Yngas . . .* , which has been abbreviated in English translation. In 1557 Juan de Betanzos finished his *Narrative of the Incas*,[1] the single most authentic document of its kind. He drew on testimony of descendants of the Inca kings who still remembered the oral history and traditions of their ancestors. The colloquial style of his *Narrative* suggests that Betanzos had no more than a secondary school education. At the time, all university students had to learn Latin, but no trace of Latin can be found in his sentence construction, nor are there references to classical scholars, as in the works of educated writers like Bernabe Cobo.[2] Betanzos reads more like the loose style of the soldier Pedro Pizarro,[3] who only had a primary school education. However, as Betanzos explains in his introductory letter, his style was affected by the fact that he was translating his material, and he tried to do as literal a translation from his informants' Quechua as possible.

Juan de Betanzos became the most respected Quechua interpreter of the Viceroyalty of Peru. It took him several years to learn the Quechua language with no dictionaries, grammars, or textbooks. In his prologue, which is a letter to Viceroy Antonio de Mendoza written in 1551, Betanzos explains that he spent six years of his "*mocedad*," or youth, on a commission preparing a Spanish-Quechua *Doctrina christiana*, a manual for priests that included the essentials of Christian beliefs, two vocabularies, prayers, and confessionals. Unfortunately, the manuscript has been lost. Nevertheless, the fact that the colonial government hired him for such an important assignment around 1544 shows that Betanzos had earned a reputation as the best Quechua interpreter and translator of that early colonial period. The *Doctrina christiana* (Lima, 1584), edited by Father Acosta,[4] shows what a formidable task Betanzos undertook in pioneering the translation of Christian concepts foreign to the Quechua language.

Some time after 1541, when Francisco Pizarro was assassinated, Juan de Betanzos married Doña Angelina Yupanque. At birth, she was taken to her uncle, the Inca Huayna Capac, who expressed his joy by calling her his mother.[5] A year later the Inca named her Cuxirimay Ocllo and declared that she would marry his son Atahualpa. Thus in 1532, shortly before the conquest, Cuxirimay, just ten years old, was taken from her native Cuzco to the northern province of Caranque, where she married Atahualpa. During the battle of Cajamarca, when Pizarro took Atahualpa prisoner, she remained nearby at the Inca's camp. Later she stayed with the imprisoned Atahualpa in Cajamarca. After Atahualpa's execution, she took the Christian name Doña Angelina and returned to Cuzco. By around 1538 she had become the mistress of Francisco Pizarro. She bore him two boys, Juan and Francisco. Juan died very young, but Francisco grew up with the great mestizo writer known as the Inca Garcilaso, who remembered playing with him when they were both about nine years old. Garcilaso also remembered Doña Angelina's marriage to the interpreter Juan de Betanzos.[6]

Marriage to Angelina meant instant wealth for Betanzos because she had extensive land grants and property in the Cuzco area. Their daughter, Maria, married in Cuzco. Doña Angelina and her family provided Betanzos with his major source of information on Inca traditions. Though the Betanzos narrative reflects the brilliant memory of his wife and family, no one, not even Betanzos, ever told what she looked like or how she acted. This great woman, married to the last Inca king, taken as part of the plunder by the conquistador Pizarro, and used for her collective memory of the Inca saga, comes down to us as a shadowy figure behind the glitter of the men in her life.

In 1551 Viceroy Antonio de Mendoza ordered Betanzos to prepare an account of Inca history and traditions. Betanzos indicates that he had finished at least up through Part I, chapter XIV, in 1551. The next year the viceroy died, but Betanzos kept to his *Narrative* until he finished rather abruptly in 1557. At this time he went to Lima to visit the new viceroy, Andres Hurtado de Mendoza, Marquis of Cañete.[7] Betanzos asked to accompany an embassy to negotiate with the Inca Sayre Topa, head of the neo-Inca state northwest of Cuzco. The viceroy granted the request, and Betanzos spent several months trying to convince the Inca to come back under Spanish rule. Since Betanzos ended his *Narrative* shortly before going on this embassy, one must read other sources to find out how Inca Sayre Topa came to Lima, got a warm reception from the viceroy, and settled in Cuzco.

Evidently, Betanzos received some compensation for translating Christian doctrine, recording Inca traditions, and acting as interpreter. Although he gives no details about how much he was paid, the tone of his introductory letter to the viceroy is more that of a paid official than of an independent scholar. His insistence on how long and hard he would have to work to translate an authentic account of Inca history and traditions sounds like justification for a handsome honorarium. He seems to have preferred working as an interpreter, however, because he requested that the viceroy grant him a place with the embassy to Sayre Topa rather than seeking another job translating. After this assignment as an interpreter, Betanzos appears to have spent the rest of his life in Cuzco.

Betanzos divided *Narrative of the Incas* into two parts. Part I covers Inca history to the arrival of the Spaniards. Part II deals with the conquest, mainly from the point of view of the Incas, to 1557. Betanzos's informants were from Atahualpa's family. They remembered some details of the mythological creation of the world by the god Viracocha and of the legendary foundation of Cuzco by Manco Capac (chaps. I–V). But from the second to the seventh Inca, the information dwindles to almost nothing (chap. V). The record of the eighth Inca relates mainly to his son, Pachacuti Inca Yupanque, the ninth Inca and great grandfather of Atahualpa (see Part I, chap. XXXII, on Pachacuti's lineage). Evidently, Doña Angelina and her family were taught epic poems detailing the life and times of their lineage from Pachacuti to Huayna Capac (see Part I, chaps. VIII, XIII, XVII, XIX, and XLI). These poems included speeches or statements by the main characters in the account. See, for example, Part I, chapters XXXI and XXXII, where Betanzos quotes Pachacuti giving instructions for his own funeral and making up a song about himself.

Pachacuti comes forth as a culture hero who defended Cuzco against overwhelming odds, successfully set out on military expeditions of conquest, and established the system of government, laws, city planning, and many of the Inca religious rites (chaps. VI–XXXII). His son Topa Inca and grandson Huayna Capac carried on the tradition of military exploits and expansion of the empire (chaps. XXXIII–XLVIII).

Part II has more of an eyewitness tone. Doña Angelina and her family saw or heard firsthand reports of the civil war between Huascar and her husband, Atahualpa. She remembered in great detail about Atahualpa's birth in Cuzco, his father's funeral, Atahualpa's military exploits and severity with anyone who dared to differ with him. Huascar, on the other hand, was born in a small town south of Cuzco, took scant interest in the military, openly slept with married women, killed their husbands if they complained, and drank to excess (chaps. I–XIV).

Doña Angelina, who, as a child of ten, spent the months after the conquest in 1532 in Atahualpa's camp, remembered the Incas' reactions to the Spaniards, their concern about whether the Spaniards were *viracocha* gods or mere men, whether they should be attacked, Atahualpa's treatment as a prisoner, and his death (chaps. XIX–XXVI). Betanzos also conferred with other eyewitnesses. He mentions speaking to Incas who were at Cajamarca near Atahualpa's litter during the initial battle of the conquest (Part II, chap. XXIII). The rest of his account covers events occurring shortly before and after Betanzos came to Peru. Betanzos probably got several firsthand reports for Manco Inca's siege of Cuzco in 1536, the neo-Inca state, Manco Inca's death in 1545, and the selection of Sayre Topa as Inca (chaps. XXIX–XXXIII). Betanzos brings his account to an abrupt end with a trip in 1557 to Lima, where he asked to be included in the embassy to Sayre Topa (chap. XXXIV).

Betanzos gives no indication that he aspired to publish his work. He did not even bother to update the introductory letter of 1551 or to add a letter to the new viceroy in 1557. Presumably, someone took the work back to Spain, but no one mentions it until Father Gregorio Garcia states in his work on the origin of the Indians (published in 1607) that he found Betanzos very valuable for Inca traditions.[8] No one else seems to have used Betanzos until William Prescott, working in Boston, mentions him briefly in his *History of the Conquest of Peru*, published in 1847.[9] Finally, Jiménez de la Espada edited the first edition from a manuscript still held in the library of El Escorial, *Suma y narración de los Incas* (Madrid, 1880). This incomplete manuscript includes only the introductory letter and eighteen chapters of Part I, which led scholars to date the manuscript at 1551.[10] A complete manuscript turned up in the library of the Fundación de Bartolomé March in Palma de Mallorca.[11] María del Carmen Martín Rubio edited the first Spanish edition of this manuscript with the Editorial Atlas (Madrid, 1987).

Unfortunately, this Atlas edition contains many transcription errors. For example, the word *çapa* always appears in the Palma manuscript with the ç (see folio 64v, line 33, Part I, chap. XXVII). *Çapa* or *zapa* means "unique," as in *çapa inca*, "unique Inca." The Atlas edition usually transcribes this word as *capa*, which is a different word in Quechua.[12] Sometimes phrases come out garbled. For example, on folio 53v of the Palma manuscript, line 30 reads: "y que aeste tal fuese llamado çapsi churi que dice hijo del comun" (Part I, chap. XXI), which translates as "this one [child] would be called çapçichuri, which means son of the community." The Atlas edition has a meaningless phrase: "y que este çapçi fuese llamado tal Churi que dice hijo del comun."[13] The Palma manuscript makes sense, for in Quechua *çapsi* means "community" or "people," *churi* means a "father's son." The passage refers to children considered to belong to the community because their mothers were prostitutes. These examples make it clear that any serious scholar interested in the Betanzos *Narrative* must work with the Palma manuscript (see the Note on the Translation).

The colloquial style of the *Narrative* suggests that Betanzos spoke with his informants in Quechua and then dictated his account to a scribe. This account was transcribed in the Palma manuscript with the regular lettering of an early seventeenth-century copyist or educated author, which makes it relatively easy to read. Each chapter has a heading in bold printing followed by a continuous stream of words, mostly in longhand, generally without periods and usually not divided into paragraphs. Phrases and sentences are repeatedly separated by the conjunction "y," meaning "and." In general, sentences are very long and contain several dependent clauses. Most lettering appears to be lowercase with random use of uppercase letters, though uppercase does appear at the beginning of some proper names. Written accent marks were not used. Each folio averages about 32 lines of about fourteen words. The few standard abbreviations can generally be recognized in context. The 152 folios make up 304 handwritten pages. Most doubtful passages in the Palma manuscript can be attributed to errors by the copyist. For example, in the Palma manuscript, f. 15v, line 8, a phrase has been omitted that appears in the Escorial manuscript (see Part I, IX n. 1 and XIV n. 1). Punctuation marks and paragraphs have been used in the English translation to make it more readable.

Careful study of the Betanzos *Narrative* adds many insights into Inca history and traditions. For example, there has long been a controversy over Inca chronology.[14] Traditionally, scholars have followed the work of the Inca Garcilaso in his *Royal Commentaries*, first published in 1609.[15] This work places much of the expansion of the empire before the ninth Inca. In his classic study, "Inca Culture at the Time of the Spanish Conquest" (*Handbook of South American Indians*, vol. II, 1946), John H. Rowe argues convincingly that the first eight Inca rulers conquered only towns near Cuzco and that Pachacuti provided the catalyst that turned a small regional state into a great empire. No matter how one interprets the Betanzos *Narrative*, it corroborates the theory of catalytic development under Pachacuti.[16]

Inca marriage customs have often been debated, especially marriage of the Inca rulers to their full sisters. The Betanzos *Narrative* indicates that the tenth Inca, Topa, was the first to marry his sister, Mama Ocllo. Whether she was his full or half-sister is not clarified. Topa's successor, Huayna Capac, seems to have done the same. However, Huayna Capac appears to be the only Inca ruler who came from the union of brother and sister. He arranged the marriage of Atahualpa to a cousin, Cuxirimay (see Part I, chap. XLVII, and Part II, chap. VI). Since Cuxirimay was only ten when the marriage took place, just before Atahualpa's installation as Inca in 1532, the union was probably never consummated and was more ceremonial than anything else. It suggests that Topa Inca's and Huayna Capac's marriages to sisters may also have been mainly ceremonial. All the Incas had numerous secondary wives for their sexual pleasure.

The Betanzos *Narrative* gives many other details about rites performed at birth, weaning, puberty, marriage, and death as well as about how the Incas performed many religious festivals. Many other important passages cover Inca administration, laws, social customs, the calendar, the post system, warfare, weapons, and engineering works. For example, the instructions for constructing a suspension bridge make it sound as though any well-trained gang of workers could do it. Furthermore, Betanzos states (Part I, chap. XLV) that he visited the great temple of Viracocha at Cachi, now better known as the temple of Racchi. His description of this temple coincides with recent studies by Graziano Gasparini and Luise Margolies in *Inca Architecture* (1980, trans. Patricia J. Lyon).[17]

Betanzos spins a dramatic and complex tale of revenge during the conquest period mainly from the point of view of the Incas. After the sudden death of Huayna Capac, the bitter civil war between his sons Huascar and Atahualpa emerges as a test of honor rivaling that of the proudest Spaniard. For example, Atahualpa's emissary of goodwill strikes Huascar as a traitor, so Huascar has him skinned and a drum made of his hide. Huascar's mother tries to no avail to keep the peace. After Atahualpa's generals win the war, he has Huascar's whole family killed—men, women, and children. Pregnant women have their wombs opened and their unborn children stripped from their bodies (Part II, chap. XIX). The arrival of the Spaniards leaves Atahualpa stunned at first, which explains the massacre at Cajamarca. However, by 1536 the Incas come to know the Spaniards. Manco Inca feels displaced by the Spaniards and, taking advantage of the rivalry between Pizarro and Almagro, takes his revenge by mounting a seige of Cuzco that lasts over a year and nearly breaks the Spaniards' hold on Peru (Part II, chap. XXXI).

Drawing from the most authentic sources, especially his Inca wife, Doña Angelina, Juan de Betanzos faithfully translated the history and traditions of the Inca rulers. Though never acknowledged as such, the feminine touch of Doña Angelina comes through in the details about rites of birth, coming of age, marriage, and death. The full and accurate details of this monumental work finally appear in English with this translation of the Palma manuscript. Both scholars and readers who study this Betanzos *Narrative* will reshape their views of Inca civilization.

Roland Hamilton

NOTE
on the Translation

The title of the Palma manuscript of Betanzos's work appeared in a brief article in the Palma de Mallorca press. The manuscript was included with some items from the famous library of the Duke of Medinaceli that had been obtained by the Bartolomé March Foundation in Palma. This news came to the attention of María del Carmen Martín Rubio. Professor Martín received permission from Lorenzo Pérez, director of the Bartolomé March Foundation Library in Palma, to have a copy made. She then supervised the first complete edition of the *Suma y narración,* which was published in 1987 by the Editorial Atlas in Madrid.

After reading the Atlas edition of the *Suma,* Roland Hamilton became convinced that it was based on a defective copy. Dr. Hamilton had previously published translations of a seventeenth-century manuscript on the Incas by Father Bernabe Cobo, *History of the Inca Empire* (University of Texas Press, 1979) and *Inca Religion and Customs* (University of Texas Press, 1990). He recognized the importance of working with the manuscript, but was unable to get a copy.

This job was given to an extraordinary Spaniard by the name of Miguel Bayón, who had successfully completed difficult tasks for both me and Dr. Hamilton. In November 1989 I traveled to Madrid with the intention of obtaining the manuscript.

First, I had to find a way to convince the people of the Bartolomé March Foundation to give us a copy. Fortune smiled on our efforts. It so happened that the director of the Royal Spanish Academy, Manuel Alvar López, had directed both Dr. Hamilton's and my theses at the University of Madrid. The Academy meets at its impressive headquarters in Madrid each Thursday afternoon during the academic year. Mr. Bayón and I met with Dr. Alvar on a Thursday afternoon prior to the General Session. When I told him of our interest in translating the recently discovered Betanzos manuscript, he expressed his enthusiastic support.

He had a secretary type a letter accrediting us to Dr. Lorenzo Pérez, the director of the library of the Fundación Bartolomé March. Armed with this letter attesting to our "rigor científico," Mr. Bayón went to Palma de Mallorca and obtained a photographic copy of the manuscript. Now we could translate from the only manuscript of the entire work known to exist.

One item remained to be done, however, before we could feel completely sure that we had all the pieces to this puzzle. It was the matter of the only other surviving manuscript of the *Suma*. The copy, in the library of the royal monastery at El Escorial near Madrid, contains only eighteen chapters of Part I. This manuscript had served for the first publication of Betanzos's work, the edition executed by Marcos Jiménez de la Espada in 1880. We felt it important to compare the only two manuscripts of the work to have survived to our day.

While in Madrid in November of 1989, I contacted the director of the Escorial library, Fray Timoteo, who invited Mr. Bayón and me to meet with him. He received us graciously and gave us permission to study the manuscript. We subsequently obtained a photographic copy.

In our attempt to compare the only two manuscripts of Betanzos's work, we relied heavily on Dr. Hamilton's expertise. He had previously located a manuscript of Father Bernabe Cobo's *Historia del nuevo mundo* (1653) in the Biblioteca Capitular Colombina, in Seville. He subsequently was able to prove it an original, executed in Cobo's own handwriting. He found that the two Betanzos manuscripts through chapter XVII of Part I seemed to be copies of an earlier version and that some passages from the Escorial manuscript clarified the Palma manuscript.

In reading the Editorial Atlas edition of Betanzos's work, we had found numerous passages baffling. A disturbing tendency of the Atlas edition also convinced us that any valid translation must be done directly from the Palma manuscript. The Atlas edition contains numerous passages marked with the Latinism *sic* to explain that the passage appears as such on the manuscript. This often is needless and misleading, since the manuscript is usually quite clear. A few examples should suffice.

Folio 78r, line 27 of the Palma manuscript reads: "deto p a yngay upangue." The Atlas rendering on page 160a, line 22 is "deto (sic) a Ynga Yupanque." Evidently the copyist got confused by the spacing. The transcription should read: "de Topa Ynga Yupanque."

Folio 83v, line 19 of the Palma manuscript says, "trayan las ajorro atandolas con gruesas maromas." This passage reads very clearly in the manuscript and makes perfect sense: "They brought the stones by pulling with thick ropes." The *Diccionario de autoridades* defines *ajorro* as "lo mismo que 'a remolco.'" The Atlas edition reads, page 170b, line 7: "traianlas a jarro (sic) atándolas." Evidently the editor was using a defective copy that reads "jarro," because we could see that the Palma manuscript reads "ajorro."

Another type of error is found in the Atlas edition. On page 189a, line 8 we find "caza y venados y ganados y vicuñas." The Palma manuscript folio 90v, line 20 reads: "mucha caça y benados y Guanacos y bicuñas." Apparently, the copyist did not recognize the word "guanacos," as he picked the word "ganados," which makes no sense here.

Some of the annotations also mislead the reader. For example, on page 244b, notes 134 and 135 imply that the names of the Inca generals Quizquiz and Chalcochima have been repeated in error. These repetitions also appear in the manuscript at folio 116v, line 25. There was no error. This repetition was used as an "apellido"—an archaic military expression in Spanish for a call to arms or a war cry.

In the manuscript, the name of the Inca general Chalcochima has always been spelled uniformly. In the Atlas edition, the name often appears as "Chalcuchima," a spelling often used for this general but never in the Palma manuscript. One further error in the Editorial Atlas transcription concerns the letters *f* and *s*. The copyist sometimes transcribes *f* for the letter *s* in the manuscript. For example, page 117b, bottom, reads "con tales guardas no estuviesen oficiosas." The Palma manuscript (folio 59r, line 16) reads "osiosas." The word "*oficiosas*" makes no sense, but "*ociosas*," idle, does.

Most spelling inconsistencies in the manuscript can be explained by the fact that the Spanish alphabet used in the sixteenth century was inadequate for making a precise transcription of Quechua. The Spanish vowels *i*, *e*, *u*, and *o* were used interchangeably to approximate two Quechua vowels that are half-way between each pair. Thus, *chumbe* or *chumpi* and *camayu* or *camayo* represented the same two Quechua words. The letters *b*, *d*, and *g* often replace *p*, *t*, and *k*, as in *tambo-tampu*, *Yndi-inti*, and *ynga-inca*. The combination -*nb* or -*np* has generally been transcribed as -*mb* or -*mp*. For example, *banba* has been transcribed as *bamba* (*pampa*). In Quechua, the sound *w* was usually represented as either *gu* or *hu*. Thus Quechua *wak'a* was spelled *guaca* or *huaca* by sixteenth- and seventeenth-century writers. Betanzos spells this word "guaca."

With regard to spelling considerations, this translation has modernized the spelling of place names such as Cajamarca and Trujillo that appear in the Palma manuscript as Caxamalca and Truxillo. Spellings of well-known Inca person-ages and titles have been modernized also. The title "Inca" appears in the manuscript as "Ynga," the eleventh Inca's name is spelled Huayna Capac in this translation but appears in the manuscript as Guaina Capac. The modern accent mark, generally not used in sixteenth-century Spanish documents, has not been added.

In the interpretation of the meaning of archaic or obscure words and phrases, we have used reference works reflecting sixteenth-century Spanish. The most important dictionaries are the *Tesoro de la lengua castellana o española* (1611) by Sebastián de Covarrubias and the *Diccionario de autoridades*

(1726–1729) by the Real Academia Española. We have employed early Spanish-Quechua vocabularies, especially the anonymous *Vocabulario y phrasis en la lengua general del Perú* (1586), and the *Vocabulario de la lengua general de todo el Perú* (1608), by the Jesuit Diego González Holguín.

Prior to embarking upon this translation, Dr. Hamilton consulted John Howland Rowe, world-renowned authority on the Incas, and gave him a copy of the Palma manuscript. Dr. Rowe had thoroughly studied Betanzos and pointed out the importance of the Escorial manuscript. Dr. Rowe graciously allowed us to use his translation of the first two chapters. We have attempted to maintain the high quality of his work. He also gave Dr. Hamilton advice for the maps.

Frank Salomon, an expert on colonial Quechua, has provided invaluable suggestions for interpreting the Quechua. He shows that Betanzos's Spanish glosses of the longer phrases in Quechua, while not literal, capture the spirit of the original. In addition, Brian Bauer, an authority on Inca history and geography, examined the maps.

It is with a great deal of satisfaction that we offer this first English translation of an important account of Inca life and history that, until recently, has not been available even in Spanish.

Dana Buchanan

MEASUREMENTS

The system of measures used by the Spaniards in the sixteenth century differs in several respects from the system commonly used today. Therefore, we have included an explanation of the terms Betanzos used. We have made an effort to be as precise as possible; nevertheless, the reader should understand that, many times, Betanzos's calculations are but rough estimates.

Each entry of the following list starts with the term or expression used in the English translation. The next item is the word or phrase in the Betanzos manuscript. In cases where an English equivalent is lacking, the word in the original remains. Finally, there is a brief definition of each term.

English	Spanish	Definition
	LENGTH	
Finger width	Dedo	Breadth of a finger, about 3/4"
	Geme	Distance from the outstretched thumb to the tip of the forefinger, about 6 inches
Span	Palmo	Distance from the tip of the outstretched thumb to the tip of the little finger, about 8 inches
	Vara	Castillian yard, about 32 to 34 inches; equals 4 spans or 3 Castillian feet, 2 cubits
	Braza	Fathom, the stretch of a man's arms, about 5 feet 6 inches; equals 2 varas; used for horizontal measurements
	Estado	The height of the average man, about 5 feet 6 inches, used for vertical measurements such as the height of a wall
	DISTANCE	
Foot	Pie	Catillian foot, about 11 inches
Pace	Paso	Approximately 3 feet
League	Legua	Approximately 3 miles, or the distance a person can normally walk in an hour
	Topo (Quechua)	4 1/2 miles, or 1 1/2 leagues
	LIQUID	
	Arroba	16 quarts, 4 gallons

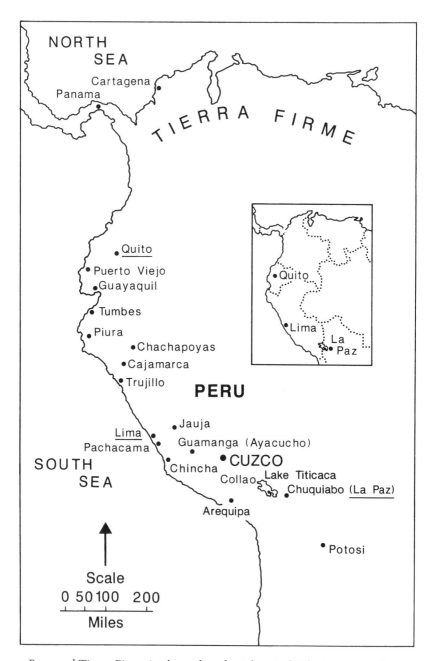

NORTH
SEA

Cartagena
Panama

TIERRA FIRME

Quito
Puerto Viejo
Guayaquil

Tumbes

Piura

Chachapoyas
Cajamarca
Trujillo

PERU

Jauja
Lima
Pachacama
Guamanga (Ayacucho)
Chincha
CUZCO
Collao
Lake Titicaca
Chuquiabo (La Paz)

SOUTH
SEA

Arequipa

Potosi

Scale
0 50 100 200
Miles

Quito
Lima
La Paz

*Peru and Tierra Firme in the early colonial period. The inset map shows
modern national boundaries. Modified from* The Men of Cajamarca *by
James Lockhart (Austin: University of Texas Press, 1972).*

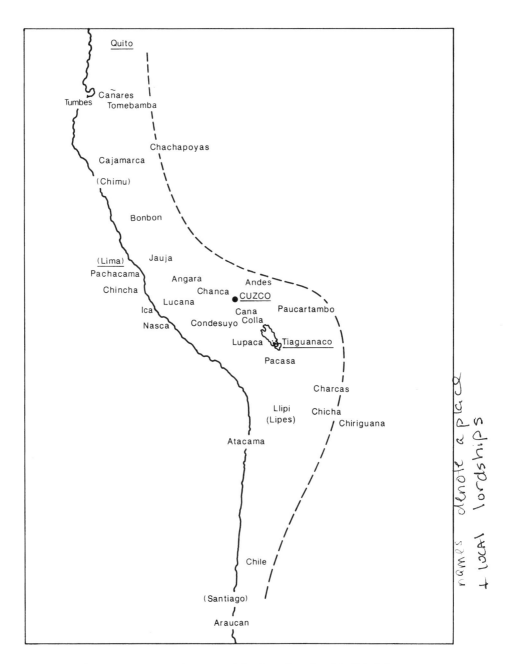

Quito

Tumbes
Cañares
Tomebamba

Chachapoyas

Cajamarca

(Chimu)

Bonbon

(Lima)
Pachacama
Jauja

Chincha
Angara
Chanca
Andes
CUZCO
Lucana
Paucartambo
Ica
Cana
Colla
Condesuyo
Nasca
Lupaca
Tiaguanaco
Pacasa

Charcas

Llipi
(Lipes)
Chicha
Chiriguana

Atacama

Chile

(Santiago)

Araucan

names denote a place
+ local lordships

Tribes, provinces, and towns of the Inca Empire. Modified from a map by John H. Rowe in Handbook of South American Indians, *vol. 2, pp. 184–192.*

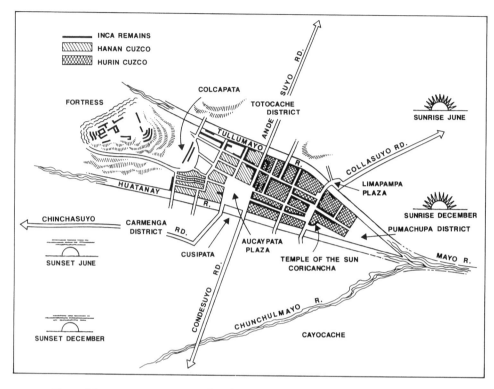

City of Cuzco in Inca times. Sketch map modified from Graziano Gasparini and Luise Margolis, Inca Architecture *(Bloomington: Indiana University Press, 1980), p. 46.*

Opposite: "La Gran Cuidad de Cuzco . . ." Poma de Ayala's drawing shows early colonial Cuzco. Names as they appear on the map of Inca Cuzco (above) correspond to the numbers inserted in the drawing: Carmenga/(1); Huatanay River/(2); Aucaypata Plaza/(3); Cusipata Market/(4); Temple of the Sun/(5); and Pumachupa/(6).

From the chronicle of Felipe Guaman Poma de Ayala,
Nueva coronica y buen gobierno.

CIVDAD
LAGRÃCIVDADICAVE

Andean
Each indiv. trying to blend the cultures

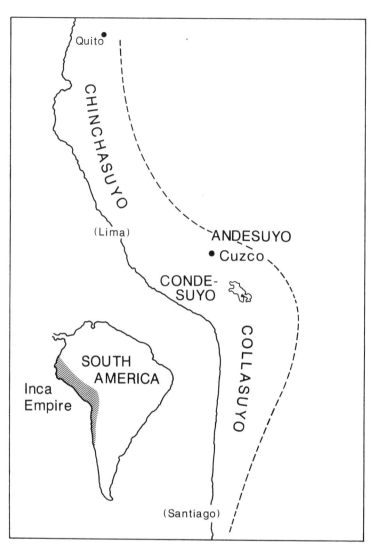

The Four Quarters of the Inca Empire.

Narrative of the Incas

PREFACE

Summary and narrative of the Incas whom the Indians called Capaccuna.[1] They were lords of the city of Cuzco and all the lands under its authority, including a thousand leagues extending from the Maule River in Chile up to that place where the city of Quito lies. They controlled and ruled it all until the Marquis Don Francisco Pizarro conquered it and put it under the yoke and royal dominions of his Majesty. This narrative contains the lives and acts of the Capaccuna Incas. It has been newly translated and compiled from the Indian language of the natives of Peru by Juan de Betanzos, resident of the great city of Cuzco. This narrative and history has been divided into two parts.

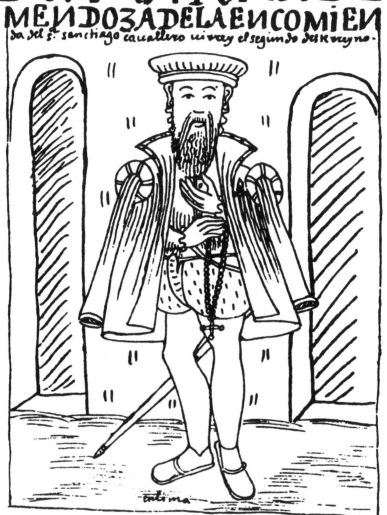

Don Antonio De Mendoza, viceroy of Peru.

From the chronicle of Felipe Guaman Poma de Ayala,
Nueva coronica y buen gobierno.

PROLOGUE

To the Illustrious and Excellent señor Don Antonio de Mendoza,[1] viceroy and captain-general for his Majesty in these kingdoms and provinces of Peru.

Your Excellency:

I have just translated and compiled a book named Christian Doctrine,[2] which covers Christian doctrine and two vocabularies, one of words and the other of notions, whole prayers, conversations, and confessionals. My mind and body were left very tired after spending six years of my youth on it. Therefore, I decided not to translate or compile another book on a topic from the Indian language dealing with the acts and customs of the native Peruvians. It seemed to me that it would be too much work because of the variety of information that I found in my inquiry. Moreover, I realized how differently the conquistadores speak about it and how far they were from what the Indians did. This I believe because at that time the conquistadores paid less attention to fact finding than to subduing and acquiring the land and also because they were unaccustomed to dealing with the Indians; they did not know how to make inquiries and ask questions because they lacked an understanding of the language. Moreover, the Indians were afraid to give them a full account. It might seem easy to prepare such books and difficult to satisfy the reader. One's eyes may be pleased with legible writing, but your Majesty's fine and experienced judgment requires an entertaining and smoothly elegant style. Considering my limitations and the history of such a subject, the gift and service that I would give your Majesty are impossible. In order to be a true and faithful translator, I must respect the style and order of the speech of these natives. In this regard, I say that in going over this present writing at times your Majesty may have to strain your eyes to read it. Although it may not be a very elegant work, it has been very difficult. In the first place, in translating and compiling it, I did not limit myself to a single informant; rather, I used many of the oldest and most respected I found among these natives. In the second place, because I knew that this work would be given to your Majesty, I have been distressed by the short time that I have had to work on it. For the other book of religious instruction, all [my effort] was necessary and, above all, having to finish this book soon added to the work, since your Majesty ordered me to do it. I am writing here about the acts and lives of the Incas that the Indians called Capaccuna, which as they explain means that there is none greater nor can anyone be greater. A list of the names of these Incas will be found at the end of this prologue. If anyone should wish to argue that in the contents of this book there is anything superfluous or left out that I forgot to include, the reason would be statements by the common Indians, who customarily say whatever they imagine or dream. Or it might be that it seemed so to such detractors when they gathered information, that the Indians meant what the detractors state now. Thus, the detractors did not understand these things fully nor even the interpreters. In the past no one knew how to inquire and ask what they wanted to find out and be well informed. I see that the customs of these Indians were childish and shallow, but I write here to state the facts since I am under orders to translate what used to happen. Therefore, let this book receive the favor of your Excellency.

May your Excellency's life be filled with prosperity and happiness.

List of the Capaccuna Incas[3] who were from these provinces of Peru
[1]   Manco Capac
[2]   Çinche Roca
[3]   Lloque Yupanque
[4]   Capac Yupanque
[5]   Mayta Capac
[6]   Inca Roca Inca
[7]   Yaguar Guaca Inca Yupanque
[8]   Viracocha Inca
[9]   Inca Yupanque Pachacuti Inca
        Yamque Yupanque
[10] Topa Inca Yupanque
[11] Huayna Capac
[12] Huascar
[13] Atahualpa
Those whom the marquis named as Incas after the death of Atahualpa:
Topa Gualpa
Manco Inca
The one who was named by the captains of Manco Inca upon his death:
Sayre Topa, who is now in the wilds.

Part One

I

Which concerns Contiti Viracocha,[1] who they believe was the creator, and how he made the heavens and the earth and the Indian peoples of these provinces of Peru.[2]

In ancient times, they say, the land and the provinces of Peru were dark and neither light nor daylight existed. In this time, there lived certain people who had a lord who ruled over them and to whom they were subject. The name of these people and that of their ruler have been forgotten.

During this time of total night, they say that a lord emerged from a lake in this land of Peru in the province of Collasuyo[3] and that his name was Contiti Viracocha. They say that he brought with him a certain number of people, but they do not remember the number. When he had emerged from the lake he went from there to a place near the lake where today there is a town called Tiahuanaco in the province of Collao referred to above. When he and his people arrived there, they say that he suddenly made the sun and the day and ordered the sun to follow the course that it follows. Then, they say, he made the stars and the moon.

They say that this Contiti Viracocha had emerged another time before that one, and that on that first occasion he created the sky and the earth but left everything in darkness. Then he made those people who lived in the time of darkness previously mentioned. These people did some disservice to this Viracocha, and since he was angry, he returned, emerging this last time, as he had done before. In his anger, he turned to stone those he created first, together with their lord, as a punishment for annoying him. In that very moment, he made the sun and the day and the moon and stars, as we have said.

When this was done, there at Tiahuanaco, he made some people from stone as a kind of model of those that he would produce later. He made a certain number of them from stone in this way, together with a chieftain to govern and rule over them, and many women, some pregnant and others delivered. The babies were in cradles, according to their custom. When he had made all these of stone, he set them aside in a certain place and then made another province of people in the manner described. In this way, he made another people of Peru and of its provinces there in Tiahuanaco, forming them of stones in the way stated.

imp. of lake b/c it's so barren
water notion life came from water

After he had finished making them, he ordered all those he had there with him to depart, leaving only two in his company. He instructed those who were left to look at the stone likenesses, and he told them the names he had given to each kind of people, pointing to them and saying, "These will be called the so and so and will come out of such and such a spring in such and such a province and will settle there and be increased, and these others will come out of such and such a cave and will be called the thus and so and will settle in such and such a province. Just the way I have painted them and made them of stone thus they must come out of the springs and rivers and caves and mountains in the provinces which I have told you and named, and you will go at once, all of you, in this direction," pointing toward the sunrise, taking each one aside individually and showing him the direction he was to follow.

II

Which concerns how the people of this country emerged under the orders of Viracocha and of the viracochas he sent to accomplish this task; how Contiti Viracocha and the two that remained with him left to do the same work, and how Viracocha rejoined his people at last after having finished, and how he put out to sea, never to be seen again.

So these *viracochas* of whom you have heard left and traversed the provinces that Viracocha had told them. When they arrived at the place where they were going in each province, they called on those whom Viracocha had pointed out to them in Tiahuanaco of stone as being the ones who had to emerge in that province. Each *viracocha* stationed himself next to the place where he had been told that these people had to come out, and then said in a loud voice, "So and so, come out and people this land, which is now uninhabited, because Contiti Viracocha, who made the world, has so ordered it." As the *viracochas* called them, the proper people came out of the places which Viracocha had appointed. So they say that these *viracochas* went along, calling and bringing out the people from the caves, rivers and springs, and high sierras, as you have already heard in the previous chapter, peopling the country in the direction where the sun rises.

When Contiti Viracocha had sent out his agents and they had gone in the manner stated, they say that he sent the two who had stayed with him in the town of Tiahuanaco to call and bring out the people in the way you have heard, dividing the two as follows. He sent one to the province of Condesuyo,[1] which is on the left, if you are at Tiahuanaco with your back to the sunrise, so that he could go and do what the first ones had done and call out the Indians and natives of the province of Condesuyo. The other he sent likewise to the province of Andesuyo,[2] which is on the right if you are placed in the manner stated with your back to the sunrise.

After these two had been dispatched, they say that Viracocha himself set out straight ahead toward Cuzco, which is in between these two provinces, traveling by the royal road that goes through the sierra toward Cajamarca. As he went along, he also called and brought out the peoples in the way you have already heard.

When he came to a province which they call Cacha, which belongs to the Canas Indians and is eighteen leagues from the city of Cuzco, Viracocha called out these Canas Indians. They came out armed, however, and did not know Viracocha when they saw him. They all came at him with their arms to kill him. When he saw them coming, he understood what they were coming for and instantly caused fire to fall from heaven, burning a range of mountains near the Indians. When the Indians saw the fire, they feared they would be burned. Throwing their arms to the ground, they went straight to Viracocha and all threw themselves to the ground before him. When he saw them thus, he took a staff in his hands and went where the fire was. He gave it two or three blows with his staff, which put it completely out, whereupon he told the Indians that he was their maker. The Canas Indians built a sumptuous *guaca*,[3] which means a shrine or idol, at the place where he stood when he called the fire from heaven and from which he went to put it out. In this *guaca* they and their descendants offered a great quantity of gold and silver. They set up a stone statue carved from a great stone almost five *varas*[4] in length and one *vara* in width, more or less, in the *guaca,* in memory of Viracocha and of what had taken place there. This *guaca* has stood there from ancient times until today, and I have seen the burned mountain and the burned stones. The burned area is more than a quarter of a league across.

When I saw this wonder, I called on the oldest Indians and leading men and asked them the explanation of that burned mountain. They told me what you have heard. The *guaca* of Viracocha is a stone's throw in front of the burned area on a plain across a river that runs between the burned area and the *guaca*. Many people have crossed the river and have seen the *guaca* and the stone statue, because they have heard the story from the Indians. I asked the Indians what this Viracocha looked like when the ancients saw him, as far as they have information. They told me that he was a tall man dressed in a white garment that reached to his ankles and was belted at the waist. His hair was short and he had a tonsure like a priest. He went bareheaded and carried in his hands something that seemed to them to resemble the breviaries that priests of today carry. This is the account that I obtained from these Indians. I asked them the name of the personage in whose place the stone was erected, and they said his name was Contiti Viracocha Pacha-yachachic, which means "God, maker of the world" in their language.

Going back to our story, they say that after he had worked this miracle in the province of Cacha, he went on, continuing his work. When he reached the place that is now called the Tambo of Urcos, six leagues from the city of Cuzco, he climbed a high mountain and sat down on the highest point, where they say he ordered the native Indians who now live there to come out of that high place. Because Viracocha sat there, they built a rich and sumptuous *guaca* in that place. Because he had sat down, they made a bench of fine gold and set the statue of Viracocha on it. In the division of spoils that the Christians made when they took Cuzco, this bench was valued at 16,000 or 18,000 pesos of fine gold.

Viracocha went on, making people as you have heard, until he reached Cuzco. There, they say, he made a lord whom he himself named Alcavicça, and he also gave the name Cuzco to the place where he made this lord. He ordered that the *orejones*[5] should emerge after he had left.

He went on, continuing his work, until he reached the province of Puerto Viejo. There he met the others whom he had sent out, as has been said. He went out across the sea with them; they say that he and his companions walked on water as if on land.

We could have written much more that the Indians have told me about Viracocha, but I did not do so to avoid prolixity and great idolatries and beastliness. Let us leave him and talk about the origin of the *orejones* of the city of Cuzco. They also follow the beastly, pagan, and barbarous idolatry that you have heard.

4 quarters of Empire

lake

Armas Propias. ynti, coya, choqui, idolo de uanacauri, Pacarictambo.
Symbols of the Incas: The Sun; the Moon; Lightening; the hill of
Guanacaure and the caves at Pacarictambo.

From the chronicle of Felipe Guaman Poma de Ayala,
Nueva coronica y buen gobierno.

GUAMAN POMA = FALCON TIGER
descendant of Uzobika
PACARITAMBO - place of caves

Which concerns the site and style used in the place which they now call the great city of Cuzco, and the origin of the *orejones, and the way it is claimed that they originated in and came out of a certain cave.*

In the place and site which is called today the great city of Cuzco in the province of Peru, in ancient times, before there were any lord *orejones*, Inca Capaccuna, as they call their kings, there was a small town of about thirty small, humble straw houses. In them there were about thirty Indians, and the lord cacique of this town was called Alcavicça. The rest of the area around this town was a marsh of sedge with sharp-edged leaves. This marsh was created by the springs from the sierra and came from the place where the fortress [Sacsahuaman] is now. This marsh was located and formed in what now is the square and houses of the Marquis Don Francisco Pizarro, who later took this city. This marsh was the same at the site of the houses of the Comendador[1] Hernando Pizarro. There was also a marsh across the river which passes through this city in the place of the Indian market, or *tianguez*, the trade plaza of the natives themselves. The inhabitants of this town called it Cuzco from ancient times. As to what this name Cuzco means, all they can say is that it was the name of this town from ancient times. While Alcavicça lived in this town, the earth opened up a cave seven leagues[2] from this town, which today they call Pacarictambo, which means house of origin. The opening of this cave would allow a man to crawl in or out. After this cave opened up, four men came out with their wives in the following order. The first one, called Ayar Cache came out with his wife, who was named Mama Guaço. After him another, called Ayar Oche, came out and after him his wife, named Cura. After this one, another came out, called Ayar Auca, with his wife, named Ragua Ocllo. After these came another, called Ayar Manco, whom they later called Manco Capac which means King Manco. After him came his wife, whom they called Mama Ocllo. From inside the cave they brought out their handsome golden halberds. The men came out dressed in garments of fine wool woven with gold. On their necks they brought out some bags, also of elaborately woven wool; in these bags they carried sinewed slings. The women also came out dressed very richly in cloaks and sashes that they call *chumbis*, well woven with gold and with fine gold fasteners, large pins about two palms long, which they call *topos*. These women also brought the ware with which they would serve and cook for their husbands; this included pots and small jars and plates and bowls and drinking tumblers all of fine gold. When they left that place, they went along the mountain range seven leagues farther on, up to a hill called Guanacaure, which is one and a half leagues from Cuzco. They descended down the back side of this hill to a small valley located there, where they planted *papas* [potatoes], food of these Indians. They went up the hill of Guanacaure one day to look out from there and discern where they could find the best place and site to settle. Reaching the very top to the hill, Ayar Cache, who was the first to come out of the cave, took out his sling, put a stone in it, and hurled it to a high hill, and it struck with such a blow that it knocked down the hill and made a ravine in it. Moreover, he hurled three more stones, and with each one he made a ravine in the high hills. These stones carried from the place where they were hurled to where they hit, as they imagine, a distance of a league and a half and of a league. Having seen these stones shot from the sling, the three other companions stopped to think about the strength of Ayar Cache. They moved a short distance away from there, and they decided to seek a way to send Ayar Cache away from their group because it seemed to them that he was a man of such great strength and valor that in time he would be giving them orders and subjugate them. They agreed to return from there to the cave where they came from, since they had left much wealth in gold and garments and other utensils inside the cave. They cunningly insisted on their need for these things inside the cave. They told Ayar Cache to go back to get it, and he said this pleased him. Reaching the mouth of the cave, Ayar Cache crawled in just as he had come out, for there was no other way to enter. As soon as the others saw him inside, all three of them put a huge flagstone there and closed up the opening of the cave where Ayar Cache had entered. Later, with many stones and mud they made this entrance into a thick wall. Thus when Ayar Cache tried to go out again he could not do it, and he stayed there. Once this was done, they stayed there until they heard Ayar Cache pounding the flagstone from inside. When the companions saw that Ayar Cache could not get out, they returned to their settlement at Guanacaure, where they stayed together for one year with the four women. Since Ayar Cache remained in the cave, they gave his wife to Ayar Manco as his servant.

IV

Wherein Ayar Manco came down from the heights of Guanacaure to live in another ravine from whence after a certain length of time he went to live in the city of Cuzco in the company of Alcavicça, leaving on the hill of Guanacaure his companion, Ayar Oche, who had turned into an idol, which will be told of at greater length in this account.

One year after they came there, it seemed to them that that place where they were was not suitable for them. They went to live half a league farther on toward Cuzco, to another ravine called Matagua, and they were at this ravine for another half year. From on top of the hills by this ravine they looked out on the Valley of Cuzco and the town where Alcavicça had his settlement. And it seemed to them that it was a good place which was inhabited by the people of Alcavicça. After they came down to their settlement, they made an agreement. They decided that it would be a good idea to settle with those people who lived in that town. They also decided that one of them would remain at the hill of Guanacaure as an idol, which the rest would worship, and that this one who remained as an idol would ask their father the Sun to protect them, increase their number, give them children, and send them good weather. Then Ayar Oche stood up, displayed a pair of large wings, and said he should be the one to stay there at Guanacaure as an idol in order to speak with their father the Sun. Then they went up on top of the hill. Now at the site where he was to remain as an idol, Ayar Oche raised up in flight toward the heavens so high that they could not see him. He returned and told Ayar Manco that from then on he was to be named Manco Capac. Ayar Oche came from where the Sun was and the Sun had ordered that Ayar Manco take that name and go to the town that they had seen. There they would find good company among the inhabitants of the town. They should settle there, and Ayar Manco would receive Ayar Oche's wife, Cura, to care for her. Ayar Manco should take Ayar Auca. After this had been stated by the idol, Ayar Oche turned into a stone, just as he was, with his wings. Later Manco Capac went down with Ayar Auca to their settlement and after they had gone down, some Indians from a nearby town came to where the idol was. When they saw the idol made of stone, which they had seen fly up high, they threw a stone at it, and the blow broke one of the idol's wings. Since one of his wings was broken, he could not fly anymore. Seeing that he was turned into stone, they bothered him no more, and these Indians who had done this returned toward their town.

Manco Capac and his companion, Ayar Auca, left their settlement, taking with them the four women already mentioned. They walked toward the town of Cuzco, where Alcavicça was. Two harquebus shots from Cuzco there was a small town which had coca and agi [hot peppers].[1] The woman named Mama Guaco, wife of Ayar Cache, who had perished in the cave, struck a blow with her *ayllos* [sling] at an Indian of this coca town, and she killed him. Quickly, she opened him up and took out his lungs and heart. In full view of everyone else in the town, she blew into the lungs, making them swell up. Seeing that incident, the Indians became very frightened, and because of the fright they had taken at that moment, they fled to the valley called Gualla, from whence the Indians have come who even today produce the coca of Gualla. After this occurred, Manco Capac and his people went on ahead. They spoke to Alcavicça, telling him that the Sun sent them to settle with him there in that town of Cuzco. Seeing Manco Capac and his people so well equipped and the golden halberds that they carried in their hands and the other golden utensils, Alcavicça realized it was true, and that they were children of the Sun; he told them to settle wherever they wanted. Manco Capac thanked him. He liked the place now occupied in this city of Cuzco by the houses and monastery of Santo Domingo, which used to be the houses of the Sun, as will be explained further ahead in this account.

Manco Capac and his companion, with the help of the four women, made a house there without allowing the people of Alcavicça to help, even though these people wanted to. The two of them and the four women stayed in the house. Having done this, Manco Capac and his companion, with the four women, planted some land with maize. It is said that they took the maize from the cave, which this lord Manco Capac named Pacarictambo, which means house of origin because, as has already been stated, they came out of that cave. With the planting completed, Manco Capac and Alcavicça rejoiced in good friendship and satisfaction.

V

Wherein Manco Capac's companion Ayar Auca died, and Manco Capac had a son who was named Çinche Roca, how Manco Capac died and after this Alcavicça died, and the lords who came after Çinche Roca up to Viracocha Inca, and the events that occurred during those times up to Viracocha Inca.

Two years after Manco Capac came there, his companion Ayar Auca died. His wife remained in the company of Manco Capac's other wives. She never bore Ayar Auca a child. Thus Manco Capac remained alone with his wife and the three wives of the companions mentioned above. Manco Capac never had anything to do with these three women as his; rather, this happened only with his own wife. A short time later a son was born, whom he named Çinche Roca. When Çinche Roca was a young man of fifteen or sixteen his father, Manco Capac, died without leaving any son other than this Çinche Roca. Five years after the death of Manco Capac, Alcavicça died. Since Çinche Roca, son of Manco Capac, was twenty years old, he took as his wife a lady named Mama Coca, daughter of a cacique,[1] lord of a town called Çaño, one league from Cuzco. With this lady Çinche Roca had a son named Lloque Yupanque, who was born with teeth. Right after birth he started walking and he refused to suckle. He said such admirable things that it seems to me that he must have been another Merlin, according to what the legends say. As soon as this one was born, they say that he picked a stone up in his hands and threw it at another boy, a descendant of Alcavicça, who was passing by with a jar in his hands at the time on his way to get water at a fountain. The stone thrown by the newborn Lloque Yupanque broke one of the legs of the Alcavicça boy. On the basis of this incident, the sorcerers said that the descendants of Lloque Yupanque would be great lords, ruling that town. The descendants of Alcavicça would be driven from that town by the descendants of Lloque Yupanque, all of which happened as foretold, as the account will tell ahead according to what was told by those who gave the report. Since Lloque Yupanque did nothing more notable during his lifetime than what has already been told, we will leave him.

After the days of Lloque Yupanque, one of his sons, named Capac Yupanque, took his place. Capac Yupanque achieved nothing greater than what his father, Lloque Yupanque, left him. After the days of Capac Yupanque, one of his sons, named Mayta Capac, took his place. It is said that Mayta Capac achieved nothing greater than his predecessors. After his days, one of his sons, named Inca Roca Inca took his place. It is said that Inca Roca Inca had six wives who bore him thirty sons and daughters. After his days, his eldest son, named Yaguar Guaca Inca Yupanque, took his place. It is said that this one was born crying blood. For that reason, he was named Yaguar Guaca, which means to cry blood. They say that he had twenty wives who bore him fifty sons and daughters. It is said that he achieved nothing greater than what his ancestors left him. After his days one of his sons, named Viracocha Inca took his place. They say that this one was named Viracocha Inca because he was very friendly with his people and affable, governing very calmly, always giving gifts and doing favors. For this reason, the people loved him greatly. On getting up one morning he went out happily to see his people, and they asked him why he was so happy. He answered that Viracocha Pacha-yachachic had spoken to him and said that god had talked to him that night. Then all of his people stood up and called him Viracocha Inca, which means king and god, and from then on he was called by this name.

VI

Wherein the many lords surrounding Cuzco took the title of king or lord in their provinces, and how a Chanca lord who was named Uscovilca rose up among them, and how he and his captains made war on the rest of the lords and conquered them, and how, knowing about Viracocha Inca, he attacked Cuzco, and how Viracocha Inca sent his agreement to obey him, and later Viracocha Inca escaped to a certain stronghold, taking with him everyone from the city.

During the time of Viracocha Inca, there were more than two hundred lord caciques of towns and provinces within the fifty or sixty leagues surrounding this city of Cuzco. In their lands and towns, they accorded themselves the title of Capac Inca, which means lord or king. Viracocha Inca did the same thing, taking the title of god, as mentioned above. Wherefore the rest of the lords saw that Viracocha Inca took a title more important than any of them. A certain lord of the Chanca nation called Uscovilca ruled over a large number of people and had six very brave captains under him named Malma, Rapa, Yanavilca, Tecllovilca, Guamanguaraca, and Tomayguaraca. Uscovilca knew that Viracocha Inca lived in Cuzco and took for himself a title of more importance than his, though Uscovilca was more powerful in men and took the title of lord over all the land. Therefore, Uscovilca decided that it would be a good idea to find out how much power Viracocha Inca had. While he was at the town of Paucaray, three leagues from Parcos, in order to find this out, Uscovilca consulted with his men about how he should proceed in this matter. Since he was very powerful, they agreed that his captains should explore the lands and provinces on the side of Condesuyo province and do the same on the side of Andesuyo province. Uscovilca himself, with two of his captains and the men who remained, should go through the middle, between these two provinces, straight to the city of Cuzco. This way he would be the lord of all the land and would himself conquer Viracocha Inca. After making this agreement, Uscovilca ordered all of his men to meet on a certain day at that town and plain of Paucaray where he was born. Thus all of his men met there on the day that had been set.

With all of his soldiers together, he ordered his captains to divide the assembled men into three units and that they all be provided with weapons, including lances, halberds, axes, clubs, slings, and round shields. After they had been supplied with these materials, he ordered that they be given ample supplies for their trip, including dried meat, maize, dried fish, and all other foods. He granted them the right to all the spoils that they would take in the war of livestock, clothes, gold, silver, women, and other captives and *yanacona* servants who would be taken in the war. Giving one group of these men to two of his captains, called Malma and Rapa, Uscovilca ordered them to leave at once and go conquering through the province of Condesuyo until they found no more people to conquer. Thus these two captains left, taking the men mentioned, and when they bade farewell to their lord, both the captains and the rest of the men gave many thanks and praise to him for the grant of the spoils he had given them. Thus these two captains, Malma and Rapa, went conquering across the province of Condesuyo with a strong force of men. These two captains were so successful that they subdued the lands from the town of Paucaray through the province of Condesuyo up to Chicha, which is fifty leagues beyond Charcas. We will leave these captains and speak of the other two that Uscovilca himself sent through Andesuyo. These captains were named Yanavilca and Tecllovilca. As soon as their lord Uscovilca gave them the other unit of men, they left from Paucaray. Just before they left, Uscovilca ordered them not to go any closer than ten leagues from Cuzco, but instead to go by at some distance because Uscovilca wanted the Cuzco undertaking for himself. Therefore these two captains left, going through the province of Andesuyo. They conquered provinces until they reached the Chiriguana. We will leave them there and speak of Uscovilca.

He had sent off his four captains in the way that you have already heard, and he personally was very anxious to go and subdue Cuzco and Viracocha Inca. He took the third unit of men who remained, leaving his land and town with the protection and security necessary so that if an attack came he could be warned to return to protect it. With this done and provided for, he left with his soldiers and two captains in search of Viracocha Inca, who was doing nothing about that menace. Viracocha Inca did not make war on anyone nor did he make any effort to take from anyone what belonged to them. As Viracocha Inca remained aloof of this war that was coming against him, two messengers sent by Uscovilca came to him. These messengers brought word for Viracocha Inca to obey Uscovilca as lord. If Viracocha Inca refused, he had better make ready, for Uscovilca would make war and intended to enter into battle and subdue him. Viracocha Inca should be aware that Uscovilca was in Vilcacunga, seven leagues from the city of Cuzco. Soon Uscovilca would be with Viracocha Inca. When Viracocha Inca understood this message that Uscovilca sent him and that Uscovilca brought a powerful force and that he had subdued everyone he had met, Viracocha Inca sent word that it pleased him to give obedience to Uscovilca and that Viracocha Inca wanted to eat and drink with him.

After the messengers were gone from Cuzco with this reply, Viracocha Inca called together his highest officials and asked them for advice about what they should do. Uscovilca's messenger had been in such a hurry that Viracocha Inca had no time to consult with his advisers about how to answer, and so he replied as you have heard. Later Viracocha Inca started his consultation. They took into consideration that Uscovilca was bringing a powerful force and that he was arrogant. If they submitted to him so easily, Uscovilca would consider them weak. To be better able to negotiate with him the things that were most important to their survival, and considering that, although they would be subjugated, they would not lose as much if Viracocha Inca resolved to leave this city of Cuzco with all of the people of the city along with the majority of the people nearby who wanted to follow them and go to a refuge seven leagues from Cuzco above a town called Calca. This hilltop stronghold and fortification was called Caquea Xaquixahuana.

At this time Viracocha Inca had seven sons. In particular, he had one son named Inca Yupanque, who was the youngest of all. At the time when Viracocha Inca wanted to abandon Cuzco, this son of his, Inca Yupanque, though young, was very proud and thought a lot of himself. He disapproved of his father's conduct in abandoning his town and wanting to submit, as he had already offered to do. Inca Yupanque thought it was a bad decision and would be considered a great disgrace by the people who got word of it. Seeing that his father and the rest of the lords of Cuzco were set on leaving, Inca Yupanque decided not to leave and to bring together as many men as he could. Since Uscovilca was coming, Inca Yupanque would not surrender. Inca Yupanque would die rather than agree to live in bondage. Perhaps by good fortune, he could bring enough men together and defeat Uscovilca. This way he would free his people. Considering what he had thought, he set out in search of three young men who were sons of lords and his friends. They were sons of those lords with whom his father had consulted about leaving and submitting to the Chanca. The names of these young men were Vicaquirao, Apomayta, and

Quilescache Urcoguaranca. Inca Yupanque met with these young lords. He discussed with them what he thought and told them that it would be better to die than live in such bondage and disgrace, since they had not been born in bondage. There together, the young men expressed approval of what Inca Yupanque had told them, and they gave him their word to do as he would do. All four of them were of the same opinion. Then Viracocha Inca left the city for his stronghold, taking with him the people of Cuzco and as many of the nearby residents as he could take with him. Inca Yupanque and the three young lords mentioned above remained in the city, each accompanied by a servant who wished to stay with them. These servants were named Pata Yupanque, Murollonga, Apo Yupanque, and Uxuta Urcoguaranca. They remained alone, and no one else stayed with them except these servants. When Viracocha Inca saw that his son Inca Yupanque remained with that purpose, he had a big laugh and paid no attention to him. He had taken his six sons with him and with them his eldest and most beloved, who was named Inca Urco, to whom he planned to leave his position and his own name.

VII

Wherein after Inca Yupanque remained in the city, Uscovilca sent his messengers to Viracocha Inca on finding out that he had taken refuge in the stronghold, and, additionally, Uscovilca also found out that Inca Yupanque was staying in the city and the reason he was, and how Uscovilca also sent his messengers to Inca Yupanque, and Inca Yupanque sent to ask for the help of his father and the rest of the provinces around the city, and what happened to them.

Once the Chanca Uscovilca found out what Viracocha Inca had done, he decided to send one of his captains, named Guamanguaraca, so that Viracocha Inca could make an agreement with him or whatever he wanted and considered right. This captain arrived, and Viracocha Inca received him very well at the stronghold where he was. Once this captain had been sent off to Viracocha Inca, Uscovilca found out how Inca Yupanque had remained in Cuzco with the three lords already mentioned, each one with a servant at his command, with the intention and desire to die and not be subdued. Once Uscovilca got this news, he was very pleased because he thought that by defeating this Inca Yupanque, son of Viracocha Inca, and the three lords with him, he could emerge victorious, capturing them within the city of Cuzco, to where Uscovilca was heading. When one of Uscovilca's captains, named Tomayguaraca, learned the news of Inca Yupanque's intention, he asked his lord Uscovilca to do him the favor of giving him this undertaking. Tomayguaraca wanted to go to Cuzco, capture and kill Inca Yupanque and those who were with him. Uscovilca answered that he wanted such an undertaking for himself, that he wanted to accomplish it with his own hands. Shortly, he sent to Inca Yupanque a messenger to inform him that Uscovilca was very pleased to know that Inca

Yupanque wanted to test his youthful strength, that he should prepare himself and those with him. Three months from that time Uscovilca would challenge him. Since he did not want Inca Yupanque to complain, he was giving him three months' time so he could better meet the challenge and at the same time prepare whatever arms and soldiers he chose. Since Uscovilca had found out that Viracocha Inca had fled the city of Cuzco and taken all his people and as many as he could from the neighboring towns around Cuzco, it occurred to Uscovilca that there would be no one who would come to the aid of Inca Yupanque, who planned to resist the force that Uscovilca brought. Once he saw what Uscovilca sent to tell him, Inca Yupanque replied that he was ready to die fighting rather than be subdued. He was born free and a lord. If his father pledged obedience to Uscovilca, he could do it for himself and for those he had with him up there at the stronghold where his father was. Inca Yupanque had nothing to do with that, but if Uscovilca was going to be lord of Cuzco and take for himself such a title, he would have to fight Inca Yupanque and defeat him to get that recognition. Inca Yupanque was happy that his father had abandoned the city of Cuzco, leaving it in the belief that he had to surrender. In the city of Cuzco no one had ever done such a thing or been defeated by anyone since Manco Capac had founded it. Once the message and reply were heard, the messenger left Cuzco and went to his lord Uscovilca, who at that time was relaxing with the lords he had brought with him there in the settlement of Vilcacunga. After Uscovilca heard the answer that Inca Yupanque sent him with his messenger, it pleased Uscovilca because he thought he would triumph in Cuzco, as you have heard. After Inca Yupanque had sent the answer that you have heard to the Chanca, he had a meeting with the three lords who were with him, and they agreed to send a certain messenger to Viracocha Inca, his father. In this way they sent word to Viracocha Inca to consider the disgrace that was coming to them and that Cuzco had never been defeated since Manco Capac had settled it. Did it not seem to him that they should defend the city and not let it be said that he had abandoned his people and later that he surrendered and gave up to his enemies? Viracocha Inca should come to the city for he promised him, as his son, that he would die in his presence if he would return and defend the city. Inca Yupanque had made up his mind to die rather than let it be said of him that he had surrendered while he was lord, since he was born free.

Later they selected one of the four servants that they had there; he was told to take the message that you have heard. This messenger left, arrived where Viracocha Inca was, and gave him the message on behalf of Inca Yupanque. Once Viracocha Inca heard what his son had to tell him, he laughed much at the message, and he said, "I am a man who communicates and speaks with god, who made me aware that I am not in a good position to oppose Uscovilca.

Having been warned in this way, I left Cuzco to be better able to make arrangements for keeping Uscovilca from doing something shameful to me and mistreating my people. This boy Inca Yupanque wants to die and assumes that I have been given bad advice. Go back and tell him that I laugh at his childishness and for him to come accompanied by those he has with him. If he refuses, I am sorry he wants to die that way because he is my son." The messenger answered these words that Viracocha told him, saying that his lord had made up his mind about that matter and that nothing would stop him and those with him from dying or winning, rather than surrendering. Viracocha Inca told the messenger to return, that was the opinion and desire of his lord, that he could fight and do whatever he wanted. Viracocha Inca thought it inevitable after Inca Yupanque's battle that he would be taken prisoner and killed in his youth for his lack of judgment. The messenger should tell his lord Inca Yupanque that Viracocha Inca would not go there, that he should never send another message like that again. After the messenger heard this, he went with the answer to where his lord Inca Yupanque was. After arriving, he told him what his father, Viracocha Inca, sent in reply to the message. After hearing everything, Inca Yupanque was saddened by such an answer because he thought that his father would send him some help and, as the people living near Cuzco saw his father Viracocha Inca giving them some aid, these people nearby would come to his aid and do him a favor. Thus as Inca Yupanque and his followers were feeling so sad because of what you have heard, it occurred to him that it would be a good idea to send his messenger to the caciques of the surrounding towns to inform them of the difficulties he was having and how he had sent his messenger to his father, who had refused to send him any help. Inca Yupanque begged them to collaborate with him by sending forces and soldiers. After thinking this over, Inca Yupanque called those four young men that he had there. He ordered each one to go separately with the message that you have heard to the caciques and lords in the area at a distance of three leagues from the city. After Inca Yupanque had divided up these messengers, one each left separately, going to the towns and caciques with the message that you have heard. The messengers reached the caciques and lords to whom Inca Yupanque had sent them. Once these caciques heard the message and plea sent by Inca Yupanque, they gave their answer to the messengers in the following way: "Return, brothers, and tell our lord Inca Yupanque that we love him with heart and soul; it would please us to give him that help he requests and to come to his aid with our soldiers and forces, but it seems to us that the forces that the Chanca Uscovilca wields over Inca Yupanque and over us are very great. Since Inca Yupanque has no more soldiers than himself and his companions and the forces and help that they could give him were also very little, they could not come to the aid of Inca Yupanque. If it came to pass that they did come to his aid with his having no more forces than he did, it would result in his losing and they along with him. They were also going to yield to the Chanca the same as his father planned to do as soon as the Chanca required it. However, up to that time the Chanca had not requested anything of them. But what they would do with Inca Yupanque was that, if he gathered somewhere or by some means a reasonable force of soldiers, they would be willing to help him in such dire straits with the resistance that he wanted to put up. This effort was not his responsibility alone, but, rather, theirs too and each one personally. At the same time, each one of them would send word to the other provinces and towns that bordered on each of theirs to ask for aid and support. They would come forth with the help and aid they promised him as soon as they saw that Inca Yupanque had some force of soldiers to offer for the resistance. For this they thanked him and begged him to do it. At the same time they would do what they said." On hearing this, the messenger returned to where their lord was. They gave him the answer that you have heard, which made Inca Yupanque very sad because he was alone. He understood the intentions and offer that the caciques had made; he considered their request fair, and it was reasonable for them to ask him to have some soldiers to go with those of the caciques and the help they would give. As Inca Yupanque was feeling this grief, it was about sunset and night was falling when he told his companions and the others, their servants, to all stay there together as they were and for none of them to leave with him. And Inca Yupanque left the lodgings alone without taking anyone else with him.

VIII

Concerning the character and virtues of Inca Yupanque and how he isolated himself from his companions, went into prayer, and, according to what the authors say, had a revelation from heaven, how he was aided, went into battle with Uscovilca, captured and killed him, along with other events that took place.

As a young man, Inca Yupanque was virtuous and affable in his conversation. He spoke little for such a young man, and he did not laugh in an exaggerated way but, rather, with discretion. He was fond of helping the weak. He was a chaste young man who was never heard to have been with a woman nor did those of his times ever find him telling lies or not keeping his word. He had these qualities of a virtuous and valiant lord, though still a young man, and he was very courageous. As his father thought over the character of his son Inca Yupanque, he was filled with envy and detested him. His father wished that his eldest son, named Inca Urco, had Inca Yupanque's character. Since his father saw Inca Yupanque's strength of character, he did not allow Inca Yupanque to come before him nor did he give anyone any hint that he loved Inca Yupanque. Since his father noticed that Inca Yupanque had so many good qualities, he feared that after his days the lords of Cuzco and the rest of the community would take him for their lord and that even if he left the title of lord to Inca Urco, these lords would take it away from him on seeing that Inca Urco was rather simpleminded and lacked the capacity and character of Inca Yupanque, whom everyone loved very much, as you have heard. After his days, their father wanted to leave his title to Inca Urco. Therefore, Viracocha Inca made the lords of Cuzco and the rest of the people treat Inca Urco with the deference and respect accorded to him personally. Thus Virococha Inca had the lords of Cuzco serve Inca Urco with the royal insignias used for him personally. No one was allowed to appear before him with shoes on, no matter how important a lord he might be, not even his brothers; rather, they came barefooted with their heads bowed all the time they were speaking before him or bringing him a

EL QVARTOCAPITAN APOMAITACINGA

Captain Apomayta

From the chronicle of Felipe Guaman Poma de Ayala,
Nueva coronica y buen gobierno.

message. He always ate alone, without anyone's daring to touch the food he was eating. Lords carried him in a litter on their shoulders. If he went out to the square, he sat on a golden seat under a parasol made of ostrich feathers dyed red. He drank from golden tumblers, and all the other service dishes of his household were of gold. He had a great many women. Inca Yupanque had no part of any of this because, as you have heard, he was detested by his father, who loved Inca Urco. When Viracocha Inca saw that Inca Yupanque had remained in the city of Cuzco, it pleased him. He thought Inca Yupanque would end his days there. When Inca Yupanque sent for the help about which you have already heard, Viracocha Inca refused to come to his aid.

Inca Yupanque left his companions the night already mentioned to you in this account. They say that he went to a place where none of his followers could see him, a distance of about two shots with a sling from the city of Cuzco. There he started praying to the creator of all things whom they call Viracocha Pachayachachic. Inca Yupanque was saying a prayer in the following words: "Lord God who created me and gave me the form of a man, come to my aid in this difficulty in which I find myself. You are my father who created me and gave me the form of a man. Do not allow me to be killed by my enemies. Give me help against them. Do not allow them to make me their subject. You made me free and your subject only. Do not allow me to be a subject of these people who want to subdue me this way and put me in bondage. Lord, give me the strength to resist them. Make of me whatever you will, for I am yours." When Inca Yupanque was saying this prayer, he was crying with all his heart. And still praying, he fell asleep, overcome by fatigue. As he was sleeping, Viracocha came to him in the form of a man and spoke to him: "My son, do not be distressed. The day that you go into battle with your enemies, I will send soldiers to you with whom you will defeat your enemies, and you will enjoy victory."

When Inca Yupanque remembered this happy dream, he took heart, returned to his followers, and told them to be happy, as he was. They should not be afraid, for they would not be defeated by their enemies. He would have soldiers in the time of need, but he refused to say more about what, how, or where, although they asked him. From then on, every night Inca Yupanque would go away from his companions to the place where he had said his prayer, where he always said it exactly as he had the first time, but not so that he would have the same dream as the first night.

However, the last night while he was praying, Viracocha came to him in the form of a man, and while Inca Yupanque was awake, said to him: "My son, tomorrow your enemies will come to do battle. I will come to your aid with soldiers so that you will defeat your enemies and enjoy victory." And they say that the next morning Uscovilca was coming with his soldiers down through Carmenga, which is a hill on the side of town toward the city of Los Reyes [Lima]. As Uscovilca was coming down with all his forces and soldiers, there appeared twenty squadrons of soldiers never seen or known to Inca Yupanque or his followers. These soldiers appeared on the Collasuyo quarter, on the road to Accha, and on the Condesuyo road. As these soldiers came up to him, Inca Yupanque and his companions were watching their enemies descend toward them. As the enemies approached, those who came to Inca Yupanque's aid surrounded him saying: "Aco çapa ynga aucay quita atixu llacxaimoctiangui cuna punchaupi,"[1] which means "Let us go, our only king, and we will defeat your enemies, whom you will take prisoner today." And so they went up to Uscovilca's soldiers who, full of fury, were coming down the hills. As they met, they unleashed their battle, fighting from morning, which was when they started, until noon. The battle turned out in such a way that large numbers of Uscovilca's soldiers died and not one entered into combat without dying. In that battle Uscovilca was taken prisoner and killed. When his followers saw him dead and saw the great slaughter that was being made of them, they agreed not to wait any longer. Returning by the road on which they had come, they fled until they reached the town of Jaquijahuana, where they stopped to rest and recover.

Having escaped this defeat, some of Uscovilca's captains sent this news right away to their land asking for aid. They also sent the news to the captains Malma and Rapa, who had gone on a campaign of conquest across the province of Condesuyo up to the province of the Chichas, as you have already been told in this account. These captains were already returning as victors, triumphant over the provinces which they had conquered. They came with great wealth, bringing their spoils. At this time, the defeated captains who were conferring together in Jaquijahuana sent their messengers to the other two captains whom Uscovilca had also sent from the town of Paucaray to discover and conquer whatever provinces and towns they could find. These captains had gone across the province of the Andes and had conquered up to the land of the Chiriguana, which is more than two hundred leagues to where they reached back to Paucaray. As these captains Yanavilca and Tecllovilca were returning as victors with great spoils, the messengers met them. When they found out about the death of Uscovilca, how he had been defeated and the way it was done, they all made their way as fast as they could to join the captains who had escaped from Uscovilca's defeat to confer at Jaquijahuana, as you have already heard. We will now leave them all together and speak again about Inca Yupanque, who was victorious.

IX

Wherein after defeating and killing Uscovilca, Inca Yupanque took Uscovilca's garments and insignias of lord and the rest of the prisoner captains that he had brought and took them to his father, Viracocha Inca, and the things that happened with his father, and how his father gave orders to have him killed, but Inca Yupanque returned to the city of Cuzco, and some time later Viracocha Inca died, the things that happened between Inca Yupanque and Viracocha Inca during this time, and about a custom that these lords had for honoring captains returning in victory from a war.

After he had killed Uscovilca, Inca Yupanque gave orders to take all of Uscovilca's garments and insignias that he had with him in the war, such as jewelry of gold and silver that he had as well as clothing with feathers, weapons, and personal equipment. Inca Yupanque got on a litter and set out to where his father, Viracocha Inca, was. Inca Yupanque took with him the three friends who had remained with him, as the account has told us, Vicaquirao, Apomayta and Quilescache Urcoguaranca, and two thousand men of war who protected Inca Yupanque personally. On arriving where his father was, he treated him with the respect that his lord and father deserved, and at the same time he placed before his father the insignias, weapons, and garments of the Chanca Uscovilca, whom he had defeated and killed. Inca Yupanque asked his father to tread on the insignias of that enemy whom he had defeated, and he also asked his father to tread on certain of Uscovilca's captains, whom Inca Yupanque brought there as prisoners and ordered to have thrown on the ground. It should be pointed out that it was customary for these lords when some captain or captains returned in victory from a war, to bring the insignias and adornments of the lords that they had killed or taken prisoner and also bring before them the captains taken prisoner in the war. When these captains entered the city of Cuzco in victory, they carried before them these insignias and prisoners and placed them before the lords. Seeing the spoils, the insignias, and the prisoners before them, one lord stood up and trod on them and stepped on these prisoners. These lords did this as a sign that those who brought them received approval and favor from their lord; and the work that had been done in defeating these enemies was accepted as service rendered. Moreover, the lord whom they asked to tread on these things and prisoners, by doing that, received and took possession and dominion over the lands that were taken and the vassals who lived there.

After this, wanting to show his father full respect even though he had not wanted to favor him, Inca Yupanque brought before him all the things that you have heard mentioned. Inca Yupanque wanted his father to accept this favor and take possession of those enemies subdued by his captains. Viracocha Inca saw these insignias before him and the captains who were brought as prisoners as a sign of victory, and Inca Yupanque asked him to tread on them as his father and lord. At this time, Viracocha Inca had with him one of Uscovilca's chiefs, who had been sent to him to make the arrangements for the surrender and the conditions that he wanted to impose. Since Uscovilca still had not sent orders, this chief remained there. Viracocha Inca had not found out what had happened to Uscovilca with Inca Yupanque, so he did not believe that what Inca Yupanque brought before him belonged to Uscovilca or that Inca Yupanque had killed and defeated him. Still unsatisfied with the evidence, Viracocha Inca ordered that chief who was with him, named Guamanguaraca, the one with whom the agreements were to be made, as you have already heard, to appear before him. Like something that he considered a fantasy, Viracocha Inca asked Guamanguaraca: "Tell me, do you know if these garments and insignias belong to your lord Uscovilca?" As soon as Guamanguaraca saw them, recognized them, and saw the captains of his lord on the ground, he looked down at the ground, started to cry, and threw himself on the ground there with them. When Viracocha Inca realized that it was true that his son Inca Yupanque had really won a victory over his enemies, he became very sad and envious because he hated Inca Yupanque, as we have told you. Inca Yupanque recognized all of this in his father, but he paid no attention to any of it except that the man was his father and lord. Inca Yupanque asked him again as his father and lord to tread on the prisoners. To that Viracocha answered that the prisoners be put in a certain room and his son Inca Urco should tread on them first. Inca Urco was the son he loved the most; to him he planned to leave his government and personal position after his days, as we have already told. To this, Inca Yupanque answered that he was begging his father to tread on the prisoners, that he had not won the victory so that such women as Inca Urco and the rest of his brothers could step on them but, rather, only the person he respected as lord and father. Otherwise Inca Yupanque would leave.

At this point, Viracocha Inca called one of the lords that he had with him. Speaking to him alone, Viracocha Inca told him to secretly take the warriors he had with him, go to a certain ravine covered with bushes and high grass, where he should wait secretly. While this lord kept the soldiers in ambush, Viracocha Inca would talk to Inca Yupanque and at the same time try to put him into a certain room, where he would take him forcibly and kill him inside there. But if Inca Yupanque escaped from there, the lord should kill him in the brushy ravine where Inca Yupanque would return. With this agreed, this lord left to do what Viracocha Inca ordered. Viracocha Inca returned to Inca Yupanque and started to talk cheerfully and smile at him. When he thought that captain had done as ordered, Viracocha Inca got up and asked Inca Yupanque to put Uscovilca's things that he carried inside that room where he had told him to put them so that his son Inca Urco could tread on them and afterward he would tread on them also. Inca Yupanque said again for his father to tread on them if he wanted, otherwise, he would leave, as he had said. Viracocha Inca realized that he could not convince him to let Inca Urco tread on them. Planning to kill Inca Yupanque inside the room, he told him to go inside the room and, while they were alone, Viracocha Inca would tread on them in his presence. At this critical moment, Inca Yupanque's three good friends arrived and, suspecting the betrayal that Viracocha Inca planned, they refused to let Inca Yupanque enter the room. Then one of Inca Yupanque's captains from his personal guard showed up and said he had seen certain warriors there at the stronghold, who had left one at a time and two at a time, that it was a large number of soldiers who had left and some of them carried lances and halberds and were headed down the road where the captains had come from. The captain suspected that those men were going to wait for their return someplace or that they were going to the city of Cuzco to steal what they had there and take it away from them. After his captain told Inca Yupanque that right there in front of his three good friends, Inca Yupanque laughed at finding out that his father wanted to kill him that way and realized that his father was filled with envy, while Inca Yupanque was asking his father to accept everything as a service to him. After hearing what that captain said, Inca Yupanque told two of his three good friends to take half of the soldiers he had brought as guards. Just as those of the stronghold had left to ambush them, he was also sending them one by one and two by two. They should follow those sent by Viracocha Inca and find out if those soldiers were going to ambush them in some brushy place or ravine or go on to Cuzco. After finding out what they could, they should report what was going on so that he, with this knowledge of the situation, could give orders to those who remained about what they should do. If perchance those soldiers had set up an ambush there, where they would find out about it, they should wait, not giving themselves away or letting the enemy know they had caught on. They should leave right away, for he would finish soon with his father, with what they would do, then he would return later.

Thus his two good friends begged him not to go alone into any room with his father so that he would not be killed by the treachery. Inca Yupanque's two friends also advised Apomayta, the friend who was staying with him, to watch out for his lord. Thus the two lords left, and they ordered two hundred Indians with battle-axes in their hands to go inside where Inca Yupanque was. These Indians were to place themselves around Inca Yupanque, watch him, and defend him so that he could not be harmed. The rest of the soldiers there were ordered to stay near the door of the room where Inca Yupanque was. If they heard any commotion of men inside, they should all go inside at once and defend their lord.

Having done this, they took the soldiers that Inca Yupanque had sent them and had fifty Indians go ahead, one by one, two by two, under cover, furtively, just like those Viracocha Inca had sent ahead. These fifty Indians went out looking for their enemies and, since they were spread out each one at some distance from the other, one of them who was going ahead, on reaching the wooded ravine where the grass was high, saw the enemies waiting in ambush. As soon as the enemy noticed him, they fell into the high grass, thinking he had not seen them. The moment this Indian saw them, he sat down on the ground and acted like he was tying a certain strap of his shoes. This deception was a sign and warning to his companions who were coming behind him. Seeing him in the way you have heard, they sent the message from one to the other until it reached the two lords who were coming behind them. Understanding that it was an ambush, they ordered all their soldiers to get together and wait there where they had heard the order, except for the fifty who had gone ahead. These were ordered to walk around there keeping an eye on those in the ambush to see if they left or moved ahead and to notify the one who was tying his shoes by sending an Indian crawling up to him. This Indian would tell him to show that he was tying and untying his shoes and other things he carried in order to disguise what he was really doing.

Leaving this like it was, let us return to Inca Yupanque, who was informed, as you have heard. He asked his father to tread on those insignias of the prisoner that he had brought there from Uscovilca. Viracocha Inca answered that he did not want to do it unless Inca Urco tread on it first. To this Inca Yupanque said that he had come there to have his father tread on that out of respect for he who was his father and to show obedience to him as his lord. Inca Yupanque also wanted to beg his father to return to his town and city. As his captain and in his father's name, Inca Yupanque had won that undertaking. Inca Yupanque wanted to leave there, go to the city of Cuzco, and enter in triumph with Uscovilca's captains and things. That had been his intention and the reason why he had come there. Otherwise he had no reason to bring what he had won so that it could be tread on by a type like his eldest son, Inca Urco. After saying this to his father, Viracocha Inca, Inca Yupanque ordered Uscovilca's garments and other things to be picked up and ordered the prisoners to rise from the ground, where they had been stretched out up to that time. Thus Inca Yupanque left angry that his father did not want to tread on the prisoner and at what you have heard. It grieved him that his father was so upset with him that he wanted him killed. Inca Yupanque saw nothing in himself to have caused his father to become so angry with him and dislike him so much. On the contrary, Inca Yupanque had tried to serve him and please him as much as possible. He realized that his father's anger and passion came from envy of seeing him surpass all of his brothers. Inca Yupanque was very upset about it.

So he left the place where his father was, thinking about these and many other things. He reached the place where his two good friends were waiting for him with his soldiers. They informed Inca Yupanque about the ambush that was to take him by surprise. Right there he told his captains to divide those soldiers into three groups and two of these groups should split up and go on opposite sides of the road and the other group should go there with him. These two groups that were separated should keep under cover as much as possible. Inca Yupanque would enter by the road and over the hill where the ambush awaited. As soon as his captains shouted "Chayachaya," which means "After them, after them," his soldiers, who were encircling the hill, should come out and give battle to the enemies. Not respecting any of them, they should not leave any alive. With these orders given, these soldiers left cautiously in the way you have heard. Inca Yupanque went to the ravine where the ambush awaited. As he went in the middle, leading his soldiers, who were forewarned of what they suspected, a stone was thrown at Inca Yupanque from the mountain. But it missed, hitting one of those carrying his litter. When Inca Yupanque and his three good friends saw this, they shouted "After them." As soon as his soldiers heard the command, having surrounded the place, they attacked those in ambush with such force that not one man escaped.

After Inca Yupanque reached the city of Cuzco, he ordered his friend Vicaquirao to return to his father, Viracocha Inca, and tell him to come to his city, that he had the things mentioned stored so that his father could triumph over them. Inca Yupanque ordered three thousand men to accompany Vicaquirao. He left and when he reached the stronghold where Viracocha Inca was, he found that he and his people were mourning the loss of those Inca Yupanque had killed at the ambush, where many important lords who had been with him were killed. When Viracocha Inca got the news that a large group of warriors was coming from the city of Cuzco, he feared that his son was coming to kill him and those with him. He entered into a brief consultation with his men and they decided that if his son was coming to make war on him, but they could come to some agreement in a discussion or, if his son wanted to make him a vassal, they should do whatever his son requested of them. In order to find out who was coming or what he was after, Viracocha Inca ordered one of the lords who were with him in mourning and crying to go out, and he also ordered ten other Indians in the same way to accompany him. They were to leave the stronghold one after another with this lord in the lead. Those following should notice how the first one was received by those who were coming. If they took him prisoner or treated him angrily, or whatever they saw, they should return to inform Viracocha Inca. So this lord left in the way stated. When he reached Vicaquirao, he made a sign of respect to him, and Vicaquirao did the same. Seeing him crying, Vicaquirao asked him what was bothering him, although he had a very good idea what it was. Vicaquirao had killed with his own hands one of the lord's brothers in the ambush. The lord told him that he was crying for his brother who was killed in the ambush.[1] Vicaquirao scolded him for all this, saying the ambush was an unfortunate mistake. The lord answered that he was not at fault, that Viracocha Inca had ordered it without giving them any choice in the matter. To this Vicaquirao answered that, if Viracocha Inca had ordered it, he could keep whatever he had won there, that he could not bring back so easily those friends and relatives that he had lost there. The lord said that what had been done was final and nothing could be done about it nor should it be discussed. Viracocha Inca had ordered it on a crazy impulse. The lord begged Vicaquirao to tell him why he was returning and what he demanded Vicaquirao told him. Then that lord told

Vicaquirao the warning and message that had been given to them, the agreement that had been made, what had been decided in the agreement, and the reason he had come out there. Hearing all this made Vicaquirao laugh out loud at him and his people who were standing by. And Vicaquirao laughed so hard that that lord laughed with them. Thus all together they headed to Viracocha Inca. After they had gone some distance, this lord asked Vicaquirao to let him go ahead to see Viracocha Inca, whom they had left upset and all of his people with the fear of what had already been told. This lord returned to Viracocha Inca and told him why Vicaquirao was coming. Soon Vicaquirao arrived where Viracocha Inca was, greeted him with respect, and gave him the message that he brought on behalf of Inca Yupanque, which you have already heard. To this Viracocha Inca answered that he would be pleased to do it, as long as he was not expected to return to Cuzco. Since he had left fleeing, this would be insulting and it would not be proper for him to enter the city after abandoning it. Since a boy such as his son Inca Yupanque had gained victory, Viracocha Inca would establish a town there at that stronghold of Caquea Xaquixahuana with the people who were with him. He wanted to die there, so Inca Yupanque should not expect him in Cuzco, for Viracocha Inca did not plan to return. Thus Viracocha Inca made a settlement at that stronghold above Calca, seven leagues from Cuzco, building a town whose houses were almost all of stone.

Virtually all the rest of those who were with Viracocha Inca in that stronghold realized that Inca Yupanque was very generous and kind to everyone, a trait which he had from childhood. Being such a great lord and having achieved such a great undertaking, he would not fail to bestow great favors on those who were close to him and wanted to serve him. Considering this, many of the people whom Viracocha Inca had there with him went to the city of Cuzco. Inca Yupanque received them with a smile. Those returning begged his pardon, telling him that if they had abandoned him it was because his father had taken them. Inca Yupanque answered them, saying that he was not angry with them. If they had gone with his father, they did it as good subjects. His father was lord over all of them. They were coming to him from where his father was. Inca Yupanque would receive them well and give them land, women, houses, clothing, and he never took away anything that they had left there when they fled with his father, including houses, land, storehouses with food and clothing which they had left in their houses. On the contrary, he told them that he had protected all their possessions. He understood that they had gone to enjoy themselves with his father so he protected all of their possessions. Each one of them should look to see if anything was missing from their houses. He had remained as the guardian so he would be responsible for everything, and no one would lose anything. Inca Yupanque had arranged for all this, and he ordered certain lords to be sure that no one go into any of the houses which were left vacant. He always believed that the owners would recognize his greatness and return to their homes. And they did return, as you have already heard. Going back to Vicaquirao, who had remained with Viracocha Inca trying to persuade him to come to Cuzco, he failed in his effort after three days that he spent there with him. After that time, he realized that Viracocha Inca was determined not to return to Cuzco. Vicaquirao returned. Arriving at the city of Cuzco, he gave Inca Yupanque the answer Viracocha Inca had given, which you have already heard, and all the rest of what had happened. All of this made Inca Yupanque sad, for he realized that his father did not want to come back as the lord that he was before.

X

Wherein Inca Yupanque had a meeting with his soldiers, divided the spoils among them, what was done with the soldiers that Viracocha had given him in answer to the prayer Inca Yupanque had made to him, how he got news of the meeting called by Uscovilca's captains , how he fought them and defeated them, how he divided up again the spoils that had been taken in this battle, and of the things that came to pass at that time.

Inca Yupanque ordered all the men who were with him at that time to assemble. They say that it must have been more than fifty thousand warriors. These were the ones the neighboring lords agreed to give him if they had men. They saw the multitude of soldiers coming to support Inca Yupanque, and since they had agreed to help him, with all their men they joined the soldiers who were coming to support Inca Yupanque. Thus these neighboring chieftains favored him. They say that after the battle with Uscovilca and the victory won by Inca Yupanque, the soldiers Viracocha sent to him soon disappeared, and Inca Yupanque saw only the fifty or sixty thousand men with him who were those the neighboring chieftains mixed with the soldiers you have heard about.

Inca Yupanque called his soldiers together and ordered all the spoils from the battle brought to him. He took what he thought would be the best to offer as a sacrifice to Viracocha for helping win the victory over his enemies. All the rest of the spoils he gave out to his soldiers according to their rank and service.

Once it was known all over this city how magnificent the new lord was and that he knew how to reward service, there was great joy in the land. Thus many caciques and people came from everywhere offering to serve him and make him their lord. As Inca Yupanque was doing what you have just heard, a messenger came to him from one of his captains, who at that time was guarding the city two leagues away, trying to find out what his enemies were doing in an assembly they called. This messenger sent word that the captains who escaped during the battle by fleeing from where Uscovilca was killed, an event about which you have already heard, were reorganized in Jaquijahuana and allied with the natives of the region. From this area many soldiers had come to their aid. Moreover, Uscovilca's other four captains, whom he had sent from Paucaray to explore the provinces of Condesuyo and Andesuyo, had arrived. Their story has already been told to you. They left the next morning to go into battle with Inca Yupanque and avenge the death of their lord Uscovilca.

After Inca Yupanque got the news, he ordered his three good friends and the rest of the caciques and lords who had come to his aid and service to bring their warriors together at once and take them, each one with his own weapons, to a certain field. There the men were to be counted one by one. After this they found out there were one hundred thousand warriors. These soldiers had come together because of Inca Yupanque's great fame, which had spread. It is said that there were almost two hundred thousand enemies. Thus Inca Yupanque ordered his men to form four squadrons and for each cacique lord of Indians that was there to act as leader of his men. He assigned each of his three good friends to act as generals of the three squadrons, taking one for himself. Since all were supplied with the necessary weapons, he ordered his troops to march out in search of the enemy. As soon as the enemy found out that Inca Yupanque had left Cuzco, they returned to Jaquijahuana, where they waited for him. Inca Yupanque arrived, and the day of the battle he came within view of his enemies. In order to go into combat with them, they say that he looked back to see his soldiers and squadrons. They were separated, and each by itself. They say that he saw so many soldiers who had come at that time to aid him that it was impossible to count them. Thus he charged his enemies, striking in the middle of them and attacking them everywhere. This battle was so cruel and hard fought that it started with the sun up high, which would be about ten, the way they tell time, and at sunset victory in the battle went to Inca Yupanque. On Inca Yupanque's side more than thirty thousand men were killed, and on the Chancas side, who were the enemies, not a man remained alive. The natives of Jaquijahuana had joined them and had braided their hair. Once the victory was known and the battle won, all those of Jaquijahuana went off together to a place, and they appeared all together before Inca Yupanque and threw themselves on the ground. Inca Yupanque's men wanted to kill them after seeing their own men die. But Inca Yupanque defended them, saying not to kill them. If they took sides with the Chancas it was because the Chancas met in their land, and they could not do anything else. They also said the same thing, giving the same explanation. Then Inca Yupanque ordered that, since they were *orejones,* their hair should be cut short right then. And they cut their own hair short, for they all saw it was the will of Inca Yupanque and that he did them a favor. The style of Inca Yupanque and of those from Cuzco was to wear the hair short. With this done, Inca Yupanque ordered them all to return to their town and live in peace. And he ordered his captains not to let anyone do any harm to these people of Jaquijahuana nor take anything from them, and if anything of their property was taken in the spoils, it was to be returned immediately.

Then he ordered all of the prisoners to be brought out in front of him. When they were there he asked them why they had done battle with him again, since he was so powerful. And there among the prisoners taken were Uscovilca's four captains who had gone out exploring, as you have already heard in this account. What made them call that assembly that they formed and go into that battle was that they had been favored by such good fortune in the journeys that they had taken and in the lands that they had conquered. They explained to him about the battles and events that had happened to each one on their journeys. They never had any mishaps on any of them; rather, they had always been victorious, and since this had happened to them, they thought they would always be fortunate. They had undertaken that battle to restore the loss of their lord and avenge his death. To this, Inca Yupanque answered that they had made a mistake. If they were wise they should have realized that, if they had won victories in the lands where they had gone, they should consider that they had won them because of the fortune of their lord Uscovilca. He had sent them on that search. Since they saw and should have known that their lord was defeated and killed, they should assume that their fortune had ended and neither he nor they had it any longer. Inca Yupanque would punish them and let others see and hear that in that place they would be punished along with all the others so that they would not call assemblies any more with which to disturb him and cause others who were innocent to find themselves in such a situation where they would lose their lives. This happened to many of those who participated in the assembly that they had called. In that place, they would be punished. Thus Inca Yupanque ordered them to be brought before him at the site where the battle took place. As a reminder of it, in the presence of all his people, he had set in the ground many posts from which they would be hanged. And after being hanged, their heads would be cut off and placed on top of the posts. Their bodies would be burned, turned into dust, and from the highest hills cast to the winds so that this would be remembered. Thus Inca Yupanque ordered that nobody dare bury any of the bodies of the enemies who had died in the battle so that they would be eaten by foxes and birds and their bones would be seen all the time. All of which was done in the way that you have heard.

With this done, Inca Yupanque ordered the gathering of the spoils and gold and silver jewels that had been taken. This was done and the spoils were brought before him. After seeing the spoils, he ordered that they be taken all together, as they were, to the city of Cuzco, where he was planning to distribute them among his friends. All of the spoils were taken, and he left with them, going to the city of Cuzco. On arriving, he handed out these spoils to his people, giving each one what he thought proper according to his rank. After this he ordered that from his stores of garments and large livestock in the city and other supplies, a certain amount be brought, which he thought sufficient for everyone. Once all this was brought, he ordered his captains to distribute it among the soldiers, which they did. When these and many other favors for his captains were done, he sent them to their lands to rest, thanking them for the help they had given him. Thus they all left, and Inca Yupanque remained in the city with his people.

As these lords were bidding farewell to him before going to their lands, they begged him to take them under his protection as his vassals and for him to take the royal *borla* fringe[1] and office of Inca. Inca Yupanque thanked them for all this, but at that time his father and lord was still alive, and it was not right for him to take the royal fringe as long as his father lived. He was there as his father's captain. But he asked them to do two things for him. The first was for them to go to his father, to respect and obey him as their lord. They said that they would do it. The second thing was for them to honor him as their friend and brother and whenever he sent to ask them for something for them to do it. They said that they had no other lord except him, and as his vassals he could have them do whatever he wanted. And he thanked them for it.

Thus they left, and Inca Yupanque stayed in the city. Those lords went straight to Viracocha Inca. After making their proper sign of respect, as Inca Yupanque had ordered, they told him how Inca Yupanque had sent them there to offer their services. Viracocha Inca saw this great multitude of powerful lords before him. This pleased him very much because at that time he greatly needed the aid of some of their men to build that town he wanted to make there. He welcomed them, rose from his seat, and embraced them all. He sat down again and ordered them all to sit down also. He ordered many tumblers of *chicha*[2] to be brought, and soon after he had brought to them a large amount of coca,[3] a valued herb that they always have in their mouths. Further ahead in this account more will be told about this herb. At this point, Viracocha Inca stood up, considering that his son had sent those lords to him; they loved his son very much and wanted him to be their lord. It was reasonable that he should encourage them. He made a speech to them in which he thanked them for what they had done for him and for his son. They knew and had heard that up to that time he had been lord of Cuzco. But he had left for compelling reasons, and from that time on his son Inca Yupanque would be lord of Cuzco. They should respect and obey Inca Yupanque as their lord. From there Viracocha Inca rejected the royal insignia and fringe. He would put it on the head of his son Inca Yupanque. After that the lords stood up and one by one they went to give him many thanks, showing that they considered his renouncing his authority and giving it to his son Inca Yupanque, whom they loved and wanted to be their lord, a great favor to them. After this they sat down again.

And Viracocha Inca told them that he wanted to build a town there in that stronghold and for that reason he needed their help and men. He begged them to honor his request by giving him that help. To this those lords answered that they had come there to see how they could serve him, as their lord Inca Yupanque had ordered. They were ready to do that or anything else he might order them to do. He should tell them the time and the month he wanted to start to do the work so that they could send their foremen and Indians to start the enterprise and construct the buildings. Meanwhile he should give them the plan for that town by having models of the buildings made from clay. They would send him master builders who knew how to use stone for whatever design he wanted. Viraocha Inca thanked them and ordered many things brought out, such as slings, baskets of coca, certain fine garments, and many other things that they value. All these things were brought before him, and he gave them to those lords with his own hands. Then he ordered drinks served and also a certain amount of coca given out. Next, Viracocha Inca stood up and thanked them for the goodwill and kindness they had shown to him and his son. He told them the month and time when they were to send him Indians and men to build his town. Thus the lords stood up, agreeing to send the help as promised. They made gestures of reverence and bid him farewell. There we will leave him and speak about Inca Yupanque.

XI

Wherein Inca Yupanque made the house of the Sun, the statue of the Sun, and the long fasts, pagan rites, and offerings that he did.

The cacique lords had left Cuzco and had gone to visit Viracocha Inca, as our account has already related to you. Inca Yupanque remained alone in the city with his people. After resting two days, he started feeling restless and decided to do some exercise. Thus, accompanied by the lords he had there, he set out one morning from the city of Cuzco. That day he walked through all the lands surrounding the city, and he did the same thing the next day. After having looked them over carefully, he noticed the bad repair and workmanship left from the time his father was there. The third day he also went out looking around with the lords at the place where the city of Cuzco was founded. Most of it was a marsh and springs, as our account has already told you [Pt. I, chap. III]. The houses in which the inhabitants lived were small, low, and poorly built without the proper design of a town that had streets. What is now the great city of Cuzco was just like a town called Cayocache located today near the city.

Inca Yupanque saw the sad state of this town of Cuzco and also of the cultivated lands surrounding it. He realized that he had time and excellent materials for rebuilding it. But before starting to build houses or assign lots in the town, he decided to build a house of the Sun, in which there would be placed a statue to whom, in place of the Sun, they could worship and make sacrifices. They hold that there is a creator whom they call Viracocha Pacha-yachachic, which means creator of the world, and they believe that this one made the Sun and everything that is created in the sky and earth, as you have heard. Since they had no writing, were blind to knowledge, and almost without understanding, they differ in this in every way. Sometimes they hold the Sun up as the creator, and other times they say it is Viracocha. Generally, in all the land and in each of its provinces, the devil has them confused. Everywhere that the devil showed up, he told them a thousand lies and delusions. Thus he had them deceived and blind. In those places where they saw him, they put stones in his place, which they worshiped and adored. Sometimes the devil told them he was the Sun, and at other times in other places he said he was the Moon. He told others that he was their god and creator. He told others he was their light who warmed them and shined on them, and thus they would see him in the volcanoes of Arequipa.

In other places he said he was their lord who had made the world and that he was called Pachacama, which means maker of the world. Thus, as I have said, he had deceived and blinded them.

Returning to our account, this lord Inca Yupanque wanted to make a house and shrine at which he and the rest of his people could worship. He wanted to make it in reverence to and in the figure of the one whom he had seen before his battle. He took into account that the one he had seen there, whom he called Viracocha, he saw with great brightness, as they say. And so much so that it seemed to him that the whole day was there before him, and its light, which he saw before him, they say gave him a great fright. And he was never told who it was. As he was planning on building this house, he judged by the brightness of the one he saw that it must have been the Sun, and on coming near the first word he spoke, "Child, fear not"; thus, his people called him "child of the Sun." Taking into account what you have heard, he decided to make this house of the Sun. After making this decision, he called the lords of the city of Cuzco whom he had there with him and told them his plan and how he wanted to build this house. They told him to explain the dimensions and style of the building. Such a house as that should be built by the natives of the city of Cuzco. Inca Yupanque told them that he agreed with them. Seeing the place which he thought best to build the house, he ordered that a cord be brought there.

After that they left the place where he and his people were and, at the place where the temple was to be built, Inca Yupanque himself with his own hands took the cord, measured and laid out the plan of the temple of the Sun. On finishing, he left there with his people and went to a town called Salu, almost five leagues from this city, where they have a quarry. He measured the stones for building this temple, after which the people of the nearby towns worked the stones pointed out to them until there were enough to build this temple. Along with these stones they brought everything else necessary for this temple. On arrival they went to work on it just as Inca Yupanque had designed and imagined it. He always supervised the work himself along with the other lords. They watched how it was being built, and Inca Yupanque along with the others worked on the building. Since the materials and equipment for it were at hand, the work on it was finished in a short time.

With this temple of the Sun finished, as you have heard, Inca Yupanque ordered five hundred maidens brought there together. He offered them to the Sun so that these maidens would always serve the Sun and remain inside there like cloistered nuns. Next he sent an old man born in the city of Cuzco who seemed to him honest, of good character and good reputation. This old man was to reside there in the temples of the Sun and act as caretaker for the Sun and the temple. Then he ordered two hundred young married men to be brought there to act as *yanaconas*,[1] servants to work for the Sun. At that same time, he designated certain lands for the Sun, which these two hundred *yanaconas* would farm.

Next, Inca Yupanque ordered the lords of Cuzco to have ready within ten days provisions of maize, sheep [llamas], and lambs along with fine garments and a certain number of boys and girls whom they call *capacocha*, all of which was for making a sacrifice to the Sun. When the ten days elapsed and everything was gathered, Inca Yupanque ordered that a big fire be built into which, after having the heads cut off of the sheep and lambs, he ordered them thrown along with the garments and maize as a sacrifice to the Sun. The boys and girls whom they had brought together were well dressed and adorned. He ordered them to be buried alive in that temple which was especially made where the statue of the Sun was. With the blood which had been taken from the lambs and sheep, he ordered certain lines drawn on the walls of this temple. All of this was done by Inca Yupanque and his three friends along with others. All of this signified a way of blessing and consecrating this temple. During this sacrifice, Inca Yupanque and his friends went barefoot and acted with great reverence for this temple of the Sun. With the same blood, Inca Yupanque also drew certain lines on the face of this man who was designated as caretaker of this temple, and he did the same to those three lords his friends and to the *mamaconas*,[2] nuns in the service of the Sun. Then he ordered all the people of the city, both men and women, to come make their sacrifices there in the temple of the Sun. So the common people made sacrifices by burning a certain type of maize and coca in that fire that was built for it. They entered one at a time barefoot, heads down. And after making their sacrifice, as they left in the same way, Inca Yupanque ordered the caretaker of the Sun to draw on the face of each one of them the same line that you have heard about with the blood of the sheep. They were ordered that, from that time until the statue of the Sun made of gold, was finished, they must all fast and not eat meat, fish, agi, salt, nor be with their women, nor eat any vegetables and eat only raw maize and drink *chicha*. Anyone who broke this fast would be sacrificed to the Sun and burned in that same fire. Inca Yupanque ordered it to burn always, day and night. Inca Yupanque also ordered the wood for this fire to be carved and that every day sacrifices be made on the fire to the idol. These sacrifices were to be made by the *mamaconas* of the Sun, who were also on a fast, the same as Inca Yupanque and the rest of the lords.

With this done and arranged, Inca Yupanque and the rest of the lords ordered the best master goldsmiths from the city to come there. Giving them all the equipment there inside the temples of the Sun, he ordered them to fashion a boy of solid gold cast in a mold. This statue was to be the size, height, and proportions of a one-year-old boy in the nude because they say that the one who talked to him when he prayed and came to him in his sleep had the shape of a shining child. The one who came to him later, when he was awake the night before he went into battle with Uscovilca, as we have already told you, was shining so brightly that he did not allow Inca Yupanque to see his form. Therefore, he ordered this idol to be made the size and shape of a boy one year old. It took one month to make this statue. During this month, they had great sacrifices and fasts. After this, Inca Yupanque ordered that lord whom he had designated as caretaker of the Sun to take the idol. This he did with much reverence and he dressed it in a tunic of very finely woven gold and wool in a variety of styles. He put a certain band on its head, according to their style and custom. Then he put on it a fringe like the one used by lords, and on top of it a gold disk and on its feet *ojotas,* as they call shoes, also of gold.

When the statue was dressed this way, Inca Yupanque came to where it was. He came barefoot and he made gestures of reverence, showing it great respect. Thus he took the statue of the idol in his hands and carried it to the chamber or place in the temple where it was to be kept. There was in that chamber a seat made of wood and well covered with iridescent feathers of various colors, which made it very attractive. Inca Yupanque placed the idol on the seat. Afterward, he had a gold brazier brought, lighted a fire in it, and placed it before the idol. Inca Yupanque had certain little birds and certain grains of maize thrown into the burning brazier, and he had a certain *chicha* poured onto the fire, all of which he said the Sun would eat, and thus by doing that he was feeding the Sun. From that time on, that custom was regularly maintained. All of this was done by that caretaker of the Sun, and as if the Sun were a person who ate and drank, they were very careful in cooking a variety of dishes and delicacies for it. These things were burned before the idol in the afternoon and in the morning over the gold and silver braziers in the way that you have already heard. From that time on they worshiped that idol, but no one went inside where the idol was except the most important lords, who entered barefoot and head down with much reverence and veneration. Inca Yupanque went in alone, and he personally, with his own hands, sacrificed the sheep and lambs, making the fire, and burning the sacrifice. When he was making the sacrifice, no other lord dared enter. They all remained in the patio, and there outside they made their sacrifices and their reverent gestures. The common people had to worship outside, not even entering the patio as the lords did. Therefore, Inca Yupanque had placed in the middle of the square of Cuzco, where the pole of the gallows is now, a stone made like a sugarloaf pointed on top and covered with a strip of gold. He also had this stone worked the same day he ordered the statue of the Sun made. And this stone was for the common people to worship, and the statue in the temple of the Sun was for the lords.

This temple was worshiped and held in great reverence, not just the statue but also the temple stones. The *yanacona* servants of the temple were thought to be like something blessed and consecrated. When they were building it, as they were fitting a certain stone, a piece about three fingers wide and long broke off the edge. Inca Yupanque ordered a certain amount of silver to be melted right away and poured into the stone, where the piece broke off in such a way that it filled exactly what had broken off the stone. The whole temple was made of stone, and the seams of the blocks of stone against stone were so fine that they looked like lines made with a nail across a stone. The most important lords were buried in the patios and rooms, except where the idol was.

The day the idol was placed in the temple of the Sun, the stone was placed in the middle of the square. Ten days after the idol was put on the seat which you have heard about, Inca Yupanque ordered a small litter made and covered with a certain gold cloth. With it ready, he ordered the most important lords, who were his three friends and the caretaker of the Sun, to take the litter, and Inca Yupanque himself went in where the idol was and put it on the litter. Then, saying that the Sun blessed the city and all of its residents, he ordered it to be carried all around the city. The lords who were carrying the litter said that it was the Sun who blessed his town and his children. Therefore, when some *orejon* noble from Cuzco left town, no matter how poor he might be, the people in the provinces worshiped him as the child of the Sun wherever he went. Thus they treated him with great reverence and respect, and they made sacrifices before him, sacrifices they call *arpa*. And they gave him food and full service with the solemnity they used in offering a sacrifice to their idols.

When the stone was placed in the middle of the square of Cuzco, first a large hole was made there where all the people of Cuzco, old and young alike, offered to the Sun as many pieces of gold as they saw fit. Afterward, they filled up the hole and built a stone font about one-half estado[3] high. All around the font they buried some small gold statues, each one about the length and thickness of one finger. Before these little statues were buried this way around the font, they made as many small squadrons as lineages of the city of Cuzco. Each statuette represented the most important lord of each of those lineages. After these squadrons were set up and put in order, all were buried under the earth by the wall of the font. In the middle of the font they put the stone that represented the Sun. Putting these statues around the font that way was an offering which they made to the Sun of the generation of the people of Cuzco and the lineages from the time Manco Capac had founded it up to the lineages of that time.

Once this was done in the way you have heard, all the people of the city sacrificed a large number of sheep and lambs. From that time until the Spaniards entered the city of Cuzco, the natives always made this sacrifice to this stone idol. So many sheep and lambs were sacrificed there to that idol from the time it was put there until the Spaniards entered the city that they do not know nor can they count them. But they say that the least number of sheep and lambs sacrificed at one time amounted to more than five hundred.

XII

Wherein Inca Yupanque brought together the lords of all the land who were under his dominion, and how he improved the lands around the city of Cuzco, made the first storehouses of food, and took other measures that were necessary for the good of the republic in Cuzco.

After giving the order and having made the idols and temple of the Sun, as you have heard, Inca Yupanque ordered in the city of Cuzco that all the important cacique lords who had pledged obedience to him and were living in the provinces and neighboring lands around the city of Cuzco attend a meeting on a certain designated day because he had certain things to communicate to them. Once the major lords of Cuzco heard the order, they sent their lord *orejones* to the provinces and neighboring places, as you have already heard. With them was sent the order that the Inca had made, and on that designated day they were all to come to the city. As soon as these lords found out about Inca Yupanque's order, they came to the city of Cuzco as soon as possible. When they were all together, Inca Yupanque told them that they could see that the Sun was on his side and that it was not fair that they be satisfied with little. It seemed to him that as time went by war would not allow them to care for their lands and conserve them in the way that once and for all he wanted the lands to be improved so that perpetually they and their descendants could farm and be supported. It seemed to him that each one of them should have designated and recognized lands to be farmed and maintained for each one by the people of their house and their friends. He said all of this to the lords and inhabitants of the city of Cuzco. And thus all together, having received this great favor that he did for them by giving them lands that would be recognized in perpetuity for each one of them, all together they gave him many thanks, giving him the title of Yndichuri, which means child of the Sun.

Then from there Inca Yupanque ordered them all to go to a certain place where the lands were painted. He gave to each one of them the land that he thought adequate for them. After doing this, he ordered that his friends the three lords distribute the lands to all the lords of the city just as Inca Yupanque had ordered. Afterward, they were all to appear again before him. Thus the lords went and distributed the lands, giving possession to those whom the Inca had favored. On their return, the Inca ordered the caciques and lords who were there to bring to him the number of Indians that each one had there with him. Soon the cacique lords counting with with *quipos*,[1] which means numerical record, brought him the total number of Indians they had. After the Inca found out how many Indians there were, he ordered the lords to distribute them by houses. This was done the next day and he ordered each one of those of Cuzco who had been lucky enough to get lands to go out and work and improve them, making canals for irrigation, all of which was repaired and made from building stones so that the construction would last forever. He ordered them to put their boundary stones high in such a way as never to get lost. Under each of these boundary stones he ordered that there be placed a certain amount of carbon, saying that, if at some time the boundary stone fell, the carbon would mark the boundaries of the lands. After this was arranged, while the lands were being improved, Inca Yupanque spent some days relaxing and watching how each one worked and improved the land he had been given. He gave help to those whom he noticed having some difficulty. He saw that the construction and improvements on those lands was taking a long time, considering the way the work was going, and since this construction could not be finished so easily, he ordered the lords and caciques who were there to come to a meeting in his house one day. They met just as he ordered. With them there in his house he told them that it was urgent that in the city of Cuzco there be storehouses for all foods such as maize, agi, beans, choclo,[2] chuño,[3] quinua,[4] dried meat, and all the other dried provisions and foods that they have. For that, it was necessary that they have it sent from their lands. Then the lord caciques said that they would be very pleased to have it brought, for him to send from the city of Cuzco some noble *orejones* to accompany the Indians that they were sending so that in their lands they could tell those who were there that it was the Inca's will to provide such supplies to the city of Cuzco because that was the first time. They were very pleased to do this service for the city and for their lord Inca Yupanque. The Inca thanked them for all of this and then ordered those lords of Cuzco to make the arrangements there in their lodgings, along with those cacique lords, for the *orejones* who for their part were to go to the towns and provinces to gather and bring the food and provisions mentioned. Thus the lords went to their lodgings and had their meeting there with the caciques. The lords designated what each province had to bring and contribute. The caciques there were assigned the storehouses that were to be made. The order was given and the time designated that every so many years they were perpetually to fill them, unless some other order was given by the Inca. All of this the caciques agreed to do because they understood that Inca Yupanque was a lord who knew well how to honor any service that might be done for him.

Next there in the meeting, the lords designated the noble *orejones* who were to go and also the caciques, leaders, with whom they were to go. Thus these noble *orejones* and leaders left to bring the foods and provisions mentioned. The lords and caciques left the meeting and went to where Inca Yupanque was. They told him what they had done and arranged, as he had suggested. They asked him to indicate the places where the storehouses were to be built. The ones which each one was to make had already been assigned. Then Inca Yupanque pointed out certain hillsides of the sierras in view which surrounded the city of Cuzco, and there he ordered that the storehouses be built there right away so that when the provisions mentioned were brought, there would be a place to put them. Then the lords went to the places that the Inca had pointed out to them. They had the work started to build the storehouses. Making these storehouses and preparing the land for them took five years because they made a great many storehouses. Inca Yupanque ordered so many because he had a very large amount of food, enough so that he would not run out. This food he had there was also for those whom he wanted to make stone structures in the city of Cuzco and repair the rivers that run through it. He thought that, by itself having such a large amount of provisions, none would be lacking to feed the men he wanted to have construct the buildings and houses he wanted rebuilt.

After the storehouses were made and supplied, the lands improved, and all this work done, Inca Yupanque ordered the caciques and lords to come to a meeting. In all that has been stated they had complied. It seemed to Inca Yupanque that it was proper for him to do them some favors and do something to please them. In the assembly he gave them many jewels of gold and silver that he had made while they were doing their work. He also gave each one two sets of the garments he wore, and to each one he also gave a lady born in Cuzco and of Inca lineage. Each of these women was to be the principal wife of the cacique to whom she was given. The children of these unions would inherit the domain of their father. Because of these family ties, they would never rebel. There would be perpetual friendship and confederation between them and those of the city of Cuzco.

After all this was done and the caciques saw the great favors he was doing for them, they were all inclined to kiss his feet and thank him very much. Then Inca Yupanque told them to go to their lands to rest and return to the city of Cuzco in one year. During this time, each of them should have a great many fields sown with all of their foods. The Inca believed it would be necessary some day. He recommended that in their lands the young men and women not be idle so that such idleness would not cause their people to imitate bad habits. They should keep their people busy all the time in farming, preparing for war, and similar pursuits such as practicing with slings, shooting arrows, handling battle-axes as if fighting in combat, and brandishing spears with shields on their arms. All of this the young men were to do in their lands, putting an equal number on each side. On hearing all this the caciques said that they would do it as ordered and that what he told them was good. Thus the Inca bade them farewell and, making their gestures of obeisance, they left and returned to their lands.

XIII

Wherein the lord caciques met a year later, Inca Yupanque had the two rivers that pass through the city of Cuzco repaired, married the young single men, and organized the supplying of food, which was necessary in the city of Cuzco and its republic.

That year, after the caciques had gone to their lands, where they had to remain, Inca Yupanque had nothing to do, so he took up the practice of hunting, which he did most days. Other days he would walk around the city looking at it and at its site, imagining by himself how he should plan it and the building and rebuilding that he wanted to do there. He saw that those two rivers that ran through the city were very damaging to it. Every year when the rains came, the rivers overflowed and cut away the land, overflowing into the city itself, which was harmful for the city and for its residents. To build the city and the houses that he planned to construct, it was necessary to repair the banks of those two rivers first. With the rivers repaired, he could construct any building without fear of these floods bringing them down.

At the end of the year, Inca Yupanque decided that it was time for the local lords to come. He sent his messenger, who told them it was time for them to come to the city, as the Inca had already told them when they were there. They were also to bring all the livestock they could and food and provisions. The time had arrived when the Inca needed it. As they heard this, the caciques already had stored what the Inca had ordered when they left him. They set out right away because they had everything together that they needed to bring. Soon they were on the road with everything, and they came to the city of Cuzco, bringing as many workers with them as possible.

On arriving at Cuzco, they paid their respects to the Inca in this way because this was the custom observed when they appeared before him. As they appeared before him, they raised their hands and faces to the Sun, showing it reverence and obeisance. Then they did the same for the Inca, neither more nor less. And the words they said on greeting him were as follows: "Oh, child of the Sun, loving and kind to the poor." Saying this they placed the gifts that they brought before him. Then they sacrificed certain sheep and lambs before him with great respect and obeisance, as befitting a child of the Sun. With this done, the Inca greeted and welcomed them, asking them if they had arrived in good health and if those in their lands were also. All of this that you have heard these lord caciques did with Inca Yupanque when they appeared before him. He himself answered them and told them what you have heard. He told them to give what they were bringing to those lords of Cuzco who were there. So they left from where the Inca was and went with those lords of Cuzco to the storehouses. They stored all of the provisions that they brought. After they enjoyed themselves with the Inca and the lords of Cuzco for five days of fiestas and celebrations, Inca Yupanque told them what he was planning to do and how he wanted to repair and strengthen the banks of those rivers that run through the city. He spoke of the damage done to the city by those rivers. They said they were willing to do whatever he might order them to do, for him to tell them the way he wanted it because they would provide whatever was necessary for it. Thus Inca Yupanque showed them the sources of the rivers and where he thought they should start the reinforcements and repairs down to where the two rivers join at the end of the city, a place they call Pumachupa, which means lion's tail. From there he ordered these reinforcements and repairs to reach Mohina, which is four leagues from this city. So these lords measured with their cords the distance from the place where Inca Yupanque ordered them to start to where the two rivers join. With the measurements taken, they divided among themselves the work that each one would do on the construction that needed to be done. After this, Inca Yupanque ordered them to bring many rough stones, for the repairs were to be done with rough stone. The mortar that they were to put between the stones, they should notice, was to be a sticky clay. Since it would be made wet by the water, it must not loosen and be cut away by the water; rather, the stones should stick together. So the caciques gave the order to go get that clay mortar and the rough stones that had been requested. After bringing all together, they started the construction, and he ordered that the construction and reinforcements reach Mohina. This river was repaired below the city where the sown fields were so that when the rains came, the increase in this river would not break the banks, overflow, and damage the planted fields.

With this done, the Inca told the lords of Cuzco that on a certain day he wanted to inform them about something that was very important for the good of the city and the republic. When they were gathered together, he told them that it was necessary to build storehouses for large numbers of garments. In order to promote that, he wanted to have a large fiesta for the caciques. He saw that the lords were pleased that he wanted to tell them and order them to have that fiesta and supply it from their lands. The lords told him that it was a good thing and well conceived. They decided to give the order to make a large amount of *chicha*. With this done and arranged, they informed the Inca. Once he found out everything was done, he said that the next day he wanted to start the fiesta. Thus he had all those caciques called, and when they were there before him he said that he wanted to relax and enjoy himself with them. They took this as a great favor.

The next morning a large amount of sedge was brought and spread about the square. Many branches were brought and were set firmly there. Many flowers and live birds were placed on the branches. Then the lords of Cuzco came out very well dressed in their finest garments, and the Inca came along with them. The caciques also came wearing the garments that the Inca had given them. Then many large jugs of *chicha* were brought out on the square. Next came the ladies, both the wives of the Inca and those of the other important men. The ladies spread out a variety of delicacies, and then everyone sat down to eat. After eating, they started to drink. After having drank, the Inca had four golden drums brought out. There in the square, they had the drums placed at intervals. Then they all, including those from both sections, joined hands. While the drums were played in the middle, they began to sing all together. The ladies, who were behind the men, started the singing. In this song they told of the coming of Uscovilca against them, the departure of Viracocha Inca, and how Inca Yupanque, saying that the Sun had favored him as its son, had captured and killed Uscovilca. They also told how he defeated, captured, and killed the captains who had brought the last forces together. After this song praising and giving thanks to the Sun and also to Inca Yupanque, they greeted him as the child of the Sun and sat down again. At that time, they started drinking the *chicha* that they had there. According to what they say, they had an immense quantity of it there. Then a large amount of coca was brought to them there and handed out to all of them. After this was done, they all got up again and performed their song and dance, the same as you have heard.

This fiesta lasted six days, after which the Inca told those lord caciques that for the good of Cuzco it was important that there be storehouses of both wool and cotton garments. It was also important that there be storehouses of *cabuya*[1] blankets, ordinary and thick ones with cords about two palms long on the corners with which to tie them around their necks or however else the Indians who got them wanted to do it. These blankets were to be distributed to the workers who were employed on the job of repairing the rivers and to the ones having to do the other construction work so that on these *cabuya* blankets they could bring the earth and stone that was necessary for the job. Since they had these blankets, they did not have to use their own, which were of wool and cotton, or their cloaks, with which they cover themselves. Hearing all this, the lord caciques who were there told Inca Yupanque that they would be pleased to do it just as the Inca had ordered.

Right after leaving there, they sent word to their lands, towns, and provinces. So that this work would be done, they ordered that many women be brought together and placed in houses and yards. Fine wool in a variety of colors was to be distributed to them and many looms were to be placed there and set up. As quickly as possible, both men and women were to make the garments that each one had been commissioned to do according to the measurements of length and width that they were given. Once these garments were completed, they were brought to the city of Cuzco. When the garments arrived, the Inca ordered them placed in the storehouses that he had requested for the garments. With this done, the Inca and the lords kept on reinforcing and repairing these banks of the two rivers of the city of Cuzco, as you have heard. The Inca and the lords were always keeping track of the workers who were engaged on this job. They made them work as fast as possible in order to finish these repairs and reinforcements quickly. They spent four years on the job, doing it and finishing up as soon as possible.

After the work was finished, the Inca called for another fiesta similar to the one that we have already told you about. In this fiesta both the lords and the rest of their subjects took part. This fiesta lasted thirty days, after which the Inca ordered a certain number of lord *orejones* to leave the city. They were to go through the lands of those lords who were there to find out about and bring him the number of unmarried young men and girls there were. He sent word to the caciques and important men to inform their foremen, *llacta camayos,* as they call them, of what the Inca wanted. He ordered them to give an account of what he wanted to know as soon as possible to the lord *orejones,* who were to return right away. All of this was done. The lord *orejones* got an account and explanation in the towns and provinces. Then they returned to the city of Cuzco. There before the Inca they explained to him what they had learned.

Once the Inca understood the number of young unmarried men and women in these towns and provinces, he ordered his three friends the lords to leave right away for those towns and provinces and to take with them all those cacique lords who at present were there with him. In their presence in each town and province where they went they should marry the young men of a province to the young unmarried women of another province and the young unmarried women of the other to the young unmarried men of the other. They should continue doing this throughout the lands and dominion of those lord caciques who were with him so that their numbers would grow and multiply and they would share perpetual friendship, family ties, and brotherhood. With this arranged, the Inca did great favors for those lord caciques, giving them many gifts.

Thus those lords left Cuzco along with the other caciques, and they went to do what you have already heard. Inca Yupanque stayed in Cuzco with the people of the city itself and some lords of those little towns within about one league, a half league, or less from the city. He ordered them and those of the city to each bring before him the young unmarried men and women that they had in their towns. When they were brought before him, the Inca himself performed the marriage of all of those young men and women. With this done, he ordered the necessary garments for all of them to be taken from the storehouses. He gave them the garments himself, handing to each one, both men and women, two sets of clothing. He also gave to each one a blanket of *cabuya* in addition to the garments that he gave them so that with the blanket of *cabuya* they could do their labor and construction and not wear out in such work the other garments that he gave them. He also gave out to them or had them given the maize, dried meat, dried fish, live sheep, earthenware with which to serve it, and everything else he thought necessary for each one of them to have a house and the necessary things to have in the house. He ordered that every four months all those of Cuzco be given the food and provisions needed. Once he knew, by [counting] the houses in the city, the number of people in each one, the necessary provisions were distributed for each household and its servants. The Inca ordered that the supplies and food be brought to the city square and placed in large piles. From there it was measured and counted out so that each one received what was necessary. He ordered that this benefit always be rendered as long as the city of Cuzco existed. This benefit and provision lasted from the time of this lord Inca Yupanque until the Spaniards entered into the city, at which time it ended.

XIV

Wherein Inca Yupanque instituted and arranged the order that was to be followed in making the lord orejones *and the fasts, ceremonies, and sacrifices that in this ordainment were to be done, establishing at this time that a fiesta of the Sun be performed; this fiesta and ordainment was called Raime.*

Once Inca Yupanque had made the arrangements for supplying the city of Cuzco and the republic, his three good friends the lords returned from where he had sent them to marry the young men and women, as you have already heard in this account. With these lords in Cuzco and the rest also there, Inca Yupanque ordered them all to meet at his house the next morning because he wanted to discuss a certain fiesta with them, which he wanted to dedicate every year to the Sun for the victory which was given to him and made him ruler.[1]

So that this fiesta would be memorable, he wanted to establish in it something that he would tell them there in the assembly. The next morning these lords met in the houses of the Inca, where he told them of the fiesta that he wanted to have. So that this fiesta would always be remembered, Inca Yupanque told them that it would be good to confer the title of *orejon* warrior with certain ceremonies and fasts. Such a thing as that was a sign and insignia that would gain them, from the youngest to the oldest in that city, recognition throughout all the land as children of the Sun. It seemed to him that from that time on those of that city should be held in more esteem and respected more than they had been before by those of all the land. Since they were to be called children of the Sun, he wanted them to be made and ordained *orejon* warriors with many ceremonies and fasts in that fiesta of the Sun. Those who had been made *orejon* warriors up to that time had their ears pierced by their parents whenever they wanted to do it. That was not a thing that should be done so easily. Therefore he let them know that it seemed to him that in that matter it was proper that there be order and ceremonies as follows. The relatives of the young man who was to be made an *orejon* warrior should assemble. The young man's father must have been born in the city of Cuzco. A certain fiesta should be performed by the father and mother if both were lords and, if not, by only the father, and if he had no father, by the closest members of his father's family. This fiesta would be for all the other members of the family. In this fiesta the request should be made and it should be stated that they wanted to make their son or relative an *orejon* warrior. The young man would ask them to be present at the fiesta with their wealth and provisions for them to show him their favor. Even though it happened that the fiesta was to be put on by the richest of his relatives, he should request that his other relatives favor him in the fiesta and other things might be offered to him with what they had. The Inca wanted them to understand that no matter how prosperous they might be, they should respect those who did not have so much. In the end it could happen that the one who at present was prosperous might become poor. And the other who had less might increase his wealth and be in a position to come to his aid. The Inca gave that order in that way so that there would always be brotherhood and consideration. And so that from that time on, besides the name he had as lord, the nickname that they and others should use every time anyone spoke to him would be Guacchaycoya, which means "kind to the poor," a title used by his descendants.

Returning to our topic, the Inca told them that, being together like that, they should indicate a day on which the wives of those relatives of the one to become an *orejon* warrior would get together. With the wives together, the parents should bring a certain black wool, enough to make a tunic for their son. Once the wool was brought, it would be handed out to the women and the next day in that same place they should spin and finish it. On the day that tunic was made, the young man in question should leave there in the morning and go on a fast in the country. He should take other young men of his family with him, and they should each gather and bring bundles of straw so that they would not be idle but, rather, learn to take orders, and if by chance they were ever in need of food they should know what it means to work and fast. After they brought the straw, it would be distributed to those women who had made him the tunic. Five days later, they should get together again and have another fiesta in which those women would make four jugs of *chicha*. These jugs of *chicha* would be ready from the time they were made in this fiesta until the end of the fiesta of the Sun. And the jugs should always be well covered, and each jug should contain five arrobas. In five more days, this young man should go on a fast to Guanacaure Hill alone, gather another bundle of straw, and distribute it to those women who made him the *chicha*. This young man would go on a fast from the time that tunic was being woven and finished until the day he was to be made an *orejon* warrior. And he will not eat anything other than raw maize nor will he eat meat, salt, agi peppers, nor have anything to do with a woman. One month after the beginning of this fast, his relatives should bring him a young maiden who has never known a man. While also on a fast, this maiden will make a certain jug of *chicha,* which will be called *caliz.* This maiden will always walk along with the young man during the sacrifices and fasts. She will serve him as long as the fiesta lasts. The relatives of the neophyte accompany him and the maiden carrying the little jug of *chicha* called *caliz.* Thus they take this neophyte to the *guaca* of Guanacaure Hill, which is a league and a half from the city. At a spring there the relatives wash this neophyte's whole body. After washing him, they shear his hair very short. After the hair cutting, they dress him in that tunic of black wool that those women made him and put on him the shoes made of straw, which the young man will have made while fasting so that they would know that if the young man were in a war and needed shoes he would know how to make them of straw and pursue the enemy with those shoes on. After he has the shoes on, they will put a black band around his head. On top of this band they will put a white sling. Around his neck they will tie a white cloak that hangs over his back. The cloak will be narrow, two spans wide, and hang from his head to his feet. After this, they will give him a handful of straw as big around as a wrist. The tips of the straw should be pointing up just as it grows. To the other end of this straw, there will be hung a small bunch of long wool, which looks almost like a small amount of long, white hemp. As the young man arrives this way where the *guaca* is, with the maiden carrying that little *caliz* jug, she will fill two small tumblers of *chicha* and give them to the neophyte. He will drink one of the tumblers and give the other to the idol by pouring the *chicha* out in front of it. This done, the neophyte and his relatives will come down from the *guaca* and come to the city. The neophyte will carry that straw erect in his hands. Once he is in the city, they will dress the neophyte in a red tunic with a white stripe across the middle from bottom to the top of the tunic with a certain blue border at the bottom of the tunic. They will put a red band on his head. With him like this, they will put a type of scapular over his shoulders. From there they will go to a *guaca* that I will point out tomorrow,[2] which will be called Anaguarque. On arrival there, they will make their sacrifice, offering a certain *chicha* and making a fire before it. In the fire they will make offerings of maize, coca, and fat. When they are there, the relatives of this neophyte, who are almost like godfathers, will carry some long halberds of gold and silver. After making the sacrifice, they tie that straw they carry in their hands to the heads of the halberds, and hang from the heads of the halberds that wool that was hung on the straw. Having tied the straw on, they will put one of these halberds in the hands of each of the neophytes. Then all of the neophytes there will be brought together and they will all be ordered to leave there all running together with the halberds in their hands as if they were chasing their enemies. This run will be from the *guaca* to a hill where this city comes into view. Certain Indians will wait in this place so that they will see how these neophyte warriors arrive running and who arrives first. The winner will be honored by all his people. They will give him a certain thing and tell him that he did it like a good *orejon* warrior. They will give him the nickname Guaman, which means hawk. These young men who make such an effort when they become *orejon* warriors will be known, for when the city goes to war, they, being the quickest, will climb on the boulders and combat the enemy.

The next day they will leave the city for a place where I will point out another *guaca* tomorrow. It will be called Yavira and will be the idol of the favors. When they are there they will have a big fire built and offer to the *guaca* and to the Sun sheep and lambs, beheading them first. With the blood of these animals they will draw a line with much reverence across their faces, from ear to ear. They will also sacrifice in this fire much maize and coca. All of this will be done with great reverence and obeisance in making the offering to the Sun. There each of these neophytes will ask the Sun to give him prosperity, more livestock, and to watch over him, and free him from any evil that might come. With this done, each one will take an oath by himself before the idol. He will take care always to revere the Sun, farm his lands, and be obedient to the Inca, always tell him the truth, be a loyal vassal, and, whenever he learns that anyone plans to betray the Inca, to inform the Inca of it. He will also be loyal to the city of Cuzco, and whenever the Inca or the city of Cuzco goes to war, he will offer himself with his weapons in that war. And he will die in defense of the city and the Inca.

With the oath taken, the lord there at the *guaca* before which the oath was taken will answer in the name of the Sun and of that idol; he will thank it. The lord should tell him that the Sun has seen fit to make him an *auqui*, which means knight. This done, the neophyte will give thanks for the honor there to the Sun. Next right there they will put a very colorful tunic on the neophyte and a very colorful cloak on top of everything. These will be very fine garments. They will put on his ears some large gold earplugs, fastened with red thread. They will place a large gold scallop shell on his chest and put straw shoes on him. They will put a very colorful band around his head, which they call *pillaca-llauto,* and on top of this band they will put a feather diadem and a gold disk. This done, they will put a new breechclout on him, which up to that time no young man could wear. If by chance he forgot to put it on there, he could never wear it again in his life. After this, they will make the neophyte hold out his arms, and his relatives, who were waiting there with him like godfathers, will beat him on the arms with slings so that he will remember and not forget the oath he took there and the favor done him. Next, dressed and adorned as they were before, they will come down all together to the square of this city. There they will find all the lords of Cuzco dressed in long red tunics that come down to their feet. They will have tanned lion skins on their backs, the heads of the lions over their own heads and the faces of the lions in front of their faces. These lion heads will have gold ear ornaments. These lords who are in the square like this will have four gold drums.

When the neophytes reach the square they will spread out in wing formation at the lower end facing toward the direction the sun comes up. On arriving, each one will drive the halberds they carry into the ground in front of them. With this done, the lords will start singing and playing the drums. After singing, they will all sit down in a wing to rest as they are and each drink two tumblers of *chicha*. Two more tumblers of *chicha* will be offered to the Sun by pouring them out in front of the halberds. Soon they will get up and return to their singing. In their song they will praise the Sun highly and ask it to protect and increase the people and the neophytes. After this song they will drink again. This they will do for thirty days from the day it begins. Well supplied with *chicha,* they will do this every night, for their main enjoyment in all the things they do is good drinking. The more they drink, the more noble they are because they have the means for it.

The Inca ordered that after the thirty days had elapsed the relatives of these neophytes should assemble there in the square and bring the neophytes with them. After thrusting the halberd into the ground, the neophytes remain standing, hold the halberd in their hands, and extend their arms; their relatives will then beat them with slings on their arms so that they will remember this fiesta. Next they will go from there to a fountain called Calizpuquio, which means spring of the *caliz.* They will go to this spring, where they all bathe, at nightfall. Then they will put on other fine tunics. After the boys get dressed, their relatives will throw some *tunas* [prickly pears] at them. Each relative will be obliged to give these neophytes certain jewels and garments. After this they will also give each one a sling. Then each one of these neophytes will return to his house, which will be very clean and well lighted. All his male and female relatives will be there. Then they will get out those four jugs of *chicha* that they made at the beginning of the fiesta. They will all drink from the jugs. And they will get the neophyte so drunk on the *chicha* that he will pass out. After that they will take him out of the house, and wherever they see fit they will pierce his ears. The next morning all of the neophytes will go out into the square in military formation as if they were going into battle with their slings in their hands. Around their necks they will carry net bags full of *tunas.* The same number will be placed on either side of the square as they start their battle or fight. They will fight this battle with the objective of learning how they should fight their enemies. It seems to me that this is the way these ceremonies should be. This rite will provide the order for making these *orejon* warriors, and not what has been done before this time.

After the lords heard what Inca Yupanque had ordered, they said that it was well arranged and planned and it should be done that way from then on, for him to tell them when he wanted the fiesta to start. The Inca said that in thirty days it should start. That would be the beginning of the first month of the year.[3] They told him that, since until then they had no system for knowing the year and its months, he should take on the task of explaining it to them, telling them where it began and the names of the months. The Inca answered that after that fiesta of the Sun he planned to organize that matter. They asked him to explain it to them. And he wanted to do it. However, at present it was not possible for him to give information about that because he was planning to establish and arrange other fiestas in those months in which all of them would enjoy themselves and make sacrifices. The Inca said that in ten days he would tell them of the months, the fiestas they were to celebrate, and the sacrifices they were to make. Saying this, the Inca and the rest of the lords left their meeting. The lords each went to their lodgings, where they started to arrange for the fiesta that you have heard about. It was to begin in thirty days, after which time they performed the fiesta in the way you have heard. And from that time they continued doing it that way up to this present year we are in, which is 1551. Though attempts have been made to suppress them in this city of Cuzco, the people go out and secretly perform this fiesta and the others that this lord established in the small towns surrounding this city of Cuzco.

XV

Wherein Inca Yupanque designated the year and the months and named them, and the great idolatries that he established in the fiestas he ordered them to celebrate during those months, and how he made sun clocks by which those of the city of Cuzco could see when it was time to sow their fields.

The ten days elapsed, after which Inca Yupanque had told the lords they would meet with him again. There he was going to give them the arrangement that they asked him to make of the year and the months and the rest of the fiestas that they were to celebrate. Inca Yupanque ordered the lords of Cuzco to meet in his house just as they had done before. After they got there, Inca Yupanque told them that many years before, he had imagined the months and times of the year and found that there were twelve months. He planned only to tell them about these months and time in their sequence to establish the fiestas that they were to have during the months. But since they had asked him, he wanted to tell them and enumerate the fiestas and sacrifices they were to have during those months. He expected them to pay careful attention and remember well. In addition, he had decided to make a certain thing that he called *pacha unan changa*,[1] which means "knower of time." We can think of it as a clock. In case they lost track of the months, by it they and their descendants would know when it was time to sow and prepare their fields.

The lords were listening carefully. Inca Yupanque told them this next month, when the boys were made into *orejon* warriors, as already stated, marks the beginning of the year; it will be called *pucoi quilla raime quis*,[2] which is our month of December. He called the month of January *hatun pocoi quis* and the month of February he called *alla pocoi quis*. The month of March they call *pacha pocoi quis*. The month of April, *ayrigua quis*. The month of May he calls *haucai quosqui quilla*. For this month Inca Yupanque ordered that another solemn fiesta of the Sun be celebrated. At this time they made great sacrifices for what the earth had given them and the maize that they would get from it. The fiesta would start at the beginning of the maize harvest and it would last until the end of June, which they call *hatun quosqui quilla*. Those who had become *orejon* warriors in December for this fiesta that he instituted for this month of June would put on tunics woven of gold, silver, and iridescent feathers. Dressed like that with this plumage, gold disks and bracelets, they would come out to the fiesta. There they would end their fasts and sacrifices, which they had made from the time they were made *orejon* warriors until then. At that time, they would start to enjoy themselves and celebrate the other fiesta that had been instituted, since it was necessary to give thanks to the Sun for the crops. This fiesta, which started in May and lasted until the end of June, as you have heard, he called *yaguayracha aymoray*. He ordered that this fiesta be celebrated in the square where the hospital is now in the city of Cuzco, which is the exit from this city called Limapampa. For this fiesta the lords of Cuzco were to come out dressed in red tunics that reached down to their feet. He ordered great sacrifices to the idols for this fiesta. They were to burn much livestock, food, and garments. And at these *guacas* they would make many offerings of jewels of gold and silver.

They called the month of July *cagua quis*. In it he did not order them to celebrate any fiesta. But he told them that during this month they were to water their fields and the next month start sowing their maize, papas [potatoes], and quinua until the beginning of September. The month of August he called *carpai quis*, and the month of September, *situai quis*. This month they say that Inca Yupanque instituted two fiestas. One of them seems almost like the one we do for San Juan. They get up at midnight; bathe until dawn and carry certain lighted torches. After bathing, they strike at each other's backs with the torches, and they say that they ward off all illness and evil that they might have. Inca Yupanque called the other fiesta Poray Upia. He also ordered it to be performed this month. He ordered that it be done for the waters and that sacrifices also be made of many garments, sheep and coca. They were to bring the flowers from all the plants in the country. He ordered it all to be sacrificed to the waters in the following way. They should take a large number of garments and throw them in that river by Cuzco where the two rivers come together. They should also bring many sheep and lambs, cutting off their heads in the place where the garments were thrown in, and offer them to the waters. Then they should make a big fire in which they would burn these sheep and lambs. The ashes of these burned animals should be thrown into the water in the same place. Next they would throw in the flowers that you have heard about. After this he ordered them to throw in much ground and shredded coca.

Then each one of the *orejon* warriors of Cuzco would throw into the river certain tumblers of *chicha*, and these warriors were also to drink other tumblers of *chicha*, acting like they were drinking with the waters.

It should be known that these lords and the rest in all the land have a custom and way of showing good manners. If a nobleman or a noblewoman goes to another's house for a visit or to see someone, the visitor has to carry behind her, if it is a woman, a jug of *chicha*. On arriving at the house of the man or woman that they are visiting, they have two tumblers of *chicha* filled, one goes to the man being visited and the other to the man or woman giving out the *chicha*. Thus they both drink. The one being visited does the same, also bringing out two tumblers of *chicha*, giving one to the visitor and drinking the other himself. This is done by the lords and it is the greatest honor that they can show each other. If this is not done when visits are made, it is taken as an insult by the person who goes to visit someone and the honor of visiting is not recognized by giving them a drink. The visitor will decline ever to go to see that person again. It is also considered an insult if one person offers a drink and the other refuses it.

Thus we return to this sacrifice that you have heard they make for the waters. They say that they drink with the waters by tossing a tumbler of *chicha* into the river. And the one who tosses one tumbler in the river drinks the other. In addition, Inca Yupanque ordered that, when this sacrifice was made, two lords of Cuzco would go on either side of the river. They should each take ten Indians or as many more as they pleased. These Indians would carry long poles in their hands so that, if the things offered for the sacrifice in the river got stuck on its banks, the Indians could push them out into the middle with the poles so that the current would carry them on. These lords who were taking the Indians to push the things sacrificed into the middle of the river were to go along the banks thirty leagues downriver so that the things would not get stuck anywhere and so they could see that the land was bearing fruit as a result of the waters. He ordered that this sacrifice be made in all the land and that on the day set there be brought as much food as possible that was in season and could be eaten. The food was to be put in the middle of the square of Cuzco. From there it would be distributed throughout the city so that the common people would realize that, by means of the sacrifice that was made to the waters and by virtue of the waters, the land bore fruit, which they shared for their nourishment. It was ordered by this lord that this fiesta be celebrated in the middle of this month that you have heard about when there was a full moon. This fiesta and sacrifice lasted four days.

This lord named the month of October *omarime quis*. During this month he did not order that any fiestas be celebrated in the city, but he allowed one by the people of Oma in their town, which is a league and a half from the city. He granted them this favor and did the same for the Ayarmacas, the Quiaios, and the Tambos. They could pierce their ears as long as they did not cut their hair so that they would be thought of as subjects of Cuzco. The *orejon* warriors were the lords and the ones to be recognized throughout all the land. They had their hair cut short and their heads tapered on top. They were known by this feature throughout the land, whenever they left Cuzco or walked through the land.

This lord named the month of November *cantarai quis*. In this month they start to make the *chicha* that they will drink in the months of December and January, when the year begins and they celebrate the fiesta of the *orejon* warriors, as you have learned in this account. Inca Yupanque gave the months the names that you have heard. He told these lords that each month had thirty days and the year had three hundred and sixty days. So that, as time passed, they would not lose count of these months and the times for sowing and celebrating the fiestas that he had already told them about, he had made those *pacha unan chac,*[3] which means "clocks." He had these clocks made during these ten days he waited before telling them what you have heard. He made the clocks in the following way. Every morning and every afternoon of every month of the year he looked at the sun, watching for the times for sowing and harvesting. Also when the sun went down, he watched the moon when it was new, full, and waning. He had the clocks made of cut stone placed on top of the highest hills at the place where the sun rose and where it went down. One clock [pillar] was put in a certain place according to where the sun set. The clock was set firmly in a place where it could be seen. Since he could tell the line along which the sun moved as it was setting straight ahead from that place where he stood, he had four marble stone pyramids made on the highest part of the hills. The middle ones were smaller than the ones on the sides. The pyramids [pillars] were each two *estados* high, square and set about one *braza* apart, except that he had the two small ones in the middle closer together, about half a *braza* from one to the other. As the sun rose, if one stayed where Inca Yupanque stood to look and calculate, the sun comes straight up and goes straight between the two pillars, and it did the same when it went down to the place where it sets. By this means, the common people kept track of time. It showed when to sow or harvest. There were four clocks where the sun comes up and four others where it goes down that mark the courses and movements made by the sun during the year. Inca Yupanque made an error by our count in picking the month that would mark the beginning and the months of the year that he designated because he picked December instead of January. However, he made himself understood and organized his republic.

XVI

Wherein Inca Yupanque rebuilt the city of Cuzco, and how he distributed it among his people.

Inca Yupanque had designated the year and months and the fiestas that were to be celebrated and had made the clocks. He had also relaxed and enjoyed the things that you have heard about during a period of two years. He spent this time in his town so that the natives and caciques who were his subjects had time to relax in their lands after the work they had done to improve the rivers of the city of Cuzco and so they would have time to sow and harvest great fields with which to replenish their food and provisions and could contribute to the city of Cuzco and to the storehouses there. Feeling that he and the others were now getting a little restless from being idle, one day he met with the important men of the city of Cuzco and told them that they had been idle long enough and it was time for the caciques and lords under him to come to the city of Cuzco with their food and supplies and to bring as many people with them as possible. He had decided to rebuild the city of Cuzco in such a way that it would be permanently constructed of certain structures that he had in mind. And after the buildings were done, they would see them. For this it was necessary for certain lords among those there to leave the city. Next they would see who among them wanted to go. He needed those who stayed while those who left were to provide the materials that would be necessary for the construction. Then ten lords with twenty *orejon* warriors were named. They left right away and went to the towns and provinces to have the materials brought, as you have heard.

After their meeting, Inca Yupanque and the rest of the lords who stayed there went around the outskirts of the city up to five leagues away. In this area they looked over the hills and places where they might find stone quarries and clay for making the mortar that was needed for the buildings. They found that there was an abundance of stone and large quarries in the vicinity of Salu.[1] Once the Inca and the other lords saw that there they already had material and a great quantity of stone, they returned to the city. Immediately after arriving there, they gave the order about how they were to bring and transport the building stones. For this purpose, they had a large number of ropes, thick cables of sinew, and sheep hide. After this was done, Inca Yupanque outlined the city and had clay models made just as he planned to have it built. Then at that time those *orejon* lords arrived who had gone to bring the provisions of food and a large number of people to construct those buildings, as you have already been told in this account. On arriving, the caciques greeted the Inca in the way we have already explained to you. The Inca received them with great affection. He decided that it would be well to relax with them for five days, and so this was done. After which time the Inca decided to give the order to start to work building the city. It seemed to him that the people who had arrived had rested as long as they needed. Then he ordered each one of the caciques to assemble his workers on a certain field and to separate each group because he wanted to assign them all the work that they were to perform and organize them on how to proceed. With all of these workers together, he assigned the jobs to the caciques, ordering some to transport rough stone for the foundations and others to bring the clay that seemed good and sticky to them. He ordered them to make the foundations of the buildings with this clay and rough stone by starting at such a level that it was the beginning and seat of the buildings. They went down so deep they hit water. For that reason, he ordered the use of rough stone and thick clay so that if the water came in over the foundation it would not ruin the clay. As we have told you, the whole seat of the city was marshes and springs of water. He ordered that all of the springs be canalized in such a way as to be piped to the houses of the city and made into fountains to supply water to the city.

At the same time, he ordered others to prepare the foundations of the houses and buildings of the city. He ordered others to bring the building stones for the structures that were to be built after these foundations were the right height, strength, and necessary size. He ordered others to make adobe blocks of clay and sticky earth. In these adobes he ordered them to put a large amount of straw, which is of a type similar to the *esparto*[2] grass of Spain. This earth and straw were to be mixed so that the adobes would be well made and solid. These adobes were to be used from the stone work upward to the height and size these buildings and houses were to have. He ordered others to bring a large number of wooden poles from long, straight alder[3] trees cut to the right length and size. When the structures were completed to the proper height, size, and shape they were intended to have, he ordered them to bring at that time a large amount of cactus that they call *haguacolla quisca*, so that the mortar that was used for plaster both inside and outside the houses would stick and not crack.[4] They were to spread the juice of these cacti over these walls. The mortar would be very well mixed with a large amount of wool and put on the walls over the surface made wet by those cacti you have already heard about. If they did not want to use wool in the mortar, they should use straw which was very finely ground. This would give a glossy finish to the walls and structures.

After each and every one of the things you have heard was stipulated, those lords and caciques got up and had the work started on the structures and supply of materials necessary for the job according to their orders. Then Inca Yupanque ordered everyone from the city of Cuzco to leave their houses, take out everything they had in them, and go to the small towns nearby. As this was done, he ordered those houses to be torn down. With this done, cleaned up, and leveled, the Inca with his own hands, along with the rest of the lords of the city, had a cord brought; indicated and measured with the cord the lots and houses that were to be made and their foundations and structures. With all of this prepared, the foundations were dug. Having brought the necessary equipment, they started to build their city and its houses. While these buildings were being made, the work went on continuously with fifty thousand Indians on the job. From the time that Inca Yupanque ordered the beginning of the improvements on land and rivers of the city and the construction of buildings until everything you have heard about was completed, twenty years elapsed.

When the city was finished and made to perfection, Inca Yupanque ordered all the lords of Cuzco and the rest of its inhabitants to meet at a certain open field. After they assembled, he ordered that there be brought there the sketch of the city and the clay painting that he had ordered made. With this in front of him, he assigned the houses and lots already built, as you have heard, to the lords of Cuzco and the rest of the residents. They were all *orejon* descendants of his lineage and of the other lords who had succeeded in power from the beginning with Manco Capac up to him. He had them settle in the following way. He had his three lord friends settle from the Temple of the Sun down toward where the rivers join in that space where they made houses between the rivers. He ordered that the section from the Temple of the Sun on down be named Hurin Cuzco, which means "lower Cuzco." He ordered that the far end of this section be named Pumachupa, which means lion's tail. In this place these three lords and those of their lineage settled. From them and from each one separately the three lineages of Hurin Cuzco were started. These lords were named Vicaquirao, Apomayta, and Quilescache Urcoguaranca. From the Temple of the Sun on up, including everything between the two rivers up to the hill which is now the fortress, he distributed to the most prominent lords among his relatives and descendants of his lineage in a direct line, children of lords and ladies of his own family and lineage. The three lords whom he sent to settle in the section below the Temple of the Sun, as you have heard, were illegitimate sons of lords, though they were from his lineage. They were born of women foreign to his nation and of low extraction. Children born like this are called *guacchaconcha*,[5] which means "relatives of unfortunate people and low offspring." Although these people are children of the Inca, they are given this name, and none of them, neither men nor women, are respected like the rest of the lords but, rather, like a common *orejon*.

You should know that the Inca who is lord has a principal wife, and she has to be from his family and lineage, one of his sisters or first cousins. They call this woman *piuiguarmi*[6] and by this other name *mamanguarme*.[7] As the principal wife of their lord, the common people call her in their greetings Paxxa yndi Usus çapaicoya guacchacoyac,[8] moon and daughter of the Sun, unique queen and friend of the poor. This lady had to be a direct relative of the Inca on both the paternal and the maternal sides without the least trace of *guacchaconcha*.[9] The Inca received this lady as his principal wife the day he received the *borla* fringe of office and royal insignia. The sons this lady had were called *piuichuri*,[10] which means "legitimate children," and the eldest of these sons was lord of the empire and the legitimate heir. If the Inca happened to die leaving this son so young that he could not govern, he would be made lord and the fringe would be put on his head, even though he was still not weaned. This child would be called *huaina capac*, which means "young king." However, those who explain this name, not understanding what it means, say it means "rich young man." You should know that *capa* without the final "c" means "rich" and *huaina* means "young man." If this name were pronounced "*capahuaina*," it would mean "rich young man." But saying "*huaina capac*," with the final "c," it means "young king."

It is also true that those who do not understand it derive another name, "*viracocha*," which we can say means "god." This name is used by them to mean "creator." Since the Spaniards appeared as very strange beings, as our account will explain to you farther ahead, every one of the Spaniards were called "*viracocha*." Trying to break this name down, those who were learning this language thought that "*vira*" meant "fat" and "*cocha*" meant "sea." Thus they stated that the whole name meant "fat of the sea" or "foam of the sea." However, it does not mean that but, rather, it means "god." When the Spaniards came to this land, they [the Incas] used this name for them and thought they were gods.

Returning to our account, this child was assigned tutors and guardians who would run the government as long as they saw he was not old enough to do so. After receiving this woman as his wife or before this one, he had fifty other women who were his sisters and relatives, but the children he had with these would never succeed him in office unless it was the son of the legitimate *piui* wife, as they say. It was their custom to marry all of their sisters. If it happened that the Inca had no children by the principal wife or, if she had only daughters, in this case, at the end of the Inca's days they gave the title to the eldest son of any of his other sisters or relatives as they saw that he showed the character and capacity to rule and govern the kingdom and republic. And if one was not fit, they should select from among his brothers the one who seemed to them best suited to govern. And they gave his sister in marriage to this one, as you have heard. She was the daughter his father had had with the *piuiguarme,* or principal wife, whom the lords of the city of Cuzco and the rest of the lords of all the land respected as the queen and principal lady over all of them.

Returning to the matter of distributing the houses of the city, Inca Yupanque gave them out in the way you have heard, taking for himself the houses and lots that he considered adequate. He ordered that in this city there be no mixing of people or offspring other than his own and his *orejon* warriors. He wanted this city to be the most distinguished in all the land and the one all the other towns had to serve and respect, like our Rome in ancient times. Those of the Alcavicça lineage, the cacique Manco Capac found settled in that site, as you have already learned in this account, were to settle there near Cuzco, about two harquebus shots from the city. And this they did. Inca Yupanque favored and helped them make their houses. After it was finished, Inca Yupanque ordered this town to be named Cayocache. Thus the people of Alcavicça were expelled from the city of Cuzco, and they ended up subjugated. Of them it could be said that a guest came who threw them out of their home.

XVII

Wherein the lords of Cuzco wanted Inca Yupanque to take the borla *fringe of state because of his great knowledge and valor, and he refused to accept it because his father, Viracocha Inca, was alive, and Inca Yupanque would not receive the* borla *from anyone but his father, and how his father, Viracocha Inca, came and gave it to him, and of how Inca Yupanque insulted his father, Viracocha Inca, in a certain way, and of the end and death of Viracocha Inca.*

After Inca Yupanque divided up the city of Cuzco in the way you have already heard, he named all the places and lots. He named the whole city lion's body, saying that the residents of it were limbs of that lion.[1] He personally was the head of the lion. The lords of the city had seen the exceedingly great favors that he had done for them and kept doing every day. They considered the vast knowledge and great zeal for the good of the republic that they saw in him. All together and each one separately the lords kept trying to imagine how to do some great service for him which would benefit him and please him. For this purpose, they met one day. In their meeting, they decided that the service that they should do for him was to give him the *borla* fringe of office and insignia of the king, which was used according to their ancient custom along with another new name. Having done all this and agreed on it, they left very pleased, thinking that they had decided on something that would please the Inca. With this agreed on they left and went together as they were to the houses of the Inca, whom they found not idle but painting and drawing certain bridges and showing the way he wanted to have them and how they were to be constructed. He was also drawing some roads that went from a town to those bridges and rivers. Since the meaning of these drawings was beyond the understanding of those lords, on arriving where the Inca was and after greeting him and making the proper show of obeisance, they asked him what he was drawing. He had seen them come before him all together in a very happy mood. He answered, "Tell me what brings you here all together and, as it seems, in a happy mood. This question that you put to me I will answer in due time and I will give the orders for each one of you according to the lot which falls to you. Do not ask me this question again because I will tell you. You must have realized that, since my father left here, I have only dealt with matters that benefit you and what belongs to you. Be assured that you can expect the same from me for as long as I live. I will always do so, as will be my custom."

The lords thanked him for that, asking him to do so and to watch out for them. Inca Yupanque asked them to tell him what they came for and to leave right away because they were wasting his time. They told him that what they came there for was to ask him when he planned to take the *borla* fringe of office because it seemed to them that it was time. They wanted to give the order and do the preparations and things that were necessary for it and for the necessary fiesta and fasting for such an event. When the Inca heard this, they say he laughed and said that they were a long way off and that their thoughts were far behind where his were moving, for his thoughts were ahead of theirs. They should not waste their time with thoughts about such a thing. He let them know that as long as his father was alive he would not put any such thing on his head. He thought that at the end of his days his father would give that *borla* to his son Inca Urco. After that Inca Yupanque planned to take it off Inca Urco's head and take off his head at the same time. This was because of what his father had said, which was for Inca Urco to tread on the insignias of the Chanca Uscovilca whom Inca Yupanque had defeated. And Inca Yupanque had promised them not to take the *borla* fringe while his father was alive unless it were in this way or unless his father came to the city of Cuzco to put it with his own hand on Inca Yupanque's head. That way he would accept it. He thanked them very much for the goodwill they had shown in that matter. He swore to them that he would satisfy the dishonor that his father had done to them and to the city by abandoning it and running away. He took this oath in the following way. He picked up a tumbler of *chicha* in his hands and emptied it on the ground, saying that his blood was spilled in the same way that he had emptied that tumbler of *chicha* on the ground, if he did not get satisfaction personally from his father for the insult that his father had done to them and to the city. Those lords understood Inca Yupanque's will in regard to what they had come to discuss. Seeing that he was angry, they did not answer anything to all that. Then he asked them if they wanted anything else; otherwise, they were to leave. The lords answered that they had not come for anything other than what they had stated.

Thus these lords left and assembled again, as they had done before. In the meeting they discussed how they could give the order for Inca Yupanque to have the *borla* of office, which they so wanted for him. Thus they agreed to send on their own and in their name messengers to Viracocha Inca to beg him to look favorably upon a visit to the city of Cuzco. They would inform him of the new construction of the city, which he would enjoy seeing. In order to do them a favor and make them happy, would he see fit to give his son Inca Yupanque the *borla* of office on that visit when he came. Viracocha had stopped using the *borla* and he told the caciques who had gone to see it that he had given it up and was giving it to this son Inca Yupanque for him to have from then on and for him to be lord of Cuzco and of everything in its dominion. For this purpose, they had gone to Inca Yupanque to beg him to allow them to put the *borla* on his head. This Inca Yupanque had refused to do because he respected Viracocha Inca as his father.

With this agreement made by the lords in the way that you have heard, they sent their messenger to Viracocha Inca, where he was established in his stronghold. When Viracocha Inca got the message that the lords sent him, he came to the city of Cuzco. When Inca Yupanque learned of his arrival, he went out to meet him on the road and greeted him as his lord and father. Thus they entered the city together. Viracocha Inca saw the city and its buildings so well planned and constructed. He understood the order and management that he had established in the city with the storehouses as well as everything else regarding the good of the republic. He also saw how much Inca Yupanque was loved by the people of the city as well as the rest of the caciques and lords for the good management with which he governed them and the favors that he did for them. Seeing the magnificence that the city and its structures represented, and in the presence of all the lords of Cuzco and caciques who were there, Viracocha Inca said to Inca Yupanque, "Truly you are the son of the Sun and I name you king and lord." Taking the *borla* fringe in his hands, he took it off his own head and put it on Inca Yupanque's head. It was customary among these lords that when that was done the one who put the *borla* on the other's head, besides putting it on, had to give the other a name, which he was to keep from then on. Thus as Viracocha Inca put the *borla* on his head he said to him, "I give you this name so that from now on your people and the other nations that you may conquer will call you Pachacuti Ynga Yupangui Capac Yndichuri,[2] which means "change of time, King Yupanque, son of the Sun." Yupanque is their lineage of origin because Manco Capac's nickname was Yupanque.

Once Inca Yupanque was named king and lord in the presence of those who were there, he ordered that a used jar be brought there. They were to bring it just as they found it in the house from which the jar was taken, without washing it. With it there he ordered it to be filled while still dirty with *chicha*. After it was filled, he ordered the *chicha* to be given to his father, Viracocha Inca, whom he ordered to drink it and drink all without leaving anything. Seeing what he was ordered to do by the new lord, Viracocha Inca took it and without answering anything he drank the *chicha*. After that he bowed down before Inca Yupanque and begged his pardon. To this the new lord answered that he had no reason to forgive him. If he was saying it because of the people Viracocha Inca had sent to kill him when Inca Yupanque went to see him, regarding that, he was satisfied; it was only done in the name of the city of Cuzco and those lords who were present there. Since Viracocha Inca acted like a woman and he was one, he should not drink from any jugs other than the jug from which he had just drank. During all this, Viracocha Inca was on the ground with his head bowed toward him, and to what the new lord was saying he answered from time to time, "Hochaymi," which means "It is my fault and I recognize my sin." Presently, he had his father get up and took him to his houses, where he gave him luxurious lodgings. Later the two ate together, and from then on the new lord took pains to make his father feel honored, pleased, and contented.

Next the lords gave the order for the provisions necessary to have the fiestas, sacrifices, and fasts that the Inca had to hold for the wife he was to receive in that fiesta. With it done and provided for, the Inca went into a room which was reserved for that, and his wife and parents-in-law were put in another. They went on a fast, eating nothing but raw maize and drinking *chicha* for ten days. And both his relatives and hers went on the same fast, although they went out walking around the city. During those days the lords of Cuzco made many and very great sacrifices to all the idols and *guaca* shrines near the city, especially at the Temple of the Sun, where a large amount of livestock in sheep and lambs was sacrificed as well as deer and all the other animals that they could get for that fiesta, including a large number of birds, such as eagles, hawks, partridges, ostriches, and all the other birds of prey they could get, even ducks and other domestic birds and many other animals, tigers [jaguars], lions, wildcats, but not foxes. They hate foxes. If they see one when they are having a fiesta like this, those who handle these sacrifices consider it an evil omen. Also offered in this sacrifice were many boys and girls, who were buried alive very well dressed and fixed up. These children were buried two by two, boy and girl. Along with each pair, they buried gold and silver service, such as plates, bowls, pitchers, jars, and drinking tumblers, along with all the utensils that a married Indian normally has, all of gold and silver. Thus they buried these boys and girls with all these utensils. These children were the sons and daughters of caciques and important people.

While these sacrifices were being made, everyone in the city was having a big fiesta and enjoying themselves in the city square. At the end of these ten days, the parents of the lady and all the relatives took the woman, dressed in garments finely woven with gold and silver, ahead of them. These garments were fastened with four gold pins each two spans long, each one of which would weigh two pounds in gold. On her head and resembling a crown she would have a gold ribbon the width of one thumb. She also wore a sash woven of fine wool and gold wrapped around her waist. On this sash there were a large variety of paintings. The outer garment was a small mantle also woven of gold and fine wool and in a variety of patterns, according to their style of dress. She wore gold shoes on her feet. She was very clean, with her hair carefully combed and arranged. As they arrived where the Inca was, her parents and relatives begged the new lord Pachacuti Inca Yupanque to look favorably on receiving their daughter and relative for his wife. As the new lord saw that it was a good thing for him, he said that he would receive her as his wife. Next he ordered the lords of Cuzco who were there with him to receive her as his wife. Then the parents of the lady thanked him very much. The lords of Cuzco said that they received her as their lady. At this point, Viracocha Inca, father of the new lord, stood up there, hugged her, and kissed her on the cheek. And she did the same thing to him. Then he did her a favor and gave her certain small towns that he had nearby as a part of his inheritance. Now Pachacuti, the new lord, hugged and kissed his wife and gave her one hundred *mamacona* women to serve her. Then she was taken to the Temple of the Sun, where she made her sacrifice; the Sun gave her, and his steward in place of the Sun, fifty more *mamaconas*. After leaving there, she was at the houses of the Inca, where the lords of the city went to offer her gifts. They gave her many sets of gold and silver ware such as gold and silver pitchers, bowls, jars, and drinking tumblers and many *yanacona* servants, who numbered over two hundred.

With this done and the fiestas over, Viracocha Inca told his son that it was time for him to return to his town. The fiestas and festivities that they had enjoyed lasted three months, during which time he had always been there. Pachacuti told him to leave whenever he wished. Being supplied by Pachacuti Inca Yupanque with all necessary provisions as well as everything else that he might need in his town, Viracocha Inca left. But Inca Yupanque told him that whenever there were fiestas in Cuzco, he should be present in them. And he said he would do it. So whenever there was a fiesta in the city, he always came to be present in it.

Ten years after Pachacuti Yupanque's coronation, while Viracocha Inca was in his town at the stronghold called Caquea Xaquixahuana, which is above the town of Calca seven leagues from the city of Cuzco, enjoying himself he fell sick of a certain illness. Four months after he got sick, Viracocha Inca died. At the time of his death he was over eighty years old. After Viracocha Inca died, Inca Yupanque honored him greatly, having his body brought in a well-adorned litter as if he were alive, coming to the city of Cuzco whenever there were fiestas. Pachacuti Yupanque would have Viracocha honored and respected by the lords of Cuzco as if he were alive. Before the wrapped body a sacrifice was made in which they burned many sheep, lambs, garments, maize, and coca and poured out much *chicha*, saying that the body ate, was the son of the Sun, and was with him in the sky. Inca Yupanque had as many statues made of as many lords as there had been from Manco Capac to his father, Viracocha Inca. After the statues were made, he ordered that certain wooden benches be made and very decoratively worked and painted. Many feathers of diverse colors were attached to the paintings. With this done, this lord ordered that all these statues be seated on the bench along with his father. He ordered that these statues be revered as idols and that sacrifices be made to them as such. These statues were placed in his houses, and whenever any lords went in where the Inca was, they made a gesture of obeisance to the Sun, then to the statues, and next went in where the Inca was. He picked out and named a certain number of *yanaconas* and *mamaconas* to serve these statues and gave them land on which to sow and harvest for the service of these statues. He also designated much livestock for the sacrifices that were to be made to the statues. These servants, lands, and livestock were given out to each one of the statues for itself. He ordered that great care be taken to give food and drink to these statues every evening and morning and to make sacrifices to them. For this purpose, he had a steward put in charge of the servants he had designated for each one of the statues. He also ordered each one of these stewards to make up songs which the *mamaconas* and *yanaconas* would sing in praise of the deeds of each one of these lords in his day. These songs were ordinarily to be sung by the servants of those statues whenever there were fiestas starting first with the song, story, and praise of Manco Capac, and these *mamaconas* and servants would sing about each lord as they had succeeded one another up to that time. And that was the order that was followed from then on. Thus they preserved the memory of them and their times.[3]

Inca Yupanque ordered that the *yanaconas* and servants should have houses, towns, and farmland in the valleys and towns around the city of Cuzco and that these servants and their descendants should always take care to serve those statues which he had designated for them, all of which was done from then until today. Now it is done in secret and sometimes in public because the Spaniards do not understand what it is. They keep these statues in *orones*,[4] which are storage bins used here for maize and other foods and others in large jars and in niches in the walls, and in this way the statues cannot be found. When Inca Yupanque had these statues put on the benches, he ordered that, on their heads, there be placed some diadems with very attractive feathers. Gold earplugs were hanging from the diadems. After this was in place, he ordered that some gold disks also be placed on the foreheads of each one of the statues. The *mamacona* women were always to have in their hands some long red feathers attached to some rods. With these they were to shoo away any flies that might light on the statues. The service articles for these statues were to be kept very clean, and every time the *mamacona* women and *yanacona* servants appeared before these statues to serve or revere them, or others, whoever they might be, they came very clean and well dressed. With cleanliness, reverence, and obeisance they appeared before these statues. Thus this lord did two things in this matter. He had his ancestors worshiped as gods and had them remembered. He did this because he understood that the same thing would be done for him after his days.

XVIII

Wherein Pachacuti Inca Yupanque assembled his subjects; in this assembly he ordered that they all prepare themselves with their weapons for a certain day because he wanted to go in search of lands and peoples to conquer and subjugate under the dominions and servitude of the city of Cuzco, and how he went out with all his soldiers and friends, won and conquered many towns and provinces, and of what befell him and his captains.

Since Inca Yupanque saw that he became lord in the way that this account has related to you and he no longer had to deal with construction in the city, after relaxing with his people, he ordered that all of the lords of the city of Cuzco and the rest of the caciques and important people assemble in the square, which they did all together. With them all there, he told them that he had information that surrounding that city there were a great many towns and provinces. For him, since he was powerful, it was bad to live with so little. Thus he had made up his mind and given the order to go out from that city two months hence in an effort to subjugate those towns and provinces to the city of Cuzco and remove the title of *capac* that was held by every one of those little lords of those towns and provinces. There should be only one *capac* and he was that one. And if it happened that during that campaign he should meet some lord with whom he did battle and lost, he would be happy to serve him. But he did not fear this would happen because, as they could see, the Sun was with him. For the campaign he would need one hundred thousand warriors. Within those two months he wanted to have them assembled in the city of Cuzco with their weapons and the rest of the provisions necessary for the campaign. To this they answered that they would be glad to give him these soldiers and serve with them, for they would go along themselves. They begged him to take them along

Pachacuti Inca Yupanque

From the chronicle of Felipe Guaman Poma de Ayala,
Nueva coronica y buen gobierno.

with him and to see fit to give them three months' time, because they needed that much time to raise the forces.

Pachacuti Inca Yupanque was pleased with this. He ordered that they leave everything in their lands with their leaders and stewards, who were to take great care to sow many large fields, because he knew that the time he planned to spend in the war would make it necessary. Then he ordered them to leave and, when they reached their lands and provinces, to give the order to assemble the forces which would come there in three months. Thus the lords left, and Pachacuti Inca Yupanque remained in the city with his people. During the following three months, he did nothing but enjoy himself with his people and make great sacrifices to the Sun and the rest of the idols and *guacas*. During these sacrifices, he fashioned a small idol that a man could carry easily in his hands. This idol was of gold, made for them to worship when they were at war and the time they spent on it. They worshiped this idol as the god of battles and named him Caccha. He gave this god as a favor to his closest relative so that during the war he could take charge of carrying it on his shoulders or however he could. On the day when they were going into battle, he would carry it in his hands all dressed and adorned with its diadem, and the bearer would wear another diadem on his head, all the while taking a young man along with him who, with a small parasol, called *achigua*[1] by them, would shade the idol whenever they stopped, exactly as they did for the Inca. This parasol would be carried on a long pole so that during the battle it would be known where the Inca was and the people would take care to watch out for him and defend him and the idol. Great sacrifices were made to this idol, from the time it was made until the end of the three months, when the people assembled. After the three months elapsed, the people gathered. The day before they were to leave, Inca Yupanque himself made great sacrifices to all the *guacas* and idols, especially to the Sun and to this idol Caccha, and ordered that the people who remained in the city always take care to offer a sacrifice to the Sun, the *guacas*, and idols, whom they were to beg for success as long as the Inca was away at war.

With this done and arranged, Pachacuti Inca Yupanque left the city of Cuzco accompanied by one hundred thousand warriors, who always repaired the roads as they went along. Up and down the slopes he had them make stone stairs so that the travelers could walk up and down more easily. When he reached the Apurimac River, which is ten leagues from the city of Cuzco, he had them build bridge pillars or towers [two on each side of the river] on which he put crosspieces of long stones and thick wooden beams. Then he had them make a cable from some twigs that, being quite thin and strong, resemble those of wicker. He had these cables made one and a half times the width of the river. The cable was a long span wide and six fingers high. He had fourteen cables made. From seven of them he had the bridge made in the following way. The bridge pillars are six feet wide[2] and one *estado* high, at the entrance of the bridge. A big hole is made in the pillars where they set the crosspieces, which extend right through, and there are two or three of them. To the first one, next to the entrance, the end of one cable was wound around the crosspiece. From there it was wound around again with the remainder of the same end. Then it was wound around the last support and crosspiece for the last time, at which point it was tied firmly with *cabuya* cords. The end of the other cable was tied in the same way. Thus he had five cables tied to those crosspieces. Then he had a thick rope thrown over these crosspieces. This rope would extend all the way across the river. And this rope was tied to the structure of these bridge pillars. At this point, he ordered that, with rafts and other Indians swimming, enough men cross to pull these cables over. After the men reached the other side, he had thick ropes tied to the other end of each one of these cables. With a small cord tied to this rope, he ordered an Indian to climb along the rope which was tied to the top of the bridge. The Indian climbed across, carrying in his mouth the end of the cord, which was tied to the other rope, which itself was tied to the cable made of twigs. Once he was on the other side with this cord, he had those who were over there pull on this cord and those on the first side release the thick rope little by little, and as the rope moved across, all the Indians on the other side pulled it and those on the first kept on releasing it little by little. Thus the rope went across as well as the cable, which was tied there, and which they took across the end of the cable, in the way that you have already heard. When they had it over there, as they stretched it forcefully, they wound it several times around the crosspieces, just as the Inca had had them do on his side.

With the five cables pulled across, in the way that you have heard, all together, even, and very tight, he had them put from the entrance of the bridge many cross poles [for the floor] each one *braza* long and the thickness of the wrist. These poles were securely tied so that the cables would not get separated. With the poles tied holding the cables together all the way across, he had another cable thrown across at the height of the entrance of the bridge on the right-hand side. He had this cable tied very securely to these pillars of the entrance to the bridge on both sides. And he had another cable thrown across on the left side, having it tied, as you have heard, to the pillars of the bridge [for guard rails]. After this he had many heavy *cabuya* ropes the thickness of the wrist made. He had this rope tied to that cable on the right side from the edge of the bridge to that cable that was tied up high [guard rail], weaving this rope from the bridge to the cable and from the cable to the bridge up and down and down and up. Then the Inca had many limbs brought and had them tied to this cable all along the side of the bridge. After finishing the strip of the right side, he had exactly the same thing done on the left side. Next, on the floor of the bridge, which is where the cross poles were tied, he had many of those ropes put down, together with as many limbs as seemed sufficient to him. Thus the bridge was finished. Then he had another one just like the first one made next to it, in the way already stated.

With these two bridges made, he ordered the men, one after the other, to cross the first one very slowly. When half of the men had crossed, the bridge swayed to one side. To straighten it, he had many large stones hung on the other side. This weight straightened it out somewhat. While this was going on, his men crossed the other bridge. With all of his men on the other side, he went with them to a settlement called Curahuasi, which is three leagues from there [the bridge]. When they went there, the Indians of those regions, the Quichuas, Umasayos, Aymaraes, Yanaguaras, Chumbibilcas, and Chancas, came out to offer them peace, obedience, and vassalage. The Inca did them many great favors and thus won them over with his powerful forces.

Thus the Inca went on his way and reached the Abancay River, where he ordered his soldiers and captains to have those who could swim jump into the river and swim across. Then they were to get to work on the supports for two more bridges just like the last ones. They acted on this order right away and made them. Right there many other caciques and lords offered peace. The Inca asked them if the people from towns and provinces that were ahead of them had news of his arrival. They said that past their towns there was a province with a very great number of people. These people were called Soras, and also farther ahead of this one there were two provinces with very many people, who were called Lucanas. Between the Soras and the Lucanas, along with other Chancas who were also from a neighboring region, they had a large assembly of soldiers. From the time they received the news that the Inca had left the city, they were stocking up on weapons. When the Inca heard this news, he said he was very pleased to have heard what they were saying. This confirmed that his excursion had not been in vain. And he asked them which one of those lords of those provinces was the one who had called that assembly. They told him that it was the lords of the Soras, and he answered them that it was well for them to guide his camp in that direction.

There the Inca told his captains and leaders of the city of Cuzco that when they went to ask him to take the *borla* fringe, it was the painting and drawing that they had seen him make of the bridges and roads that they had made up to there. And he ordered them to have roads constructed and bridges made over the rivers, just as he had done up to there, wherever they went on military campaigns. Thus he left there with his army. He gave the order to march to the province of the Soras. Thinking they were powerful and planning their defense and resistance, when they got word that Pachacuti Inca Yupanque was coming against them, they had readied their forces, barriers, and forts through all their land, which had big ravines, mountains, and very rough terrain with high cliffs and bad roads.

When Pachacuti arrived with his powerful forces, he divided his squadrons and made war from all sides, in such a way that very quickly he defeated them, subjugated them, and captured the lords of those towns and provinces. After this was done, the Inca had his men divide into three groups. He put two of the groups under certain captains of his who were lords of Cuzco. He ordered them to leave there and for one group to go in one direction, not going off very far from the city of Cuzco, to conquer and subjugate the people of the province called Condesuyo today. The other squadron of soldiers, along with the other lords of Cuzco and captains to whom he had given command, were to go across the province today called Andesuyo, winning and subjugating the towns and provinces they might find. He also ordered them not to go too far from the city of Cuzco. They might run into some provinces with so many soldiers that they could not overcome them and for that reason would need help. If so, they were to send him word of it. And he would come to their rescue. They asked him where the messengers they would send would find him if they found themselves in such straits. He told them he planned to relax there for a few days. From there he would return to the city of Cuzco. Therefore they should send their messenger to the city of Cuzco because there they would be able to inform him of what was happening.

So that he could receive messages better and faster, he ordered each one of the lords from there on to the city of Cuzco to put runners in their territory along the road. There were always to be runners there who would be provided by the communities as necessary. The post stations were to be close together so that news would reach the city of Cuzco quickly and his captains could keep him informed. For this purpose, he immediately ordered an *orejon* lord of the city of Cuzco to start setting up these post stations. Each one should have little huts set up in the places designated. Then that *orejon* lord who had been given that assignment asked the Inca how far one station should be put from the next. The Inca showed him a certain distance, which was one-quarter of a league [less than a mile] and not very far. Then the captains left with their men, going across the provinces that you have heard about. And that *orejon* lord left to set up the post stations. Finally, the Inca remained with that other part of the soldiers whom he had ordered to stay as his personal guard.

XIX

Wherein Inca Yupanque returned to the city of Cuzco after defeating the Soras, and how he met with his captains in Jaquijahuana, and how he entered the city of Cuzco triumphant over the Soras as well as the rest of the lords his captains subjugated, and of the things that they did on his return.

Inca Yupanque remained in the province of the Soras after having sent his captains and arranged for what you have already heard about. He ordered brought before him the insignias and garments of those lords that he had taken prisoner and subjugated. When these things were brought before him, he ordered that a number of red *borla* fringes one *geme* long be made. After many of these red *borlas* were finished, he had them attached and sewed to those garments and things that they had taken there. After this was done, he ordered all of it placed beneath his feet. He also ordered that some large tunics reaching down to the feet be made. He ordered that many *borlas* be attached and sewed to the tunics from the bottom to the top. These tunics and *borlas* were to be red. After this was done, he ordered brought there before him the lords that he had defeated and subjugated. And there before him he ordered them to put on those tunics, splash a certain amount of *chicha* over themselves, and put some crumbs made of maize flour on their heads. He gave this order, saying that by doing those things he was taking possession of those lords, as well as the towns and provinces controlled by them.

After this he ordered the wives of the lords of Cuzco to come out immediately and sing there, before him and those prisoners, a song that he had selected there. The song went as follows: "Ynga yupangue yndin yocasola ymalca chinboleisola ymalca axcoley haguaya guaya haguaya guaya,"[1] which means "Inca Yupanque, son of the Sun, defeated the Soras and put *borlas* on them" with that jingle of "Hayaguaya," which is like the "tanarara" that we say. Then certain drums were brought there. The lords of Cuzco who were there put on their garments and plumage, just as when they had entered that province to fight with the Soras. Being all together there with those prisoners among them dressed as you have heard, they started their song and fiesta which lasted one month. Finally, Inca Yupanque decided it was time to return to the city of Cuzco. He did so with all his warriors, and he took ahead of him always those prisoners dressed in the way already stated. Preceding him, as you have heard, these prisoners were greatly embarrassed.

Thus Inca Yupanque returned with the prisoners and the rest of the spoils, leaving under his control the provinces of Soras and Lucanas, which are fifty leagues from the city of Cuzco. And the captains that he sent across the province of Condesuyo conquered and subjugated the lands up to Arequipa. From there they ascended toward Cuzco, where they subjugated the towns and provinces of Collaguas, Canas, and those of Urocache. From there, having made the bridges of Quiquijana and many others that they had made across the rivers that they found in the provinces where they went, they came to the city of Cuzco. On arriving they found out that the Inca had not entered the city; they did not do it either but remained outside of it. The other captains who also had gone up to the province of the Andes, won and conquered up to the province of Caxaroma, which is in the Andes and its woodlands, forty leagues from the city of Cuzco. When they reached there, they decided it was time to return to see their lord. Thus they returned, leaving subjugated as many lords of the Andes as they could as well as provinces and valleys of coca. From that expedition they brought back many tigers [jaguars] and big snakes that they call *amaro*, some of which were as thick around as the calf of the leg of a fairly large man. Some of the snakes were four *brazas* long. They brought them rolled up on litters, always feeding them meat. They had found that the lords of the Andes had these snakes in their houses, where they had tamed them. And they had done the same thing with the tigers. When they approached the city of Cuzco, they found out that the Inca had not arrived yet. They continued on without entering the city, and stayed nearby awaiting the Inca. As they went by the city of Cuzco, they found out that their companions, the other captains, had passed by there the day before with many prisoners and great spoils that they had captured in their campaign. They had just as many prisoners and spoils. As they were going by, they had news that Pachacuti Inca Yupanque was coming the next day to Jaquijahuana, which is four leagues from the city of Cuzco. The captains who had passed by had also arrived at Jaquijahuana. They received the news, and as they had it that they were waiting for him there, these captains went quickly and reached Jaquijahuana.

The Inca was happy to see his captains, who approached the Inca and each made gestures of great reverence and obeisance. After this all of the captains of the squadron that had gone across Condesuyo, since they had arrived there before the other group, had a big fire built before the Inca. In this fire they sacrificed sheep, lambs, fine garments, maize, and other provisions that they had taken in the war. Afterward, they put the fire out there. Then they brought out before the Inca the insignias, garments, and weapons of those prisoners that they had defeated and subjugated. They humbly begged the Inca to tread on it. To all of this the Inca ordered them to bring out many of the *borlas* that you have heard about. With this done, the Inca stood up, tread on it, and put it under his feet. Afterward, he ordered the prisoners brought before him. When they appeared before him, the Inca ordered them dressed in other large tunics with many *borlas*, just as he had ordered done to the lords of the Soras, along with the other ceremonies of pouring *chicha* on them and crumbs that were put on their heads, just as you have heard. With this done, these captains stepped aside. Thus the other captains arrived who had gone to the province of the Andes. They did the same thing the others did before the Inca, who did the same with them and their prisoners. The Inca was very pleased to see the wild animals that they brought out before him, and he ordered them not to give the animals anything to eat that day or the next day. The next day he ordered them to strike camp and all march to the city of Cuzco. Pachacuti Inca Yupanque went on his litter with the prisoners ahead of him dressed the way you have heard and the rest of the spoils there, too.

When they came within sight of the city of Cuzco, he ordered the captains to assemble there all together with him and to enter the city singing, each one in order about the things that had happened on the expeditions that they had taken. In singing all this, those who had stayed with Inca Yupanque started with the song that you have heard about the defeat of the Soras. After they finished, the other captains started singing about what had happened to them in the province of Condesuyo. And the same thing was done by the captains who had subjugated the Andes. At the same time, he ordered the prisoners to cry and declare their guilt and crimes in a loud voice and how they were subjects and vassals of the son of the Sun and that no forces could resist him, starting first of all with the Soras and then the rest.

In this way the Inca entered Cuzco where, as he reached the square, he found there the statue of the Sun, the statues of the rest of the *guacas* and of the ancient lords, which he had made. On arriving, the Inca made his gestures of obeisance and sacrifices. Afterward, he ordered that those tigers be placed in a house that he had designated for a jail, which he named Çanga guaçi.[2] With these fierce animals in there, he ordered that the prisoners be thrown in there so the tigers would eat them. And he ordered that the prisoners be kept in the company of these fierce animals for three days. If after three days the tigers had not eaten them, the survivors were to be let out. Since the tigers had not eaten for two days, they say they ate I do not know how many of them. Those who were found alive after three days were taken out. Afterward, they lost their properties, authority, and power. And they were given as servants to the statues there. The Inca ordered the insignias and things of this sort that were brought from the war when these people were taken prisoner to be placed in a house. In it were to be put similar things taken in war by him. The Inca designated that house and ordered that it be named *llaxa guaçi*.[3]

With this done, he ordered an audience with the lords and caciques who had offered peace to his captains. He did them many special favors. Then he ordered that they bring all of the spoils taken in the war, including livestock, garments, jewels of gold and silver, Indian men and women, all of which he ordered his captains to distribute among the warriors who had served him on that campaign. First the Inca took what he wanted. Then he gave whatever he saw fit to his captains. After this, all the rest was divided up among the common soldiers who had served him. Next he named certain caciques to be lords of those towns and provinces of the ones the tigers ate and he had dispossessed. After this he realized that it was time for all those caciques and lords to go rest and enjoy themselves in their lands. So he brought them all together before him and told them to take care from then on to serve and give tribute to the city of Cuzco with everything they had in their lands and to be sure that every four months they brought some of each of their foods to the city. These foods should be piled up in the city square so that from there the foods could be distributed in the way he had ordered to the people of the city of Cuzco. The caciques answered that they would obey. They were his vassals. The Inca should designate what each one was to bring in tribute and how much.

The Inca ordered them to tell him what they had in their lands and what each one could produce. And they were to tell him the truth, for the Inca had given orders to place in each province of each one of them an *orejon* lord born of the people of Cuzco. Each one of them was to respect this lord in their land as if he were the Inca. This lord would know what each one possessed, and if the Inca found out that someone lied to him, no matter who it might be, they should understand that the culprit would die. Then the caciques sent for the *quipos*, records that they keep, and also for paintings of what they had and of the type of land and province of each one of them. Some said that they had livestock, others, great fields of maize, others, gold mines, others, silver mines, others, much wood, and so forth for the rest of the things and products. Having seen this, the Inca called the important lords of the city whom he had designated to keep track of what those lords and caciques brought in as tribute.

And being there he ordered many woolen cords in a variety of colors. Bringing each cacique before him in the presence of those lords of Cuzco and making knots in those cords, he made a record for each one of them of what he was to bring in tribute to the Inca and to the city of Cuzco. He ordered some of them to bring in tribute maize, others, sheep, others, garments, others gold, and so forth for the rest of the things. He designated a moderate tribute for each one so that they could comply without annoyance or bother. The Inca ordered two of each one of these *quipos* and records to be made, one for the cacique to take and another to remain in the possession of those lords. Next the Inca named the *orejon* lords who were to reside in those towns and provinces, where they were to keep track of everything that happened and grievances that might come up among the people. These lords were to take care in distributing the lands every year to the local residents and also to have the young unmarried boys and girls assemble every year. With them together the Inca was to be informed so that he could provide lords to join the youth in marriage. The lords were also to take special care every four months to have sent to the city of Cuzco the foods that they were ordered to bring to supply the city. They were also to have brought the garments, gold, silver, livestock, and the rest of the things that they were to bring each year in tribute.

With this stipulated and ordered by the Inca, as you have heard, the caciques and natives of these lands had lost their liberty and were in perpetual subjugation as they lived until the Spaniards came to this land. After finishing this, the Inca ordered them all to go to their lands, rest and enjoy themselves. He reminded them always to take care to sow large fields of maize and all other foods. As long as they had enough to eat, they could do anything. With this done and ordained, the caciques set out for their lands, each one taking along an *orejon* lord of the city of Cuzco, who was to live with them in their lands for the purpose already stated. Thus they left, and the Inca remained in Cuzco with his people.

XX

Wherein Pachacuti Inca Yupanque was in the city of Cuzco enjoying himself with his people for a certain time at the end of which he had the people assemble to go across the province of Collasuyo because he had news that this province was heavily populated and had a lord there whom everybody respected and revered; this lord called himself king, unique lord and son of the Sun, just like the Inca.

As Inca Yupanque remained in his city and town of Cuzco, seeing that he was lord and that he had subjugated the towns and provinces, as you have heard, he was very pleased. He had subjugated more and obtained much more importance than any of his ancestors. He saw the great apparatus that he had so that whenever he wanted to he could subjugate and put under his control anything else that he wanted. Seeing also that he succeeded at anything he tried or wanted and since he was pleased on seeing himself lord, he decided to enjoy himself in his town with his people for twenty years. During this time he kept busy watching how his people sowed and harvested, making sacrifices and holding fiestas that he created; making a household idol of each thing that he considered necessary, just as the Romans did. The Inca made a maize god whom he called Çaramama,[1] saying that was the mother of maize, another *chicha* idol, and many others for similar things. And he had these idols in his house with him for he had made them of gold.

There were more than two hundred of these idols because he made idols for animals, birds, waters, plants, fruits, and herbs, and of all the other things that he could imagine. He had them in that room in his house, where he had the statues of the ancient lords that he had made. Each time he made one of these, he had great fiestas, sacrifices, fasts, and idolatries, just as he had done when he made the first idols of the Sun, which you have already heard about. And during this time his wife, the one he took when he put on the *borla*, had two sons. He named the first one Yamque Yupanque and the second, Topa Inca Yupanque. With one of his other wives he also had another son, whom he named Capac Yupanque. For the birth of each of his sons he had great fiestas, merriment, and sacrifices. At this time he also took as wives twenty more ladies, daughters of those lords of the city, from both Hurin Cuzco and Hanan Cuzco, which mean lower Cuzco and upper Cuzco, which were separated and bordered by the Temple of the Sun and the two rivers, as you have already learned in this account.

After the twenty years had gone by, the Inca got news that past Lurucache, which is twenty leagues from Cuzco in the direction of Charcas, there was a province and town called Hatun Colla. In it there was a lord named Ruquiça-pana. This town of Hatun Colla and the lord already mentioned had subjugated and controlled a great many other lords within twenty to twenty-five leagues of Hatun Colla. This lord also called himself Capac Çapa apo yndi chori,[2] which means king and unique lord son of the Sun. He was very powerful and had very powerful forces that were very warlike. When the Inca received this news, he was very pleased. What he wanted was to find in his times another lord who had the audacity to do battle with him. Then the Inca could prove his forces and power against this adversary. After receiving this news, the Inca thought over what he would do in this campaign. Then he ordered all the lords of Cuzco to assemble in his house on a certain day because he wanted to communicate certain things to them. With them all together he told them that he had news that past Lurucache there was a province and towns where there was a certain lord who called himself lord, just like the Inca. This lord was very powerful and had very powerful forces. The Inca had decided to do battle with him and for that purpose it was necessary to assemble a large number of soldiers. Since he had decided to do this, they should prepare and send a messenger right away to all the *orejon* lords spread out over the provinces and to the caciques of the provinces for them to bring together as many warriors as possible. As soon as they had them together they should leave at once and come to the city of Cuzco. For this purpose he gave them three months' time from the day that the messengers left the city of Cuzco.

Next, certain young *orejones* were called there. They were ordered to leave and go out to all the towns and provinces with the orders from the Inca that you have just heard. Without giving them any explanation about why these soldiers were to go, the messengers ordered them to leave at once. In his meeting the Inca ordered that this news be kept secret. Thus the messengers left. The

Inca and his men left their meeting. And then each one of them gave the order to get the weapons and provisions ready that would be needed for the campaign. At the end of the three months the warriors arrived at the city, where the Inca ordered a review. He found that there were one hundred fifty thousand men, not counting the rest of the servants that they brought. The Inca and his soldiers were ready, and it seemed to him that he had enough men for the campaign.

The next day he made sacrifices to his idols according to his custom and, taking his war idol that he had, as we have already told you, he left in search of this lord of Hatun Colla across the province of Collasuyo, where as he passed he conquered and subjugated the towns and provinces that he found on his way. When the lord of Hatun Colla got the news that such powerful forces were coming against him, he had a meeting of his men where they say he assembled more than two hundred thousand warriors. With them he waited in his town of Hatun Colla. When the Inca reached there he attacked. The battle was so fierce and bitter that though it started in the morning victory was not in sight until evening. In this battle it is said that more than one hundred thousand men died from both sides. At the end of the battle the Inca and his men won the victory. That lord of Hatun Colla was captured and killed in the battle. The Inca ordered that lord's head be preserved to keep it intact.

The Inca also ordered that the rest of the lords taken there be made captive, carefully tied up and put under guard. He also ordered that no one dare to bury any of the enemies' bodies and that all of the spoils be brought together and guarded, including livestock, garments, gold and silver, jewels, and slaves, male and female Indian servants known as *piñas* by them, that were taken there. The spoils were very extensive, all was to be collected and put in a safe place.

When night came, the Inca went to rest. And all of his men, after putting everything mentioned under guard and having cared for those wounded there, also went to rest that night, for they had gotten very tired that day. The next morning they took the bodies of their friends and put them in sepulchers, not with the thought of leaving them there, but, rather, so the bodies would remain there for a time while the Inca was subjugating those provinces. One of the favors that they had asked of the Inca was that the bodies of those who had died in the war, after it was over, be returned to their land. A lord of Cuzco had asked this of the Inca in the name of everyone else. The Inca promised it to them because these Indians have an expression that they say in the following way: "Cay pacha tu coptin atarixunxi llapan chic runa caoçarispa aichantin ymanamcuna canchic,"[3] which means "When this world comes to an end we will all rise up with life and with this flesh as we are now." Someone made them understand this; they know it very well. With this purpose, that lord begged both for those of Cuzco and for the rest that the bodies of the dead be brought back both to Cuzco and to the other lands.

As soon as the Inca saw that the bodies were picked up, he had the bodies of the dead enemies taken far away from the place where they fought the battle. With them out of the way, he had a small temple of the Sun built on that site. In that house he had a statue put in the place of the Sun. To this statue he had a great sacrifice made. Then he sent word by messenger to the city of Cuzco to inform them of his victory and to tell them to offer great sacrifices to the Sun, the idols, the statues, and the *guacas* near the city. The message arrived very quickly because it was carried by the post service that he set up along the road by which he had come. With this taken care of, he had camp broken, and from there he left for the provinces of Chiquicache, Moho, Callavaya, and Asangaro, all of which offered to obey him. And he did many favors for them.

With all of this subjugated along with the rest of the towns and provinces that are in that region, he returned to the city of Cuzco, where he entered triumphantly, as he did the other time when he returned from the Soras and had the prisoners thrown into the house with the wild animals. The Inca had the head of the *Colla* with all of his regalia that he had when he was killed along with the rest of the things that were taken from the captains when they were taken prisoner. All of this was put in the other house, called *llaxa guaçi,* where before they had also put the things that they had taken in the defeat of the Soras and that of the other provinces. With this done and after finishing all of the sacrifices, fiestas, solemnities, and ceremonies that in entering the city like this and in the following thirty days he customarily performed, he ordered that all the spoils taken in this campaign be brought before him. With it all there he divided it between himself and his men, as he had done with the spoils from the Soras.

After this he told all of his caciques to go to their lands, rest, and enjoy themselves. Then those caciques left, taking with them the *orejon* lords who were supposed to be with them. Each one of the *orejones* was given the title of *tocorrico,*[4] which means "inspector." The Inca also ordered that the bodies of the dead, as soon as the bodies were preserved, be taken by them to the wives and children of the dead. He ordered that they be given a certain part of the spoils. For this purpose he had distributed from the amount that was given to him for those who had died. He also told the *orejon* lords who were going to live in the provinces that, when they distributed land or something in the name of the republics of those lands and their towns, part of the best should be given first to these widows and orphans and not to anyone else. After counting the poor, part of the lands should be given to them and other widows as needed. After this, lands should be given to the caciques and lords and then to the rest of the community. After these orders had been issued, the caciques and lords left and the Inca stayed in his lands with his people in the city of Cuzco. After returning from Collao [Collasuyo], the Inca spent another twenty years without going to war. He enjoyed himself in idolatrous vices and in doing some things for the good of his government, as this account will explain to you in the next chapter.

XXI

Wherein Inca Yupanque, after returning from subjugating Collao, spent some time in the city without considering another war but instead enjoying himself; during this time he organized and established certain laws and ordinances for the good of the people of the city and its republic.

After Inca Yupanque had bid farewell to his warriors and sent them to their lands and provinces, he remained in his town. Having relaxed in the city for a year, he went out through the city, saw it, looked at all of it, its streets as well as the damage that the waters and rains were doing there. He saw that the currents and waters that came in the rain and fell from the roofs of the houses, removing the earth from the edges of the streets, did damage to the streets and went under the foundations of the houses. Thus, so that this could be prevented, he ordered, at the base of the walls in the places where water fell from the roofs of the houses, that many flagstones all the same size be placed closely together. These flagstones were to be placed evenly. The Inca also ordered that in the middle of those streets there be made of stone some small channels about one *geme* wide and also that much gravel be thrown there and sandy soil in the space between this channel and the flagstones that came right up to the walls. From the walls up to the channel there should be some slight slope so that the water from the rains would run off.

With this done, one day it occurred to the Inca to look into the behavior of the inhabitants of the city in their houses. Wanting to see this, he went out of his house one morning, taking only two young servants. If some lord met him on the street and wanted to accompany him, the Inca would not consent to it, saying that he was taking care of something and wanted to be alone that day. In this way he went to all the houses of the city and every room in them, without announcing himself to anyone or explaining what he was looking at. Moreover, at night he disguised himself by the clothes he wore. Thus he went through all the streets of the city and the surrounding area at night looking at and listening to what his people were doing and saying. He kept this up for ten days.

Based on the things that he had seen before and on what he saw and understood during those days, he thought over the vices of the city. And it seemed to him that the same would be true of the rest of the common people of all the land and its towns, that it was reasonable to find a remedy for this and establish the order and reason that should be followed. In view of what he had observed, the Inca ordered a meeting of all the important nobles of the city. When they were before him all together, he told them of the vices and failings that in the whole town he had seen, in the people's houses, and in each one of them. With the desire to put a stop to this he had told them to assemble there so he could give them the rules that they were to follow and the things they were to do, which are as follows.

He ordained that, since the city's roofs were straw and its houses and buildings rather close together, everyone should be careful with their fires. If it happened that any house caught fire because of the negligence of its owner, all the nearby neighbors and anyone else who could get there should put out the fire at this house. Those who put out the fire in this way could freely take any goods and property that they found inside the house; the owner had no right to protect it or to ask for restitution. If the house was burned down by someone who wanted to do evil to its owner, this delinquent would be caught and thrown into the house of the wild animals, to be killed there and torn to pieces. The property of this delinquent would be given to the owner of the house. If this house burned by chance, everyone should help the owner, either by putting out the fire or by helping to put it out. If, because this happened suddenly, the goods in the house were taken in the way mentioned, such goods should be kept by those who got them but they should not use any of them until the truth of the case be revealed. If the owner of the house was found not to blame for the fire, his goods would be returned to him and the inhabitants of the city would help him put on a new roof and rebuild his house as he had it before. And if something burned which he had been given from the public storehouses, he should be given the same amount of goods as was burned.

There were accidental events like the one just mentioned and other similar ones. If one's properties were lost, the situation could become desperate where one could see no way to regain the position that one had. For redress in this case, the Inca ordained that there be many large storehouses around the city full of all necessary things, including each thing and type of thing for these provisions and benefaction. But if someone, by virtue of being a man of ill repute and unsavory habits, lost his property, he would be sent out of town to serve in the wars and not be relieved of duty unless he had performed such services to the Inca and to the city of Cuzco that for those services he would deserve to return to Cuzco. On his return he would be done favors. But it would remain to be seen, in spite of all this, whether he had given up misconduct and unsavory habits. If so, from the storehouses mentioned above, his property would be restored.

These storehouses were so well supplied with all of the things necessary for their lives and needs that in them there was even footwear for rams made of *cabuya,* which is used like hemp in Spain. There were not only storehouses for garments and wool and the other necessities, but there were also large corrals of livestock along with this. The corrals, just like the storehouses, were well supplied for these provisions and benefactions. Before this the Inca had three *repartimientos*[1] of Indians near the city. These he had designated as belonging to the city so that they could do the things that were needed in the city. Thus these *repartimientos* were charged with protecting and pasturing this livestock, which belonged to the city. Each year these caciques who were in charge of this livestock were obliged to report to one of the lords of the city who was chosen for this purpose. This lord was a very close relative of the Inca and very important in the city. These caciques reported to this lord the increase in the herds, the wool taken, and the animals that had died that year. The dead animals, dehydrated and preserved, were brought before the lord. They even brought the cloth in which the lambs were wrapped at birth. All of this they brought dehydrated and preserved, and in this way they gave an account of everything by bringing it there with them. If it happened that the report was not reasonable and it was found that the cacique in question had failed to register one single sheep for which he was responsible, the Inca ordered that this man be publicly hanged for contempt of the property and goods of the republic.

The Inca ordained the following. Since the city of Cuzco and its buildings were so distinguished, if any stone or wall fell down from where it was placed, it should be rebuilt and the straw of the roofs of the houses should be replaced if it was so old and rotten that rain came into these houses. In addition, the channels and fountains of the city streets should always be kept clean. They should also take care, almost like a night patrol, to watch at night who entered and who left the city, and no one should dare to leave at night. The one who was caught leaving at night, whether man or woman, whether noble or plebeian, even if it were one's son, should be taken prisoner so that the next day that person could give a full explanation of what he was doing. For these purposes, he designated one of those lords, giving him a *repartimiento* and town near the city. Thus the city was kept clean, its buildings well maintained; no one dared go out at night for fear of being caught, put in jail, and punished.

The Inca ordained that to maintain tranquillity in the city no one should dare cause an uproar, nor should they act shamelessly, nor start a riot. They should be alert for any of this by watching and finding out what was going on in the city and in each house both at night and during the day. Both for him as well as his government and the order of the republic, twelve lords in whom he had confidence would be appointed. He gave these lords twelve hundred Indians so that each month one of these lords would have one hundred Indians to see and find out about the things in the city mentioned above. Everything that was heard and observed on a certain day by the one designated for that month would be explained to the Inca, including what was going on and what was said in the city. These lords mentioned above were ordered to be vigilant so that in the republic and town there would be a good example of virtue and the vices of women and young men both on days of their fiestas and fasts as well as on the rest of the days of the year, would not be allowed to perform these vices and if the vices persisted, punishments would be meted out for such behavior. Each one of these lords should take special care during the month for which he was responsible to look throughout the city and its houses with his Indians at both the lords and those who were not lords, at women and at men who were acting immature and who were talking with women and at women who were talking with men. When they were seen by those guards who had this responsibility, the guards should come up close to observe those things and without saying anything to them, the guards should go right up to both of them and take something from each one, and the guards should remember well the signs and things that they saw done and the words that they heard spoken. With this clearly in mind, the guards should leave them and pay attention to which days they had observed them doing those things, whether it was fiesta days or not. And the things picked up by the guards should be taken home with them to keep. The guards should also take care to go through all the houses on fiesta and fasting days and look on those nights at who was sleeping with women, even if it were their own wives. During those days no one was to dare to do it. And even if the ones that they found were lords, the guards should take a jewel or an article of clothing from each of the ones found in that way. The guilty persons whose things had been taken should not dare to ask for these things nor try to keep them nor even say a word to the one who took the things. If one of the culprits did such a thing, that person would be hanged without a hearing. And the guard who took the thing would not speak or say anything to the culprits, but, rather, either during the night or the day anyplace in the city, quietly seeing these persons who were transgressing, come up to them carefully, having seen the transgression, and take right there some jewel or article of clothing. Then the guard would leave silently with it and the delinquents would let it go without resisting or saying a word. If the delinquent should request that the one with this duty should return to the owner what had been taken because that person was a lord, the son of the Inca, a friend, or if that person offered a gift, the delinquent would be hanged at once. Thus in this case no one could dare resist, even though it were the principal wife of the Inca who begged the Inca for someone's life, even though it were the Inca's own son who was condemned for this offense because he refused to give up what was taken in this way, this piece of clothing or jewels that were taken.

At the end of the year and the last day of the month of that year, the Inca would come out to the square with all of his wives and his retainers, from the oldest to the youngest, leaving none of them at home, and all of the lords of the city would do the same. While they were all out there together, four designated lords would be stationed in a certain part of the city where they had this meeting; these lords would hear about the offenses that had been committed that year, and they would sentence each one according to the misdeeds of which they were guilty on the basis of what was said by those who were in charge of seeing and finding out about such things. According to the excuse that each one gave, and for the witnesses and information about it, the loads of clothing and jewels would be brought. Each lineage of the city had a designated place where that was done. Those of the lineage remained there during the proceedings and it was determined whether each one of them would be freed or found guilty.

With them all ready, those lords mentioned above came, each one in his turn with his people, entering the square just as when they started in the year. The first one to enter placed before the Inca and those four lords piece by piece the clothing and jewels. And as they were bringing out those things, they also presented before the Inca and those lords the owners of the things. With the person there present, the offense that he had been found committing was stated. The one who deserved death according to the offense was taken prisoner there and carried off to jail. With this done, those who were found less at fault according to their offenses and what had been found out about them were sent separately to a certain place.

The Inca designated and ordered that there be houses in certain places where the offenders would be placed, and it was understood that, according to the offense that each one had committed, that person would be put in one of these houses. The Inca indicated the punishment that was to be given in each one of the houses to those people who were put there. If the person got the death penalty, the Inca ordered that person put in one of the houses; for the one incurring a lesser offense, in another house; for one incurring a still lesser offense, in yet another house. Thus the Inca designated for each house the punishment to be given to each one, as you have already heard. It should be known that those whose offenses were considered most serious and most severe were the ones found in whatever way speaking of love, making merry, or actually sleeping with a married woman or with a *mamacona* priestess of the Sun or of the Inca or of any of the statues of lords dead and gone.

Thus all of them were punished in the presence of everyone who was there in accordance with the offenses that had been committed. And if it happened that some son of the Inca was found guilty of an offense punishable by death, the Inca himself would kill the offender right there in front of everyone, saying that the one who should make an example, like the sons of the Inca and the other lords, should not transgress. And the Inca ordered that if one of the principal lords of the city were guilty and deserved that punishment, the most important member of his lineage would kill him right there in front of everyone. The rest of the common people, both men and women, were to punish and bring to justice everyone else. They were empowered to do it. In this way, this lord kept his city free of all vices and other disturbances.

The Inca ordained that, to keep the young men who were unmarried from going after married women and *mamaconas,* there should be a certain house outside the city in which there would be placed a certain number of women of those taken in the wars with whom these young men could converse. And if a married man were found who went to that house with those women, he would be bound hand and foot in the square. There the relatives of his wife would censure him and take his wife away from him for a certain length of time. If one of the women of this brothel got pregnant while she was there, her son would be brought up elsewhere and this child would be called *çapçi churi*,[2] which means "son of the community." They consider that if two or three men sleep with a woman in an hour or so and the woman gets pregnant, the child is engendered by all three. In order to ensure that the children engendered in the brothel would be reared, the Inca ordered that there be in a house certain women of the provinces and towns whose children had died. These women would bring up the children born like this.

The Inca also ordered the lords that he had designated to watch after the activities of people have much straw thrown at the edge of the water under the bridges of the river that went through the city. It should be ordered that the children born secretly to *mamaconas,* married women, or daughters of lords should not be killed but, rather, on giving birth to them at night, the mothers should have the children placed under these bridges. Everyone was advised that if they found anyone at night taking some child to place it under the bridge, whether it were a man or a woman carrying the child, if the night watch asked, "Who goes there?" the man or woman carrying the child would answer, "I am carrying a child to put under the bridge." In this case, that person should not be asked who they were nor give their name. That person should be allowed to go freely and return. None of the watchmen should dare find out where that person lived. Every morning these guardian women should carefully look under those bridges. If they found any child, it should be taken to those women already mentioned who were designated to rear such children. After these children were grown, the Inca ordered that they should be taken to the valleys of coca, where they would work in cultivating coca. And this was what the Inca stipulated with respect to what has just been stated, and he ordered that the prostitutes be paid.

Taking into consideration the laziness and great pretentiousness in which the young men of Cuzco were reared, the Inca ordained the following. When a boy reached five years of age, his parents and relatives should impose on him part of their work and servitude. They should send the boys out to bring firewood and straw, to collect snails and mushrooms, and to catch birds. They should also be sent to the fields to irrigate, cultivate, and do other farmwork. These boys should be told to carry their slings, *aillos*,[3] or bolas, and little hatchets in their hands so that these boys would know how to serve, be disciplined, and would be accustomed to using their weapons in a war. From the time these boys reached the age of fifteen years, they would be sent to fight in times when the Inca was at war. With regard to girls, at five years of age their mothers should require that they go to the fountains for water, not alone but, rather, accompanied by their servant girls. These little girls should also go to the fields to pick vegetables that they eat. They should also be taught to cook, spin, and weave garments for both men and women.

So that this work would be done with care, the Inca designated certain lords who were charged to check up every ten days on the bundles of straw and firewood that these boys had brought. These lords were to look over the little hoes and equipment that their parents made for them to find out if these tools were used. The lords should also see if the boys could handle and throw a sling and how the boys could handle the rest of the weapons. And the father who did not take care to train his son would be taken prisoner and put in jail for some days. So that the girls would be seen and tested in what has been stated, the Inca ordered that there be designated certain *cozcoy naca cuna*,[4] which means, as we say, "Roman matrons." The Inca ordered that his own sons and daughters from that time on be trained and disciplined in that way.

The Inca ordained that if anyone were caught stealing in fields where the maize was green or dry, the thief, whether man or woman, would be completely undressed. The one who caught the thief would keep the garments. The Inca also ordered that everyone should have guards for their fields.

The Inca ordained that if someone stole something, whether a small or a large amount, from any other, the thief should be tortured severely. Twice the amount of what was stolen should be returned to the owner. If the thief were unable to replace the stolen thing, the thief would be given as a perpetual servant to the lord whose thing was stolen. But the thief would not be given as a slave because among them it was not customary to deal in slaves but, rather, perpetual servants. And the descendants of these servants would serve the children of these lords. These servants are called *yanaconas*. Prisoners of war were also perpetual servants. If a lord did not want to take the thief as a *yanacona*, the thief would be killed.

However, if it were determined to be a lie that a theft had taken place, to make up for the disgrace that the person had suffered by being called a thief, the one who had informed the Inca should give to the accused twice the value of the thing supposedly stolen. And if the slanderer did not have enough to pay, the one slandered should go into the house of the slanderer and openly take everything there. The one slandered would also make the slanderer retract the accusation before everyone and offer a sacrifice there before everyone. With this the honor of the accused would be restored.

The Inca ordained that if someone testified against another and as a result of the testimony the accused suffered infamy, the one who testified falsely would be killed.

The Inca ordered that if anyone lied to him about anything, whether something they were discussing or some news the person brought, that person would die.

The Inca ordained that every four months food be given to the residents and lords of Cuzco for ordinary use in their homes, for their servants, and for fiestas that they had. In addition, every year garments should be given to each one, for their personal use as well as for the young men and women who served in their house. And it should be ordered that the storehouses also be filled. He also ordered that each one have storage places in their houses of what was harvested from their fields and of what was handed out to them. The Inca ordered that what was brought in for one year be stored for the future. If they came to be in need, because of a war or loss of food in a frost, they would have a sufficient supply to sustain themselves in that time of shortage.

The Inca ordained the following. The servant women of Cuzco and the *mamaconas* left everything very dirty, including the tumblers, cooking pots, and plates in which they had served and cooked. They were accustomed to a great deal of filth. These servant women always let their hands, arms, legs, and feet get dirty. In order to ensure that these servant women kept themselves and the tumblers with which they served clean, there should be certain stewards. They all ate out in the square. These stewards should take care to watch the serving women and be sure that when the women came out on the square to serve that they kept everything clean. If they did not, then before everyone a container of water, which they call a *virqui*,[5] would be brought. In front of everyone, this woman, even if she were the daughter of the Inca, would wash her hands and arms and feet in this water. No matter how dirty the water was, this woman would drink it so everyone could see. And this order would be spread by these stewards so that these serving women and *mamaconas* could not give the excuse that they had not heard the order. Therefore from then on this service and these servants would be very clean.

The Inca ordained that the married woman or *mamacona* found guilty of adultery when proven guilty would be stoned to death by everyone outside the city in a certain place that he designated for that purpose, which was where the two rivers that run through Cuzco meet. And if the testimony could not be proven, the one who had given it would die in the same place and in the same way as the adulteress would have died.

The Inca ordained that anyone who entered the city and brought gold, silver, or fine garments adorned with jewels and personal finery could not take them out but had to leave them in the city. As one was leaving the city the guards at the bridges would search their bundle and what one was carrying. If the guards found any of the items mentioned above, they would take the things, return them to the city, and put them in the storehouses.

The Inca ordained that no cacique in all the land, no matter how important he might be, could wear fine clothing or feathers or own valuable litters or wear wool strings on the shoes, only *cabuya*, unless the garments or feathers or litters had been given by the Inca for their services. And anyone who wore such garments without receiving the things from the Inca would die. Any *orejon* warrior who found someone like that would hang the person right there on the spot. This was to ensure that there would not be equality and the vassals could be identified and so that they would not try to be equal to the lords of Cuzco.

The Inca ordained that no one could have their own sister as their wife, except for the Inca. No one could marry on his own authority without the Inca marrying him. If the first husband of a woman died and the woman wanted to marry, she would be married to the closest relative of her husband. If children remained from her first husband, she should rear them as her own. If the first husband left no children, the second should be from the same lineage and the lineage would continue and the blood of those of Cuzco would not be mixed with that of some other nation or disappear.

The Inca ordained as follows. Those of his lineage and descendants on both the father's and the mother's side from inside the city of Cuzco were *orejon* lords. He said this because he had given certain of his daughters to cacique lords, and he had also given many other daughters of lords of his lineage. He had married these girls so the caciques would come under the dominion of Cuzco. What he was ordering now did not apply to the sons of these women. Those of his lineage were to carry one or two hawk feathers on their heads as a sign so that they would be recognized and respected in all the land as his descendants. If any other person wore such a feather or insignia like those of Cuzco and the great lords, he would die for it.

The Inca ordained as follows. He designated one who was *capac* and lord, Inca lieutenant, in his place. The people would come before this one with the business of the land and also that of the city. Due to his greatness and stature, no one was to come before the Inca lord with any business. This lieutenant would explain to the Inca the business and news that were brought in so that the Inca could tend to them and resolve them as he saw fit. And the Inca ordered that this lord be named *Apo Ynga randi rimaric*,[6] which means "the lord who speaks in place of and in the name of the king."

The Inca ordained that from all around the city and all of the nearby places all the men and women should come to the city of Cuzco with the things that they had for food, fruits, and other necessities and in the public square of the city they should hold a market in order to sell and trade. The Inca ordered that this market be named *cuxipata cato*,[7] which means "the fortunate pleasure," where it was ordered that no one would dare take anything that was brought there without paying for it and without the consent of the person selling it. The penalty for forcibly taking anything publicly was that there where the thing was taken the culprit would be whipped.

XXII

Which concerns the things and laws that the Inca ordained for his warriors, their proper supplies, and what was to be done in the provinces under his authority.

The Inca ordained that an army captain who was winning and conquering provinces should not leave any province where he feared a rebellion would take place. As the captain continued to conquer provinces, he should establish post stations together one after another all along the road along which he passed. These stations should be maintained by the local Indians and the provinces he passed. The station should be supplied with the necessary food by the local provinces themselves. They should order that fields be cultivated to supply these stations. For each province there should be named a supervisor in charge of organizing the stations, changing the messengers, and making an inspection every ten days. If any messenger failed to report or left without a relief, he would be hanged at once at the site of the station, and the cacique of the province would lose his command if the messenger failed to report because of the cacique's fault or as a result of bad management. By means of these messengers the Inca was informed of what was happening to this captain who was off at war.

It should be known that these messengers traveled so fast that in eight days the Inca had word in Cuzco of what was happening in Quito and its provinces. And it is more than three hundred leagues from Quito to Cuzco.

The captain who went out conquering would put the insignias and garments of those of that province in his houses for personal adornment, as a man who won it, like our coat of arms, and he would take a nickname and surname from it if he wanted. The provinces had different languages. Thus the captains should order the lords and natives of the provinces to join in learning the general language of Cuzco so that it would be possible to understand them.

The Inca ordained that each army captain be sure to order the people of the province to make a *tambo*[1] lodging on the royal road in each of the provinces that they were conquering as soon as they arrived there. A *tambo* is a lodging for soldiers. A certain number of *mamacona* women should be placed there. These women would be charged with preparing the food and *chicha* for the lords of Cuzco who were passing by there and for the soldiers who were going somewhere on the orders of the Inca. In these *tambos* there should be store-houses of food of the kind grown in that province. And the caciques of the province should take care to learn if some *orejon* lord left Cuzco and headed down the road to his province. Once they got this news, the cacique or caciques should make preparations to provide the lord with every service and reverence due a lord of Cuzco from his vassals. These vassals should take care to provide there in the *tambos* Indians ready to carry the burdens of these lords. These Indian carriers should not go from one *tambo* to another, and if they left any *tambo*, the cacique of the province and *tambo* where this happened would be given twenty blows on the back with a stone with all the strength of the man giving the punishment. This was to ensure that the caciques would never again let the Indians who carried the loads leave their *tambo*. If the cacique let the Indian carriers leave his province and *tambo* again, the cacique would be considered incorrigible and so would be hanged in his *tambo*.

The Inca ordained that the captain who took soldiers have large storehouses made by the *tambos* every forty leagues from the city of Cuzco to the last place he reached. These storehouses should have all types of food, including maize, *chuño*, papas, quinua, agi peppers, salted dried meat, fish, and livestock. This food was for the soldiers who arrived on a conquest campaign or who were pacifying some province that had rebelled. Each of these soldiers should be given as much of this food as he needed to make it to the next *tambo*, forty leagues from there, where he would be given more food. And the distance from one *tambo* to another where this food was given out the Inca had named *xuco guaman*,[2] which means "one flight of a hawk." And every year the local caciques of these *tambos* took care of these storehouses and had them filled for the purpose already stated.

The Inca ordained that the captain who leads soldiers take great care to maintain strict discipline over the soldiers. If any soldier took any woman by force in any town he was going through, right there where the offense took place the delinquent would be hanged publicly. If any of the men the captain was leading entered the house of some resident of the town they were passing through and forcibly took something, though it was only a handful of maize, he would be punished according to what he had stolen. If any of these men the captain was leading strayed off the royal road as much as one shot of a sling, this man would have his foot cut off. It would be presumed that this man intended to steal something. If any of these soldiers passing along the royal road entered into some maize fields and picked an ear of maize, the man would have his hand cut off and put on a long pole in the place where the ear of maize was picked. That same ear of maize clasped in the man's hand would be left there on the pole for everyone to see. And the same would apply to anything that was harvested. If any man on a campaign stole a sheep, he would be hanged in the presence of the other soldiers. The same sheep would be slaughtered and the skin filled with straw, as if it were alive, and the sheep would be strung up right next to the man who was hanged. If the captain leading these men did not carry out these orders with his soldiers, even though the captain were victorious, he would be hanged publicly, for disobeying orders of the Inca, and he would not be buried or honored in any way.

The Inca ordained that in each town a man be identified who was the most able and diligent of the town and of good judgment. If the town were large, one man from each *parcialidad*[3] of the town would be selected. This man or men would be in charge of keeping track of male and female children born each year as well as those who died. Each one would keep track of the people of their town. He should know about the lives of everyone and how they made their living, what livestock they were raising. Those who raised livestock were to have an insignia of it hanging on their door, such as a sheep's leg or jawbone. If they had birds, they should have its feathers and eggs hanging from the door of the house where they lived. If the man were a hunter, a fisherman, or a farmer or had any other trade, he should hang on the door of his house some insignia of it.

The designated man should take care to know what each person harvested from their fields and the livestock that each one had as well as the increase of it. And each one should keep track of increases and what was acquired. This was done so there would be no idle people and each one would give tribute to the Inca and to Cuzco of what he had. The Inca ordered that the man who had these responsibilities be named *llacta camayo*,[4] which means "town official" and partly steward in charge of the town. These men were in charge of collecting tribute from each person, but no one was to contribute more than he could reasonably give. And it should come from the labors of each one and from products of his fields. The *llacta camayos* from the small towns should give an account to those of the larger ones of their province where their meeting place was. These stewards should explain the things mentioned above and the tributes to the *orejon* lord who was in those provinces. This *orejon* lord should order that the children of each one of these towns and provinces from a young age be taught by their parents the farming and jobs done by their parents. From a young age these children should be accustomed to serve Cuzco and to avoid idleness.

These *orejon* lords should take care to inspect the roads and bridges in their province and have these roads and bridges repaired whenever necessary so that if the Inca decided to go to that province he would not need to get off his litter because of the road conditions. The *orejon* lord should also inspect the *tambos* and storehouses to make sure everything necessary was ready both for the soldiers and for what the Inca ordered. Furthermore, these *orejon* lords and each one personally should have made in the major towns where they resided many storehouses of much food of the kind harvested in those provinces so that the soldiers would have a stock of food and the Inca and his people would have the same if they came by there. This was prepared and kept in the storehouse so that the natives of the province would not feel it burdensome.

The *orejon* lords were also charged with inspecting the borders and lands of each province and maintaining boundary stones in place. If any neighboring town or province needed more land because it had too many people, they should send a painting of the lay of these lands and provinces so that an equitable adjustment could be made and boundaries set. The caciques of these provinces would be sent before the Inca, who would divide these lands, giving and taking, and give as compensation to the lord of these lands something which was good for him and for his people. In addition, the Inca required the *orejon* lords in charge of these provinces to look over the area between these provinces and Cuzco, and the unpopulated lands there were from these provinces up to Cuzco. Houses should be made in which to store the tributes that were brought and these tributes should be brought every year.

The Inca ordained that there be certain designated houses in the provinces and principal towns. In them a certain number of young virgins would be placed. These would be the wives of the Sun who faithfully fed the Sun and made sacrifices to him every day. This lord also sent to the provinces many idols which the people of these provinces could worship and honor with sacrifices, just as he had done in the city of Cuzco. These sacrifices would be made in these provinces to the idols in the same way as was done in Cuzco before the idols. He ordered that the statues of the Sun which he sent to these provinces be placed in those houses where the *mamaconas* were, that storehouses of food and garments be made and fields be designated for this service of the Sun and sustenance of these *mamaconas*. All of this was to be put in the name of the Sun.

In addition, other houses should be made where there would be placed other *mamaconas*, virgins, daughters of lords. These would be called the wives of the Inca. They should also be given lands and storehouses made for all their provisions. In order to provide for all this and to be its collectors, certain men of the town were designated. And those who had dealings with these *mamaconas*, both these and the others, and the guardians who looked after them were castrated Indians. And that *orejon* lord would take great care to order that all this be carried out.

The Inca ordained that every year an important lord of the city of Cuzco who was a son of the Inca would go out to inspect these provinces and the treatment of the natives of these provinces by the *orejon* lords who were in charge of them and by the caciques of these provinces. If this lord found any of these *orejon* lords or caciques negligent, he should punish them as he deemed fit, remove them from office, and put others in their place.

The Inca ordained that the captains who went out to conquer lands and provinces, after conquering a province, should make the caciques of these provinces and towns understand that the Inca and the city of Cuzco sent them out to conquer. These people were now vassals of the Inca. They were no longer lords of these provinces, for the Inca was the only lord. By the grace of the Inca, they were to receive women and land. If they did not agree to this, one of the Inca's sons or another lord of Cuzco who would do it on his orders and in his place would come to impose it. They should tell the people how from then on they should serve and give as tribute to the Inca of all the kinds of things that were produced in their lands.

The Inca ordained that the captains who were going to war order that about forty or fifty men be placed in the provinces closest to the bridges. By turns of ten men at a time, these bridges should be guarded. There where they were guarding the bridge, these men should make cords of *cabuya* and ropes and cables of those twigs so that when the bridges needed to be repaired they would have the materials ready and these guards would not be idle.

XXIII

Which concerns Inca Yupanque's age at the time when he made the laws and of his sons and daughters; seeing that it was reasonable, he sent his sons on a war of conquest.

Inca Yupanque was in consultation with his people about preparing the laws that you have just heard. They say that he spent one month in making them up, preparing them, and presenting these laws to those lords. During this time, the Inca normally consulted with the lords every day. These sessions lasted from after he had eaten until time for supper. During these meetings, the Inca made up and arranged for the laws that you have heard and many others that they say no one remembers; there were many more, but their lack of writing does not allow them to remember more.

The way the Inca had of expressing these laws to his people is as follows. He had some long strings of beads brought. With the beads there, the Inca said the rationale for each law that he enacted and set aside the beads that represented each part of the rationale, law, and constitution that he made. With this done, he called those lords one at a time and showed them the laws by counting the beads. In this way they understood them by his saying the laws in words as he counted the beads. So during those thirty days the Inca enacted the laws and explained them to his people.

At the time that Inca Yupanque enacted these ordinances and laws, he was seventy years old, and he had three hundred sons and daughters of all ages, two hundred boys and one hundred girls. And it is not surprising that he had so many sons and daughters because he had countless wives, all virgins when he took them. At that time Yamque Yupanque, Amaro Topa Inca, Paucar Usno, and three or four others were grown men. All the rest were children. Inca Yupanque realized that since his sons were grown, it was time for them to act like men and conquer the rest of the lands beyond where he had arrived and conquered. For this purpose he ordered his people to assemble. When they were together, he told them what he had decided and how he wanted to send his sons and some of them on a war of conquest across the province of Collasuyo. They answered that what he had decided was good, that they were eager to do what he commanded, and that he should name from among them those who were to go on the expedition and the lords, his sons, in whose company they were to go. Then the Inca said that his sons who were to go on the expedition were Amaro Topa Inca and Paucar Usno, and the others who were to go were six lords. Then he picked them out from among those at the meeting. And he also gave the number of soldiers whom they were to take with them, which was one hundred thousand soldiers; fifty thousand of them were to be from the province of Collasuyo and the other fifty thousand from the rest of the towns and provinces. After the men left the Inca's meeting, they sent to the towns and provinces for the soldiers. For this they were given a period of three months. When they saw the Inca's command, the *orejon* lords who were in the provinces gave the order to send the soldiers whom the Inca had requested of them. After they got them together, they left for Cuzco. The *orejon* lords arrived there within the allotted time with all the necessary equipment, provisions, weapons, and everything they were ordered to bring.

As soon as the Inca saw those soldiers there, he ordered his two sons Amaro Topa Inca and Paucar Usno to take those soldiers and go out to discover and conquer as far as they wished. He gave the necessary provisions to his sons and the rest of the lords. After making the sacrifices and holding the ceremonies that they were accustomed to doing when they left on such journeys, they left for the province of Collasuyo, conquering and winning as far as the province of the Chichas. When they arrived there, the lords of the Chichas had a type of fort. Inside of it, all the Chichas were waiting for these sons of the Inca. All around the fort there was a deep trench filled with a great deal of firewood. When Amaro Topa Inca and Paucar Usno arrived with their soldiers, they laid siege. As soon as the Chichas saw that they were surrounded, they set the wood in the trench on fire. It seemed to Paucar Usno that one could jump over the fury of that burning trench and go on to fight the Chicha lords. Since he had made up his mind, he gave it a try. As he jumped the ditch, Paucar Usno fell into the fire, and his men could not rescue him; he burned in the fire.

After Paucar Usno was burned, Amaro Topa Inca was left in command of the soldiers. They say that he remained there with the Chichas surrounded for so long that the Chichas surrendered for lack of food. Thus the Inca won his victory. He took the Chichas prisoners along with others that he held from before. He returned to the city of Cuzco, where he entered in triumph. There he found his father, Inca Yupanque, to whom he gave the prisoners he brought. These prisoners were dressed in the red garments and with the *borlas* that you have heard about. Then they were thrown into the jails with wild beasts, where some of them were eaten. Among those who were eaten were two Chicha lords who had given the order to build the fiery trench in which the son of Inca

Yupanque, Paucar Usno, was burned. Three days after they were put into the house of the wild beasts, the order was given to take out those who were still alive. The Inca ordered them brought before him. When he saw them he received them well and treated them kindly. They swore loyalty to the Sun, the Inca, and Cuzco.

Inca Yupanque ordered that the burned body of his son, which they had brought to him, be taken back to the provinces of the Chichas where he had been burned. It was called Nasavacollo. The Inca did the favor of giving this province to his burned son. Many lords and ladies of Cuzco accompanied the body and resided with it as long as they stayed there. This body was held in great veneration in this province, and the whole province, with everything they had, served the body as if it were alive. Thus every morning they brought to this body for sacrifice many lambs, sheep, birds, maize, deer, fruit, honeycombs, jugs of honey, and all the things and game that could be obtained. All of which was brought before the body. And as if it were alive, they begged it with much efficacy and persistence to accept the offerings and eat them. The Chichas stayed there until a lord of Cuzco, who had gone with the body for that purpose, came out. Then the lord of Cuzco ordered much carved wood brought and many paintings made on the wood. This wood was carved expressly for sacrifice. He ordered that a fire be made with it in a golden brazier before the body. In it they burned whatever they saw fit. After the offering burned, the Chicha lords left, showing that they were very pleased and saying that their lord Paucar Usno had eaten and accepted their offering. With this done, as at first, they brought in another serving of food of the things already mentioned. This was distributed to the wives and children of this lord Paucar Usno and the rest of the other servants and lords and ladies of Cuzco who were there. All of this was done from then until the Spaniards came to this land.

XXIV

Wherein Inca Yupanque sent another two of his sons to conquer through the province of Chinchasuyo, and of the things that happened to these two sons of the Inca on this expedition.

After Inca Yupanque had taken care of the Chicha lords with the body of his son Paucar Usno, whom he ordered them to serve, he ordered his soldiers to assemble. Before them he ordered this son Yamque Yupanque to take charge of those soldiers, go with them across the province of Chinchasuyo, conquer as far as he could, and take one of his brothers with him, whichever one he wanted. This Yamque Yupanque was the eldest son of Inca Yupanque, the son Inca Yupanque loved the most and the one he planned to leave in his place when his days were ended. They say that from among all of his brothers Inca Yamque picked out one of his brothers who was called Capa Yupanque. They say that this brother was fifteen years old. With everything necessary ready, Yamque Yupanque set out accompanied by Capa Yupanque. After leaving, they headed straight for the province of the Soras, which their father had won and subjugated. From there Yamque Yupanque started winning the war of conquest up to Cajamarca. There they decided it was time to return, leaving soldiers for full protection and provisions to defend what they had won to that point.

They returned along the valleys of the *yungas*.[1] They say that on the way, Yamque Yupanque looked over the lay of the land in the valleys, their fruits and people. It occurred to him that in the Cuzco area there were places and valleys where these fruits, foods, and provisions could be grown and produced. After making his observation, he ordered the caciques of each valley to give him a leader with some Indians who should take from their lands all the seeds of their fruits as well as the rest of their foods and provisions. Thus he brought with him to the city of Cuzco these *yunga* Indians in the way just stated. Yamque Yupanque and his men entered the city in triumph over the towns and provinces that they had won and subjugated. And his father, Inca Yupanque, received him, tread on the things they brought, and called for the customary sacrifices and idolatries to be made in this case, as this account has already told you. In the city of Cuzco, this Yamque Yupanque was enjoying himself with his father, the rest of his brothers and relatives in their fiestas, sacrifices, and idolatries for three years. And he put the *yungas* Indians as *mitimaes*[2] in the valleys surrounding the city of Cuzco.

XXV

Wherein Yamque Yupanque once again set out for conquest and of the things that happened to him.

After the three years had elapsed in which Yamque Yupanque had enjoyed himself with his father, Inca Yupanque, Yamque Yupanque told his father that it seemed to him that it was time for him to set out again for conquest and move ahead. It seemed to Inca Yupanque that his son was right. So he ordered the soldiers to assemble. When they were gathered together, Inca Yupanque ordered his son Yamque Yupanque to take with him on this second expedition another of his brothers. He should leave Capa Yupanque behind because it was the intention of Inca Yupanque that his sons from an early age be exposed to the rigors of war by his eldest son, Yamque Yupanque. Thus if Inca Yupanque should die, Yamque Yupanque would be accompanied by his brothers, who would be familiar with matters of war. If any province were to rebel after Inca Yupanque's days, his son would have brothers to accompany him in wars of conquest and increase their dominions.

For this campaign they say that Yamque Yupanque selected his brother Topa Inca Yupanque.[1] Taking his soldiers, as he should, and with the necessary supplies he left from the city of Cuzco. On arriving at Cajamarca, where he had left his men at a garrison, he took them along with the rest whom he had with him. He left there with his brother Topa Inca Yupanque to conquer all the towns and provinces that they found both in the sierra and on the coastal plains. On this expedition they conquered all the Guancavilcas and Indians of both the sierras and the *yungas* up to the province of Cañaripampa, where the Cañares live. When Yamque Yupanque had arrived there, he realized that his father was very old and that while they were at war he might die with them absent at the time of his death. Yamque Yupanque had news that his father was rather sick. With this in mind, he took all precautions and left as many soldiers as they felt necessary with captains and lords of Cuzco to protect everything they had won. They were to await further orders from Cuzco.

With all of this done and arranged, Yamque Yupanque took the people that he needed and returned from their campaign. On it Topa Inca Yupanque had conducted himself like a man thirty years old or older. He was twenty-five years old when he left the city of Cuzco to go on this campaign to conquer and subjugate the lands and provinces already mentioned. From the time they left Cuzco until they returned took five years. On returning, Yamque Yupanque and Topa Inca entered the city of Cuzco together, each one on a very richly decorated litter with much gold and many paintings. They were carried in these litters on the shoulders of caciques, leaders, and lords subjugated to Cuzco.

When Inca Yupanque got word that his sons were entering the city in triumph and that they had before them the caciques and lords that they had taken prisoner and subjugated on their campaign, as was their custom, their father, Inca Yupanque, came out to meet them. As he saw them entering with so many prisoner lords ahead of them and found out about the many lands and provinces that they had subjugated, the Inca was very pleased. As their father approached, his sons both stepped off their litters and made all their soldiers stop. As his father approached them, Yamque Yupanque made gestures of obeisance to his father, as was their custom on returning from this campaign. With this done, Yamque Yupanque asked his father with much reverence and humbleness to accept that service and for him to please tread on the insignias that he brought in the morning. This account has already told about this custom of theirs. The Inca said that he was very pleased with it. So that his son would understand that he accepted this service and that Yamque Yupanque really was his son, the Inca came up to him, hugged him, and kissed him on the cheek. And his son did the same to him.

After this Inca Yupanque took the *borla* fringe that he had on his head. Then he put it on his son over the one he already had. Next he ordered the lords who were present there to obey, respect, and revere his son as the *capac* and lord that he was and told them to give the order to celebrate the fiestas, sacrifices, fasts, and ceremonies that in this case were customary. All of which would have to be done after performing the sacrifices and ceremonies for the triumph in which his sons returned.

Right after arranging this, the lords of Cuzco and the other brothers swore obedience to Yamque Yupanque as their *capac* and new lord. Next, another *borla* and headband was brought to Inca Yupanque. He stepped between his two sons, ordered them to get into his litter, and entered the city with them as if he had come in from the campaign. Wishing to honor his sons, he made sacrifices to the Sun and to the idols. Then his sons made the same sacrifices for him. This time Yamque Yupanque spent another three years enjoying himself with his father, who was old at that time. To increase his father's years, Yamque Yupanque made every effort to make his father happy and do things with him that would please him.

Topa Inca and Mama Ocllo carried on their litter.

From the chronicle of Felipe Guaman Poma de Ayala,
Nueva coronica y buen gobierno.

XXVI

Wherein Yamque Yupanque went again on a campaign of conquest, and of the lands and provinces that he subjugated this time, and what happened to him on this expedition, and of the birth of Huayna Capac.

After the three years mentioned in this account elapsed, Yamque Yupanque realized that his father was strong enough to live some time longer than he had thought and that it was now right for him to return to his campaign of conquest. He told his father that he wanted to return to his war duty and his quest. He was well informed that ahead of where he had arrived there were extensive lands, provinces, and people. To this the father answered that he was his son, what he had been saying pleased him very much, and he should give the orders for it. He should take into consideration the time always in everything he did and try for brevity.

Therefore Yamque Yupanque told his brother Topa Inca Yupanque and the rest of the captains whom he planned to take with him to bring together as many soldiers as possible and prepare because he wanted to return again to his military campaign and conquest. The soldiers that they were taking that time and all of those of Cuzco who were going with him should take their wives and the rest of their gear from their houses and things that they needed, except food. He had arranged ample supplies for their needs on the road where they were to go. But he did not know where they would end up that time. Assembling the soldiers that he felt were necessary, they bade farewell to his father, who told them that he would inform them by messenger of anything that happened, whether concerning his health or anything else.

Thus Yamque Yupanque left the city of Cuzco, taking with him his brother Topa Inca Yupanque as his first in command. They traveled for several days until they reached Tomebamba. There they found their people well, on the alert, and without having suffered any misfortunes. And they say that this time on leaving Cuzco, Yamque Yupanque gave one of their own sisters to his brother Topa Inca Yupanque as his wife. She was much loved by their father, Inca Yupanque. She was the younger sister. Her older sister had been given by their father to Yamque Yupanque for his wife when he was given the *borla* fringe, as was customary among them. This sister who had been given to Topa Inca Yupanque for his wife was called Mama Ocllo. When they reached the land of the Cañares, the order was given to the soldiers, and from there both brothers went on their campaign of conquest, subjugating everything they found on their way until they reached the province they call Yaguarcocha, some leagues past the city of Quito.[1]

They spent three years on this conquest. At the end of this time, as they continued their campaign, a messenger arrived from Cuzco. The messenger told them that their father sent word to them that he wanted to rest and go with the Sun his father and for both brothers to return right away from the place where they received the message. Once Yamque Yupanque heard the news, he separated as many soldiers as he felt he needed for the return trip. He ordered the rest of his soldiers to remain in the city of Quito. He had the number he felt adequate settle in the city and the rest nearby. He fortified the city with the forces and forts that he felt necessary. He ordered the natives of Quito and the rest of the nearby inhabitants and provinces in the area and the Guancavilcas, Cañares, and Yungas to give him fifteen thousand Indians, who were to leave with him on the road he was taking. These Indians were young married men with their wives, their things, and seeds from their lands so they could be placed as *mitimaes* in the valleys and lands surrounding Cuzco. *Mitimaes* means people from one province settled in another.

Those of Quito and the surrounding provinces gave him the Indians that were required of them to be placed as *mitimaes* in the way already stated. Then they sent to the rest of the towns and provinces which he had designated that the others were to come from.

With this done and settled, he and his brother went from the city of Quito to the city of Cuzco. They entered it in triumph, as before, about which you have heard. They put before their father all of the booty and things that they brought. Their father was now very old; his arms trembled; he was too old to remain standing; he had no teeth. It pleased Inca Yupanque very much to see his son Yamque Yupanque before him. Yamque Yupanque told him about the conquest he had made and how he felt he should leave the people he had brought to settle in Quito and its provinces as a precaution, since it was so far from Cuzco. The road measured more than one hundred *topos*.[2] As you have heard, each *topo* is one and a half leagues. He also felt that he should bring fifteen thousand men, all young and married, to place as *mitimaes* on the land surrounding Cuzco, and all should bring the seeds for their maintenance from their lands.

Inca Yupanque answered that what he had done was good, that he was about to rest and wanted to go with the Sun. He should take very good care of his land and office. Inca Yupanque feared that after his death all the land would rebel. Yamque Yupanque told him that he was also old and before his father died he wanted to leave the *borla* fringe and the state to the one his father chose. Inca Yupanque told him to leave it to his grandson, son of Yamque Yupanque himself. This grandson Yamque Yupanque had from that sister of his whom his father had given him when he received the *borla*. The boy was also called Yamque Yupanque like his father. To this Yamque Yupanque answered that his son was not of age and very young and that it seemed to him that he should give it to his brother Topa Inca Yupanque, who had gone with him. Topa Inca Yupanque deserved the *borla* more than anyone else. He still had not arrived because he had stayed behind with his wife Mama Ocllo. She had given birth to a son in Tomebamba. The child was beautiful and looked very much like Inca Yupanque. The child was certain to grow to be a good man for the child was conceived and born at war. Once Inca Yupanque heard what his son Yamque Yupanque said, he was very pleased with it and with the news that he had that grandson. Inca Yupanque became very anxious to see his grandson so he ordered a messenger to go tell Topa Inca Yupanque to come as soon as possible and bring the child, his son, and the mother. With this arranged and sacrifices and solemnities for the conquest done, Yamque Yupanque ordered the lords of Cuzco to make all the preparations for the fiestas and sacrifices that were to be done when Topa Inca Yupanque arrived.

XXVII

Wherein Topa Inca Yupanque was named as capac, and what this name capac *means.*

When Topa Inca Yupanque and his wife Mama Ocllo reached the city of Cuzco, then he went straight to where his father was. On coming up to him, Topa Inca Yupanque made his gestures of obeisance and kissed him on the cheek. Topa Inca Yupanque's wife Mama Ocllo did the same, for she was the daughter of Inca Yupanque himself. Inca Yupanque ordered her to go to the house and lodging where her other sisters, the maidens, were, which is where she used to spend her time, and for her to stay there. He ordered the child that she was carrying be brought to him. When the Inca saw the child, he took him in his arms, saying: "Caiñoc ap randi canga. Caiñoc ap randi cachun,"[1] which means "This one will take my place, let this one take my place." When Yamque Yupanque saw what his father wanted, he got up from his chair and in the presence of his father and the rest of the lords who were there, grasped Topa Inca Yupanque's hand and took him where his father was. As they got there, he took the *borla* fringe that he himself was wearing on his head and put it on Topa Inca Yupanque's head. Then Yamque Yupanque ordered that Topa Inca Yupanque's chair be placed by his father's chair. When he went over there, his father asked him to sit down. When he was seated, Yamque Yupanque told him to take the oath, as was their custom, to be obedient to the Sun, not to subjugate the lords of Cuzco, to work the fields of the Sun, make war on anyone who attacked Cuzco, look after the welfare of the city and the republic, as well as of the rest of the land in the way that his father, Inca Yupanque, had arranged.

Making him take this oath and everything just stated, Inca Yupanque ordered that his daughter Mama Ocllo, the one he had previously ordered to be placed inside, be brought out. She had been dressed in the way that was required for such an occasion. She came out in garments made of gold and fine wool, as if she were a maiden. When he saw her brought there, as if he were her father, Yamque Yupanque took her by the hand and gave her to Topa Inca Yupanque, asking him first to accept her as his wife, making the plea that her parents would have made if they were of lesser social status than he, since it was customary among them. Topa Inca Yupanque said yes, he did want her.

Then all the lords of the city of Cuzco got up, and Yamque Yupanque did it first, before anyone. They made their gestures of obeisance and reverence to their lord and *capac*. Then the customary sacrifices were made to the Sun, to the statues of their grandfathers, the former lords. Thus Topa Inca Yupanque had the allegiance of the lords of Cuzco. Inca Yupanque ordered, after these fiestas that he had ordered, another solemn fiesta that they should arrange, all of which was done.

The lords assembled. With them there he said that the fiesta that he wanted to have before his death was to name the lord who would take the place of Topa Inca Yupanque after his days. And with this as it was, the lords told him that for their part it would be satisfactory and proper for him to name anyone he wished. Then they brought that child there who had been born to Topa Inca Yupanque and Mama Ocllo in the war. With the child there and in the presence of all the lords of Cuzco, he took a *borla* and headband made to fit the child's head and put it on the child's head. This *borla* was made like the one he had on his head. This was the insignia of the king and lord. When the *borla* was put on him, the child was six months old. With the *borla* placed on the child, Inca Yupanque said that the child should be named. Yamque Yupanque said that he would call the child Huayna Capac and that this would be his name.

The word "*inca*" rightly means king, and it is the name applied to all the *orejon* lords of Cuzco and to each one of them. In order to distinguish between the *orejones* and the *inca* king (and when one wants to talk to him), he was called Çapa Inca, which means unique king. When one wants to give more importance than king, he is called Capac. The meaning of *capac* is a matter that each one presumes what it is. What I understand about it is that it means a rank much higher than king. Some who do not understand this language stop to consider what Huayna Capac means. Summing up what they have thought, they say that it means "rich young man." But they do not understand it. If one were to say *capa* without the final "c" they would be right, because "*capa*" means "rich." "*Capac*" with "c" means a title much higher than king. And this was the title given this child by Yamque Yupanque when the *borla* was given to this child Huayna Capac. When they want to say what we call emperors or monarch, they say "*capaccuna*."[2] So this is what *capac* means according to what I understand of their speech.

With this done, Inca Yupanque told Topa Inca Yupanque and Mama Ocllo, since they were the parents of Huayna Capac, to offer the sacrifices and do the fasts in the child's name, as he would do them if he were a man. Thus they did the sacrifices and fasts. With this done, Inca Yupanque took that child, his grandson, in his arms. Taking the old man and the child on a certain bench, they put them in his room. The old man never left there, but reared his grandson Huayna Capac. With this done and two years had elapsed since they were in the city of Cuzco enjoying themselves, Yamque Yupanque appointed as governor of Quito and its provinces a lord of Cuzco whom he thought to be completely loyal and of good judgment.

XXVIII

Wherein Topa Inca Yupanque left the city of Cuzco to conquer the province of the Andes, and how he subjugated as much of it as he could, and of the things that happened to him there.

Yamque Yupanque noticed that his brother Topa Inca Yupanque was now a lord and that in Cuzco they had been idle for a long time. Since nothing was known about the province of Andesuyo, it seemed to him that it would be a good idea for his brother Topa Inca Yupanque to go out with his soldiers, seek out this province and its people, and see what kind of land was there. After making up his mind about this, one day when they were both together, Yamque Yupanque told Topa Inca Yupanque that now he was a lord, and it seemed to Yamque Yupanque that Topa Inca Yupanque should, as the lord that he was, go out across the province of Andesuyo, conquer and put under his dominion the people he found there, and see what kind of land there was.

Topa Inca Yupanque heard what his brother said and agreed with him. He said that he was pleased and ordered his soldiers to assemble. He heard that the land lacked salt, so after his people came together, all kinds of supplies were provided. This included as much salt as they could carry from each one's storehouses. Topa Inca Yupanque ordered his camp to make ready. Thus he left the city of Cuzco and went across the province of the Andes. Yamque Yupanque remained in the city of Cuzco looking after whatever seemed most appropriate for the well-being and health of his father, Inca Yupanque. They say Yamque Yupanque gave up the *borla* of the state with the idea of remaining in the city of Cuzco. He realized that all of his brothers were young men and his father, Inca Yupanque, could not govern because he was so old. He also saw that the lords of the city of Cuzco were numerous and that conceit grew in them day by day. His brothers were also young men, and it could happen that with both him and his brother Topa Inca Yupanque engaged in a war, their father, being so old, might die while they were out of the city. Then it might come to pass that upon his death the lords of Cuzco, relatives of the mothers who had children with Inca Yupanque, might want to name as lord one of those illegitimate sons. Because of this and with this situation in the city, there might be divisions and wars among them. But this could be prevented by his giving up the state and turning it over to Topa Inca his brother. Yamque Yupanque would always stay in the city of Cuzco, and by being in the city he would be responsible for providing whatever might be needed for the well-being of the city and its inhabitants from everything available in the whole land. His brother Topa Inca Yupanque was waging war, but to do the same would cause Yamque Yupanque annoyance and harm.

Since Yamque Yupanque remained in the city, soon he gave the order to have the people he brought from Quito populate the valleys and the vicinity of Cuzco. Thus he made *mitimaes* of them. During all the time Topa Inca Yupanque spent on his conquest and discovery, Yamque Yupanque occupied himself in taking superb care of his father, giving him the things he considered the very best to eat. Yamque Yupanque also cared for the welfare and sustenance of his people and what was under his jurisdiction and governed it well. Since Topa Inca Yupanque had left Cuzco with the warriors in the way you have already heard, he reached the town of Caxa Roma, which is forty leagues from the city of Cuzco. This place had been under the dominion of his father for a long time. Topa Inca Yupanque found out from the inhabitants of the town of Caxa Roma what the people were like beyond there, straight along the path he was following as well as to the right or left, and whether it was a land of sierras or forest, as he had seen up to there. In any case, they told him that it was a land where it always rained and that the towns of the people in that land had only one big, long house, which was full of people. Each of these houses had room for one to two thousand people. There they lived all together, but inside these houses each one had his own arrangement and living quarters where they lived. These people went naked because the climate was so hot, and they were very dissolute and did little work. They always carried their bows and arrows and hunted the parrots, monkeys, and birds, which they could take. They also ate human flesh. And all the others engaged in wars with each other, not with the aim of subjugating each other. Those who were taken prisoner, from whichever group, were taken to the captor's towns, where they had a great feast and ate the prisoners. These people were so warlike that if by chance they took some woman prisoner in battle who struck their fancy, she would be taken as wife, and after she gave birth once or twice, he would call his relatives whenever he pleased, and they would kill this woman. They would have a great feast and they would all eat her.

These people cultivated some fields of maize and *yuca*[1] and planted some squashes. This was the food they had. They had no graves. When one of them died, all of the relatives got together. They would not cry, but, rather, show that they were sad all together. They showed their feelings in a certain way without shedding tears. Having done this, they cut the body up in pieces, distributed the parts among themselves, and ate them. After gnawing the bones clean, they gathered together and hung the bones on top of the wall of the house where the deceased had lived. On that side of the living quarters, they hung the deceased's bow, arrows, and feathers.

All that land lacked salt, no matter where one might go to look for it. Once the Inca found out about this, he sent the order throughout his whole camp to guard with great care the salt that each one carried. The Inca ordered his captains to have each one ration the salt he was carrying, and when the captains saw that the troops in their camp, those going on that conquest, had eaten three-quarters of the salt they were carrying, the captains should inform the Inca because, from the place where they let him know, he would return. Presently, he ordered his camp to continue and he went on through that province of the Andes, taking his people all spread out over that land and dispersed from one side to the other. As they proceeded thus, some came upon houses like those of the report and others found people at the edges of rivers staying in shacks they had made. Thus the Inca went subjugating all those that he could find and take.

As word spread throughout that whole province about how the Inca was conquering it, some of the caciques of these Indians came in peace to the Inca. When they came out in peace, they gave him parrots, monkeys, and other odd creatures that they call "*perico ligero,*"[2] which have long snouts and tails and a clumsy walk. They also gave the Inca some feathers, plumage, and some gold dust. Since this land is very mountainous and rocky where the Sun reverberates and burns as it comes up, this province is a land of gold, and there is gold in it. They also offered the Inca pieces of sweet cane filled with honey, and painted bows and arrows. These people who gave him obedience were given salt, which they valued more than anything that could be given to them. Seeing that these people went naked, as was their custom, they were given tunics and cloaks and made to dress. They wore the clothes that day and in the evening went to their shacks. The next morning they appeared naked, as was their custom, before the Inca, and the Inca laughed. Then he proposed to bring all of them, both those who came in peace and those taken in war, to the city of Cuzco.

He ordered his people to spread out on both sides in a wing because the land is rough and overgrown and has large rivers and ravines. He had two objectives. On the one hand, since the land lacked food, if the people went that way, some of them would likely run into food. On the other hand by traveling all spread out, some of them would run into people in those woodlands because there were no roads through there nor could towns be seen. In this way the Inca traveled through those woodlands and provinces of the Andes conquering those who acted belligerently and treating well those who acted friendly until his captains told him that, for what there was to conquer out there, they had already traveled enough. The captains were not involved in anything but making roads and cutting down woodlands on the orders of the Inca, who always went on a litter. The rest of the people were looking for food. And when they ran into some people, they quickly took them under their control and that of their captains. The Inca saw that it was time to return, for he had no news of many people from there on ahead, and the men he was taking along were starting to fall ill. The Inca went back to the city of Cuzco.

The Inca brought there many of the odd creatures and parrots already mentioned and some gold dust, tigers [jaguars], and large snakes that they call *amaro*,[3] as well as a few prisoners and other people who for their part came to him in peace. The Inca took two years on this journey, and on his return he found his father alive and well because of the great care that he had been given by his brother. Thus the Inca entered the city in triumph, as was their custom. When he came before his father he showed his respect for him, placed before him what he had taken on that venture, and begged him to tread on it. Inca Yupanque told two lords, sons of his who were there, to pick him up bodily because he wanted to tread on that, honor his son, and accept from him the service he had done.

He ordered Yamque Yupanque to tread on it also, and he did it as the lord that he was also. Then Yamque Yupanque ordered that the tigers and *amaros* be thrown into the houses of the wild animals and together with them the prisoners who had been brought. He also ordered the lords to make the sacrifices and fiestas that were customarily done when one entered the city in triumph. With this done, Topa Inca Yupanque ordered that a strip two and a half spans wide, very thin, and the thickness of a small tin plate be made from the gold that had been brought. This strip was to be as long as the distance around the lodging where the Sun was. After it was made, the strip was put around that lodging of the Sun. It was placed on the outside, from where the straw roof reaches up to the masonry of the house, which makes the strip of gold as wide as the distance from the straw roof to the masonry. Thus he ordered it be placed on what there was from the masonry to the straw roof, which was so thick itself and so well put together that the ends of it seemed more like a thing made of mortar than of straw, and the wood that was placed inside was covered with straw ropes all very well twisted and made. On top of this was laid mortar of mud, made in such a way as to preserve the wood so that even though it should remain there another two thousand years, it would not be damaged for three reasons. For one, it is kept in such good repair that no water or even wind damages it. For another, it is in a cold land where wood is preserved very well as long as no water falls on it. For the other, it must have been cut opportunely and at such a time of the moon that it be very well preserved.

XXIX

Which concerns the things that Inca Yupanque

said to his sons and to the lords of Cuzco, and how

he gave away his daughters and all the rest of his

possessions once he realized that he wanted to die.

After three weeks had passed since Topa Inca Yupanque had returned from his journey through the Andes, it seemed to his father, Inca Yupanque, that he had reached the end of his days. Inca Yupanque ordered all the lords of Cuzco and all of his children to assemble and with them all together he told them that he was ready to rest and that he wanted to go to the Sun. What he entrusted them to do was look after the lords whom he had left for them, who were Topa Inca Yupanque and the child Huayna Capac. The rearing of this child as well as the governance of the whole kingdom he had entrusted to his son Yamque Yupanque. For as long as he lived, his son Topa Inca Yupanque would be charged with going to war, subjugating and pacifying provinces that rebelled. He let them know that after his days the provinces of Collasuyo and Andesuyo would surely rebel. After the days of his grandson Huayna Capac there would be *pachacuti*, which means "change of the world." Those lords asked him if that change of the world would be from floods, fire, or pestilence. He told them it would not be for any of those reasons but, rather, because white, bearded, and very tall men would come. They would go to war with these men and in the end these men would subjugate them. There would be no more Inca lords like them. What he was telling them was to enjoy the good life as long as they could because few lords would survive after the days of his grandson Huayna Capac. Those lords asked him from what direction those people would come. He answered that he did not know if they would come from where the sun comes up or from where it goes down. He just knew that these men would come, but he did not find out from where.

Then he had his daughters brought before him. They were all maidens, and with them present he gave them to the principal lords of the city of Cuzco who were there for women. He ordered some of his daughters to be married to certain cacique lords, principal men of the land. With this boon he increased their esteem for his son Topa Inca Yupanque. After this, he gave out all of his property as seemed best to him. Next he told the lords who were present there and his sons to learn how to survive after his days, and that to survive well they should govern themselves in the following way. In their nation and in the rest of the nations of the whole land, they should treat the people justly and not allow any discord among them. If anyone rebelled against them or if any of the lords of Cuzco committed some act of treason, even though he were Inca by birth, he should be killed. If he were pardoned, he could never be a friend, and sooner or later he would return there. The only way to protect themselves against such a person would be by killing him. Whenever they went to war or did anything else, they should first consider the danger and discover it before doing or putting anything into effect. That way the thing would be well done. Whenever they could do a good deed for their people and give them something from their wealth, they should do it routinely.

Saying that previously idle people tore the nation apart, they should tolerate no idleness in their nation or in the other nations and provinces but, rather, all should work and practice all kinds of activities. When they elected an Inca king or named some lord of the town to an office, they should make sure such a lord was a reserved man and not a gossip. When these lords were angry, they should not dispatch things without counsel. When they were with warriors going against some province, they should not stop to tell them ugly things but, rather, try to speak well and harmoniously to them. If it happened to be necessary to increase by a large amount the population of Cuzco or if they needed to take people from there to some other place, these people should live together. They should not consent to these newcomers' having any conversation or mixing with people of low rank. They should always endeavor in their speech and in everything else to be virtuous and do good works, saying that, by the works of each one and in accordance with the works, good fortune or bad would come. The lords of Cuzco with whom they should take counsel should be the most ancient ones. It should be understood that they were the most reasonable and had more experience in war.

There he said to Yamque Yupanque that he should always make Topa Inca Yupanque go out to conquer and subjugate lands and provinces. If he continued in this way throughout his youth, he would see more lands and things that would improve his mind so that when he came to reside in his city he would have experience for reigning and governing his people. They should punish bad people who did ugly things in the city because words fly more than the wind. If they covered up the crimes of the delinquents, these things would be heard throughout the land and the people would do the same thing everywhere. For this reason, some task might fall to them that they wanted to avoid and could not. When they went into battle with their enemies, before doing it, they should consider first how to go about it, no matter how powerful their forces were for it. They should never threaten anyone. If someone deserved punishment, he should be punished without being threatened so that they would not come to regret it later. It could happen that, on threatening someone, if the person heard of the threat, he might go to a place where he could not be found.

In the city more care should be taken to provide for and oversee what was necessary for the women, children, and homes of those who were at war than for those who were at home. They should not allow the youth to be gluttons. If they were to give an office to someone to rule and give orders in the republic, they should look first at how he managed his own home, how he lived there, what orders he gave for the rest of his property and farm, and from that they would see if they should give him such an office. They say this lord said many more things and ordered his subjects to follow them for their right living and sustenance. But at the present time they do not remember any more.

XXX

Which concerns the pagan rites that Inca Yupanque established at the time when he wanted to die, and the subject will be divided into three chapters.

Inca Yupanque ordered that when he should die, in his house there should be no light, and no *agi* or salt should be eaten. Everyone in his household should take off their fine clothing. The men should not put any bands on their heads or wear any plugs in their ears. The women should not use gold or silver pins to fasten their clothing but, rather, they should do it with thorns. This fast and mourning should last for three days from the day he died. After he died, all the lords of the city should be called secretly to his palace without the common people's knowing of his death. With all the lords present then at that time, they should elect the one he had named as Inca and lord in his place, and again his eldest son, Yamque Yupanque, should name him or it could be he if he wished. Afterward, the new lord should go out to the plaza with the majesty of such a lord, and the election of the new lord should be made public. After doing this, his death should also be made public. If the people found out about his death and that there was to be a new lord, they might get violent and try to organize an uprising.

With this done, the new lord should send word to all the land ordering all the caciques, as soon as they heard from the messenger, to come to the city of Cuzco to swear obedience to the new lord and offer him their gifts. They should bring lambs and sheep and make a sacrifice to the new lord as a sign of obedience, since it was for the son of the Sun. Three days after his death, when the fast was suspended, all the lords, the members of his household, and those of his lineage should go to a fountain that he had designated. Everyone, both men and women, should bathe there. This bathing meant that his death ended in him and that he alone died from his lineage and none other.

After this they were to dress as before, to grind a certain green herb, all smear it on their faces, and go like that all together to their homes. They should ask the wives of the Inca which ones wanted to go with him, and the same should be asked of his sons and daughters. Those who wanted to go with him, both men and women, should be dressed in fine clothing with jewelry of gold and silver, according to their dress. And these who were to go with him should dance and sing and have a great feast that day. They should drink much *chicha* and get intoxicated, and while they were drunk they would be strangled. With their jewelry on, as each one of them was wearing the things they used, they would be buried. And it will be made known that the things that the dead wore were as follows. The women wore jewels and carried small jars full of *chicha*, bags with coca, and pots full of toasted and cooked maize as well as plates, bowls, jars, and tumblers for service, all of which was of gold and silver. The men dressed according to the offices that they had in the Inca's house. Even the porter, if he wanted to go with his lord, would be buried at the door of the tomb. Thus all the dead and strangled were buried with the things already mentioned and in the manner stated.

He ordered that after this was done, all the lords of Cuzco should go out into the plaza and cry for him there and, crying, tell in a loud voice of his famous deeds such as planning the city and subjugating and acquiring lands and provinces under his dominion as well as the organization he had in ruling and giving orders for the well-being of the city as in everything else of all the land. After preserving his wrapped body, it should be placed along with the bodies of the previous lords which were there. Then they should send out throughout the entire land and have a thousand boys and girls brought. All these children should be from five to six years of age. Some of them should be the children of caciques. They should be very well dressed, paired up male and female. As married couples they would be given all the table service, which would be of gold and silver, that a married man would have in his house.

These children would be collected from all over the land and would be carried in litters together and by pairs to be buried in pairs with the table service that they had been given. They would be buried all over the land in the places where the Inca had established residence. And some of them would be thrown into the sea in pairs with the table service mentioned above. They called this sacrifice *capa cocha*,[1] which means "solemn sacrifice." The Inca ordered that as these were buried and sacrificed, it would be said that they were going where the Inca was in order to serve him.

He ordered that after this, to all the lord caciques who had come to give obedience to the new lord, a Cuzco *orejon* should be sent with each one so that in the land of each cacique sacrifices would be made and mourning for the Inca's death in the following way. Once the cacique and the Inca *orejon* had arrived at the province, they should call an assembly of all the principal men of the province as well as all the other people, both boys and girls, the rest of the principals together, the common people together, and the boys and girls together. Each *parcialidad,* or social unit, should mourn him in all the towns of the provinces. After this, a distribution should be made of all the maize and clothing in the storehouses of each province among this whole community and in each province of the land, distributing among every four of these a sheep and as much would be given to the children as to the adults. Much *chicha* would be made and given to these. All this would be made as a sacrifice to the Inca and he would receive it as such. This should be done on a designated day throughout the land. At the same time, the lords of Cuzco along with the rest of its inhabitants should do the same mourning, which would last ten days from that first day when they started. When they did this mourning, everyone in the whole land, both men and women, would dress in the poorest and most ordinary clothing they possessed. When they were mourning this way, they should all have their faces smeared with a brown pitch.

XXXI

Concerning the sacrifices and idolatries that Inca Yupanque ordered to be done after his death.

Inca Yupanque ordered that at the end of a period of one year after his death, they should have a certain fiesta, which is almost to canonize him as a saint. In this fiesta he ordered them to make so many ceremonies and to disguise themselves in so many costumes that because of the prolixity of them we will not tell of them all here but only of ones that it seemed to me I should describe to avoid being too brief. He ordered that this fiesta be held in the city of Cuzco and in another place, and it was to last one month. This fiesta was to be put on by the lords and ladies of Cuzco in the following way. On the first day they were to start by having all those of Cuzco leave in their squadrons, with both men and women having smeared their faces with a black color. They were to go to the hills surrounding the city. They were also to go to the lands where the Inca planted and harvested. They should all go crying and each one, both men and women, should carry in their hands the clothes he wore, his personal adornments and weapons with which he fought. When they had all arrived at the places where he stood and the ones where he sat down when he was alive and walked through there, they should call out to him in loud voices, ask him where he was, and speak to him of his deeds. Each one of them would talk with his possession they had in their hands. If they had a tunic, they should say, "Look here at the garment that you used to wear," according to what garment it was. If it were the one he wore in the fiestas, they should acknowledge that. If it were weapons with which he fought, they should say, "See here your weapon with which you won and subjected such a province and so many caciques who were lords there." Consequently, they would tell him of what he did when he was alive with everything they were carrying in their hands. This they were to do for fifteen days from morning to night across the hills, lands, houses, and streets of the whole city. After they finished with what each one had to tell according to what they were carrying in their hands, they were to call him in a loud voice. The most important lord of those who were going there would answer, saying he is in heaven with his father, the Sun. Then they should answer this call, asking him to remember them, send them good rainstorms, and take sickness from them and any evil that might befall them. After all, he was in heaven.

Fifteen days after they had been doing this, they made him a fiesta which he had named Purucaya.[1] On the first day, four men came out into the plaza dressed in certain feathered garments and heavily painted faces with other makeup. These garments should be made in such a way that no one would recognize these men and everyone would be frightened of them. It is true that I saw this fiesta done in the city of Cuzco for Paulo[2] one year after he died. These men disguised like this seemed to me in their dress and things like images made by demons and not people or heavenly angels.

Returning to our story, the Inca ordered that these four men carry tied to their belts some long cords made of gold and fine wool. Also they should each bring with them ten women dressed and adorned in valuable garments. Each of the women would come grasping the cord that each one of the men had tied to his belt. Two of these men would be on one side of the plaza and the other two on the opposite side, separated by a short distance. Each of these men would have a boy and a girl with him in the middle. The girl would carry over her shoulder a small coca bag, which was and had to be of gold or silver. The boy would carry some *aillo*[3] bolas in his hands, which he would drag on the ground. Each one of those four men would go around the plaza from one place to another grimacing, and the ten women would be in one place quietly holding in their hands the cord to which the disguised man was tied. When the disguised man moved some distance from the women, they would release part of the cord, as much as they saw fit. When he came back toward them, they would pull in the cord. From time to time, the girl who was carrying the coca, taking it from that little bag of gold or silver, would put coca in his mouth while he continued grimacing. This girl, carrying a little stick in her hands and threatening him with it, would go hopping to one side of the disguised man as if she wanted to hit him on the arm. The little boy would put that little *aillo* cord, which they say represents the stance they take before their enemies in battle, on the ground. The girl with the coca represents a woman who gives him coca when he is fighting. The boy with the *aillo* bolas received it from her along with other weapons she gave to him by hand when they fought like this.

You should be aware that this *aillo* is a little cord made in a triangle. At the tips of the two ends there is tied a ball the size of an orange and as round and at the other end of the other branch another, not more or less. The balls are made of metal stones. They grasp one ball then let the other two hang down. When they want to throw the balls, they twirl them in the air the way one does to throw a sling. They are good marksmen for hitting whomever they want. If it is at a man, they throw them at his legs, wrapping them around him in such a way as to entangle him and prevent him from taking a step unless help comes to untangle the cord. The one who is like this cannot cut it quickly enough to prevent the enemy who got him from taking him and killing him. The same thing will happen to the arms if it is thrown at the arms. The ones for war are one and a half *brazas* long and made of sinewy cords. They have other smaller ones for throwing at birds on the fly. If they happen to hit the mark, they grab the birds because the bird gets too tangled up to fly. They are very good marksmen with these bolas because they use them from the time they are children, and it is a wonder if they miss their mark.

Returning to this story, they say that the ten women represent the will of that lord. If his will gave him a long piece of cord with which he was tied, he acted like a free man. If it was pulled up short, he did not do another thing, as he did when he was given a long piece of cord, he would say that his will had him tied. And these people were tired when they left the plaza. Then great mourning was done in the plaza by the new lord and by the rest of the people who were there. When this was done, two squadrons of warriors came out, one with people from Hanan Cuzco and the other from Hurin Cuzco. One squadron came out from one side of the plaza and the other from the other side and did battle. The people from Hurin Cuzco acted like losers and those from Hanan Cuzco, representing the wars the lord had in his life, like winners.

After this all the lords of Cuzco held hands in mourning, spoke in a loud voice, and told of the lord's victories and greatness. Then two more squadrons of women came out in men's clothing over their own garments. On their heads also they also wore men's headbands and, in addition, they had feathers on their heads. And one squadron of women carried large shields and the other long halberds in their hands. These women walked around the plaza at a moderate pace, as they do in their dances. Among the women there were some men carrying slings in their hands like males. When I ask what this means, they say that this lord is going to heaven with these ceremonies. When I ask how they know that, they say that Inca Yupanque said it when he arranged for this.

With this done, the month is over from the day they started, and Inca Yupanque ordered this to end by having all of them go to wash away the mourning that they wore all year. Then they were all to come to the plaza and bring there all the garments and possessions with which they had mourned for him. In the plaza there would be built a great fire on which they would throw all those garments and possessions. Then they would bring there a thousand sheep dressed in vestments of all colors.[4] "There in that fire the sheep will be sacrificed to me. Then they will bring another two thousand sheep without vestments, which will have their throats cut and be offered to me. The meat of these will be handed out among all the people of the city who have shown their feelings for me. Then they will bring another thousand lambs, which would be sacrificed to me in that fire. Another thousand will be sacrificed throughout the whole city in my houses where I have slept and in the rest of the places where I have been, burning them in fires in each one of these places. In addition, a thousand boys and girls will be brought and will be buried for me in the places where I slept and where I usually enjoyed myself. With this done, all of my table service of gold and silver will be placed in the earth with me and in my houses. All my livestock and stores will be burned in the places where I had them." The Inca said that everything was going with him, and after that he was in heaven with the Sun. After all these fiestas were over, the new lord would have the deceased Inca's body wrapped and kept in his house, where all would worship it because with the ceremonies and idolatries that you have heard the deceased Inca's body was canonized and held a saint.

XXXII

Which concerns the death of Inca Yupanque, where he was sent for burial, and of the lineages that those of Cuzco made after the death of this lord.

Since there were instructions for the idolatries and activities that you have heard about, Inca Yupanque ordered that immediately after he died these activities and sacrifices should be done. In addition, as soon as this was done, word should be sent to all the land, and from all the provinces and towns they should bring again all that was necessary for the service of the new lord, including gold, silver, livestock, clothing, and the rest of the things needed to replenish all the storehouses that, because of his death, had been emptied for the sacrifices and things he ordered to be done, and it should be so abundant because he realized that the state of the one who was thus Inca was growing greater.

While Inca Yupanque was talking and ordering what was to be done after he died, he raised his voice in a song that is still sung today in his memory by those of his generation. This song went as follows: "Since I bloomed like the flower of the garden, up to now I have given order and justice in this life and world as long as my strength lasted. Now I have turned into earth." Saying these words of his song, Inca Yupanque Pachacuti expired, leaving in all the land justice and order, as already stated. And his people were well supplied with idols, idolatries, and activities. After he was dead, he was taken to a town named Patallacta, where he had ordered some houses built in which his body was to be entombed. He was buried by putting his body in the earth in a large new clay urn, with him very well dressed. Inca Yupanque ordered that a golden image made to resemble him be placed on top of his tomb. And it was to be worshiped in place of him by the people who went there. Soon it was placed there. He ordered that a statue be made of his fingernails and hair that had been cut in his lifetime. It was made in that town where his body was kept. They very ceremoniously brought this statue on a litter to the city of Cuzco for the fiestas in the city. This statue was placed in the houses of Topa Inca Yupanque. When there were fiestas in the city, they brought it out for them with the rest of the statues. What is more laughable about this lord Inca Yupanque is that, when he wanted to make some idol, he entered the house of the Sun and acted as though the Sun spoke to him, and he himself answered the Sun to make his people believe that the Sun ordered him to make those idols and *guacas* and so that they would worship them as such.

When the statue was in the city, Topa Inca Yupanque ordered those of his own lineage to bring this statue out for the feasts that were held in Cuzco. When they brought it out like this, they sang about the things that the Inca did in his life, both in the wars and in his city. Thus they served and revered him, changing its garments as he used to do, and serving it as he was served when he was alive. All of which was done thus.

This statue, along with the gold image that was on top of his tomb, was taken by Manco Inca from the city when he revolted. On the advice that Doña Angelina Yupanque[1] gave to the Marquis Don Francisco Pizarro, he got it and the rest of the wealth with it. Only the body is in Patallacta at this time, and, judging by it, in his lifetime he seems to have been a tall man. They say that he died at the age of one hundred twenty years. After his father's death, Topa Inca Yupanque ordered that none of the descendants of his father, Inca Yupanque, were to settle the area beyond the rivers of Cuzco. From that time until today the descendants of Inca Yupanque were called *Capacaillo Ynga Yupangue haguaynin,*[2] which means "lineage of kings," "descendants and grandchildren of Inca Yupanque." These are the most highly regarded of all the lineages of Cuzco. These are the ones who were ordered to wear two feathers on their heads.

As time passed, this generation of *orejones* multiplied. There were and are today many who became heads of families and renowned as firstborn. Because they married women who were not of their lineage, they took a variety of family names. Seeing this, those of Inca Yupanque ordered that those who had mixed with other people's blood should take new family names and extra names so that those of his lineage could clearly be called *Capacaillo* and descendants of Inca Yupanque. When the Spaniards came, all of this diminished, to the point where they all say they are from that lineage. And they answer yes, as you have heard, when the Spaniards ask them if they are of the lineage of the lord Inca Yupanque. Though the matter will not be dealt with more, they say that in the year that the Spaniards were asking those of Cuzco, among the elders who remember such things, there was no end to the stories of the greatness of this lord Pachacuti Inca Yupanque. Now we will speak of his son and successor, Topa Inca Yupanque, who in his life and deeds tried to emulate to some extent his father, Inca Yupanque.

XXXIII

Wherein one year after his father's death, Topa Inca Yupanque got word of an uprising against him, how he assembled his men and left to pacify and subjugate, taking with him two of his brothers, and of what happened on this expedition.

Topa Inca Yupanque was in the city of Cuzco making arrangements himself, along with his brother Yamque Yupanque, for the good government and provision of the things needed in the city and the rest of the provinces and towns under his dominion. After a year had passed and the fiestas were over that his father had ordered them to perform after his days, one of those *orejones* whom they had left on guard for support in the province of the Andes arrived at the city of Cuzco. On arrival, he went straight to where the two brothers were. After making the demonstration of respect that was done when someone came to them, he told them that the province of the Andes was in rebellion because they had found out about the death of their lord Inca Yupanque. Since they were in rebellion, one night they surrounded all of those who were on guard, and so many men surrounded them that not one man could escape except him. Since the guards were caught unawares and so many men came, in a short time all the guards were killed. And when they were dead, their flesh was handed out among the rebels. He had escaped by submerging himself in a river. With his head covered by some trees and bushes he saw the rebels come to wash the flesh of the dead. In this way he had escaped coming up the river by night.

When Topa Inca Yupanque learned the news about the rebellion of Andesuyo, he got very angry. He had honored them in conquering them and by doing it himself. He immediately ordered an assembly of his warriors and two of his brothers, Inca Achache and Gualpa Rimache, to go out and conquer Andesuyo again. The warriors went off together, leaving in the city his brother Yamque Yupanque to handle the governance of the kingdom, and besides he was very old. Topa Inca Yupanque left Cuzco with his warriors very well equipped and prepared, along with the two brothers mentioned above.

He was going to punish the province of the Andes, traveling through there across forests and taking his soldiers as best he saw fit. The land is very mountainous and has big rivers. He went conquering and defeating everyone he found, and once the lords of the Andes found out he was coming against them, they decided to assemble and wait for the Inca. Since they were all bowmen, they thought that the Inca would not defeat them all together. When Topa Inca found out about the assembly, it pleased him to know that they were all together and he did not have to look for them in the forests. Thus he ordered his army to march on them. Walking along like this one day, one of the Inca's brothers named Inca Achache headed alone into the brush, where he ran into a tiger [jaguar]. As soon as he noticed the beast, he grabbed a battle-ax that he was carrying and went after the tiger which charged him. But Inca Achache was so skillful with his ax that he struck a blow on the tiger's head between its ears. The blow was such that the tiger instantly fell dead. The deed of killing this tiger heartened him so much that Inca Achache took it on his shoulders and went to where the army was marching. He arrived carrying the tiger, but since his brother Topa Inca Yupanque was close enough to see his enemies, Inca Achache put the tiger down in front of his brother and the whole army. He cut the tiger into pieces with his ax. And in order to frighten the enemy, after cutting up the tiger he started eating a piece of the meat, raw as it was. Then Topa Inca Yupanque ordered his men to charge the enemy, and as Inca Achache heard the order, he took a piece of the tiger in his mouth and his ax in his hands. Going well protected with a small shield he was carrying, he noticed a principal lord of the people of the Andes who stood before them.

It is said that at the time he left the place where he cut the tiger up in pieces, he swore he would not leave the Andes until he had eaten the flesh of the lords of the Andes who had killed his friends and relatives and eaten them up. Thus Topa Inca Yupanque attacked with his men, going ahead of Inca Achache, who charged the enemies so fiercely that in view of all of them he captured a captain of the Andes and cut him to pieces and started right away eating him. The enemies saw what Inca Achache had done and that he had a piece of their lord and captain's flesh in his mouth and that he was doing great damage with an ax that he carried in his hands. Seeing that he was cutting them to pieces, the other lords and warriors fled. Thus the Inca's soldiers chased them down, capturing and killing all the lords of the Andes who had rebelled against the Inca.

Once Topa Inca Yupanque achieved victory and inflicted the damage he saw fit, he returned with his soldiers to the city of Cuzco, where he entered in triumph, according to their custom. When he reached the place where Yamque Yupanque was, they greeted each other, and Topa Inca Yupanque begged Yamque Yupanque, as his elder brother and the one who had made him lord, to tread on the insignias that they brought from the war. Yamque Yupanque did it because he saw that it pleased his brother and also because he saw that it was appropriate because his brother was in command and governed in the kingdom. Then the sacrifices and idolatries his father had arranged were performed. While they were performing these sacrifices and fiestas, a messenger arrived for Topa Inca Yupanque. The messenger told him that the province of Collasuyo, which his father had won with his brothers Amaro Topa Inca and Paucar Usno, was in rebellion and was coming with a great force of soldiers against the city of Cuzco. Once he was informed of the news of this turn of events, he went into consultation with his brother Yamque Yupanque and the rest of the lords of Cuzco in order to see and agree on what should be done in this situation.

XXXIV

Wherein it was stipulated in their resolution that certain lords, sons of Inca Yupanque and brothers of Topa Inca Yupanque, would be governors of the provinces of Condesuyo, Chinchasuyo, and Andesuyo, how each one of them was given all the provisions and warriors that they felt were necessary for it, and how they also provided in their resolution for Topa Inca to go out in person to punish the province of Collasuyo, and the things that happened on this expedition.

Topa Inca Yupanque made a resolution with his men in the city of Cuzco. In order to keep the province of the Andes from rebelling, they decided to send Inca Achache with a certain number of warriors to that province, which had already been pacified. They named him Uturungo Achache[1] for the tiger he killed, which means the tiger Achache. It was decided that Topa Inca Yupanque would go in person to put down the uprising in Collasuyo. It was also decided that, if by chance, while Topa Inca Yupanque was putting down the uprising in Collasuyo, Yamque Yupanque should die, since he was very old, seventy years of age, and worn down by the hardships of the wars to subjugate Quito, after his days they would name as governor, in place of his lord Topa Inca Yupanque, his brother who was called Sopono Yupanque. It was also decided that three brothers of Topa Inca Yupanque, who were called Tambo Topa, Gualpache, and Huayna Yupanque, would go to the province of Chinchasuyo in order to govern up to Quito. They were given a certain number of warriors for their guards as well as to cover the need that might come up to put down a rebellion in some town. They also decided to send two other brothers of the Inca to govern the province of Condesuyo so that they could keep it quiet and at peace. They were given as many warriors as seemed fit. The lords who went to Condesuyo were called Inca Quiço and Caimaspi. With this arranged, they set about complying by gathering as many warriors as they could, which took them three months. During this time, Topa Inca Yupanque and the residents of the city spent their time preparing their weapons and making sacrifices. After two months, the warriors were assembled who numbered one hundred and thirty-six thousand.

The Inca and his lords separated twenty thousand men of those from Andesuyo, Cana and Canches of Collasuyo. Then they sent with these twenty thousand men those three lords who were selected for governors of the province of Chinchasuyo, who, being supplied with all their necessities, left the city. With this taken care of, they separated ten thousand men from the provinces Andesuyo, Cana, Quivios, and Canches. Then they sent with these ten thousand those two lords who were selected as governors of the province of Condesuyo, who, being well supplied with all their necessities, left the city. With this done, they separated another six thousand natives of the province of Condesuyo, who were given to Uturungo Achache. Then he left for the province of the Andes with those men in order to protect it and govern it. Having been given all of the provisions of salt and the rest of the things, they left the city of Cuzco. Having taken all the precautions necessary for the defense, governance, and sustenance of the three provinces, as you have heard, Topa Inca Yupanque ordered the lords of Cuzco who had been picked for his personal guards and captains of his people to prepare because he planned to leave the city of Cuzco in three days. After the three days passed, since all was ready that they needed in the way of provisions for their expedition and the warriors were also prepared with all they needed, Topa Inca Yupanque left to put down the uprising of the people of Collasuyo, and he took with him one hundred thousand warriors, natives of all Chinchasuyo. He also took with him as his personal guards, five thousand men, one thousand *orejon* lords from the city of Cuzco, and four thousand from the towns closest to the city, as well as his friends.

Thus he went against his enemies, who were now approaching nearby. Topa Inca Yupanque met with them in the province and town of Asillo, where they gave him battle. In it, since Topa Inca Yupanque took his enemies very lightly, he threw himself courageously into battle, but since the enemies were very numerous, they killed all the men of that company, charged the Inca, and grabbed him. One of the Inca's captains named Rarico Inca, who was keeping watch on his lord and saw what had happened, attacked suddenly with ten thousand men whom he had on the side where the Inca had entered and had been taken captive. Since this captain and his men were killing so many of the Collas so swiftly, the Collas released Topa Inca Yupanque from danger. As soon as he saw that he was free, he picked from the ground an ax of one of the fallen. With it the Inca started to defend himself so well that very soon he cleared the area around him. Thus his captain Rarico Inca arrived doing as much damage as his lord, and together they both led their men in the fray. Seeing that the time was ripe, the other captains charged suddenly with all their squadrons together, hitting their enemies from different places. When the enemies saw the ravages being inflicted on them, the Collasuyos turned tail, giving victory to Topa Inca Yupanque.

Once the Collas saw themselves defeated, they fled and went to build a stronghold on the crag of Pucarane, where they assembled again. The Inca ordered his army to move from the town of Asillo and march to the strongholds. When the Inca reached there, he did battle with his enemies again. Defeating and putting them in disarray, he took the stronghold. The enemy escaped from there and went to Arapa, which is another six leagues from that stronghold. Since the Inca had word that the enemy was building strongholds again in Arapa, the Inca ordered a certain number that he thought sufficient of *orejon* warriors whom he had brought with him to stand guard on that stronghold. With this arranged, he ordered his captains to have the army march to the town of Arapa, where his enemies were waiting for him. On arrival, the Inca found the enemy on all the hills, where they had fortifications and thought they were safe there. In addition, they had on a small island which is near the town of Arapa in a lake there a large fortification at the entrance to the island on a causeway that goes from terra firma to it.

When Topa Inca Yupanque arrived, he started to fight them, distributing his squadrons in the way his enemies were distributed so that his men could fight them and drive them out of those strongholds that they had. Topa Inca Yupanque's people saw the Collas there. They had already defeated them two times, the first of which was when the enemy was the most heartened and the Inca's people rather disheartened. Topa Inca Yupanque's men realized this and charged, defeating them quickly and driving them out of the strongholds that they had there. After that, the enemy made strongholds again at a site which is in the province of Chuquiabo in a town called Surocoto. When Topa Inca Yupanque got news that the enemy had taken up positions again, the Inca sent one of his captains called Camaque Yupanque against them with thirteen thousand warriors. This captain was to go through the unpopulated regions of Asangaro toward the town of Cotocoto and see if any of the enemy had remained hidden in those unpopulated regions in order to ambush his rear guard. After this captain left, the Inca took his army toward Surocoto, where his enemies were reassembling. Since that captain went ahead, the people of Cotocoto got news of it. Since the captain had so few men, they ambushed him, killing him and all of his men except a few who escaped and gave the news to Topa Inca Yupanque. The Inca had his army march over there, where he did not let any of them who had angered him escape, and he took his army ahead to where his enemies awaited him in Surocoto. When the Inca arrived, there was another battle in which he routed them. In the aftermath of this defeat, the enemies fled. The enemies had a three-day head start because Topa Inca Yupanque's army had been reassembling and gathering the spoils of that battle. Thus they did not have time to follow their enemies right away. At the end of the three days, Topa Inca Yupanque ordered his men to strike camp and went in pursuit of the enemies.

XXXV

Wherein Topa Inca Yupanque followed his enemies, did battle with them, took them prisoner and punished them, and continued on from there on an expedition that led to Chile, and of the things that happened on it.

Topa Inca Yupanque followed his enemies, but they had a considerable head start on him, and they headed into the province of the Mayosmayos Indians to a stronghold there next to a town called Tongoche. Since the enemy had been thrown into disarray, as soon as they arrived, they had a meeting with the natives of that whole province and with those from nearby. All of this Topa Inca Yupanque found out about, including the fact that strongholds had been built and the enemy awaited him there. This pleased the Inca, and when he approached he laid siege to them, going into battle on all fronts. When the enemy saw that Topa Inca Yupanque had them surrounded and they needed to defend themselves, they did everything in their power to do so. Since Topa Inca Yupanque had so many men and gave battle continuously, four days after the siege had been laid, Topa Inca Yupanque won his victory over them, took them prisoner, killed all those lords who had risen up against him, and had their heads preserved.

After this was done, the Inca had all of his soldiers assemble, letting them know that he was pleased and that he was anxious to enlarge his kingdom. So he told them that with their advice and help he wanted to forge ahead and conquer farther on. To this they all answered that they would follow him until they saw where the Sun comes up, which made the Inca very happy. Wishing to pay them for the services that they had rendered to him to that point and for that very good will they showed him, he did great favors for all of them by giving them many women, valuables, and livestock, all of which had been taken as spoils from the enemy.

After doing this, being so far from Cuzco, because it was about two hundred leagues from there to Cuzco, the Inca decided to send his messengers to his brother Yamque Yupanque, letting him know what had happened to that point and that he intended to continue. When those messengers reached the city of

Cuzco, many great sacrifices were to be made to the idols. Giving the messengers certain jewels and things for Yamque Yupanque, the Inca sent them off. The messengers gave the news to Yamque Yupanque and to the rest of the lords of Cuzco. The whole city was very pleased to receive this news. And the sacrifices and fiestas ordered by Topa Inca Yupanque were made. With this done, Yamque Yupanque sent his messengers to his brothers in all of the provinces where they were governors, giving them the news of Topa Inca's good fortune and ordering them to have in all the towns and provinces under them great rejoicing and sacrifices to the idols for the good fortune of his lord and brother. All of which was done.

Returning now to Topa Inca Yupanque and his expedition, after sending the messengers that you have heard about to the city of Cuzco, he ordered his captains to prepare his camp and warriors because the next day he planned to leave there in search of Chiriguana, a province which, according to his information, had great warriors. The next day he and his army left. On reaching there, he had a battle with them and renewed the attack. Having won his victory over them and leaving them under his dominion, he pressed on to where he heard about the province of the Suris. He ordered his army to head over there. When he arrived, he had a battle with them and renewed the attack, defeating and subjugating them in the end. This great province had majestic mountains and lands with many ostriches [rheas]. Most of the clothing worn by the people of this province is made of feathers.

Once the people of the Suri nation were subjugated, he pressed ahead, reaching the big river said to be the Plata.[1] On arriving there, he saw how wide it was and did not cross it. He went along the river's edge to where it rises, which is said to be behind Chile toward where the sun comes up. Pressing on from there to the right as he did, he came to passes in high snow-covered mountain ranges, where he subjugated everything he found on his way. Thus he reached Chile, where he found a bellicose people who were very rich in gold. He went into battle with them and sujugated them. After having pacified them, he asked them where they got so much wealth in gold. They answered that it came from some mines that they had. Becoming very anxious to see these mines, he went there and saw them.

The Inca asked what kind of people there were ahead and what the land was like. They told him that ten days' journey ahead there was a river called the Maule. Up to the river there were a few people, but six days' journey beyond the river there were a great many people who had some small sheep, and the people were very well treated. Bearing this in mind, he became anxious to continue, and he ordered his army to move. After covering fifteen or twenty leagues, he stopped and sent his captains with a certain number of men to see how wide the river was and what the land was like. The captains went there, saw the river, and returned to their lord, telling him that the river was very wide and populated in places with a few people. The Inca told them that a long time had passed since they had left the city of Cuzco and, since they had seen what there was up to there, it seemed to him that they should return. His captains already felt like returning home so they told him that they agreed with him. Thus the Inca returned home from Chile.

XXXVI

Wherein Topa Inca Yupanque returned from the province of Chile to the city of Cuzco, learned at the entrance to the city of the death of his brother Yamque Yupanque, and how he mourned and what happened to him on that return.

Before returning from the nation of Chile, Topa Inca Yupanque reflected on how warlike the people of that province were and that it would be well to leave a garrison of warriors there so that what had been won and conquered would be kept quiet and peaceful and so that from that province his tribute of gold would be brought to him at the city of Cuzco. With this in mind, he designated enough of his troops to keep that province under control. With this done, he ordered those whom he had designated to remain for the purpose already stated and all the lords of Chile, Copayapo, and all the rest of the surrounding towns and valleys to assemble for the Inca to give them his speech. He told them what they would have to do from then on and how they were to serve and give tribute. He gave them many jewels of silver, which is the metal they do not have there and the one they valued more than any other thing that he gave them.

Having done them great favors, the Inca ordered his captains to have their troops ready to march the next day along the road from Chile to Copayapo, which is sixty leagues from Chile on the way to Cuzco. When the Inca reached Copayapo, he found out that from there to Atacama there were large stretches of desolate, sandy land without water and in that wilderness there were some waterholes called *xagueyes*[1] with very little water. When a number of people traveled, they would divide up in such a way that when one group reached the first *xaguey* another group that had been there before would be at the next *xaguey*. This was the way the people traveled when they were going to trade with those of Atacama or vice versa.

With this news in mind, the Inca immediately ordered the natives of those provinces to take as many soldiers as possible and go to the province of Atacama, where he had been told the people were very warlike. The natives should carry their weapons and open up the *xagueyes* on their way, making large pools of water so that the Inca's soldiers could cross and so that if the soldiers of Atacama wanted to attack his men as they were leaving the desolate lands in small groups, those natives of Chile and Copayapo who had gone ahead should protect them from attack. Thus the natives of Chile and Copayapo set out to do what has been stated. Then the Inca ordered that many skin bags be made from the hide of the legs of their sheep so that his people could carry water in these skins, enough water to last them throughout their crossing of that wilderness in successive groups so that they would not lack water. Thus the Inca crossed the wilderness, taking all of his men with him and leaving word there in Copayapo to store those skins for water to be brought by those who would bring tribute from Chile to the city of Cuzco.

When the Inca reached Atacama, he made sure to find out what that whole land was like and what roads left there for Collao to see the way he should travel on the road he selected. After getting the information, he divided his men in four groups. With this done, he ordered three of these squadrons to leave there right away. One squadron was to travel along the plains of the seacoast until reaching the province of Arequipa. Another was to go across the Caranga and Aullaga. The other one was to turn right and continue to Caxa Vindo and from there cross the province of Chicha until it reached the place where the body of his brother Paucar Usno was. From there they were to march until entering the province of Collao, where he ordered his captains to wait for him if they arrived first, and, if he arrived first, he would wait for them so that they could all go together to the city of Cuzco.

With this settled, those three parties and captains left in the way just explained. The Inca also left at the same time, going in the direction that suited him. Thus he marched for a number of days until he came to a province called Llipi in which he found a people with insufficient food. Their sustenance was toasted quinua, which is a very small white seed, and some papas [potatoes]. The walls of their houses were covered with [roofing made of] soft poles that are the heart of some very light and poor hawthorn wood. The houses were small and low, the people, inferior. What these people had were mines of many fine colors for painting, including all the colors we have. They also had a certain amount of livestock. Additionally, in that land there were many ostriches [rheas]. Furthermore, the natives of these villages drank from small *xagueyes* and springs. The Inca ordered these people to send him tribute of those colors and livestock. And they did it.

The Inca and his men left there, going through lands devoid of water and food, flat land without forests and the rest of it salt beds. On leaving this bad land, the Inca came upon a province called Chuquisaca whose people and surrounding areas were very warlike, and they were called Charcas. The Inca subjugated them in a short time. Having them under his dominion, the Inca was informed by his warriors that these Charcas were lords who had much silver. The Inca asked them where they got the silver, and they told him that they took it from a hill called Porco. The Inca wanted to see it so he ordered his men to march there. On reaching the mines, he gave the order to require a certain amount of tribute from there. Then he gathered as much silver as possible and left that province of Charcas.

The Inca came to a place called Paria, where he had a *tambo* constructed. He left there with his men and marched toward Chuquiabo [La Paz]. On getting word that there were certain gold mines in that province, he collected as much gold as he could. Giving orders about how that gold should be sent to him in tribute, he left for the city of Cuzco, going straight to the town of Chucuito and on to Hatun Colla, where he found the captains who had traveled along the seacoast going up through Arequipa. He also found those who had gone through Caranga. Both of these parties brought with them the caciques whom they had taken in the towns and provinces through which they had gone. The Inca received them benignly. Since the captains had not arrived who had gone through Chicha to come out where the body of Paucar Usno was, the Inca waited there in Hatun Colla for five days, after which those captains arrived, worn out and with one-third fewer men than they had at first. The Chichas tried to defend themselves and put up many battles. Although the Chichas killed one-third of their soldiers, in the end the Inca's warriors had their victory over them all. Even if the Chichas had killed a third of their soldiers, they got their satisfaction by killing and subjugating the Chichas. They also brought with them all the caciques and lords of all the towns and provinces through which they had passed. When they reached the town of Hatun Colla, where the Inca was, the Inca received well his captain and the caciques he brought with him.

The Inca ordered his troops to march toward the city of Cuzco the next day. Thus the Inca left, taking with him great riches from when he had gone out to do battle with the soldiers of Collasuyo and also taking with him all the caciques and lords of all the provinces and valleys that he had subjugated from Chile to the city of Cuzco and from the seacoast over to the province of the Andes. From the time he left the city of Cuzco this time until he returned there, he conquered six hundred leagues. On returning through a town called Moyna, four leagues from Cuzco, he received the news that his brother Yamque Yupanque, whom he had left in his place and who had named him lord, giving him the *borla* of state, had expired that morning of a grave illness. This lord Yamque Yupanque, eldest son of the Inca Yupanque, had lived for eighty-five years. On receiving this news, Topa Inca Yupanque was deeply saddened.

Although he was a very stern man, he could not cover up such sadness as he received this news of the death of his brother, so he wept and shed some tears. Since the news spread throughout the camp, the rest of the lords and ladies made so many lamentations that nothing else could be heard. This lasted all that day and all that night while many drums were played. The same was done throughout the city and surrounding towns.

Thus the next day the Inca dressed in mourning, made a black stripe the width of a finger down his forehead, and took off the *borla* of state as a sign of grief. Then everyone in his camp, both men and women, dressed in mourning. The color for mourning was brown, which they call "*paco*,"[2] made of wool from wild animals. Both men and women smeared their faces with black pitch. Next the Inca ordered his soldiers to leave for the city. So they pressed on until reaching there. Both the Inca and the rest of the people, always playing their drums, made many signs of grief.

With this news the Inca refused to enter the city of Cuzco in triumph, as he would have liked to do. When the Inca was within about a quarter league of the city, all the inhabitants of the city came out to meet him, all of them, both men and women, formed in a squadron. They were all dressed in mourning with their faces smeared, as has already been stated, crying in loud voices and playing their drums. As the Inca was coming with the rest of his people, the townspeople raised their voices much higher in crying than they had up to then. They sang a song which contained all the deeds that lord had done while he lived. When this was done, each of the lords of Cuzco showed their respect for the Inca separately, and the Inca received them benignly, giving his welcome to each one, asking them about their health and that of their families.

After this was done, the Inca ordered all the citizens to prepare everything necessary that night because the next day he wanted to start the mourning that needed to be done for his brother in accordance with their custom, the same way it was done when his father, Inca Yupanque, died. Thus these lords left with the arrangements made and went in their order singing and mourning the death of Yamque Yupanque. Shortly after the citizens entered the city, the Inca entered, also going straight to the houses of Yamque Yupanque, where he found his body already dressed and adorned for burial. The Inca also found his household members expressing their grief and fasting, as had been ordered by his father. When the time came for the burial, the Inca had it done like the body of his father. The Inca also had a golden image of Yamque Yupanque made, which was placed on top of the tomb. The Inca himself put a *borla* fringe identical to his own on the head of the golden image. The Inca had a statue of Yamque Yupanque's fingernails and hair made like his father's, which the people worshiped. It should be known that in their lifetimes these lords were worshiped and revered as children of the Sun and after death their images were regarded as gods. Thus sacrifices like those made before the statue of the Sun were made before them.

After their ceremonies and rites, which they customarily performed according to the order of Inca Yupanque and the fiesta called Purucaya, which means almost to canonize, the dead Inca was considered a saint. With these pagan rites finished, Topa Inca Yupanque had brought before him a surviving son of this lord Yamque Yupanque, whom he ordered to be named Yamque Yupanque, the same as his father. This boy was fourteen years old. With the boy in his presence, the Inca did him great favors, giving him all of his father's property, houses, land, and livestock that his father left when he died. The Inca ordered this boy to be brought up and remain in the company of his own son Huayna Capac, who was twelve years old himself and the boy's first cousin. These boys were reared together, but we must leave them until the time comes to speak of them in this account.

Let us continue with the account of Topa Inca Yupanque, of whom we are speaking now. After he had finished having the feasts that you have heard about for his brother, he ordered an assembly of those who had served him on that expedition. The Inca divided up among them the spoils of the war he had brought and did them many other favors. Then he ordered them to return to their lands for a rest. After these subjects had gone, the Inca ordered to appear before him all the lord caciques whom he had brought with him after they came to him or to his captains in peace during that expedition. He also had the prisoners and delinquents punished in his presence, as was their custom. Then and there he named others as he saw fit to be caciques and lords of those towns and provinces where the delinquents had held office. With this done, the Inca did great favors for those he had named caciques as well as to those who had come in peace. He also gave to each of them women from among the daughters of the lords of Cuzco and his own sisters, who were young when their father died. These gifts and favors pleased the lord caciques, who never once rebelled against this lord Topa Inca Yupanque during his lifetime. Afterward, he sent them back to their land in the province of Collasuyo, and those lords left. It took Topa Inca Yupanque seven years from the time he left Cuzco to pacify this province of Collasuyo until his return to the city of Cuzco.

XXXVII

Wherein Topa Inca Yupanque built the fortress
of Cuzco and its structure, which is
magnificent and famous.

After Topa Inca Yupanque returned from pacifying and putting down the uprising of the province of Collasuyo, as this account has already told you, he remained in the city of Cuzco for a period of four years, resting and enjoying himself with his family in their fiestas and pagan sacrifices. The Inca had visited distant lands and had seen many different things there. One that stuck in his mind was that few of the towns that he had visited and subjugated lacked a stronghold or fortress where those of that town or province took refuge and defended themselves from those who wanted to harm them. On returning to the city of Cuzco and observing the magnificence of its buildings, he realized that, as the center of the whole land, everyone would have their eye on it. It would be possible for some province or provinces to rebel just as the rebellion of the province of Collasuyo, which he had recently put down. If it came to pass that a province rebelled and attacked the city of Cuzco, though the entire city and buildings were solid, there was no stronghold in which the citizens could take refuge and defend themselves against attack.

Having taken these facts into consideration, at the end of the four years, the Inca decided that he should build in this city for its defense an impregnable castle or stronghold whose lodgings, including the entire construction and walls, would follow the model of the buildings of the city of Cuzco and its greatness. Thus the Inca wanted to make it memorable, and it seemed to him that it would take some time to make such a construction as he had it outlined in his imagination. With this in mind, he ordered an assembly of the caciques of all the land, sending out the order for each one to bring all those in their land who knew how to make buildings and were most skilled at it. He wanted to explain to them about a certain building he wanted to make in the city of Cuzco and start construction after they arrived. Then *orejones* and other Indians were sent to all the lords of the land. As soon as they heard the Inca's order, they all assembled in the city. The Inca went there and consulted with them about the construction project, telling them that it was for the well-being and safety of his people. After those lords realized what the Inca had in mind and heard what he wanted to do, they told him they were eager to get the plans so they could go to work as soon as they were told the site where they were to build.

LA DEZÍMACOIA
MAMAOCLLO

Reyno guanoco   guay llas atapillo

The tenth Coya, Mama Ocllo, wife of Topa Inca and mother of Huayna Capac.

From the chronicle of Felipe Guaman Poma de Ayala,
Nueva coronica y buen gobierno.

Then the next day Topa Inca Yupanque went out and looked over all the hills and sierras surrounding the city. It seemed to him best to build on a hill called Sacsahuaman Urco above the city.[1] Then he made the plans and gave them to the lords of the city and the caciques of all the land. The next day the Inca went up to the site where the fortress was to be built. He ordered that measurements be taken with cords in his presence and plans be made according to what he had imagined and said. Then the craftsmen and technicians took their cords and measured the fortress, its enclosures and walls. The day after this was done, the Inca ordered them to prepare for the foundations and for the rest of the people to bring the foundation materials from all the quarries of Oma, Salu, and Guairanga, towns surrounding the city within five leagues. It took them two years to bring the stones, work them, make the rest of the preparations, including ropes and mixtures as well as opening and preparing fountains. With everything ready, the Inca ordered work to start on the foundations and walls. On this job, ten thousand men normally worked in orderly groups, some making the mixtures, others working the stone, and still others setting them in place. The largest number of workers had to bring the stones from the quarries already mentioned and set them in place.

One would think that these stones that they carried like this were stones that ten or twenty men could pick up and bring on their backs. In fact, most of these stones are so big that five hundred men carried one of them, and others required a thousand Indians. These stones were pulled with thick ropes made of braided sinews and braided sheepskin. These stones were so well worked in the wall of the fortress fitted up to one *estado* and two *estados* of the structure that it is a sight to see and consider how such huge stones were so well placed in such a high structure. This is no fabrication but quite true. In fact, on the flat place behind the fortress there is a very big stone. It was brought like the others from the quarries; this stone came from more that a league and a half from there. They put it down a stone's throw from the fortress on the flat place mentioned, and they could never move it from there. Topa Inca Yupanque ordered the whole multitude of Indians who were there to pull on the ropes that were tied to it and used to put it in that place and take it from there to the place for which it was brought. But they could never move that stone from there or even budge it. Seeing this, the Inca said that stone had gotten tired and that it should be called the tired stone, which is the name it bears to this day. It still remains there on the flat place a stone's throw from the fortress. Within this fortress two strong turrets were built as well as its cisterns for water, enclosures and walls. The turrets were of these large, rough stones.

This was such a magnificent construction that it could be considered one of the marvels of the world. Today most of it has been knocked down to the ground, which is a shame to see. They say that from the beginning of construction until completion took six years. With it finished, Topa Inca Yupanque ordered an assembly of all those who had worked on it. He gave many presents and did many favors to each one according to his station. Then the Inca ordered them to go rest in their lands.

XXXVIII

Wherein Topa Inca Yupanque had a town, which he named Chinchero, built two leagues from the city of Cuzco behind the fortress on the road to Yucay.

During the two years after building the fortress that you have heard about, the Inca enjoyed himself by celebrating great feasts and offering sacrifices to the Sun and the rest of the *guacas*. Then he decided that it would be good to build a town to be populated by the growing number of people in Cuzco, so that he would be better remembered, so he and the lords of Cuzco would have a place to go for recreation, and so it would be said that he had built this town for himself and for his recreation. Then he ordered the lord *orejones* to go throughout all the land and in a designated month arrange an assembly of all the caciques from all the land with the number of people the Inca called for in the city of Cuzco. These *orejones* left and in the month designated for them, they went together to the city of Cuzco with their men, which they say amounted to twenty thousand. When they arrived, the Inca gave to the lords of Cuzco the plan of the town. Leaving this city of Cuzco, the Inca went to a flat place two leagues from this city where there is a big lake and decided that it would be a good place to build this town mentioned above.

Then the plan that the Inca prepared was brought there. After seeing it, the technicians and master builders took their cords and measured the town. After the measurements were taken, with the houses and streets outlined, Topa Inca Yupanque ordered the foundations to be made. Then he had the lords of Cuzco arrange for the construction of that town, giving instructions to each one about what they needed to have built. This town was made of stone and very well constructed buildings according to their workmanship. Then Topa Inca Yupanque gave the houses to the lords of Cuzco. The Inca and the rest of the lords had some of their women in these houses, where the Inca and lords went to relax during the months and at the times they saw fit. The construction of this town took five years. The Inca ordered this town to be called Chinchero.

XXXIX

Wherein Topa Inca Yupanque returned to the city of Cuzco, the things he did and provided there before he died, and of the preparations made after his death.

After Topa Inca Yupanque parceled out the town of Chinchero to the lords of the city of Cuzco in the way you have already been told, he enjoyed himself there for a certain length of time. At the end of this time, he decided that, since he was old and tired, he would go to the city of Cuzco, where, following in everything every single one of the commandments set down by his father, he stayed to look after the well-being of his people and the republic. At the same time he made sure to send many gifts to the cacique lords of all the land, sending to some of them valuable clothing, to others, women of the Cuzco nation, from whom their descendants and successors would come, and to others, tumblers and jewels of gold and silver, as he saw fit. Topa Inca Yupanque did all of this to sustain their friendship and to keep them from rebelling, disturbing him, and putting him to the trouble of pacifying and subjugating them once again. He was old and his past efforts had left him weakened. Two and a half years after the founding of the town of Chinchero, he suffered a grave illness. Seeing that he was worsening, he felt that he was coming to the end of his days and that he should give the order as to what the lords of Cuzco should do after his days because his son Huayna Capac was very young and in the Inca's opinion still not capable of governing the kingdom.

After deciding this, he ordered an assembly of the lords of Cuzco there where he was so that he could consult with them and give them the orders he wanted regarding matters of the kingdom and its governing and name governors who would rule after his days. His illness was severe and getting worse every day, so he thought he would die of it. With the lords present he gave them the explanation you have just heard, to which they answered that he should order whatever he saw fit for them to best sustain themselves. Then he ordered his son Huayna Capac and his nephew to be brought. With them there the Inca had the *borla* of state brought and he gave it to his nephew Yamque Yupanque so that he could place it with his hands on the head of his son Huayna Capac, whom he named the only king. Then the boy Yamque Yupanque, first cousin of Huayna Capac, took the *borla* in his hands and put it on the head of the new lord, Huayna Capac, naming him Çapa Inca. Then Topa Inca Yupanque ordered the lords to go out to get the sheep, lambs, and birds, make the customary sacrifice before the new Inca, and show him the respect and obedience that was given to the lord they elected.

Then the lords left and brought back everything necessary and made their sacrifices to their new lord, giving him their obedience as the new lord. Next Topa Inca Yupanque did Yamque Yupanque, his nephew, a favor by naming him chief purveyor of all the livestock held by Cuzco in all the land. Each year he would keep track, with all the cacique lords of all the land, of the increase in livestock, provide for the lords of Cuzco to see how they benefited from it, and by his hand the supply of livestock would be made that would be consumed in Cuzco for fiestas, rejoicing, and sacrifices, and that no more would be consumed than he saw fit and decided to have consumed. He would keep a record of it all by putting on his *quipos* and registers the livestock that each cacique had in his land and what he had sent to be consumed in Cuzco. Seeing the favor that his uncle Topa Inca Yupanque was doing for him, Yamque Yupanque rose from his seat of a lord that he had, went to his uncle, and kissed him on the cheek as a sign of his love and gratefulness for this favor.

Yamque Yupanque sat down again in his seat, and then Topa Inca Yupanque favored his son Huayna Capac by making him, in addition to lord, purveyor of the livestock of the Sun and having him take care each year to get an account from all of the caciques of the land about the increase in the Sun's livestock, so that by his hand the livestock for the sacrifices to the Sun would be provided. He would be named keeper of the Sun's livestock. Then the new lord Huayna Capac rose from his seat, kissed his father on the cheek, and accepted the post and favor his father did for him. They say that sometimes as a pastime Huayna Capac enjoyed taking the livestock out to pasture himself.

Then Topa Inca Yupanque designated as governors of the kingdom, while Huayna Capac was a youth until he was mature, a nephew of his named Apo Gualpaya, who was a man with excellent administrative skills and very intelligent, and also his brother Uturungo Achache, the one we've already said who, during the conquest of the Andes, killed and dismembered tigers and people and ate them. The Inca told these two to take charge of the governance of the kingdom, increase the grandeur of Cuzco, take special care to watch over his son Huayna Capac and his nephew Yamque Yupanque so that they would not turn out to be dissolute, teach them the ways of virtue, not presumption, and how to be affable with their vassals. They should also take good care of his wife Mama Ocllo, the mother of Huayna Capac, for everyone to respect her as the Inca's mother and what she said or asked for, if it seemed to them appropriate for the good of Cuzco and its support, they should do it for as long as she lived.

After her days, a gold statue of her should be made and the fiesta of Purucaya, with all its formalities and sacrifices, should be performed for her.

Then the lord governors called Apo Gualpaya and Uturungo Achache rose from their seats and kissed Topa Inca Yupanque on the cheek, making the proper show of respect for him and thanking him for the favor he did them by making them governors and leaving entrusted to them his wife Mama Ocllo, his son, and nephew, whom he loved very much. With this done, the Inca ordered them to go home and for the next day prepare the fiestas and rejoicing for a new lord that were customary among them. They should also make preparations to send sacrifices to all the *guacas* and idols throughout all the land and the sea. Then the lords left and gave orders for what they had been told to do. Four months after this election and appointment, during which time they had celebrated and the new lord had done great favors for the lords of Cuzco, as was their custom when a new lord was appointed, the good Topa Inca Yupanque died, having lived seventy years and won and conquered the provinces and lands that you have heard about and having done great favors for all of his people. The Inca's death was deeply mourned by all the people in all the land, as was their custom, and they had good reason to mourn for a lord who had loved them so much and done so much good for them.

The governors gave the order to make the sacrifices and ceremonies that were customary when such a lord died, strangling those who wanted to accompany him, sacrificing livestock, burying children, as was done on the death and according to the orders of Inca Yupanque. You should know that those who say they want to go with the Inca for they love him so much rush those who do the strangling so much that, on seeing that they do not get strangled as quickly as they want, with the ropes around their necks they would strangle and hang themselves and their women with their sashes called *chumbes*,[1] tying the sashes around their necks and down their backs to their ankles, making the sash as short as possible. Tied in this position they would straighten out their legs, which they had bent, and in this way they would strangle themselves, saying that they were going to serve their lord who had died and be with him in heaven with his father the Sun.

One year after the day that Topa Inca Yupanque died, with all the lords of all the land together, they performed for him the fiesta of Purucaya, which is his canonization. After the fiesta they made the statue of his fingernails and hair, which was worshiped and adored as a lord. They made the sacrifices to this statue that were customarily made to the dead lords of the past. With solemnity and a show of respect as if it were alive, they would give food and drink to it as a sacrifice at the same times that the Inca ate and drank during his lifetime.

XL

Wherein Huayna Capac and the lord governors provided inspectors who did an inspection of the kingdom and considered the well-being of all, and of how the governors gave up their post and Huayna Capac became the only lord.

After they finished the sacrifices and fiestas for the death of Topa Inca, the lord governors decided that it was time to take action on things relating to the common good and the government. They told Huayna Capac to order an assembly of advisers so that together they could see what should be done in such a situation. Then Huayna Capac and the governors began their deliberations together with the rest of the principal lords of the city there in the assembly along with the rest of the lords of the people. There they agreed to send four lords of the people and principal lords of the city of those who where there in the assembly. They were selected, and each one was to go to a province that was designated there. They were each told separately that in each province they were to examine the precautions and care taken by the stewards selected by the now deceased lord for handling tributes, as well as the storehouses, widows, orphans, poor people, whether the young men and women were taught the ways of virtue and work by their parents, according to the order laid down by the Inca Yupanque, and whether they took care in those provinces to make the customary sacrifices to the Sun and the rest of the *guacas* and idols, as the lords of Cuzco had ordered.

With this done, those four lords left the city of Cuzco. One went to the province of Collasuyo, the other to Condesuyo, the other to Chinchasuyo, and the other to Andesuyo. Having sent these lords out on their inspection, Huayna Capac along with the governors occupied themselves in looking over the city and its republic. All of this being done both by the inspectors who went to the provinces and by Huayna Capac and the governors, the inspectors returned. Huayna Capac and the governors ordered great gifts of clothing, sheep, tumblers of gold and silver, and women of the Cuzco nation to be sent to all the caciques and lords of all the land. As soon as the order was given, it was acted on. This was done to maintain the friendship and loyalty of the vassals and keep them happy always, which is what the governors did to keep the peace as long as they governed. Ten years after the death of Topa Inca Yupanque, the governors realized that Huayna Capac was capable and had the stature he needed; it was time for him to rule them alone. All the lords of Cuzco and the governors assembled in the house of Huayna Capac, and in his presence the governors all together resigned the post that Topa Inca Yupanque had given them. With this done, the governors who had served together with the lords of Cuzco swore obedience to the new lord and made a great sacrifice.

XLI

Wherein Huayna Capac sent these lords of the city of Cuzco to do an inspection of the four provinces and again gave the order as to what was to be done both in the city of Cuzco and in all the land.

Huayna Capac left the meeting in which the governors had resigned the post they had held up to that time. The next day the Inca ordered certain lords of Cuzco to go throughout all the land on an inspection tour of all its provinces to find out if the customary care was being taken throughout the land to obey and serve the city of Cuzco as they should. Since it was the maternal city of all the land, they were to make announcements as the Inca ordered and install stewards in the name of the Inca in all the provinces, ordering these stewards to be changed from one province to another. Having taken care of this matter, the Inca sent for the caciques who were in charge of maintaining the city buildings. After their arrival, the Inca went with them to look over the whole city and its buildings, bridges, and the work on the river, which seemed to him somewhat deteriorated by the weather and the rains. He ordered this work to be done again. With this finished, he went thought all the farmlands, those of both the Sun and the city people. He saw the work done there and the channels and ditches for irrigation. Whatever seemed to him broken down or ready to collapse, he had made over and strengthened.

After finishing this work, the Inca sent word to the lord in charge of the property of the Sun that on a certain day he should have his report ready and the service and property of the Sun together and the service of the idols, *mamaconas*, and *yanacona* youths in the service of the Sun and its temple. The Inca wanted to see and find out what method was used to perform this service and whether anything was neglected or done improperly. Then that lord steward of the Sun left and arranged for what the Inca had ordered. On the day already mentioned, when the Inca was to see it, he went to the temple of the Sun. As he arrived at the door, the Inca took off his shoes and with his head somewhat bowed, he made his show of respect to the Sun. Then in a brazier of gold before the image of the Sun, the Inca himself lighted a small bundle of firewood the servants of the Sun brought. This wood was carved, of four edges, and on it were painted birds, butterflies, and other things that he found pleasing. He set the fire and burned a lamb, sacrificing it to the Sun and beheading it alive first. He offered that blood from the lamb to the Sun.

After this he left there making his show of reverence to the Sun, going into the temple in a certain chamber where the steward of the Sun put him. At the same time, his cousin Yamque Yupanque and the two lords who had been governors went in with the Inca. No one else went in. That lord steward of the Sun explained to the Inca the things and wealth of the Sun that were under his care. Seeing how careful he was, the Inca did certain favors for him and sent for all of the eunuchs who were charged with serving and looking after the *mamacona* nuns of the Sun. The Inca ordered them to take him and the lords with him where the *mamaconas* were. The Inca went in, saw them, and asked for an account of the tumblers each one had and the garments that they kept with which to serve and dress the statue of the Sun. Seeing the great care they took in this, the Inca ordered them to be given certain gifts of gold and silver jewelry and garments for them to wear. Having seen that in everything there were ample provisions and care, the Inca told them not to be negligent in the service and sacrifices to the Sun. After this he left and increased the number of *mamaconas* beyond the number there had been and also increased the number of certain other *yanacona* youth who were servants of the Sun, as well as the service of gold and silver tumblers and many other provisions.

With this finished, he gave the order throughout the city and all the houses of all the lords and ladies who were in charge of the statues of past lords to have them ready, for he wanted to see them, do an inspection of them, and find out how the valuables of these statues were used and how the sacrifices were done for them. After doing and arranging this, the Inca started making a list of those who were in charge of administering the service for these statues. The Inca started to do an inspection of them, from the one of Manco Capac to the one of his father, Topa Inca Yupanque, who was the last lord who had died at that time. The first statue, that of Manco Capac, being ancient, was poor. It seemed to the Inca that, since that man had produced all the lords up to him, for that reason he should be honored. Then he doubled the service it had of *mamaconas, yanaconas*, garments, and tumblers of gold and silver.

The Inca ordered that, since he was looking into the things of these lords, the *mamaconas* and servants of each lord should sing his history and past deeds. Thus as he was inspecting the images and their houses, whenever he noticed anything lacking, he would provide it for them. When he reached the house of Inca Yupanque, hearing the song of his history, the great deeds and livestock of this lord, the Inca stayed for one month holding great feasts and making sacrifices to the image of Inca Yupanque, his grandfather. To this image he gave great gifts, a great number of *mamacona* maidens, as well as many *yanacona* youths. He ordered them to settle in the valleys near Cuzco and that from there to bring what they cultivated and raised to the house of Inca Yupanque. Thus they brought fruit, fresh maize, and birds. These were placed before the image of Inca Yupanque as if he were alive and with the same show of reverence as when he was alive. Moreover, he ordered the Soras, the Lucanas, and the Chancas of Andahuaylas put in the service of this image because they were the first provinces that this lord Inca Yupanque conquered and subjugated in his life.

After this the Inca went into the house where the image of his uncle, Yamque Yupanque, was kept. Then he heard his story in his song of praise. Remaining there ten days and with great reverence to him, the Inca made sacrifices, left provisions, and gave him great gifts. He gave him a certain *repartimiento* in Vilcas. From there he went into the house of his father, and in his story and song of praise he heard and learned of his great deeds and of the lord who was fond of subjugating lands and provinces. The Inca remained there one month making great sacrifices and doing service. Next he ordered all those in charge of *guacas* and idols and their property, sacrifices, and rites to give him an account of this, which he took down from them all. Seeing that all his things were good, including the order of his sacrifices, he did favors for the stewards of these *guacas* and idols. The Inca made his sacrifices and offered his father many gifts.

XLII

Wherein Huayna Capac went out twenty leagues from the city of Cuzco and did an inspection of the towns and provinces in that surrounding area, and the things that he did on this inspection tour.

After Huayna Capac had done his inspection of the city of Cuzco, as you heard in the last chapter, it seemed to him that he should go out to see the towns and provinces in the area within twenty leagues of the city. With this in mind, he decided that it would be well to take some things with him to give as gifts to the caciques of the towns and provinces that he saw. Then he ordered the preparation of the things that he was to take. With this done, he left the city, ordering those lords whom he was taking with him always to be sure to make his arrival known before he reached a certain town or province so that the people could come out to meet him on the road and to get him a garment like the ones used in that town. The custom in Cuzco was for everyone to wear their hair very short and cut off. The Inca did the same. Since sometimes they would go to a town where they wore long hair, the Inca ordered that, along with the garment, a hairpiece should also be brought for him to wear. Thus the arrival was awaited by the lords of the province where the Inca was to arrive with the garment and hairpiece in this way. If they wore their hair in braids, the Inca ordered that the hairpiece have braids.

When the Inca arrived, they offered him that garment. The Inca received it and put it on and also put on the hairpiece. He looked like a native of that province. Thus he entered the most important town, where they had in the plaza a certain seat which resembled a high platform and in the middle of the platform, a basin full of stones. On reaching the town, the Inca climbed up on that platform and sat there on his chair. From there he could see everyone in the plaza, and they could all see him. They brought out before him many lambs whose throats they slit in his presence, and they offered them to him. Then they poured out much *chicha* into that basin which was there for sacrifices. The Inca drank with them, and they with him. Then he came down from there, danced and sang with them, clasping their hands, joining to make a circle, and he ate with them.

After this, he gave them what he brought and did them favors. Then he ordered them to bring him an account of the number of widows and orphans.

He wanted them and also the poor people brought out before him. Then they reported what each one of these had, and they told him the truth, for no one dared tell him a lie. For the one reported to be poor, the Inca gave provisions from the storehouses that were in each town for this purpose on the orders of Inca Yupanque. Thus they did not live in want because the orphans as well as the widows and the rest were given enough to live on from then on without want.

After doing this, he left that province, and in the next one they found out that the Inca was traveling. When he reached the border he found that they had the accustomed garment ready there. The Inca took off the garment of the town he had just left and put on the other one. Thus he entered every province in the local attire, and the Inca celebrated with them as if they were his equals. To some he gave women, to others, livestock, to others, tumblers of gold and silver, and to others, valuable garments like the ones he wore as well as other things which they liked. In this way he traveled the country surrounding Cuzco for a year, until he came to the Valley of Yucay, which he liked, though it was unpopulated and there was nothing there but ravines and wild country. From there the Inca went to Cuzco.

XLIII

Wherein Huayna Capac erected the buildings of the Valley of Yucay and made the river flow on along a new course, and afterwards he went to do an inspection of Vilcas.

On returning from this inspection tour that we have just told you about, Huayna Capac ordered that one hundred thousand Indians, or as many as possible, come from all the land. Then his order was sent out to all the provinces, and within six months one hundred fifty thousand Indians assembled in the city of Cuzco. When the Inca saw them, he ordered the lords of Cuzco to go with those workers and take them to the Valley of Yucay. The Inca himself also went with them and started the work of improving the valley. He had the river moved along the side facing Cuzco, making it stronger and making a bed where it went. Along the path of the river the Inca had hills leveled. Thus he made the valley flat so that it could be planted and harvested. There he had houses built and lodging where he could go to enjoy himself. In this valley he gave farmlands to the lords of Cuzco, both to the living and to the dead lords whose statues were there. They sent their young *yanacona* servants to cultivate their vegetables and other things for their enjoyment. There Huayna Capac had many small towns of twenty, thirty, and fifty Indians built. In these towns he put many *mitimae* Indians from all the nations and provinces of the land. *Mitimae* means people, including them and their descendants, transplanted from their birthplace to reside permanently there where they were placed.

With this finished, the Inca went to the city of Cuzco. There, after having rested, he gave the order for an inspection of Vilcas and its province, to rest and enjoy himself. Thus he left and when he reached there he did his inspection of the towns and surrounding areas, doing much good for young and old alike as best he could. He was always affable and not pretentious, for which his fame spread throughout all the land. He was greatly loved by all for being so affable and frank with both old and young alike. He was just as attentive when some poor Indian came to speak to him as with his cacique. After having stayed for a period of one year in the province of Vilcas, which is forty leagues from Cuzco, he returned to Cuzco.

XLIV

Wherein Huayna Capac, after he returned from Vilcas, went to hunt wild game in the province of Collao [Collasuyo] and, on returning, went on the conquest of the Chachapoyas Indians after his mother died, and of the events that befell him.

After returning to the city of Cuzco from Vilcas, Huayna Capac remained in the city amusing himself with fiestas and celebrations. Learning that in the province of Collasuyo there was good hunting of deer, guanaco, and vicuña, which are mountain sheep, and other wild game animals, he left the city of Cuzco and enjoyed himself hunting in that province until he arrived in the town of Ayavire, which is thirty-five leagues from Cuzco. When he reached there, he hunted the wilderness areas of that town. From there he went to another neighboring town called Horuro. So he spent six months hunting in that province. At the end of that time, he returned to Cuzco, where he deposited a large quantity of game.

He spent a month there, but he did not wish to amuse himself that month because he found his mother, Mama Ocllo, ill. She died of that illness at the end of the month. He was so affected by her death that he did not leave his lodgings for a month, grieving. The love he felt for his mother increased.

From there he ordered the nobles of Cuzco to perform the accustomed mourning and sacrifices. When six months had passed since the death of this lady, Huayna Capac secretly called together the nobles of Cuzco and told them that he wanted to go and purchase coca and *agi* in the province of Chinchasuyo so that upon his return he might perform the fiesta of Purucaya for his mother.

You should know that, when Inca Yupanque created this fiesta to be observed after his time, he ordained that all that was used in it should be purchased. Someone should send out and purchase throughout all the land in the year following her death, since at the end of that year the fiesta must be performed and all would have been gathered together that was necessary. Nothing must be used in that fiesta that wasn't purchased. The reason was that, if it were purchased, it meant that the deceased would go to a good place where the Sun was, and if it were not purchased, he would not go to a good place.

From this came the custom that when some lord or lady died, they would then go to buy the provisions for the fiesta of Purucaya.

Therefore, Huayna Capac said that he wished to go and buy the provisions for the fiesta for his mother and that they should likewise send to Collao to purchase their share of the requirements. Since he did not know how far he had to go, he wanted to take one hundred thousand warriors with him as his personal guard.

He left as governors his first cousin Yamque Yupanque and his uncle Hilaquita, a younger son of the Inca Yupanque, and Topa Inca, his brother, until his return. The nobles told him that they would send to purchase provisions for the fiesta and that they would watch over the city until his return and that he should tell them how far he was going. He told them that he did not know, since he was buying those provisions, and he would return later.

So he left, taking with him one hundred thousand warriors and marching until he arrived in Labando in the province of the Chachapoyas. He waged war upon these for three years and after these three years he returned to Cuzco. He always maintained his mourning and sadness at the death of his mother. On both the going and the return he ordered that none of his men should dare paint his face red or any other color than black, which is what the Inca wore as a sign of mourning, under penalty that anyone doing this would have his nose cut off. Several young men were caught painting themselves red and their noses were cut off.

When he returned to Cuzco after this war with the Chachapoyas Indians, he did not want to enter in triumph. Rather, he entered lamenting and ordered that all his people enter in the same way, crying as he did for the death of his mother.

The day after he arrived, he ordered the lords and ladies of Cuzco to make preparations, since he wanted to begin the fiesta of Purucaya for his mother. Huayna Capac then began that fiesta and ordered some women to come out and, in imitation of his mother when she wished to spin something, spin fine gold with spindles and distaffs of gold. Other women would emerge with little golden pitchers and tumblers. They would pour *chicha* from the little golden pitchers into the tumblers and give it to the Inca. This would symbolize his mother giving drink to his father, Topa Inca Yupanque. Other women would emerge with small golden pots and gold spoons and with plates and small golden bowls. These were in remembrance of his mother's giving food to his father.

You have heard of the other ceremonies and sacrifices customarily performed in that fiesta. When these were completed, they made a statue of Mama

Ocllo and placed it in her house. They painted a moon in the place where the body was. This meant that she was going to where the Sun, her father, was and that she was another Moon.

These festivities lasted for two months from the day they began. Then Huayna Capac and the rest of the nobles, to wash away the mourning, went to a fountain constructed for the purpose by the Inca Yupanque. When this was done, the Inca went to Yucay to rest.

XLV

Wherein Huayna Capac left the city of Cuzco and did an inspection tour of his country during which he reached Cochabamba, and of the births of Atahualpa, Huascar, and Paulo, and of the many other things that he did and that took place during that time.

After Huayna Capac had rested in the Yucay Valley for the time he wished, he left there and went to Ayavire, where he spent three months hunting and in recreation. From there he returned to Cuzco for one month before leaving again. Upon his return he found that a son, Atahualpa, had been born.

He was very pleased with the birth and celebrated a solemn fiesta. Afterward, when Atahualpa reached his first birthday, his father ordered that his hair be cut so that the lords of Cuzco could perform this ceremony and offering because cutting the hair of such a recently born child was their custom.

So they cut his hair and performed a solemn ceremony. All the lords and ladies of Cuzco offered their gifts. In this hair cutting ceremony his father named him Atahualpa. You should know that they had a custom to celebrate a fiesta four days after the birth of a son. One year after the birth they celebrated another in which they cut his hair.

At that ritual hair cutting all his kin, including his mother and father and other lords and ladies who attend that fiesta, offer him large gold and silver jewels. Each one gives according to his ability. In this fiesta he is given a name he will use while he is a boy.

When he attains manhood and the age when he can be admitted into the ranks of the *orejon* nobility, they ordain him with the rites already described.[1] The child's ears are pierced for earplugs. There they give him the name by which he and his lineage, if he is from Cuzco, will be known. Thus this fiesta was held for Atahualpa.

After Huayna Capac rested in Cuzco, he decided to do an inspection of the province of Collasuyo. When this had been decided, he left the rearing of his son Atahualpa to his first cousin Yamque Yupanque, his uncle Hilaquita, and his brother Topa Inca. Naming these men as governors of the kingdom until his return, he left for his inspection of the province of Collao. He had heard it praised as a very flat land with many people and filled with livestock.

He left Cuzco and when he reached the province of Cacha, eighteen leagues from Cuzco, he saw the *guaca* shrine of Viracocha that we have described to you,[2] there in the midst of a plain. He asked why that *guaca* was in that plain. The people of the province told him of the miracle that Viracocha had performed there and of the fire that fell from the sky and burned the hill. When he heard this and saw the burned area, he decided that the remembrance of this event should be greater and ordered the erection of a large building near the burned hill.

This was done and it was so large that there is no larger building in all the land. The building is eighty feet wide and one hundred paces long.[3] The construction is as follows. Because of the great width there were no timbers long enough to reach across. In the middle of this building a wall was erected from one end to the other with many well-wrought doors and windows. From this middle wall to the outer wall of the building, there is a width of forty feet. In the middle of this width he built some round and tall pillars [one row on each side of the middle wall]. Across the tops of these pillars a lengthwise beam was mounted. This building was covered with a sloping roof because the cross timbers reached from the outer wall to that lengthwise beam on the pillars and, from the pillars, other beams reached to the top of the wall in the middle [which was higher than the outer walls].

Thus it was finished and they held fiestas and sacrifices there to Viracocha. They also built many other houses around this building, in which were placed many *mamaconas* whom he had gifted together with many *yanacona* servants and all their service.

When this was done, he left and continued his journey, visiting and inspecting the provinces, towns, and lands that each province contained. He marked the boundaries of all of them and gave order, reason, and good government to all. He went about doing good to everyone and bestowing great benefits and kindnesses, and he always did so.

Engaged in these works, he proceeded through the entire province of Collao until he reached the town of Cochabamba, which is one hundred and sixty leagues from the city of Cuzco. When he arrived, he saw and inspected the garrisons of soldiers that his father, Topa Inca Yupanque, had left in that province and its towns.

After seeing and learning of the security, he always provided for more according to what to him seemed best for them and in the best interests of preserving his land and kingdom.

When this was completed, he returned from there to Cuzco. When he arrived at a town called Tiaguanaco, eighty leagues from the city of Cuzco, a son named Paulo was born. He performed there a great celebration for the birth. When this was done, he left for Cuzco.

Arriving at a town named Huascar in a place they call Mohina, another son was born. This son was named Huascar, since he was born there in this town called Huascar. This Huascar was the one who had a dispute with Atahualpa.

XLVI

Wherein Huayna Capac was resting in the city of Cuzco, and of the birth of Cuxi Yupanque, his nephew, the son of Yamque Yupanque, his first cousin.

Huayna Capac arrived in Cuzco upon his return from Cochabamba and the inspection of Collao. On that journey he spent four years. He found his son Atahualpa already quite grown and at that time well-loved by all the lords of Cuzco.

When Huayna Capac returned from that journey he seemed somewhat aged. The lords of Cuzco knew that he was given to making inspections throughout the kingdom and to waging war. Since he was old, it was possible that he would die of some illness without being able to name a successor to carry on after his days were done.

They came to Huayna Capac all together and after greeting him with due respect, they offered him the gifts they brought. You should know that the Inca Yupanque had made a rule that no one, no matter how important a lord or lady they might be, could appear before the Inca with empty hands. Each time that they would approach him to perform the greeting and to see him or conduct some business with him, they would bear something in their hands to offer him, whether it be fruit, vegetables, flowers, birds, or some other thing. This is done to this very day among the nobility of the city of Cuzco.

When these men reached Huayna Capac, they said to him: "Unique lord, may you live long! As you know we are all mortal and someday your father the Sun will call you and will wish to take you with him. We have come to beg you that at your age now you name the son you desire to be your successor after your days."

He replied to them, asking what they had seen in him that caused them to come and say those things. Did they see him as old, as was his grandfather, the Inca Yupanque, whose hands and arms had trembled from age? He was worried about that and as soon as he saw fit, he would pick a ruler of his choice to govern them properly.

He had his son Atahualpa brought before him. He was a beautiful boy whom it greatly pleased him to see. He said that in facial features he resembled his own father, Topa Inca Yupanque.

After this he told the lords: "Why do you come to me with these words? Even if I did die outside of this city, as you say, do you not have here this boy and other sons of mine whom you could name after I am dead? If it so happened that I died outside the city and my sons were too young to govern you, are there no lords who would be able to rule the kingdom until you could name that son of mine you felt was the most capable to rule and to be the lord?"

The nobles refused to answer anything they had been asked. They finally told him that he had many sons born of noble ladies from the city of Cuzco and of his line.

Atahualpa was the son of a noble lady of Cuzco called Pallacoca of the lineage of Inca Yupanque. She was Huayna Capac's second cousin and the great-granddaughter of Inca Yupanque. Her father was called Llapcho and he was Inca Yupanque's grandson and a son of Yupanque's own son. There were Atahualpa's fathers and grandfathers. He was part and parcel of the family and lineage of Capacaillo, which they say was of the line of the Inca Yupanque.

Huascar was the son of a woman they called Ragua Ocllo of the nation of those of Hurin Cuzco and a distant relative of Inca Yupanque. She was related to many who were rulers from the group of Hurin Cuzco and likewise were the principal lords of the city. Similarly, Huayna Capac had many sons and daughters who were related in the way described above.

The lords observed that there was no man among these sons and that all were children. If the father were to die at that point, some confusion would occur, since no one of these had been named as ruler. During the selection process, some controversy could arise because the kinsmen of one would wish that son to be the lord, since they were related to him. This would also be the case with the others.

This situation could cause among them a fight to which they were already predisposed. To this end, they had come to Huayna Capac to ask him to name a ruler to take his place after his days were done. And he, not wishing to concede anything they asked, answered what you have heard.

At this point, a lord of Cuzco came forward and said to him: "Only king, you know that the wife of your first cousin, Yamque Yupanque, has given birth to a son." He was greatly pleased at this news and ordered that the woman and his recently born nephew be shut up for four days in a room where they would not see the Sun. After the four days passed, all the nobles of Cuzco would assemble in the plaza and hold a great celebration with sacrifices to the idols for the birth of this nephew.

So it was that the woman and child were confined and at the end of the four days Huayna Capac and Yamque Yupanque, his cousin and father of the boy, and all the rest of the nobles went out to the plaza. They performed their celebration with rejoicing and sacrifices. Huayna Capac spent ten days in this fiesta and granted this baby great gifts since he was his nephew.

A year after his birth the day for his hair cutting arrived. Huayna Capac and the rest of the nobles held a great celebration and they cut his hair. The hair cutting was done in this way: all the noble lords and ladies of Cuzco assembled and formed a circle, with the men seated in front and the women behind them. They brought out a bundle of straw recently obtained from the field and placed it on the ground in the middle of the circle formed by those nobles. They brought a blanket woven of fine wool and gold and placed it on the straw that lay in the middle.

The mother of the baby arrived, carrying the boy in her arms. She sat, holding the child, on the blanket. As she sat there, a golden knife was placed before her. Huayna Capac arose and approached the child. Taking the knife he cut a tuft of hair with it. When this was done, he offered the child a gold jewel. He also did him the honor of placing him in charge of the idol of the god of battle, a charge that he himself had held. This idol was called Caccha.

He also commanded that they call this boy by the name of Cuxi Yupanque now and after he was made an *orejon* warrior. Yupanque was the family name of the boy's great-grandfather and Cuxi means *ventura*, "happiness." The full name means Ventura Yupanque. Then the rest of the lords and ladies cut a bit of his hair and gave him their gifts. Thus he was completely shorn in the way you have heard. When this was done, the celebration ended.

XLVII

Wherein Huayna Capac remained in the city of Cuzco engaged in work for the benefit of the city, and of all the land, and of the birth of Doña Angelina Yupanque, and of the things that occurred during this time.

When Huayna Capac had rested and enjoyed himself with the ceremony of his nephew's hair cutting, it seemed that he should look over and again do an inspection of his city and the entire realm. Therefore he ordered eight lords to leave Cuzco. Four of them would be responsible for looking to see how well and in what way the governors and overseers placed by him throughout all the land and its provinces administered and governed them. They would also find out if these officials kept the commandments of his grandfather, the Inca Yupanque, for the well-being, preservation, and increase of the natives. And if those governors had done some injustice, they were to set it right and to mete out punishment.

The other four were to take an inventory from all the leaders and nobles in all the land of the animals they had in their charge, including those belonging to the Sun as well as those of the city of Cuzco, which were controlled by Huayna Capac and his cousin Yamque Yupanque.

When this was done, Huayna Capac engaged himself in looking to all the rest of the things and estates. In all of this he spent two years creating storehouses and commanding the repair of roads and the construction of a great many buildings and bridges.

Finally, the eight lords he had sent as judges and inspectors to all the realm returned. While they were giving their report to the Inca about what had happened to them and what they did, an *orejon* arrived and spoke to Yamque Yupanque, who was there near the Inca. He told him that his wife, Tocto Ocllo, had given birth to a daughter. Yamque Yupanque was pleased to hear it was a daughter.

Huayna Capac saw how the *orejon* lord had come and had spoken to Yamque Yupanque and he saw that he was happy. He asked him what had happened. Yamque Yupanque told him that the *orejon* had said that his wife had given birth to a daughter.

When Huayna Capac heard this he said: "That is my mother and I want her for myself." He immediately ordered preparations made because, as soon as the four days were over, he wished to celebrate a great fiesta for that girl. Thus it was done.

A year after her birth, Huayna Capac and the rest of the lords and ladies performed the fiesta for her. They cut her hair and offered her their gifts. Huayna Capac said at that fiesta that he wanted her for himself and that she would be his son Atahualpa's *piuiguarme*[1] meaning that she would be the legitimate and principal wife of his son Atahualpa.

He ordered that this niece of his be named Cuxirimay Ocllo. Ocllo means the same as *doña* [lady]; Cuxirimay[2] means "speaks good fortune." All together the names mean: "Lady who speaks good fortune." He commanded that she be Atahualpa's wife if she lived because on their father's side they were cousins; and on their mothers' side they were first cousins because their mothers were sisters. Huayna Capac named her "Speaks good fortune" because he intended to make a journey when the festivities were done.

This girl was Doña Angelina Yupanque, whom the Marquis Francisco Pizarro took for his own and with whom he had two sons. They were named Francisco Pizarro and Juan Pizarro. Juan Pizarro died but Francisco Pizarro remained.

Let us now return to our story. After having rested in Cuzco during these and other festivities and engaged in work for the good of his city and realm, Huayna Capac felt that he should go to the province of Quito to do an inspection of it and to see what it contained.

XLVIII

Wherein Huayna Capac left the city of Cuzco for the province of Quito, and of the wars that he fought and the conquests he won there, at the conclusion of which he died, and of the election that was made of the lords who were to follow him after his days.

Since Huayna Capac had already decided to go the province of Quito, he put his plan into action and, leaving the instructions he felt necessary to protect and preserve his city, he left it, taking with him fifty thousand warriors. He also took with him his son Atahualpa, who was at that time thirteen years old. When Huayna Capac left Cuzco to make this journey, he was sixty years old and he left his son Huascar in Cuzco with the rest of his sons and daughters. He took with him Huascar's mother, who was pregnant and gave birth on the road to a daughter whom they called Chuquihuipa.

Huayna Capac went through his provinces doing much good for all those he met. He was accustomed to doing this for the poor, the widows, and orphans. Even today they love him for the great familiarity that he displayed to all. They say that his solemn demeanor was the same with everyone, the most important and the least important. He answered all who brought him questions and pleased them. No one who came before him left unhappy.

Traveling through his provinces in the above-described way, he reached Tomebamba, the province of the Cañares, where Huayna Capac himself had been born. He spent a month there resting and then left for Quito, where he marshaled his forces.

After having rested for some time in the city of Quito and leaving it well guarded, he left in search of the province and the lake that they call Yaguarcocha, sending his son Atahualpa ahead with twenty thousand warriors.

When the men of Yaguarcocha learned that warriors were coming against them, they came out on the road to resist their enemies. When they met the men that Atahualpa was bringing ahead of the others, they offered battle. The men of Yaguarcocha defeated him and Atahualpa returned in flight.

When Huayna Capac learned that his son was retreating, he hurried his warriors, which at that point numbered more than one hundred thousand men. When he saw the soldiers that his son had taken fleeing, he tore his clothes, ripping them in front. He rebuked them, calling them cowards and saying that women were worth more than they. He asked from what they were fleeing; was it from unseen animals, since those from whom they fled were not men like they; why did they flee?

Saying these things to them, he forced them to return and ordered Atahualpa to go at their head with Huayna Capac himself. The men he had with him attacked their enemies with great energy. Since the enemies were spread out in pursuit of Atahualpa, Huayna Capac met them with great strength. He vanquished and captured them.

Pressing his victory, Huayna Capac himself entered a town which contained the house of that leader who was his enemy. He entered these houses intending to capture him. When he entered he found a pile of many blankets one on top of another. Thinking that the enemy leader he was chasing was hiding under them, he began with his hands to remove the blankets. He took down the mound of them and found a very small Indian dwarf underneath.

When Huayna Capac uncovered him, the dwarf said: "Who has uncovered me? I wanted to sleep!" When Huayna Capac heard these words and saw the height of the dwarf, he was so amused that finding the dwarf pleased him as much as the victory that they had achieved over their enemies.

Later he told all his men that since he had captured that dwarf in that battle all should regard him as his eldest son. Thus from that point on they all called the dwarf the eldest son of the Inca. And the dwarf called the children of the Inca brothers and sisters.

After having conquered and subjected these Indians of the province of Yaguarcocha, Huayna Capac returned to Quito with his victory. According to their custom, he entered the city triumphantly because of the victory he had achieved. He remained for six years in the city of Quito, resting and amusing himself, as he had in Cuzco.

At the end of those six years in Quito, he fell ill and the illness took his reason and understanding and gave him a skin irritation like leprosy that greatly weakened him. When the nobles saw him so far gone they came to him; it seemed to them that he had come a little to his senses and they asked him to name a lord since he was at the end of his days.

To them he replied that he named as lord his son Ninancuyochi, who was barely a month old and was in the province of the Cañares. Seeing that he had named such a baby, they understood that he was not in his right mind and they left him and went out. They sent for the baby Ninancuyochi, whom he had named as lord.

The next day they returned and entered and asked him again whom he named and left as the ruler. He answered that he named as lord Atahualpa his son, not remembering that the day before he had named the above-mentioned baby. The nobles went immediately to the lodgings of Atahualpa, whom they told was now lord, and they gave him their respects as such. He told them that he had no wish to be the ruler even though his father had named him. The next day the nobles returned to Huayna Capac and in view of the fact that Atahualpa did not wish to be ruler, without telling him anything of what happened the day before, they asked him to name a lord and he told them it would be Huascar his son.

The nobles immediately placed Ragua Ocllo, the mother of Huascar, and her daughter Chuquihuipa in a room so that they might fast according to their usage and custom when some noble was named and the woman who was to be his principal wife.

Two nobles of Cuzco who were brothers of this Ragua Ocllo, called Xauxigualpa and Amurimachi, learned that Huascar had been named Inca and that Atahualpa did not wish to be. They sent the news to the nobles who were in Cuzco and to Huascar via the post service.

Huascar retired for a period of fasting after he heard the news in Cuzco. Here we will leave him and return to Huayna Capac, who was in his final days. After having named Huascar as ruler in the way we have described, he died in four days. After he died, the messengers who had gone for the baby who had been named as ruler by Huayna Capac returned. The baby had died the same day they arrived of the same leprous disease as his father.

A short time after these messengers arrived, others sent by the leaders of Tumbes arrived to see Huayna Capac. These messengers gave news of how some white and bearded men had arrived at the port of Tumbes. They came in a *ganbo*,[1] which means a ship. It was like a building, so large that no one would get sick on it. They themselves had entered it and found them to be men who did no evil to anyone. They gave them those things that the messengers brought. These were *chaquira*,[2] diamonds, combs, knives, and things from bartering, all of which the leaders sent to Huayna Capac. They found that he was dead and had died at that moment.

You should know that they were speaking about the Marquis Francisco Pizarro and that was when he arrived the first time at Tumbes with a single ship and fifteen or twenty men and with the sailors and all with him. From there they went up to Payta, from whence they returned to ask his majesty for the governorship [title of governor]. Here we leave him and return to our story and to the death of Huayna Capac.

When he died, the nobles who were with him had him opened and took out all his entrails, preparing him so that no damage would be done to him and without breaking any bone. They prepared and dried him in the Sun and the air. After he was dried and cured, they dressed him in costly clothes and placed h.m on an ornate litter well adorned with feathers and gold.

When the body was prepared, they sent it to Cuzco. All the rest of the nobles who were there went with it, including the mother of Huascar and her daughter. Atahualpa remained in Quito with one hundred nobles from the city of Cuzco, all kinsmen of his.

Part Two

Here begins the story of the two sons of Huayna Capac who were named Atahualpa and Huascar, and of the wars and disputes that occurred between the two brothers regarding which of the two would be lord and rule. That dispute was caused by the fact that neither was legitimate because Huayna Capac had no male child with his principal wife. Rather, he had a daughter who was named Asarpay. At the time her father died, Asarpay was quite elderly and, since Huayna Capac had no male issue with his principal wife, discord arose between these two brothers; since each one laid that claim to the state, they were mutually suspicious. What most worried the leaders of Cuzco was what would happen to them after Huayna Capac's death, as you have heard in Part I, chapter XLVI of Huayna Capac's history.

I

Wherein Huascar was named lord, and of those things that he did after he became lord, and how the body of Huayna Capac came to the city of Cuzco, and what was done with it.

As the time of fasting had passed in preparation for the investiture of Huascar with the *borla* fringe and office of *capac*, the lords of Cuzco who were there at that time went to Huascar's quarters. After paying their respects, as was due such a lord, they placed the *borla* fringe on his head and named him Topa Cuxigualpa. And the lords who were present called him the only lord.

When he became lord, he went out into the square and declared that henceforth the lands of coca and maize production that had been owned by the Sun and the bodies of the dead rulers, including those of his father, Huayna Capac, would be taken from them. All these he took for himself, saying that neither the Sun nor the dead nor his father who was now dead ate. Since they did not eat, he had need of their lands. This action horrified the lords. And they were saddened because they had permitted him to become lord.

He was quite given to all the vices and most of all to drink. Very few days found him not drunk. While drunk he would do a thousand foolish things. Since he was a young man and very promiscuous, if he fancied one of the wives of the lords who were there with him, he would have her placed in the nearest room and would sleep with her. If any of the lords would come and attempt to stop him, he would have him killed later. Thus no one dared to speak or tell him not to do anything because in this he was a youth not given to accepting advice on anything, no matter how difficult it might be.

His clothing was of costly cloth and woven with gold and silver, and the footwear the same. He ordered that no one was to be married in all the land and that all the young girls of his time be placed together in certain houses in all the land.

When the body of his father was arriving, he saw his mother there and he went up to her and greeted her with these words: "Whore, how is your boyfriend Atahualpa? How is he with whom you take your pleasure and he with you? When you leave him there, wretch, it is so that he might rebel and name himself lord in Quito."

To these words his mother did not reply but went sobbing with those noble men and women who were mourning the death and accompanying the body of Huayna Capac, whose body entered the city of Cuzco on its litter.

Before the litter marched all those leaders whom he had captured and subjugated in Quito. Among them was a dwarf called Chimbo Sancto, who had been captured by Huayna Capac in one of those towns of the Yaguarcocha when he entered the house of the leader of Yaguarcocha. All these prisoners and the dwarf entered Cuzco as prisoners of war and prisoners of Huayna Capac and marched before his litter. The lords and ladies of Cuzco, *ñacas* and *pallas*, and the princes and princesses saw the dwarf and observed him, dressed in that red outfit with fringes even on his feet, preceding the litter.

They knew he was a prisoner and, recognizing him as such, all of them, men and women, with a great shriek and cry attacked the dwarf with the intention of tearing him to pieces. Amid their yells and sobbing they called him a miserable and luckless wretch who had not enjoyed the luck of being a man, how could the Sun have taken our lord and father who so loved us and did us so much good and given us in his place a being as vile as you.

When the men carrying and accompanying the litter saw the attack of the women of Cuzco with the intention of killing the dwarf, they placed themselves in front and stopped it, and when the women saw that the dwarf had been taken from them, they shouted amid their tears and cried of the great valor and the goodness of this good man, Huayna Capac.

Later the men placed his body in Caxana, Huayna Capac's own house. This done, they ordered that the crimes and the defeat of the prisoners who had preceded the litter be proclaimed and those of the dwarf with them, and then they were thrown in prison, where it was the custom for the tigers and lions and bears and serpents to eat them.

They remained in the prison three days and the animals did not harm them at all. Later they were removed and were rendered great honors by the men of Cuzco and were sent to populate the Valley of Yucay. The dwarf was given women so that he might have descendants. The dwarf had some children and among them were two dwarf daughters and the rest were men of good stature.

The lords of Cuzco placed Huayna Capac's body in a burial site in the Valley of Yucay. Huayna Capac himself constructed the grave near the river and below it during his lifetime. A large sum of gold and silver and great riches were buried with the body. The Spanish never have been able to find this treasure nor has anyone else ever found the body.

When this had been done, the lords of Cuzco celebrated the fiesta of

Purucaya with great solemnity. They took the fingernail clippings and the hair cuttings that were cut from Huayna Capac during his lifetime and made many statues, which they adored as divine objects. When they finished making the statues, they placed them on the benches with feathers and well-worked gold. Here we finish speaking of this good man and we will speak of his two sons, who concern us here.

II

Wherein is told how Atahualpa in Quito and the nobles who were with him celebrated as many rites of mourning and sacrifices in the memory of the death of his father [as Huascar], and how he sent certain tribute to Huascar as a sign of servitude and vassalage, and what Huascar did with it and to the messengers who carried it.

Since Atahualpa remained in Quito with the rest of his noble kinsmen, when he saw that his father's body was taken to Cuzco, he ordered the nobles who remained with him to prepare themselves, as he wished to conduct the accustomed mourning and sacrifices in his father's memory and wished to celebrate the fiesta of Purucaya. He also wanted to prepare statues of the hair and nail clippings that were left over and some of his father's flesh, which he had retained when the body was preserved in order to take it to Cuzco.

The nobles arranged things and as all was prepared, Atahualpa conducted the fiestas and the mourning of Purucaya. Lastly, he prepared two statues of his father's relics. One was to accompany him when he journeyed anywhere and the other was to be left in the city of Quito in his father's house where he had died. Therefore, he placed a statue in this house and had it served and sacrificed to as if it were alive. There this statue was worshiped and respected as if it were living.

After doing this, he ordered that twenty very elegant men's suits be woven with fine hammered gold. When they were completed, he ordered a Cañare noble of those who were with him to take them to Cuzco and give them to his brother Huascar. He was to tell him that his brother and vassal Atahualpa sent that clothing as a tribute from the city of Quito to his lord. He asked Huascar to send him his measurements so that he might prepare clothing that would fit and that he should send his orders regarding what he should do in Quito.

Thus commanded, this messenger left Quito and took with him ten Cañare

Indians laden with the clothing and some other Indians also from the Quito nation. When this noble arrived in Cuzco, he found Huascar drinking in the plaza. He was drunk from the *chicha*, as he usually was.

When the messenger arrived, he paid his respects in this way: he raised up his clasped hands to the sun and said to the Sun: "Oh, Sun, oh, Day, give light." Then he bowed his head with some burden borne on his back. Barefoot and with his eyes on the ground he paid his respects to the Inca by raising his hands and saying: "Oh, unique king, lover of the poor and son of the Sun." He did this because this was their accustomed way to pay respect to the lord when they appeared before him.

He placed the clothing before him, saying that his brother and vassal Atahualpa sent that clothing to him as tribute from Quito and that he should order what he wanted done in his name and that he should send his measurements so that clothing could be prepared in Quito and sent to him. When Huascar, being drunk on the *chicha*, saw the clothing before him, he rose and took some of the clothes in his hands and went over to the nobles who were present, those who had brought the statue and body of Huayna Capac from Quito, and threw the clothing he was carrying in their faces, saying: "Take this clothing that Atahualpa sends for you and not for me so that you may put it on and enjoy it. For it he asks you to rebel and make him Inca." He then took others in his hands and ripped them to shreds. He ordered the nobles who had been with him when his father was in Quito to rise and to trample and tear them up, and they rose and trampled and tore up the clothing.

His mother, Ragua Ocllo, stepped forward then and told him that he should not do that and that Atahualpa sent it to him as the true vassal he was, to his lord and brother. And that proceeding in this fashion he would alienate the people rather than attract them to his friendship. To this Huascar replied: "Just look at the whore who left her lover in Quito and who now sees her possessions and returns for them." And his mother replied: "Atahualpa is good and your brother wants to do you some service and to please you. And you goad him to do that which he does not intend to do. I advise you not to do that but, rather, that you receive his things well and with goodwill, since he only wishes to serve you. If he wanted to be king he would only do so if you were no longer here, if something happened to you. Therefore, don't complain because I advise you what is best for you."

Angry at these words, Huascar took one of the tunics of those that had been torn and threw it in his mother's face and forced her to leave, insulting her and saying slanderous words to her. He later had the leader who had brought him the clothing beheaded. When he was dead and had been beheaded in his presence, he ordered that he be flayed. When this was done, he ordered the skin to be prepared and made into a war drum with which he intended to amuse himself when he raised an army against Atahualpa.

He ordered the rest of the Indians who had accompanied that gentleman to be cruelly bound in his presence with rope and tortured. After the torture, he ordered them to be sent as *mitimaes* to Vilcacunga, which is seven leagues from the city of Cuzco.

He then commanded that no one consider him a member of the group of Hanan Cuzco, because Atahualpa was of Hanan Cuzco, descended from the lineage of Inca Yupanque, and he no longer wished to be of that lineage. Although he was indeed of that lineage, henceforth he would say that he was not but, rather, from Hurin Cuzco, because those of Huascar's hometown where he was born were of the Hurin[1] Cuzco lineage and that he was also. Henceforth he wished them to recognize him as from Hurin Cuzco because he intended to kill Atahualpa and all his kinsmen and lineage that was of Hanan Cuzco and form a new lineage of Hurin Cuzco.

III

Wherein Huascar leaves Cuzco to build the town of Calca, and how he raised an army and sent it against Atahualpa.

After ordering that no one recognize him as being of the house of Hanan Cuzco but, rather, of that of Hurin Cuzco, he commanded that a large group of men be assembled with whom he left Cuzco and went to a place that today is called Calca. Once there, he built and settled a town and named it Calca.

When he had completed the greater part of the construction, it seemed to him that it was time to raise an army against Atahualpa. Therefore, he ordered Atahualpa's kinsmen to be brought, among whom were found Cuxi Yupanque, brother of Angelina Yupanque, and the children of Yamque Yupanque. When all had been assembled before him, Huascar rose and told them: "I have news that your kinsman Atahualpa is rising in rebellion and wants to make himself king." This was a lie and the product of hatred and the imagination of a man who often had poor judgment. "I wish to send all of you, his kinsman, to kill him. Bring me his head because I wish to drink from the skull. If you do this, I will hold you as friends and will grant you favors. If you do not bring it to me, none of you should return, for if you do I will tear you all to pieces."

To this they replied that they were glad to obey and they requested that a captain be named to lead them. He named Cuxi Yupanque as captain, who then left with that group that numbered some three hundred nobles of Cuzco.

Huascar commanded that Cuxi Yupanque go to Jaquijahuana and there await further orders. Cuxi Yupanque left the town of Calca, taking with him the statue and battle idol that Huayna Capac had placed in his charge since childhood, as you have heard in the first part of this history.[1] This idol was called Caccha Inca.

Huascar remained among the nobles with whom he was friendly and had them bring him the war drum that he had ordered made of the skin of the leader and messenger sent by Atahualpa. When it had been brought, he ordered a festival and rejoicing, during which he had a good time having someone play the war drum of the skin of the messenger. When this celebration in Calca was done, Huascar named one of those he had with him named Hango as captain-general for the war that was beginning and over the army he was sending. He then ordered six thousand soldiers outfitted. He commanded that the rest of the men be raised from the provinces of Jauja, Tarma, Bonbon, Huanuco, Huailas, and Cajamarca in order to take ten thousand warriors to Quito.

With these went Cuxi Yupanque and all those kinsmen of Atahualpa's lineage so that they might march and quickly arrive in Quito to capture and kill Atahualpa and return with his head. Meanwhile, Atahualpa remained in Quito, unaware of these passions or of the army that was being raised against him.

IV

Wherein is described how Hango left Huascar with his men, and how he gave battle to Atahualpa, during the course of which battle Atahualpa was victorious and Hango was killed, and the rest of what happened to him.

Hango left the town of Calca with the soldiers that Huascar had given him and joined Cuxi Yupanque in Jaquijahuana. The two then marched together and thus arrived at the province of Jauja, where Hango began to gather his soldiers. From there he sent messengers to the aforementioned provinces all the way to Cajamarca. Through these messengers he informed the caciques of these provinces that he was gathering warriors, giving them the number he required and all the food and supplies needed for the army, and that they should prepare those that he would take from their towns.

This news spread in such a way that it arrived at Quito because the Cañares learned of it and told Atahualpa and the nobles who were with him. When he learned the truth of this and what had happened and that his messenger had been killed and made into a war drum, he was astounded. He ordered the nobles gathered for consultation. In that meeting the order was given that named Quizquiz, Chalcochima, Unanchullo, Rumiñagui, Yucuragualpa, and Urcoguaranga captains for the duration of the war. Leaving this meeting, they arranged for those soldiers who were at the garrisons guarding Quito to be assembled. Atahualpa ordered that the greatest number of soldiers possible be raised from the provinces of Quito. Sixty thousand warriors joined those from the garrison.

When the Cañares learned that Atahualpa had already raised an army, they sent messengers to Hango and Cuxi Yupanque informing them that Atahualpa had an army and was rapidly raising more and that they should hurry before he had more men than they could oppose.

When Hango and Cuxi Yupanque learned of this, they hurried their march as much as they could. As quickly as they could, they arrived at Tomebamba, where they found the Cañares all prepared with their arms to fight for Hango and to go against Atahualpa.

When Atahualpa learned that the Cañares were against him, he took a glass of *chicha* in his hands and, pouring it on the ground, swore an oath. He said that his blood would be spilled on the ground like that *chicha* if, after conquering Hango, he did not give a punishment to these Cañares that would be remembered.

When Atahualpa learned that Hango was in the province of the Cañares, he ordered Chalcochima and Quizquiz to take warriors from the city of Quito. When they were outside town, Atahualpa himself, with the rest of his captains, left with the warriors. He left some nobles in the city of Quito as a guard with the appropriate soldiers.

When the Cañares learned that Atahualpa had left Quito, they advised Hango and Cuxi Yupanque to also go in search of Atahualpa. Thus they left and the armies met on a field near the town called Mochacaxa. There they did battle, during which Hango was killed and Cuxi Yupanque was captured.

When Atahualpa recognized that Cuxi Yupanque was his cousin, he embraced him and paid him many honors and asked about his sister, Doña Angelina. Cuxi Yupanque told him that she was being brought there, that she would not be left with the enemy. Atahualpa later sent some of his officers and soldiers to the site where the enemy had their baggage to find Cuxirimay Ocllo, who was Doña Angelina, and to bring her. He ordered them to be careful not to harm her in any way. His captains went and found her crying with all her *mamaconas*, thinking that her brother Cuxi Yupanque had been killed in the fight.

When those captains arrived and paid their respects and told her how her brother Cuxi Yupanque was alive and that they came on behalf of her brother and of Atahualpa, she went with them. When she arrived where Atahualpa was, she paid her respects to Atahualpa, who embraced her. At that time she was ten years old. Afterward she went and sat behind her brother Cuxi Yupanque. After this battle Cuxi Yupanque was made Atahualpa's captain-general and second-in-command. This battle had been so fierce and cruel that no one escaped except the Cañares and one of Hango's captains named Aguapante, who was an *orejon* from Cuzco. He escaped with the Cañares and went with them to their country. He made them all leave that province ahead of him. He sent a message to his master, Huascar, informing him of the defeat and the death of Hango and how Atahualpa had declared his enmity. He told of how Atahualpa had triumphed in that battle and had so utterly destroyed his enemies that none were left alive. As a memorial of this battle, he had ordered the bodies of the dead to be taken and piled on the descent from the Hampato summit. He made two piles of bodies. One was of the native-born *orejones* who had left Cuzco and the other of commoners whom Hango had gathered from the provinces.

When this was done, Atahualpa ordered Chalcochima and Quizquiz to follow the retreating army, and when they got to the land of the Cañares, they were to capture anyone they found there, including men, women, and children of all ages, and to send them under guard to him wherever he was. After this was commanded, Atahualpa returned to the city of Quito with few men because he had given the majority to Chalcochima and Quizquiz, whom he had sent in pursuit of his enemies.

V

Wherein Atahualpa returns to Quito, and a certain province rebelled, and an army was raised and sent against it. During this journey he ordered a royal residence built in the province of Carangue. He then punished the Cañares and sent messengers to Chalcochima and Quizquiz.

When Atahualpa's captains had left the place where this first battle took place to pursue his enemies, Atahualpa and Cuxi Yupanque left for Quito. When they arrived, Atahualpa learned how the Pastos Indians in the province of Rata had rebelled. Hearing word of this new rebellion, he sent Cuxi Yupanque to raise an army. The officers were in the garrisons and they gathered six thousand warriors. Atahualpa left Quito with these and sent Cuxi Yupanque ahead with two thousand men. He ordered him to await him in Carangue, the land and province of the Cayambes.

Cuxi Yupanque arrived and awaited Atahualpa, who arrived there in a few days. On his arrival, Atahualpa found all the nobles of that province assembled. He told them that he wished to build a royal residence there. He ordered them to make all preparations for this construction.

The leaders told him that if he laid the plans they would build it. Then he himself with his own hands and with Cuxi Yupanque and the rest of the nobles took up a cord and measured and traced out the house. When he had finished this, he ordered Unanchullo to carefully oversee the work and make sure that the construction was done properly.

Unanchullo commanded the nobles of that province to lay the foundations and begin the construction. So it was done. And Atahualpa ordered that the statue of his father, Huayna Capac, which he always took with him, remain in that building.

While he was engaged in these activities in the town of Carangue, some *orejon* warriors arrived who brought with them all the Cañare prisoners that Chalcochima and Quizquiz had been able to capture. They found Atahualpa there because he had been greatly delayed by the duties he had in ordering and providing for the construction. Those who do not know the truth say that Atahualpa was born in that house. It will later be explained why Atahualpa built it there.

When the Cañares, whom he greatly wished to punish, had arrived, he ordered the principal leaders among them separated from their people and placed apart. When they had been separated, one of them, an important leader of the Cañares named Rocosaca, who had but one eye, was placed in a prison with another leader from Cuzco who was a *mitimae* in Quito named Atoc. He had committed great treason by carrying messages to the Cañares regarding what Atahualpa did in Quito so that the Cañares and Huascar and his captains might be warned of what he was about in Quito.

While Atoc was a prisoner, Atahualpa learned from him of his treason and that of the Cañares; he became even more enraged against the Cañares. When these two were placed in prison, he had three of the principal leaders from those he had separated brought before him. When they appeared, he ordered that their hearts be pulled out while they were alive. He said he wanted to see the color of the hearts of evil men.

When the hearts had been removed, Atahualpa cried in a loud voice that if the Indian subjects of these three leaders had good hearts and wished him well, they would arise and eat the evil hearts of their leaders. They then arose and cut the three hearts of their leaders into pieces and distributed them among all of them. The pieces were very small so that all might have some. Then they ate them, raw as they were, in front of Atahualpa. He was greatly pleased by the quickness with which they rose and ate the hearts of their leaders.

When this was done, Atahualpa commanded that some Quillaycingas Indians be brought there so that they might eat the bodies and flesh of the three dead leaders in the presence of the Cañares. The Quillaycingas Indians, who eat human flesh, came before Atahualpa and all the Cañares, built a great bonfire, took the dead bodies, cut them in pieces, and placed them upon their roasting racks. They brought a small kettle full of hot peppers, salt and water and with some straw brooms brushed the roasting meat, wetting it with the hot pepper and salt mixture.

When the meat was done, a great quantity of toasted and cooked corn was brought. The Quillaycingas all together sat down in a great circle and in the presence of all the Cañares ate the three leaders.

When the Cañares saw this, they made a show of demonstrating great pleasure so that Atahualpa would understand that those three leaders were criminals and enemies as far as they were concerned. And they took pleasure in seeing the punishment that was exacted. This done, Atahualpa commanded that these Cañares be placed in the province of Huambo, which adjoins that of the Rata, as *mitimaes* and there live and serve him. These Cañares were then taken and placed in the province of the Huambo as *mitimaes*.

When this was done, he sent Chalcochima and Quizquiz a messenger to warn them to be careful in their enterprise. They should not neglect anything, but should carefully attend to each detail. Especially they should not pardon anyone, no matter what his station, any crime that he should commit. Neither should they allow any crimes by the people in the province that bordered those of the rebels and enemies. They should exact great punishments so that they might be feared and thus in the war they would be victorious over their enemies.

If any province came to them in peace, then those leaders of that province should be well received and loved in such a way that both the punishment and the good treatment would be broadcast to all.

The warriors who would be given them and taken from these provinces that welcomed them in peace would be placed in the vanguard in the most danger-ous place during the battles that would be fought. In this way, they and their officers could see if the obedience they had given was true or given with reservation.

Nor should they trust these for their personal guard but, rather, entrust that duty to the warriors they had brought from Quito and that he had given them. By the post service or by whatever method was deemed best, they should always keep him informed of all that happened on their expedition.

In this way they informed him that those in the province of the Pastos had rebelled. He was going there with an army to attack them. When he had punished them, he would try to advance and see the peoples not seen or conquered.

When this messenger had been dispatched, he ordered the departure from Carangue and ordered Unanchullo to remain in that province and, as quickly as possible, to build the house, because on his return from that conquest he intended to celebrate the fasts and fiestas and receive the royal *borla* fringe of state there.

He now left the house with the walls already one *estado* high. He ordered Unanchullo to tend to the prisoners named Atoc and Rocosaca in such a way that they not escape and ordered their food to be restricted so that they would die of hunger and thirst in that prison. And the food given them should be vile because they were renegade officers. This was done and they died in prison.

When Atahualpa had finished giving orders regarding the construction of the house to Unanchullo and to the rest of the nobles, he left to punish the Pastos Indians.

VI

Wherein Atahualpa punished the Pastos Indians, and continued his journey, and passed through the mountains called Cinnamon. On his return, he conquered another province and from there he returned to Carangue and was invested with the borla *fringe of state. From there he went to Quito, where he received news from his captains; he went to help them.*

When Atahualpa had left the province of Carangue in search of the Pastos Indians, they learned of it. Since they knew that Atahualpa was coming for them, they prepared their weapons and other requirements and fortified their strongholds. When they were thus prepared and warned, Atahualpa arrived with his host and encircled them.

Thus besieged, the Pastos Indians defended themselves well, and when Atahualpa found that he could not breach their fortifications, he commanded one night that large fires be lighted in his camp and that the soldiers act as if they were carefully guarding it. When he knew the location of the enemy camp, Atahualpa ordered his warriors, guided by spies, to march. Leaving the fires lighted in his camp, they left.

That night at the hour of the dawn watch, they fell upon the camp and the Pastos warriors, who were well fortified. They were caught off-guard. Because of the fires they had seen, they did not expect an attack that night. Atahualpa and his army fell upon them at the hour you have heard and overran the fortifications. Such was the uproar and terror caused by the suddenness of the raid that they disbanded and the leaders were captured and killed that night, along with a large number of the soldiers.

That morning Atahualpa commanded that all those still alive be brought before him. When they were thus assembled, he ordered them to take heart and he pardoned them for their uprising. Henceforth they would correct their former behavior and serve him.

He commanded that those leaders who had been killed the night before in the battle be eaten by the Quillaycingas in front of their people, and it was thus done, as had been done with the Cañares before.

After resting some time and giving appropriate orders regarding the service that those of the province of the Pastos should render him in the future, he left and entered the mountains called Cinnamon.

Many of his soldiers died of hunger in these mountains. Finding no people there to subjugate and seeing that the farther he entered the more soldiers died and were lost, he decided to return.

When he had left the mountains, he gave orders for his soldiers to march toward the province called Toquiri. When he arrived, he attacked and subjugated it, leaving there the detachment that seemed needed. He returned to the province of Carangue, where he found that Unanchullo had already finished the construction of the house and walls, with the exception of the roof. Atahualpa had the roof made and, once it was roofed and completely finished, he entered it.

Here he, Cuxirimay Ocllo, and Cuxi Yupanque fasted. When they had finished, Cuxi Yupanque, speaking for Huayna Capac's statue, which was there, took the *borla* fringe of state that had been readied and placed it on Atahualpa's head in the presence of a great number of lords both from Cuzco and from all those towns and provinces of Quito. *how old was she?*

When this was done, Cuxirimay Ocllo, dressed and prepared in the required manner of the previous lords you have already heard in this account, was brought forward. According to their usage and custom, Cuxi Yupanque and the rest of his kinsmen and relatives there assembled begged Atahualpa to see fit to receive her as his *piuiguarme mamanguarme,*[1] which means "principal wife." The Inca Atahualpa answered that he accepted her as such. When this was done, they began their sacrifices and fiestas. The accustomed duration of this fiesta was two months.

This was the house in which those who have been misinformed say that Atahualpa was born. But he was born in Cuzco and from there went to Quito with his father, as this account has related.

When he had remained in this house these two months after receiving the *borla* fringe of state there, he decided that Chalcochima and Quizquiz should be sent for. They were making war on Huascar's captains. When he decided this, the Inca Atahualpa commanded that an *orejon* lord of Cuzco named Quiço should remain in that province of Carangue as the governor to watch over those houses. When this was done, he left there and returned to Quito.

When he arrived he had news that his captains Quizquiz and Chalcochima were now in the provinces of Bonbon and Tarma. With this information and finding himself lord, he ordered that a statue be prepared of his own nail clippings and hair, which was a representation of his person. He ordered that this statue be called Incap Guauquin,[2] which means the brother of the Inca.

Once this statue was completed, he had it placed on a litter and charged one of his servants named Chima with guarding and watching over it. Giving this statue many other young men as servants, he ordered that it be taken and carried on its litter by the messengers to where his captains Chalcochima and Quizquiz were so that the peoples of the subjugated provinces could render obedience to that statue in place of his person. Thus this statue was carried and given to the captains, who received it and were very pleased with it. They performed many and great sacrifices and served and respected this statue as if the very person of Atahualpa were there.

One should understand that the constitution of this statue in this way was ordained by the Inca Yupanque. When he sent some captains or his sons on a conquest, they carried one of these statues through the towns and provinces they passed. The statue was received and served by the natives of these towns and provinces as if it were the Inca in person.

Let us now return to our story. As Atahualpa was invested with the *borla* fringe of state, Cuxi Yupanque and the lords there assembled gave him the name Caccha Pachacuti Inca Yupangue Inca. Caccha[3] is the name of the idol of battles and in giving him this name they were saying that he imitated the idol in warfare. Pachacuti means change of the world, or cataclysm. Inca Yupanque was for his great-grandfather Inca Yupanque. The last "Inca" meant king. This is the name they gave him when they invested him with the fringe.

Since he was in Quito, it seemed to him that he was too far from his captains to give them assistance if something happened to them. Cuxi Yupanque ordered his warriors to get ready, since he wished to leave in four days. Cuxi Yupanque gave the order in the camp and to the warriors and arranged all necessary food and provisions. After four days, Atahualpa commanded that an *orejon* lord from Cuzco, an uncle of his named Cuxitopa Yupanque, rule Quito and its provinces. When the orders had been given regarding what should be done in Quito and its provinces, he left in search of his captains. He ordered his camp and his army to march to the province of the Cañares, where his captains had gone.

We will leave them there and speak of Huascar and the provisions that he gave from Cuzco and of Chalcochima and Quizquiz, who left Quito to make war on Huascar's soldiers.

VII

Which concerns how Aguapante was captured in the first battle launched by Atahualpa and then escaped from this captivity and informed Huascar of his defeat, and how Aguapante gathered an army and awaited Atahualpa's captains. Atahualpa's captains defeated Aguapante and Huascar sent him assistance. Other nobles from the city of Cuzco arrived, sent by Huascar, all of whom were defeated by Atahualpa's captains, until they reached the province of Jauja.

The first of Huascar's armies sent from Cuzco, with their captains called Hango, Atoc, Aguapante, and Cuxi Yupanque, were defeated. Hango and Atoc were killed in this first battle and Cuxi Yupanque was captured and Aguapante escaped. Since Cuxi Yupanque was Atahualpa's cousin, he was well received and honored. Aguapante later was imprisoned in the Cañare region and placed under guard in a house. At nightfall Aguapante dug through the foundations of the house and escaped that night.

After he escaped he was able to gather some of the lords of the Cañares and when they assembled he sent a messenger to Huascar to inform him that they had been defeated and to tell him of the captains' deaths. He also told him how things were in the land of the Cañares and asked him to send a relief column because the Cañares had declared themselves enemies of Atahualpa and Huascar's servants.

When this news reached Huascar, he ordered fifteen thousand warriors raised. With them he sent one of his brothers named Guanca Auqui to accompany that army to Tomebamba, where they would find Aguapante. When they arrived there, he was to gather the Cañares and then go to Quito and give battle to Atahualpa, who was *auca*,[1] which means "enemy" and also "traitor." In order to further censure Atahualpa, Huascar commanded his brother always to refer to him in the provinces they passed as Atahualpa *auca*.

Guanca Auqui with his fifteen thousand men left and arrived in the land of the Cañares, where he found Aguapante, who had already assembled as many Cañares as he could. Joined now with Guanca Auqui, he was very pleased and later the two of them gave orders to leave for Quito to do battle with Atahualpa.

While they were thus engaged, Chalcochima and Quizquiz arrived and encircled Guanca Auqui and Aguapante with their army. At the dawn watch, they fell upon Guanca Auqui and his army and defeated them. They captured some of the Cañare lords and sent them immediately to Atahualpa. Guanca Auqui, Huascar's brother, escaped, fleeing with Aguapante and some five thousand men of those they had brought from Cuzco together with some of the chiefs of the Cañares, among them Ucoxicha.

When he found himself defeated, Guanca Auqui sent a messenger to Huascar and asked him for assistance. When Huascar learned of his brother's defeat, he sent him a captain named Llasca with thirty thousand warriors. This captain Llasca found Guanca Auqui in Vilcachaca, which is part of Cajamarca.

Guanca Auqui and his men were retreating from Chalcochima, who was catching up with them. Whenever Guanca Auqui found a stronghold, he stopped and waited. But this gained him little. When Chalcochima and Quizquiz arrived, they defeated him and continued to skirmish with him and, even though the Indian persisted, they never wavered in their pursuit. Thus Guanca Auqui awaited the arrival of help in any stronghold he was able to find. Thinking that with the arrival of the relief brought by Llasca, he would be able to do something, he thus awaited Chalcochima at the bridge called Vilcachaca.

Llasca arrived full of valor and pride and with the intention of destroying Chalcochima and Quizquiz. He then awaited the battle with Chalcochima. When Chalcochima arrived, they began their battle and, since Llasca was full of daring, he went ahead and was cut to pieces. When the leaders of that province saw that Huascar's forces were not faring as well as Atahualpa's, they and their men decided to pledge obedience to Chalcochima, and so they did. Guanca Auqui escaped, as before.

Finding himself once more defeated and with Llasca dead, Guanca Auqui sent a message to Huascar to inform him that they had been defeated and Llasca had been killed in battle. He asked that men be sent because he was retreating and awaiting help.

When Huascar learned this, he sent another captain, named Coriatao, a native of Mayo, who took another thirty thousand men and found Guanca

Auqui at the Bonbon bridge. Since Chalcochima thought little of Guanca Auqui's defensive forces, he sent one of his captains with just a few men to that bridge to catch Guanca Auqui. Quizquiz came at his leisure with the rest of the soldiers and leaders of all those provinces that had made peace.

Chalcochima's captain, unaware that Coriatao had reached Guanca Auqui with fresh troops, fell upon Guanca Auqui. Coriatao killed Chalcochima's captain and destroyed and killed his whole army. When Chalcochima and Quizquiz learned of this defeat of their man, they sent an officer with a detachment of ten thousand warriors. He was to take a certain road and fall upon Guanca Auqui from behind. This was done by the captain.

Chalcochima and Quizquiz pretended to retreat because of the defeat of their captain, and it seemed to Guanca Auqui and Coriatao that they had emerged victorious, so they gave pursuit.

When Chalcochima was told by his captain that Guanca Auqui had been outflanked, both Chalcochima and Quizquiz turned and fell upon Guanca Auqui and gave battle and defeated him on a field called Chancha. Guanca Auqui, Coriatao, and Aguapante escaped and went to Jauja.

Chalcochima and Quizquiz, both exhausted by the battle, decided to stay there to rest for a few days. Even though they emerged victorious from the battle of Chancha, they had lost many of their men. After some time spent in regrouping, Chalcochima and Quizquiz left in search of Guanca Auqui, who had escaped with the rest of his officers and gone to the province of Jauja.

When Guanca Auqui arrived, the nobles of Jauja gave them a good reception and later ordered that as many warriors as possible be assembled. They gathered Indians from Guanca, Yauyo, and Angara and from the rest of the provinces. In all that region, forty thousand warriors joined the survivors of the Chancha battle. When Guanca Auqui found himself with that army, he ordered all his baggage and service personnel to remain in Jauja. He and his warriors, thinking they would take them unawares and weakened by the battle of Chancha, hastily left in search of Chalcochima and Quizquiz.

VIII

Wherein Guanca Auqui left Jauja and ran into his enemies and gave battle; he was defeated by Chalcochima, and Quizquiz, who entered Jauja. Another battle took place on the rise to Picoy, and they went from there to Vilcas.

Guanca Auqui had left the province of Jauja in search of his enemies and met Chalcochima and Quizquiz, who had come seeking him with the same thought of finding him unprepared. They met two leagues from the Tambo de Jauja[1] on the road that drops into the valley. The battle was as bitter and hard-fought as the others they had.

Guanca Aunqui and the rest of his captains escaped and fled, as was their custom, and after they made good their escape, they went to the bridge of Angoyaco, which is twelve leagues from the site of the battle. While they were fleeing, Chalcochima ordered that a captain and some men pursue them until reaching the Angoyaco bridge, which they were to destroy. Then they were to remain there on guard until Chalcochima and Quizquiz could leave Jauja.

This officer left in pursuit of Guanca Auqui until he forced him to cross the Angoyaco bridge. When he had crossed, Chalcochima's captain cut the bridge and remained there, as he had been ordered. Chalcochima and Quizquiz came to Jauja and there captured many caciques from Yauyo and Guanca and inflicted great punishment on them.

Chalcochima ordered that the principal leaders captured there be placed in a prison until he returned from Cuzco. He then intended to make war drums from the skin of their bellies, since they were quite fat. Thus he would amuse himself. Many other leaders pledged obedience to Chalcochima.

Chalcochima and Quizquiz remained in that province for some time and regrouped their army, which had been decimated and exhausted by that battle. When the army was regrouped and had the necessary provisions, they decided to leave in search of their enemies, who had crossed the Angoyaco bridge, as we have said.

Guanca Auqui sent a messenger to Huascar to inform him of their continuing defeat and asked him to send aid. When Huascar received this news, he gathered thirty thousand warriors and placed them under the command of one of his cousins, the son of Topa Inca, who was named Quilisca Auqui. He left with this army and found Guanca Auqui in Picoy, which is two leagues from the Angoyaco bridge.

Quilisca Auqui arrived, thinking that Chalcochima would cross the bridge and he could take him on the slope to Picoy. There he waited. Since Chalcochima and Quizquiz already knew of the arrival of this Quilisca Auqui and that he was waiting for them on the slope of Picoy, they decided to bypass him by crossing the Rumichaca bridge and to take the high ground.

Thus they outflanked them and took the heights and fell on both Guanca Auqui and Quilisca Auqui, who were defeated. Since Guanca Auqui was already quite practiced, he escaped with his soldiers. However, since Quilisca Auqui was but newly arrived, he was captured. He was an important leader and the blood cousin of Atahualpa and thus was neither slain nor insulted. He was sent to Atahualpa in Quito as a prisoner in bondage.

Since Atahualpa was on the road, they met. When Atahualpa saw Quilisca Auqui, he received him well and sent him as lord to Quito to govern there in his place together with his other kinsmen that he had left there before, as you have heard.

Let us now return to our account. Guanca Auqui, after his defeat in Picoy, fled with his soldiers to the province of Andahuaylas, which is thirty leagues from Cuzco, where Huascar was. When he crossed the Vilcas bridge, he burned it and from there sent a message to Huascar. He asked for aid.

When Huascar learned of Quilisca Auqui's defeat and his capture, he was saddened. He was so affected by it that he commanded his men to assemble and he had a grand drunken celebration that lasted for two days. When it was over, he ordered that all the leaders of Cuzco prepare themselves and he assembled fifty thousand men, and when they were assembled, he commanded the men and the lords to leave Cuzco. The Cuzco lords who left to aid Guanca Auqui were Inca Roca, Atao Inca Yupanque, and Chui Yupanque and many others whom I will not name in the interest of brevity.

They arrived at Andahuaylas, where they found Guanca Auqui, Aguapante, Atecayqui, Guacço, and Soto, a Chui lord. All of them amounted to sixty thousand warriors, not counting the Cuzco lords and caciques, who numbered more that three hundred. There they awaited Chalcochima and Quizquiz, who they had heard were coming.

Quizquiz and Chalcochima had already arrived at Vilcas, which is fourteen leagues from where the others were. They knew of the assembly at Andahuaylas in support of Huascar and that the bridge had been burned. Chalcochima and Quizquiz commanded that all their baggage be left there in Vilcas and that the entire camp leave on a forced march over the Omapampa wilderness, which leads to Andahuaylas, where the other camp was. Thus Chalcochima and Quizquiz left in pursuit of their enemies, where we will leave both of them until another time. Let us now speak of the Inca Atahualpa.

IX

Wherein Inca Atahualpa left the city of Quito to find and assist his captains, and of the great cruelties and destruction he wrought upon the peoples of the towns and provinces through which he passed until he arrived in the province of Guambo.

Atahualpa left Quito with what he felt were enough warriors for the enterprise and, celebrating and enjoying himself as he went, traveled through all those towns and provinces until he arrived in Tomebamba in the province of the Cañares. In this province he found no Indian, neither man nor woman, since, as we have said, Chalcochima and Quizquiiz had visited upon them a great punishment; it was there that Guanca Auqui had been defeated. He had sent as many of them as he could to Atahualpa, and those who remained fled and hid themselves as best they could to protect their lives and sustain themselves.

Thus when Atahualpa arrived, he found no one, neither young nor old, nor did he find any food, and he passed on from there. Those who have been misinformed say that when Atahualpa arrived, the Cañares came out to receive him. And in front of everyone came the small children with bouquets in their hands to welcome him. And that Atahualpa had all the children killed who had come with flowers.

When I learned of this, I spent much time with all the oldest nobles and gentlemen of Cuzco, the majority of whom had been with Atahualpa and his father, Huayna Capac, during their time in Quito. They said that this never happened. They also said that Atahualpa was never a prisoner of anyone, was not captured by the Cañares, nor did they tear his ear, and he did not escape from his captivity by breaking through the foundation of a house where he was held. The one who was a prisoner in the Cañare region was Aguapante, Huascar's captain.

When I asked them who tore Atahualpa's ear, they said it happened when he was a young man when his father, Huayna Capac, was alive. He was frolicking with a young lady and tried to force her to sleep with him. She reached up and grabbed his ear with her hand and tore it. He bandaged it with some cloth and when his father saw him with the bandage he asked what had happened. Atahualpa replied that a boil had appeared on the ear and had burst.

His father was angry and upbraided him, saying that if the boil had been so bad that it left his ear torn, why did he not advise the physicians and surgeons who were employed to cure sicknesses and wounds.[1]

They told me that Atahualpa was not captured and that he was never a prisoner or imprisoned during any of his days as an adult. The child Atahualpa stayed with his father in Quito. He was always with his father during the Quito war. Until his father died, he never left him. And after Huayna Capac died, Atahualpa remained in Quito with the nobles from Cuzco and never left Quito until he left to give battle to Hango, Huascar's first officer. Let us now return to our account.

They say that as he passed through the province of the Cañares, there were some captured Indians and nobles whom he greatly wished to have. He ordered them returned to the site of the battle that had been fought and he had them buried alive in a fenced place. They were to be planted, as were trees and plants in a garden. He said that he planted that garden with people of evil hearts. He wished to see if they would produce their evil fruit and works. He ordered that this garden be called Collana Chacara,[2] "excellent sown field." They say that all this was done to honor the memory of that battle.

When this was done, he commanded his men and their camp to take the same road taken by Chalcochima and Quizquiz. On this road from the province of Hoyaci to that of Palta, he suffered great hunger because he took with him many people and Chalcochima and Quizquiz had been inflicting such destruction on the people of the provinces through which they passed that everything was consumed in fire and blood.

When Atahualpa arrived in the land of Palta, he found them in rebellion and his warriors spread out over the countryside, and he found some food. From there they proceeded to a town and province called Çoçora, where Atahualpa found the people of Palta and those of the surrounding provinces had joined and taken refuge on a mountain near there, since they did not wish to surrender to or serve him.

When he arrived and learned of that assemblage and that all those from the provinces he and his men had passed through with such suffering were together there, he was greatly pleased. He ordered his warriors to surround that mountain in such a way that no one could escape. This they did and they captured all those they could lay hands on.

There were so many prisoners that they could not count them all. After they were taken, Atahualpa ordered them killed, and so the warriors killed them all, not sparing the life of young or old. Atahualpa commanded that pregnant women be opened alive and that the babies be taken from their wombs, and it was done.

News of the cruel massacre spread through all the region. When this massacre was made public in all the surrounding provinces, it inspired great fear in the caciques and lords of these areas. When he left that province of Çoçora, he marched forty leagues, which is the distance to the province of Guambo. In these forty leagues he did nothing but kill the natives of these areas. However, he ordered that the women taken in war not be killed but, rather, that the captains and caciques with him should take them for wives. The rest of the women would be given to his men. Thus, they were all well provided with women.

Their arrival at the province of Guambo was preceded by news of the destruction and massacre they were creating. Because of the great fear that all the land had, those of the province of Guambo and all the surrounding areas came out in peace. When Atahualpa saw they came in peace after all he had wrought, he received them with honor and relaxed there with them for five days.

X

*Wherein Atahualpa left the province of Guambo
and went to punish some yunga Indians who
had rebelled, and how he received news
of Chalcochima and Quizquiz, and of the
things that happened from the province
of Guambo to Cajamarca.*

After Atahualpa had rested in the province of Guambo for five days, he received news that the yungas[1] of the Çaña Valley were in rebellion. When he heard this, he ordered his camp to descend into that valley. When he arrived, he captured many people of the valley and exacted great punishments and massacres. When this was done, he returned to the mountains and came out at Cajamarca.

Here the nobles and leaders of Cajamarca received him in peace, and he honored them greatly and spent a year with them. At the end of the year, a messenger sent by Chalcochima arrived. From him he learned that things were going very well and nothing blocked his advance. The most valiant [enemy] they had found in their battles was a Cañare named Ucoxicha, who always told them that he was saddened because Atahualpa did not go there so that the two of them could engage in personal combat. Chalcochima wanted to know what to do with him if he were captured.

When Atahualpa learned of this Cañare, he smiled and said, "He must be brave and he wanted to fight me; do not kill him but take him alive and show him respect, since he has been such a good man and always resolutely fights against me." Ucoxicha was later captured by Chalcochima and he was granted the respect that Atahualpa had ordered. Later, this Ucoxicha was a great friend of the Christians.

But let us return to the mission of Chalcochima's messenger, who told Atahualpa that Chalcochima sent him to request weapons, arrows, lances, and slings from the munitions that he had with him because those he had taken from Quito had now been used up. Upon hearing this, Atahualpa became very angry and had the messenger not been such an important lord and kinsman of his, he would have had him killed. Atahualpa said: "What is Chalcochima trying to say in asking me for arms, labeling me as a weak man of little worth while he makes war." The messenger told him: "Unique lord, I tell you that in Chancha, Guanca Auqui gave us such a fight with the help that came to him from Cuzco that we found ourselves in great difficulty. This was because we arrived from the prior battles with our weapons used up." To this Atahualpa replied: "You were the victor in these battles. If we were victorious, why didn't the pillaging of the enemy provide arms?" The messenger said: "Unique lord, they were always found broken to pieces because there has been no battle between our enemies and ourselves that has not been highly contested in which we might have found arms that weren't broken."

Atahualpa was very attentive to and angry at everything the messenger told him. When Cuxi Yupanque saw how angry the Inca was, to avoid having the messenger harmed, he ordered him to leave the Inca's presence. Later, Atahualpa had Cuxi Yupanque, his captain-general, prepare his warriors, since he wished to leave for Cuzco. And he ordered twenty Indians, great and able carriers, brought to him. He wanted to send them ahead, loaded with strong and thick ropes, under an important lord. When they arrived where Chalcochima was, they were to tie him with those ropes and bring him as a prisoner under strong restraint. Quizquiz was to continue with the warriors.

Cuxi Yupanque picked out an *orejon* lord and ordered him to find twenty Indians, load them with ropes, appear before the Inca, and see if he ordered anything else. When the lord was prepared, he appeared before Atahualpa, who then ordered him to leave and to capture Chalcochima for insulting him. He was to bring him back as a prisoner bound by those ropes he carried.

This lord departed and received news that Chalcochima was leaving Vilcas, which is forty leagues from Cuzco; the lord understood he would find Chalcochima in a battle with Huascar. The lord would not press the matter and did not bother to hurry. He arrived in the province of Jauja and there awaited the arrival of Atahualpa or his order on that matter. Atahualpa had ordered preparations made for departure, since he already had his warriors prepared with the necessary provisions and had already spent a year there in Cajamarca. He thus decided to leave and ordered his men to march directly to the province of Guamachuco, where we will leave him for now.

Let us now speak of Chalcochima and Quizquiz, whom we left in Vilcas on the road in search of the lords of Cuzco who had gathered in Andahuaylas.

XI

Which explains how Chalcochima and Quizquiz left Tambo de Vilcas to fight the lords who gathered in Andahuaylas on behalf of Huascar, and how they destroyed Huascar's men, and how, before the battle, Huascar's men split their forces and some of them went to burn the baggage that Chalcochima and Quizquiz had left in Vilcas.

When Chalcochima and Quizquiz learned that the bridge at Vilcas had been burned and that those assembled at Cuzco were in Andahuaylas, they decided to go there from Vilcas through the Soras wilderness and come out at that of the Chancas of Andahuaylas. They left taking this road, as you have heard.

When Huascar's captains learned that their enemies had left Vilcas, they agreed to see what they could do and decided that Inca Roca and Guanca Auqui would depart with forty thousand men through the wilderness of the Chancas, a place called Chaquipampa where Chalcochima was coming. And they would give him battle there.

Atecayque and Aguapante, the one who escaped from prison there in the Cañare region of Quito by boring a hole through a wall, and Soto, a Chui lord, and Guacço, all these would leave for Vilcas with twenty thousand warriors and burn all the men and baggage that Chalcochima and Quizquiz had left there. Then they would proceed by forced march on the road that Chalcochima and Quizquiz had taken and fall on their rear guard.

Inca Roca and Guanca Auqui would attack the vanguard and thus they would destroy their enemies. Since these lords of Cuzco found their plan to be a good one, Inca Roca and Guanca Auqui left to meet Chalcochima. Atecayque, Aguapante, and the rest of the lords departed with their warriors on the royal road straight to Tambo de Vilcas.

On arriving in Vilcas, they found the baggage of Chalcochima and Quizquiz, who had left there quickly to prevent so many men from assembling in Andahuaylas who could threaten them. When Atecayque and the rest arrived, they killed all they found, sick and healthy and women, and stole the best of what they found. The rest was burned.

Chalcochima and Quizquiz had hurried their march through the Sora wilderness so much that they were in the middle of Chancas territory, about to come out at Andahuaylas, when they met Inca Roca and Guanca Auqui. Since night had fallen when they met, they stopped and all agreed to postpone the battle until the next day.

When Chalcochima saw that the night was almost gone and that it would soon be daylight, very quietly he roused his troops, after having been fully informed by spies of Inca Roca's camp. With a certain battle cry, he fell on Inca Roca's camp. Inca Roca and his men were caught off guard, not expecting that attack, since they had agreed to fight the next day; the surprise and terror were so great when Chalcochima fell on them that they were defeated. Inca Roca and Guanca Auqui fled and didn't stop until they had crossed the bridge at Apurimac, which they then cut.

At this time, Atecayque and the rest at Vilcas wanted to leave and fall on Chalcochima's rear guard, as they had agreed. The news of Inca Roca and Guanca Auqui's defeat and how they had escaped the battle by fleeing reached them. When they learned of this, it seemed that it would be better to flee and not to wait. So they turned from Vilcas with the loot and spoils they had and entered the mountains that stretch above Andahuaylas and Curamba. Thus they came out at the Apurimac bridge, where they found Inca Roca and Guanca Auqui. They were awaiting a certain messenger they had sent to Huascar for aid. While they were waiting, the messenger they had sent to Cuzco returned and told them that Huascar Inca was engaged in a grand and drunken party and that the messenger had found him drunk and had left him and returned.

XII

Wherein Huascar's captain Aguapante left the bridge at Apurimac for Cuzco to carry to Huascar the news of what had happened, and of the great lamentations that occurred in the city when this was known, and of how Huascar ordered the assembly of his warriors.

Since Aguapante and the rest of the lords were told in Apurimac that Huascar, their lord, was celebrating in the city of Cuzco during that period in which they were fighting and losing and that the messenger they had sent to Huascar had been unable to inform him, they decided that Aguapante would go to inform their lord of what had happened. Aguapante left there for Cuzco and found that Huascar still had not arisen, even though it was near noon; the night before he had gone to bed late because of the party he had attended.

Since Aguapante arrived and found Huascar sleeping, he entered directly into his bedroom, where he was sleeping, and woke him and said: "Unique lord, this is not the time to sleep nor to go to another party but, rather to battle Chalcochima and Quizquiz, who have defeated us in the wilderness of Andahuaylas."

When Husacar saw Aguapante, whom he had not seen for a long time, he was very pleased and believed what he told him. He ordered him to sound the alarm in the city and to gather the warriors. Aguapante then went out into the plaza and in a loud voice told the nobles who were there how the enemies and the soldiers of the auca Atahualpa were already at the bridge which is ten leagues from the city of Cuzco. They should leave the city with their wives and children and with all the rest of the people they could muster to resist them if they wished to remain the lords of Cuzco. If they did not, they and their children would be enslaved and killed. Then the nobles of Cuzco arose and very quickly gathered the warriors. This news terrified both the city and the surrounding areas so much that they did not understand nor did they know what to do.

During the great celebrations and drunken revels in which Huascar had kept them occupied until that moment, they had been quite ignorant of the things of war. When the *ñacas*,[1] which means "matrons," heard this news, the cries that they raised in the city all that day were so great that nothing else got done. Huascar even came out and tried to calm the women. He told them they were there to tear their enemies to pieces, no matter how many there were. If the enemies had reached a point only ten leagues from the city, it was because he had so ordered his captains to let them approach that close because he himself, with his own hands, wished to tear them all apart.

The women saw that Huascar was but a young man who, since childhood, had more experience in drinking than in the things of war and that he had few men. They knew of the power of the enemy and above all that Huascar was not given to accepting advice or counsel and that he was governed only by his will. These *ñacas* paid no attention to what Huascar or the other lords told them but, rather, increased their lamentations and cries.

Next, Huascar commanded that they find out how many warriors there were in the city. They found there were thirty thousand men. Huascar ordered the lords of Cuzco to leave with these men and go to the Valley of Jaquijahuana.

XIII

Wherein Huascar leaves Cuzco and instructs his warriors in the way that they should fight, and of the other things that Chalcochima and Quizquiz did after they fought the battle of Andahuaylas, and how Huascar left with his men in search of his enemies and crossed the bridge at Cotabamba and captured one of the captains of Chalcochima and Quizquiz who was coming to find out about Huascar. And of how Huascar found out from that captain about his enemies, and how he came looking for them.

Huascar had ordered the warriors to leave the city and go to the Valley of Jaquijahuana. When they were out of the city, he himself left the city together with the rest of the nobles who had remained with him. With these he marched to a position above the Cotabamba bridge. When he arrived there, he sent Aguapante to call the rest of the nobles and warriors who were at the Apurimac bridge. These were the ones who had escaped the battle in the wilderness of Andahuaylas, gone to Tambo de Vilcas, and burned the baggage of Chalcochima and Quizquiz. All together, some thirty thousand men assembled in Apurimac with whom Atecayque and the rest of the lords came to where Huascar was waiting for them at the Cotabamba bridge.

We must here leave them and recount what Quizquiz and Chalcochima did. When they broke off the battle with Inca Roca in the Andahuaylas wilderness, they went from there to Tambo de Andahuaylas and sent for the men and baggage they had left in Vilcas.

These men who went for the baggage arrived in Vilcas and found nothing because Atecayque had burned everything and killed all the Indian men and women he found there, the warriors that Chalcochima had left to defend the provisions, and the service personnel. No one escaped. He found some women Chalcochima and Quizquiz made pregnant. These he had opened and the babies taken from their wombs and hanged from the arms of their mothers. The mothers he then had hanged from high trees.

When the Indians who had gone for the baggage of Chalcochima and Quizquiz returned, they reported what Atecayque had done. This caused great anger, and Chalcochima swore by the Sun and the Earth not to leave Cuzco until he had captured Atecayque and exacted revenge. He would administer a punishment that would be famous.

They ordered their warriors to rise and set out from there to Curahuasi where they say the people are Lucanas. When they arrived there, they sent out their spies to find Huascar and his men and to learn whether Huascar had left Cuzco and where he was coming from and what he was doing. The spies returned and reported to Chalcochima that Huascar had left Cuzco and that the captains who were at Apurimac by Huascar's orders had gone to join him. They said that Huascar was proceeding by the Cotabamba road and that he had already crossed the bridge at Cotabamba.

When Chalcochima received this news of Huascar, he ordered a captain with five hundred warriors to leave Curahuaci and proceed by the Cotabamba road to find out whether Huascar was coming in search of him or waiting for him in Cotabamba. The captain left Curahuaci and went on his assigned task down the Cotabamba road.

Chalcochima and Quizquiz prepared their army and arrayed their squadrons according to their custom. They dispatched another captain with another five hundred men and ordered two hundred of them to serve permanently as sentinels one league from camp. The remaining three hundred would do the same duty as sentinels one-half league from camp. When this had been ordered and carried out, Chalcochima and Quizquiz left Curahuaci with their well-ordered and positioned warriors and, preceded always by those two captains with five hundred men apiece, arrayed as you have heard. Let us now leave them here and speak of Huascar.

Huascar was already at the Cotabamba bridge with Atecayque and the thirty thousand men from Apurimac. He inspected his army and found that he had sixty thousand warriors. He divided them into three squadrons this way. He ordered the thirty thousand men that Atecayque, Aguapante, Ataurimache, and Guanca Auqui had brought to separate themselves from those who had come from Cuzco with him. From these thirty thousand men he formed four captaincies, which he gave to those captains who had brought them. He appointed Atecayque general over these thirty thousand men and he commanded that one squadron be formed of these men.

He then ordered that twenty-five thousand men from those who had left Cuzco with him be separated. When this was done, he formed four captaincies of them. One he gave to a lord of Cuzco called Chui Yupanque, another to a lord of Cuzco called Atao Yupanque. Another went to lord named Guaçço and the last he gave to a native lord of Charcas called Soto. Over these he named Chui Yupanque general and ordered him to form a separate squadron.

When this was completed, he formed two captaincies from the five thousand men who remained. One he gave to one of his brothers, Topa Atao, and the other to one of his cousins, Inca Roca. These he ordered to separate themselves, with their men, from the others.

When they had done so, he called the generals and the rest of the captains together and told them: "You should know that I intend to go forward always with these five thousand men that my brother Topa Atao and my cousin Inca Roca have. And I want you with the rest of the army and squadrons to come after me. Since I will be ahead, the enemy will see that I have few men and when they see me thus, they will attack me with all their fury, thinking that I don't have more men. They will abandon discipline in their attack and be scattered.

"When I see them approach in the way I have told you, I will stop and order the canopy of my litter lowered. When you see that the canopy has been lowered and has been removed from my litter, you will all come together and with good discipline and as quickly as you can. Thus we will attack our enemies and destroy them."

When he had ordered and carried this out, he commanded his brother and his cousin to set out with their five thousand men and cross the bridge. They should stop and wait on the plains above. Then he ordered the rest to begin their march and cross the bridge at Cotabamba.

When this had all been ordered, he commanded his bearers who carried him on a litter, natives of the province of Lucana, to march. Thus he left, leading his army, and crossed the bridge. He arrived on the heights where his brother, who had already crossed, awaited with the five thousand. When they were all present, he sent his runners and spies and men to find the enemy camp. When this had been done, he ordered his men who were all with him to march and take the heights of Cotabamba. So they marched and he with his five thousand men was always ahead.

When they were on the high ground, the runners returned and told him how one of Chalcochima's captains approached with very few men. This was the man that Chalcochima and Quizquiz had sent, to find out about Huascar, from Curahuasi in the province of Lucana.

When Huascar learned of this captain who approached, he commanded his army to remain there until he sent them orders. He left there with his five thousand men when the sun was setting. While he was on the march night fell. When it was fully night, a spy came to him and told him that Chalcochima's captain was but half a league away and coming fast. When he heard this news, he ordered his brother to march with the men.

They went very quietly, all marching with discipline. They met Chalcochima's captain, and Huascar was so astute with his five thousand men that he captured him and the five hundred. None of them escaped whom Huascar did not kill. From this captain, Huascar learned that Chalcochima and Quizquiz were coming from a league and a half away.

XIV

Which concerns how Huascar, after having killed the captain of Quizquiz and Chalcochima, continued with the five thousand men he had without waiting for his army. He intended to capture and kill Quizquiz and Chalcochima, but they captured him and killed one of his brothers.

When Huascar found himself victorious after having captured and killed that captain of Chalcochima and Quizquiz and his five hundred men, whom he had taken unawares, he thought he could do the same with Quizquiz and Chalcochima, since they were so close. When he learned all he wanted from the captured captain, he ordered him killed and commanded that no one return to give the news of that victory to those captains who were behind with fifty-five thousand men.

He ordered the march to continue and, a quarter of a league from where he had killed the captain, he encountered the two hundred men the other captain had ahead as Chalcochima's sentinels and field guard. Since they were so few, he captured them all except for four or five who escaped. They went to their captain who was half a league from there with three hundred men as a camp guard.

When this captain learned how Huascar was coming and that he had killed the sentinels placed as forward guard, he quietly alerted his men and arranged them in order. They circled the camp and he left them like that with orders that no one was to leave to give the news to Chalcochima because he wanted to go and see who these men were. He thought that perhaps it might be his companion, the other captain, who was returning from learning of Huascar's activities. Perhaps he had met those sentinels and thought they were Huascar's. Alarmed, he had returned with that news.

This captain left after having advised his men. Very carefully he went to find out who these soldiers were. When he got there, he recognized that they were Huascar's, since there were more than four thousand men and warriors, and his companion didn't have more than five hundred.

He saw that there was a litter in their rear guard with a canopy and in it something the size of a man. He heard Huascar ask his bearers what time it was and they answered: "Unique lord, it will soon be daylight." When Chalcochima's captain heard them say "Unique lord," he knew it was truly Huascar and that his companion, the captain who had been in the forward position, was dead with his two hundred Indians.

Not waiting any longer, he returned to his men, who had remained as cautious and careful as he had left them. He took them from there and with all speed and as quickly as he could, he went to where Chalcochima and Quizquiz had their camp. They were a league away.

When they reached the sentinels, they gave the password, approached them, and told them in passing what had happened. They then proceeded to where Chalcochima and Quizquiz were and gave them the news and a report on Huascar's coming. He told of the men he had and what he had seen and the words that he heard. When he heard him ask what time it was, he knew it was Huascar.

Chalcochima and Quizquiz roused their men and formed two squadrons, one of six thousand men and the other of one hundred thousand whom they took from Quito and the provinces along the road, that had come out in a show of peace. He placed the best and most daring men from Quito in the squadron of the six thousand men. These were well armed with quilted cotton tunics, helmets, battle-axes, clubs, halberds, *macanas*,[1] lances, and shields.

When these men were ready, their captains ordered them to position themselves in the middle of the road by which Huascar was approaching. They told these six thousand men that when Huascar arrived and attacked them, they should make a show of resistance and then flee down the road together as if in a rout.

Chalcochima told Quizquiz to take as many men as he needed and to position himself where the six thousand fleeing men had to pass. They should come forward, join them, and turn on Huascar. Then his men should use the war cry "Quizquiz, Quizquiz."

Chalcochima would place himself behind a certain hill there with the rest of the army and, when he saw that Huascar had run past in the chase, he, using as password "Chalcochima, Chalcochima," would come out with his army. In this way, they would have Huascar in their hands with all of his men. None would escape.

Everything was done as you have heard and the captain of the sentinels who had come to warn them before they returned and once again met Huascar returned again to warn Chalcochima and told him that Huascar was but an eighth league away and his men were very silent and well ordered and, attempting to avoid any sentinels, approached through ravines, clumps of weeds, and rock outcroppings. They were moving as fast as they could. This news placed the army of Chalcochima and Quizquiz on its highest alert.

At one hour before dawn, Huascar arrived and fell on the six thousand men who were thus prepared in the middle of the road. These were pretending to be asleep. When Huascar attacked, they all arose and pretended to fight. So they continued for a while and when they thought the time was right they fled, as they had been ordered, and went to where Quizquiz was. When he saw the six thousand fleeing men approach, he joined them and all turned on Huascar with the war cry of "Quizquiz!"

Chalcochima, shouting his name as a war cry, came out behind Huascar's squadron after they had passed. When they were all together, they took Huascar and his men in their hands. One of Huascar's brothers who was there, Topa Atao, received so many wounds that he died the next day. The warriors thought that he was Huascar. He died even though he was treated. Chalcochima learned of him, that he was a noble, wished he would escape, and had him treated.

Huascar was badly wounded and his clothing was ripped to shreds. Since the wounds were not life-threatening, Chalcochima did not allow him to be treated. When daylight came and it was found that none of Huascar's men had escaped, Chalcochima's troops enjoyed Huascar's loot. The tunic Huascar wore was removed and he was dressed in another from one of his Indians who was dead on the field.

Huascar's tunic, his gold halberd and helmet, also gold, with the shield that had gold trappings, his feathers, and the war insignias he had were sent to Atahualpa. This was done in Huascar's presence. Chalcochima and Quizquiz wanted Atahualpa to have the honor, as their lord, of treading upon the things and ensigns of enemies who had been subjected.

When the messengers had been sent with these ensigns and messages, they asked Huascar where he had left his men and captains, and why had he come with so few men to give battle. Did he think them so unworthy that he felt that those five thousand men would be enough to rout and capture them?

XV

Wherein is told how Huascar told Chalcochima and Quizquiz why he had left his men, and of the ruse and signal he left with them, and how Chalcochima routed Huascar's captains with the information that Huascar gave them.

When Chalcochima and Quizquiz asked Huascar what he had done with his army and why he had attacked them with so few men, Huascar showed neither the valor nor the character or wisdom required by the circumstances. When they asked him, he explained the whole story of how he, thinking to take them while they slept that night, as he had killed their captain with his five hundred men, had come to attack them of his own free will. He had left his army two or three leagues from where he had been taken prisoner. He had commanded them not to move from there without his permission and order.

He told them that when they saw the canopy on his litter lowered, they should come to him. With this signal, they would understand that their enemies were now close by him and prepared to attack.

When Chalcochima heard this, he ordered his warriors to arise, explaining to them that the war was not yet finished because Huascar's army was together but two leagues away. They were unaware of the capture of their lord. It might be that they would go on the defensive or there might be something that would prompt them to take up arms. Therefore, Chalcochima's men should proceed with great caution, in ordered ranks and with their arms prepared.

This done, Chalcochima separated five thousand men, and when they had been separated, Chalcochima took Huascar's litter and got on it and ordered that Huascar's canopy be attached to the litter, as it was when he came. They tied Huascar up very well with strong rope and, thus bound, placed him on a kind of stretcher which they had quickly tied with straw rope. And to think that he had come there on an expensive gold litter.

When Chalcochima was on Huascar's litter, he ordered that they place him amid his five thousand men, and so they placed him there. He commanded them to march forward a little until it appeared to him there was space on his wing for more warriors so that, when Huascar's army saw him, they would think he was Huascar and that the squadron coming up behind were the enemy.

Thus, Chalcochima and Quizquiz left, as we have said, bearing on a stretcher a bound Huascar dressed in very ordinary garments, which were picked up on that plain and wilderness where he was captured called Guanaco Pampa, territory belonging to the town of Cotabamba.

Chalcochima and Quizquiz marched for three leagues and arrived where Huascar's captains had their camp. When they saw Chalcochima's warriors approach, they saw the litter of their lord Huascar at a great distance from the camp and they recognized the canopy. They thought that it was their lord Huascar who was coming. They prepared themselves and awaited the signal that had to be given for them to aid him and attack their enemies.

When Chalcochima saw Huascar's men, he ordered Quizquiz's warriors to stop there and pretend they were preparing for battle as if they had seen the enemy. They stopped and made a show of preparing to fight. They tied on their blankets and took up their shields on their shoulders. They brandished their slings and waved their lances about. Chalcochima placed himself with the five thousand on the ridge of a high hill with slopes running both to Huascar's troops and to his camp. Once there, he had his canopy lowered, and when the captains saw that they had lowered the canopy, they all left together.

When Chalcochima's army saw the enemy camp leave and come to them, they also left and came to the hill where Chalcochima was. When they were within a sling's shot of Chalcochima, he ordered them to stop and remain under cover.

When Huascar's men had approached within six sling shots from Chalcochima, he ordered a Lucana Indian of those who had borne Huascar's litter to leave there as if he were escaping. He should flee and tell Huascar's captains how Huascar was a prisoner and was carried there bound, and that Chalcochima came on the litter, and that he had made the signal because Huascar had told him about it when they captured him.

Chalcochima did this so that the lords and captains, who were arriving as fast as they could, would lose their will to fight and so would be routed when they learned this news and saw their enemies so close.

Then the Lucana left the litter that he had carried on his shoulders and fled as if escaping his enemies. Because of the battle and his lord's capture the night before, his clothes were ripped to pieces and covered with blood from wounds. So too he was covered with mud as if he had crawled on the ground as a vanquished one in the battle.

When Huascar's captains saw this Lucana, who was well known to them, so mistreated and in the shape he was in because he was fleeing, they asked him what had befallen him and why, escaping in this way, he had left his lord and come to them. He gave them the news and reported on what had happened, as you have heard.

When the captains heard the bad news and knew that their leader was a prisoner, without further delay they threw their weapons to the ground and turned and ran as fast as they could. They wanted to hide where Chalcochima's men could not catch them.

When Chalcochima's men saw their enemies in flight, they chased them to the city of Cuzco, where we will leave them and speak of Atahualpa.

XVI

Which concerns how Atahualpa left Cajamarca for the province of Guamachuco. When he arrived, he ordered a sacrifice to a guaca *there that they might know of his great success. When he received an answer from the* guaca *that he did not want to hear, he became enraged at the* guaca *and went to wage war upon it. And of the things he did there and how he sent Cuxi Yupanque from there to the city of Cuzco to punish those who had been against him.*

Since Atahualpa was angry at the messenger Chalcochima sent to ask for a supply of weapons, as this history has already recounted, he had ordered Cuxi Yupanque to prepare his army to leave Cajamarca. When he was ready, Atahualpa left Cajamarca and ordered his army to march to the province of Guamachuco, where, upon his arrival, the lord caciques of that province came out in peace.

He remained resting in that province ten days, after which he learned that there was an important *guaca* and idol there. He ordered a sacrifice made so that from it his great success and good fortune might be known. This *guaca* was on a hill on top of a very high mountain. The idol in it was made of stone about the size of a man. There was also a very old man who spoke with this idol and it with him.

The lords that Atahualpa had sent to make a sacrifice in his name arrived at the *guaca,* they made their sacrifice to the idol, and asked it what Atahualpa had commanded that they learn from it.

That old man who was there and spoke for the idol gave them an answer. He said the Inca, son of the Sun, should not kill so many people because

Viracocha, who had created the people, was angry about it. He wanted him to know that from it no good would come to Atahualpa.

These messengers then left there and went to Guamachuco, where Atahualpa was, and told him the answer they had had from the idol. When Atahualpa heard it, he was very angry at these words and said: "This *guaca* is also as much an enemy *auca* as Huascar."

He ordered Cuxi Yupanque to rouse his warriors, have them in battle array, and to leave there on a direct route to the *guaca*, because it was his enemy. Cuxi Yupanque then broke camp and left there in the morning. They slept that night in a wilderness area called Ñamoc Pampa. The next day Atahualpa left there, and he and his camp arrived at the *guaca* at sundown.

When they arrived, he ordered his warriors to surround the *guaca*'s hill and mountaintop so the idol would not escape. When the hill was surrounded, Atahualpa himself, in person, climbed to the *guaca* where the idol was. Atahualpa gave the idol such a blow in the neck with a battle-ax he carried that he cut off the head. They then brought there the old man, who was held as a saint and who had given the idol's reply to the messengers. Atahualpa also beheaded him with his battle-ax.

When this had been done, he ordered fire brought and he had a great amount of firewood that was around the *guaca* piled on the idol and on the old man. He had them set fire to the idol.

The next day when the idol was well burned together with the top of the hill where it had been, he ordered the fire put out. They brought a great amount of water and extinguished the fire. When it was out, he commanded that they grind the idol and the old man's bones down to dust with stones.

When the idol was reduced to dust, he commanded that it be strewn into the air from the top of the mountain. Then he ordered that all that the fire had consumed on top of the hill be similarly thrown away. This was done and thrown off the hill.

While he was engaged in this, a message arrived from Cuzco that told him how Huascar was a prisoner. In celebration of this news, he ordered that a great amount of firewood be gathered and that a fire be set on the *guaca*'s hill, as had been done before, to totally flatten it. He said no man could insult him, not even his idols and *guacas*. That hill is a half league around and twenty lance lengths high. They again built such a fire that was so bright, it turned night into day.

Since he had the news of Huascar's imprisonment, Atahualpa ordered Cuxi Yupanque to prepare himself to leave alone the next day for Cuzco on the post road to mete out justice to all those men and women who had been angry with him. When Cuxi Yupanque was ready, he asked Atahualpa's permission for a cousin, Tito Yupanque, to accompany him so that he would have someone to talk to. The Inca said to take him and that they should go on the post road in a pair of hammocks, changing Indian bearers at each province they reached. Cuxi Yupanque and his cousin then prepared for the journey.

When night fell, Atahualpa took Cuxi Yupanque aside and when the two were alone he told him: "Look, Cuxi Yupanque, I am sending you to Cuzco for you to mete out the punishment that I would administer if I were there. I trust no one but you. I want you to go because I want no noble left alive among those prisoners in Cuzco who has been against me and is found to have been on Huascar's side.

"You must understand that the punishment you administer has to be in this manner. You are to assemble all of the sons and daughters of my father, Huayna Capac. You must punish and kill all the males you find who know how to use a sling. They were the ones who were there in Cuzco before Huascar brandishing their weapons, saying, 'Let the *auca* Atahualpa die," and said to Huascar, 'You are the only lord.' Kill them and all those nobles captured in Cuzco. Pay no heed that they are my brothers or whether they have been against me anywhere else.

"You should also assemble all of the daughters of my father, Huayna Capac. Find all the maidens and send them under strong guard to me. All the others who have known a man, order them killed. Pay no heed that they are my sisters because you should know that, since they have known a man, Huascar has had them as wives, sleeping with him, and in his bed. Huascar would have been unable to leave them alone; he would have discussed with them this war he and I have had. With Huascar, they would have called me *auca* and would have approved of the war. They must not enjoy themselves; they have enjoyed themselves enough in the times of Huascar; it is my will that Huascar's women die. Kill all his sons and daughters, making the punishment widely known.

"After you have done this and have restored the discipline that should habitually reign in the city, you should return because, after I have brought down this *guaca* and mountain, I intend to go from here to Cajamarca.

"Also tell Chalcochima and Quizquiz that they should depopulate the city of Cuzco and remove the natives from thirty leagues around. They should send them to me because from Cajamarca, I intend to go to Quito, where I will build a new Cuzco. These peoples from there should come and populate the area.

"You must send me Huascar, his mother, and his principal wife, Chuqui-huipa, because I intend to speak with Huascar and his mother and find out from them why they sent to Quito to make war on me. I was relaxing, enjoying the fact that he was lord and offering myself as his vassal in Quito. I sent him gifts as a sign that I accepted him as lord. These gifts I sent he threw in my face, dishonoring me personally and making a drum from the skin of the leader I sent him with the gifts.

"All this you tell him when you see him because I will speak to him more at length here. Leave tomorrow morning."

Cuxi Yupanque arose in the morning and went to Atahualpa and kissed him on the cheek. After making the accustomed reverence, Cuxi Yupanque took his leave of Atahualpa and from there went to his sister's[1] chambers. So, too, he took his leave of her, and Cuxi Yupanque left, taking with him his cousin Tito Yupanque. They proceeded in their hammocks on the post road, changing Indian bearers in each province until they arrived at the city of Cuzco. Here we will leave them and speak of Atahualpa, who had remained at the *guaca* fulfilling his duties.

XVII

Wherein Atahualpa, while he was engaged in destroying the guaca, *learned of the arrival of the Marquis Francisco Pizarro and of the rest of the people who came with him, and how Atahualpa left and went to Cajamarca, and of the things that happened during this time.*

Atahualpa had sent Cuxi Yupanque to the city of Cuzco to punish those in Cuzco that he found on Huascar's side and against him. Atahualpa remained at the *guaca*'s hill. He commanded his captains and men to do nothing while they were there but burn and level the *guaca*'s hill. He was engaged in that work there for three months without moving his encampment.

After three months, three yungas Tallane[1] Indian messengers arrived from Tangarala and told him: "Unique lord, you should be aware that some white and bearded men have arrived in our town of Tangarala. They bring a kind of sheep on which they ride and travel. These sheep are very big, much larger than ours. These men come so well clothed that no skin appears but the hands and the face. And half of it only because the other half is covered with a beard that grows on it.

"These men wear a certain kind of sash over their garments and from this sash they hang a piece of silver that looks like those rods that the women place in their warps [threads] to tighten what they are weaving. The length of these pieces that they bear would be almost a *braza*." This is how they described the swords.

The Inca asked them: "What do these men call themselves?" They only knew that they called them *viracocha cuna*,[2] which means "gods." The Inca asked them: "Why have you named them 'Viracocha'?" They told him that in olden times Contiti Viracocha made the people. When he had finished, he entered that ocean ahead.[3] He had not returned, according to what their old men had told them.

Some of these new men had come to Payta in a *guambo*, which means boat. This *guambo* was very large and had returned from there. This was when the

Marquis Francisco Pizarro came down along the coast in a single ship looking for lands to discover and he reached Tumbes. He sent Captain Candia to land to see what this place was like, what kind of population it had, and if there were any sign of riches.

Let us now leave this and speak of the illustrious Marquis Francisco Pizarro of glorious memory, who conquered these realms. When he reached Tangarala on his return from Spain, there he learned of Atahualpa, his greatness, power, and wealth. He decided to send him four Indians from that Tallane village. He sent some pearls and diamonds with them and some knives, scissors, combs, and mirrors.

He also sent a message to him saying he came from Spain to seek a meeting with him because he had heard that he was a great lord. Pizarro said that he came on behalf of an even greater lord than himself. The task he was charged with he would relate to him when he saw him. And he sent them *chaquira* beads and the other things that he would receive. Pizarro was shortly going to go to where Atahualpa was. Here we take our leave of him and return to speak of Atahualpa.

When the two Indians reached him with news of the arrival of the marquis and the rest of the Spaniards, he was engaged in the destruction of the *guaca*. When he heard that news, he ordered his captains to break camp and march to the village of Guamachuco. They had already razed half of the hillside of the *guaca*. His captains broke camp and returned to the village of Guamachuco.

When the Inca and his people reached the town of Guamachuco, he found the four Tallanes there that the marquis had sent. After they had completed the required formal greetings, they laid out before him the things the marquis had sent. When the Inca saw what the marquis had sent him, he was greatly pleased by it and by seeing the Indians that brought it. He wanted to know about the marquis, his men, and what kind of men these were to figure out what should be done.

He went to one of his captains and had him take those messengers and place them in lodgings and see that no one spoke to them because he wanted to interrogate them alone. These Indians were then taken to the Inca's quarters.

After the Inca rested there that day, he arrived the following day and he and his captains retired to a house. He ordered that the four Tallanes be brought there. When they were before him, he asked them who the lord was who had sent them and those things to him and what the Indians called him. The Indians told him they called him by the name they had heard him called, which was "capito." They were attempting to pronounce "capitan."

The Inca asked them what type of man he was and how he was dressed and what kind of garments he wore and how they looked. He asked what his men looked like, what they did, and how and what they spoke.

The Indians told him that the "capito" was a tall man with a full beard and was totally wrapped in clothing from his feet to his neck. They said this because of his dress, and that he had a "*chuco*,"[4] which means a "cap," on his head. His hands did not appear except when he ate and he wished to show them, because he had them covered with other hands made of leather. Half of his face was visible and the other half he had covered with a beard that grew upon it.

He was girded with a kind of sash from which hung a long thing that they could not explain. His men were similarly dressed no differently from him. They saw some of his men draw out that long thing that hung at their waists and shone like silver.

They brought some sheep to that "capito," he divided them among his men, who were seen to cut off their heads and kill them with those long things. The Inca asked them how they had cut with them, and they told him how they drew them from their belts and delivered a blow to the neck of the sheep and jolted the head of the sheep that received the blow. The sheep then fell to the ground dead, and they proceeded to slit its throat. They also cut up the meat easily with those long things that cut.

The Inca was amazed to hear this and remarked that those long things that cut would be what was called "*macana*."[5] The Indians agreed that this might be. The Inca asked them if they ate the meat raw or cooked it. The Indians said they cooked it in their pots and they ate it when it was very well cooked. Part of the meat they roasted and ate when it was well done.

The Inca asked them if they ate human flesh and they said that they had seen them eat only sheep, lambs, ducks, pigeons, and deer. They ate these with some cakes made from maize. The Inca asked them for many other details. Afterward, he marveled at the cutting of the swords and the size of the horses that they told him of and how they rode and raced on them.

When the Inca learned of these things, he was very frightened. Fearful of what would later happen to him and of what he would hear from the messengers, he entered into consultation. He wanted to hide himself in the province of Chachapoyas in a place called Labando. His advisers told him he should not do this until he saw what these people were. Were they gods, or men like them, and did they do evil or good? He should not do anything until he saw this. Once he had seen them, he would then determine what he should do.

If they were "*runa quiçachac*,"[6] which means "destroyers of peoples," then, unable to resist them, he would flee. If they were "*viracocha cuna runa allichac,*"⁷ which means "gods who are benefactors of the people," then he should not flee them.

When the Inca heard this opinion from his captains, he recovered from the terror that had gripped him and said that he was happy that in this age and time gods would come to his land. They could not but do good.

Atahualpa then commanded that the Tallanes Indian messengers return and tell the great Viracocha, the "capito," that he was pleased with his arrival and considered him his father. He should go and await him in Cajamarca. He would leave later for there. He was greatly pleased with what he had sent him and requested that he receive in a similar way other things that he would send him, which consisted of feathered garments, tunics, and blankets of fine wool.

When the messengers had been dealt with and provided with food, they left for Tangarala whence they had come. When the Inca finished his consultation and had dispatched the messengers, he ordered his captains and the village leaders to make ready to celebrate that day and the next because the day after he intended to go to Cajamarca and see the "capito."

Thus it was ordered and after celebrating the coming of the Spanish there in Guamachuco, he ordered his captains with their men to begin the return to Cajamarca. Here we will leave them and speak of Chalcochima and Quizquiz, who were chasing Huascar's men back to the city of Cuzco.

XVIII

Which concerns how Quizquiz and Chalcochima,

after capturing Huascar, chased Huascar's captains

to the entrance of the city of Cuzco, and

of the things they did in the city.

While Huascar's captains were fleeing and were being chased by the army of Quizquiz and Chalcochima, Guanca Auqui, one of the captains escaping and one of Huayna Capac's sons, fled to the Valley of Yucay, where he intended to escape. This valley is four leagues from Cuzco.

When Chalcochima's men, who were chasing them, arrived in Yucay, they captured Guanca Auqui. The rest of the captains were taken in Cuzco, except Guacço, who escaped and hid himself three leagues from Cuzco.

When the captains were in the city of Cuzco, Quizquiz and Chalcochima ordered their warriors to assemble in order to provide them lodgings. When they had gathered and were housed, the order was given that they be provided with all they required and that no one, under penalty of death, steal or sack anything from the city, since they had been given all they needed in great abundance.

With this done, they called together all the city's residents and those from a league around. When the great mass of people were gathered, the captains ordered it proclaimed in a loud voice that, in the name of the Inca their lord Atahualpa, they pardon all those who had been against him, captains and others alike, if they would but come and pledge obedience in the name of their lord the Inca within ten days. The homes and property that they had lost would be returned. If they did not come, they would be held as "*aucas*" and would be punished as prisoners of war.

When this had been done, they ordered everyone to return to their homes, and this pardon was later made known all around Cuzco. When this pardon reached the ears of Guacço, he came within the time limit ordered by the captains. They received him peacefully.

Because the Cayambes and Indians from Quito were rounding up those who were found to be delinquent and because this was one of Huascar's captains who came to render allegiance, Chalcochima caused a white ribbon to be sewn on his tunic just under the neck opening. It was sewn on the inside so that those who were in charge of the capture would not seize him or accord him bad

*Huascar Inca taken prisoner by Atahualpa's generals
Quizquiz and Chalchochima.*

From the chronicle of Felipe Guaman Poma de Ayala,
Nueva coronica y buen gobierno.

treatment when they saw it. This was also done to many others who came to give their obedience. Huascar, his principal wife, Chuquihuipa, and his mother, Ragua Ocllo, were separated in prison until the will of the Inca Atahualpa about what to do with them was known.

Here we take our leave of them and speak of Cuxi Yupanque, the captain-general, who had left the *guaca* to go to Cuzco to punish those found to have opposed the Inca.

XIX

Wherein Cuxi Yupanque, Atahualpa's captain-general, entered the city of Cuzco, and of the great cruelties and punishments that he meted out there on the children of Huayna Capac and upon the children and wives of Huascar and the rest of the leaders, captains, and common people who were found on Huascar's side, and of the things that he arranged and ordered done in the city of Cuzco, and how he sent Huascar to his lord Atahualpa as a prisoner.

When Cuxi Yupanque left the *guaca* from where Atahualpa had sent him to the city of Cuzco, he traveled night and day, changing the Indian bearers of his hammock in each province. He arrived in Cuzco in seventeen days. When Cuxi Yupanque arrived, Chalcochima and Quizquiz came out to greet him at Xicllapampa, which is two leagues from Cuzco.

When they met, Cuxi Yupanque asked them to tell him what had been done with Huascar and his people. They told him that Huascar and all his brothers and sisters, sons and daughters, and wives, and, indeed, all those who had been found guilty were prisoners under heavy guard. He could order whatever justice suited him.

Cuxi Yupanque told them that his lord the Inca would remember their services. When Captains Chalcochima and Quizquiz heard this, they gave thanks to the Inca. After rendering great obedience to the Sun, they left for the city of Cuzco. When they arrived, Cuxi Yupanque commanded that the leaders of the area surrounding the city be gathered together on a certain day.

When that day arrived, Cuxi Yupanque spoke to them, telling them of the love the Inca his lord had for them and how he would maintain and sustain them with reason and good government. As a sign of gratitude, the leaders who heard this arose and gave thanks to the Sun and to the Inca and worshiped the Sun in the name of the Inca as his father.

When this explanation was finished, Cuxi Yupanque ordered them to send out to the four provinces of Andesuyo, Collasuyo, Condesuyo, and Chinchasuyo and find all those who had been rebels and warriors against this Inca his lord. He commanded that they do nothing but capture them and bring them bound as prisoners before him for punishment.

When the caciques departed from the meeting, they ordered their Indians to go throughout the land of the four provinces and search out all those who were guilty. These would be the children and wives of Huascar as well as his kinsmen, captains, and the leaders of Cuzco whom Quizquiz and Chalcochima had not been able to capture.

They searched in the manner they had been commanded, as you have heard, and many were captured and tied with ropes and brought before Cuxi Yupanque. He ordered them placed in the jail with the rest. Many, when they learned of the orders that had been given and that they could not escape, hanged themselves or took poison to kill themselves before they found themselves in the power and hands of their enemies, who would take vengeance on them. All the more so because Cuxi Yupanque had been sent by Huascar in an insulting manner from Calca to fight with Atahualpa and was regarded by Huascar as unreliable because of the rank he had and his being such a close relative of Atahualpa. Therefore, they feared his fury and could expect no pardon or mercy. Because of this, they hanged and killed themselves, as you have heard.

As they had been ordered to seek out such criminals, many of Huascar's children and wives were captured, as were the sons and daughters of Huayna Capac and those of many other lords and leaders who had sided with and served Huascar. The only exception was Manco Inca, who was later named Inca by the marquis, as this account will relate. At the time, he was a lad of fifteen years and those of his mother's lineage hid him well. She was the daughter of a woman native to the town of Anta [Jaquijahuana].

In this captivity, Paullo Topa was imprisoned. He later became a Christian and was given the name Cristobal. He later rejected this name and asked that it be taken from him and that he be given one more in keeping with his real one. They named him Don Paulo Topa.

He was a son of Huayna Capac and of a woman they called Añas, a native of Guailas. He escaped from the imprisonment because he proved that he had been mistreated by Huascar because he had shown himself to be a friend of Atahualpa's. This was a lie. Huascar had ordered him captured because he had been found with one of Huascar's wives. Huascar had him thrown in jail, where he was kept tied and was to die by slow starvation, what we call "to eat by ounces."

When Chalcochima and Quizquiz entered Cuzco, they found this Paulo in jail and, since he told them he had been imprisoned because he was a friend of Atahualpa's, they released him. When Cuxi Yupanque arrived, they recaptured Paulo and when he proved to the captains that he had been imprisoned for being a friend of Atahualpa's, Cuxi Yupanque ordered him released.

Marcachimbo, Quispiquipi, Suriti, Yunga Nusta, and Quiçpiciça, together with many other daughters of Huayna Capac, were also brought before Cuxi Yupanque. He ordered them released and placed where they would be cared for and overseen because these were young girls who had not known a man. Because he found that all the rest were Huascar's women, he ordered them to remain with the rest of the prisoners under firm restraint until the arrival of a certain day that he had selected when justice would be done with them.

When that day arrived, Cuxi Yupanque commanded that many stakes be placed on both sides of the road that leads from Ticatica, which is a fountain about one-eighth of a league from Cuzco, to Xiclla-pampa, which is between a league and a half and two leagues from Cuzco. When this was done, he ordered Huascar's wives and all the rest of the delinquents brought out except Guanca Auqui and another two or three of Huascar's captains, because these would have to go as prisoners with Huascar to where Atahualpa was.

So all these were brought to a place called Quicpai, where he ordered that each and every one learn the charges against him or her. Each and every one was told why they were to die. When this was done, he ordered Huascar's wives separated. When this was done, he commanded that those who were pregnant have their babies torn alive from the womb, and some of them had other children of Huascar. Cuxi Yupanque ordered these women opened alive also. These and the rest of Huayna Capac's daughters were hanged from the highest of those stakes. And the babies taken from their wombs were attached to the hands, arms, and feet of their mothers, who were already hanging on the stakes.

The rest of the lords and ladies who were prisoners were tortured by a type of torture they call *chacnac*,[1] before they were killed. After being tormented, they were killed by smashing their heads to pieces with battle-axes they call *chambi*,[2] which are used in battle.

A great number of the sons and daughters of Huayna Capac were killed, as were all the rest of the main lords of Cuzco and all the children and wives of Huascar. After these lords and ladies were dead, Cuxi Yupanque ordered that their flesh and bodies be thrown out, where they would be eaten by birds and foxes. This was done.

After this punishment, Cuxi Yupanque told the captains that he wanted to communicate something to them and that they should meet him at his home. When the three were assembled alone, Cuxi Yupanque told them: "You should know that the Inca our lord does not intend to come to this city but, rather, to return to Quito from Guamachuco and to populate a new Cuzco there. Therefore, he commands that you impose order here. All these Indians from both this city and from the surrounding thirty leagues will be taken to Quito, where the new Cuzco will be created. This city and thirty leagues around it will be depopulated. As this area was populated, that area will be settled in the same way.

"Moreover, I must tell you that while I was with the Inca at the *guaca* in Guamachuco from whence I left, two Tallanes came to him from Tangarala and they carried news that Viracocha had emerged from the sea and many other *viracochas* came with him. It is believed that they are the ancient *viracochas* that created the people.

"The Inca was pleased by this news. Since he was told that they had emerged from that place, he wants to return to Quito and meet them on the road to find out what orders they have for him and what he must do for his preservation."

When they heard this they were amazed and believed that Cuxi Yupanque told them the truth. They were gods and the creator. Their lord would benefit from them. They were greatly pleased and gave thanks to the creator they call Viracocha and to the Sun in place of the Inca. They later sent out a call to their captains that all the caciques and the principal men from the towns and provinces for thirty leagues around the city of Cuzco be gathered in the square.

These captains then left and ordered that all the chiefs and caciques of the Cana, Colla, Chanche, Quivio, Papiri, Chilqui, Chumbibilca, Yanaguara, and Quichua and the rest of the provinces around Cuzco be gathered. Soon they were all together because they were all there. With them assembled the three captains together went out to the square where the caciques were and ordered them to depopulate their lands and villages and to get prepared because the Inca wanted them to settle Quito, where they would build a new Cuzco.

The caciques agreed because they were forced to do so. They asked for time to prepare themselves and to provide the supplies for the journey. They were granted twenty days and ordered to prepare themselves and provision themselves for the trip. This they did, and Cuxi Yupanque later commanded some Indians from Quito to ready themselves to carry Huascar to their lord Atahualpa.

The next day, the Indians were in the square with their weapons and, when they were assembled, Cuxi Yupanque ordered Huascar brought out with his mother and his wife and Guanca Auqui and the rest of the lords who were in prison. They were brought to the square, and Cuxi Yupanque ordered some cages to be made of stakes. When they were completed, he commanded that Huascar be seated in one because that was how he would go.

Huascar seated himself and then some sinewy cords were brought with which his hands and legs were bound to the bars of the cage. He was bound in such a way that he could neither lie back nor forward on his chest. Rather, he had to remain seated at all times.

Cuxi Yupanque charged Guanca Sumari, a captain whom Atahualpa trusted, to take Huascar to Atahualpa. Thus he took him and the rest of the prisoners. Here we leave this and speak of a messenger that the marquis sent to the Inca Atahualpa.

XX

Wherein the marquis sent a messenger named Ciquinchara to the Inca Atahualpa, and of the great misfortunes that this messenger imparted to the Inca, which caused Inca Atahualpa to change his mind, and how Ciquinchara returned to the marquis on behalf of Atahualpa.

When the marquis arrived in Tangarala, he found there an *orejon* warrior, a native of Jaquijahuana, who was placed there on behalf of the Inca Atahualpa. He was called Ciquinchara.

When the marquis saw him and learned that he was an *orejon* warrior, he was quite pleased, for he had heard of them and knew he was Atahualpa's servant and conducted his business. He did him appropriate honors. When the marquis left Tangarala, he took him along. Both in Tangarala and on the road, the *orejon* dealt with and communicated with the Spaniards. He saw how they were and saw their hair, dress, harquebuses, swords, and all the rest.

When the Spanish saw how well the marquis treated this *orejon*, they did also. With many conversations and the good treatment accorded him, he came to have a low opinion of the Spanish and looked for the opportunity to meet with Atahualpa to give him a report on what he had seen and to dispel the errors Atahualpa had learned from the Tallanes.

When the marquis had climbed the mountains and arrived in Caxas, he ordered this *orejon* to prepare himself because he wished to send him from there to where Atahualpa was. Ciquinchara said that he was prepared whenever he wished to send him to his Inca.

The marquis sent Ciquinchara on his mission to where Atahualpa was, some two or three days' journey from Cajamarca in a village they call Ychocan. After this, Ciquinchara arrived in the presence of the Inca and, when he had finished paying his respects, he explained to him the things that the marquis had charged him with.

When the Inca saw Ciquinchara, he was greatly pleased because there was much he wished to know and he wanted to be fully informed about everything. Since Ciquinchara had come from the marquis, the Inca wanted to be certain

who these people were who had recently entered his lands. He was greatly
pleased with Ciquinchara and took him aside in a room.

When they were alone, the Inca said to Ciquinchara: "Tell me, Ciquinchara,
what kind of people are these who have recently come into my land? If they are
the gods who created the world, I should serve and worship them as such. Let
me tell you that I am highly pleased at their arrival and for having come in my
time in order to validate and uphold my government. It is not by accident that
they come in my time. Now tell me what you think about these people because,
based on what you tell me, I will decide what I will do."

Ciquinchara said to the Inca: "Unique lord, you ask me and command that
I speak. I have so greatly desired to do so, since I found out from the Tallanes
who left from here and misinformed you. I don't blame them because when the
lord of those *viracochas* arrived, the one they call *capito*, I did not understand
either who they were. I was also as ignorant as they.

"Let me tell you, unique lord, that I have accompanied them all the way to
Caxas. While I was with them I tried to learn what kind of people they are in
order to determine if it were the Contiti Viracocha and the *viracochas* who
came in ancient times and created the world and the people in it.

"Since I had wanted to find out about this, I saw and understood that they
are men like us because they eat and drink, dress and mend their clothes, and
have relations with women. They perform no miracles nor do they raise or level
mountains nor create people nor produce rivers and springs in areas that need
water. When they travel through arid regions, they carry water with them in
jars and gourds.

"The Viracocha that created the world in ancient times made all this that I
stated. These people don't do anything like that. Rather, I have seen that they
covet all they see and if it be to their liking they take it whether it be young
women, gold or silver tumblers, or fine clothes.

"In the same manner, they have Indians bound with *quilla guascas,* which
means "iron ropes," who bear their burdens and *petacas* that contain their
clothing. These Indians are treated badly. Wherever the Spaniards go, they
appropriate everything, leaving nothing. They take it so easily you would think
it were theirs.

"They are very few. I have counted between one hundred and seventy and
one hundred and eighty. Their number does not surpass two hundred. To me
they seem to be *quitas pumarangra,*[1] which means 'leaderless people wandering
about and thieving.'"

The Inca was stunned by what he heard. Since he had taken them for gods
and wanted to serve and worship them, he was saddened at having learned this
news and he said to Ciquinchara: "Tell me, then, why do you all call them

Viracocha?" And Ciquinchara said: "I don't call them *viracocha* but, rather, *supai cuna*,² which means 'devils.'" And the Inca said, "Well, who calls them Viracocha?"

The Indian replied: "The beastly yungas call them this, thinking they were gods." The Inca said: "It is true that the Tallanes they sent me told me they were *viracocha*. And it did not occur to me to ask them what they had seen in them to cause them to think they were *viracocha* and call them such. But since you have seen and understood them, tell me what they are like as you have seen them because I want to know."

Ciquinchara said: "Çapa Inca, which means 'unique lord,' you should understand that they bring some large and tall sheep that they ride. Wherever they wish to go, these sheep carry them there. And if they wish, these sheep run with them on their backs. When they run, they make such a noise that the earth shakes and it resembles the thunder in the sky when it rains.

"They also carry something hollow that seems to be made of silver. They place something in it that looks like ashes and light it on fire through a small hole in the bottom. When they light this silver thing, a great flame issues from the hollow and it makes such a roar that it resembles the thunder in the sky and seems very much like it.

"When I saw and heard it for the first time, I was truly afraid. But now that I have seen them do it often, I no longer fear it, for I saw that the thunder of the sky killed people and this they have doesn't kill anybody, but only frightens.

"They are white and bearded and dress in a way we have not seen people dress before. And those who have not seen them as I have would think that they are gods. But I tell you, Çapa Inca, they are mere itinerant, disorderly thieves."

The Inca asked him what he though they should do with them, and he replied that they should all be killed because they were thieves and evil men. The Inca asked him how they could all be killed, and Ciquinchara told him that he could kill them easily without risking anything. The Inca said to him: "Well, how would you do it?"

Ciquinchara told him: "Unique lord, you should know that these men usually lodge together in a house and also sleep together within. It seems to me that a large house with many walls, rooms, and corridors should be provided them. When it is completed, they will lodge there and while they are inside we can seal the entrances at night and burn them all. In this way, Çapa Inca, we will be rid of them all."

The Inca considered what Ciquinchara told him and it seemed to him something that could be done easily by a man who had come from where they were and had spoken to them. He believed what he had been told. The Inca understood that the Spaniards loved gold, so he ordered two tumblers of gold prepared and said to Ciquinchara: "I really want you to return to these men and take them these two tumblers of gold from me. You should give them to the *capito*, their lord, and you should tell him that I like him very much and that I want to see him. I wish we could figure out this matter and find out whether they are gods or another kind of people who could be gods and arrive angry and do the things you have witnessed.

"Now, return there and give these tumblers of gold to the lord of these men on my behalf. Be very observant and see what kind of men they are. I don't want something to happen to us because we do not understand what it is."

When the Inca had dispatched the messenger, as you have heard, he left for Cajamarca. He arrived three days after leaving Ychocan. When the Inca reached Cajamarca, he ordered his captains not to stay in the town but to continue on to the hot baths some two leagues from there.

When they arrived at the hot baths, he ordered them to prepare themselves there because the time had arrived for the fiesta of Raime, which is the ceremony when they create the *orejon* warriors. He wanted to make the *orejones* there, which is similar to conferring knighthood, because he had with him many young men who were the sons of the native nobles of Cuzco and he wished to make them *orejones*.

He prepared for the fiesta and, while he was engaged in it, an Indian reached him who told him that Viracocha and his men had arrived in Cajamarca. Here we leave the Inca and speak of the marquis and of the thieving messenger who went about sowing dissension.

XXI

Wherein the marquis arrived in Cajamarca and learned that the Inca Atahualpa was engaged in a celebration at the baths two leagues from there, and how he sent one of his captains to call on him, and of the things that happened between the captain and his men and the Inca at the baths.

Ciquinchara left the Inca and went to where the marquis was. He arrived and made a great show of reverence and prostrated himself on the ground as a sign of obedience. He gave the marquis the tumblers he carried from the Inca and told him that the Inca, his son, sent him those tumblers and greatly desired to see him.

The Inca had ordered all the caciques from the surrounding areas through which he would come to render him service and provide him with all he needed. His son, the Inca, awaited him in Cajamarca.

When the marquis saw the messenger, he was greatly pleased and asked him if he had given the Inca what he had given him to carry to him, which were some *chaquira* beads, combs, and other assorted things of small value. Ciquinchara told him that he had given them to the Inca and that the Inca was well pleased with them because they had been sent by his father.

The marquis then had food brought and attended to all his desires. The marquis wanted to send him again to ask the Inca to prepare rooms for him and his men. Ciquinchara said that he was tired and he had not intended to return except when he went with the marquis.

When the marquis saw this, he was pleased that Indian had shown him love and had stayed with him out of the love he had. He was also pleased that he was the mediator between him and Atahualpa. In reality, the Indian deceived the marquis because he wanted to remain to carry out the Inca's orders and find out more about the Spaniards.

The marquis, taking with him this Ciquinchara who, when he arrived, learned that the Inca was resting at the baths, continued on his journey in stages and arrived in Cajamarca.

When the marquis learned that the Inca was not there, he ordered one of his captains to go with thirty or forty horsemen and an interpreter[1] and Ciquinchara. The captain left with the men you have heard described and Ciquinchara and the interpreter and went in search of the baths where the Inca was.

Here we will leave the captain and we will speak of the Inca, who was resting at the baths when the messenger that Quizquiz and Chalcochima sent him arrived with Huascar's clothing and emblems. When Atahualpa saw these things, he was greatly pleased and ordered that many red tassels be attached to them. When this had been done and they were prepared, they were brought before Atahualpa. He placed Huascar's things under his feet and walked on them.

He was thus engaged when another messenger from Cajamarca arrived, who told him how the Spaniards were in Cajamarca. The Inca was pleased by this because he wished to see them. Later, another Indian who had been sent by Ciquinchara came. He told him how one of the *capito*'s captains was coming to see him and that he brought thirty men with him and that the *capito* had remained in Cajamarca. This captain came to speak with him on the *capito*'s behalf. Ciquinchara also came; he would tell why the captain was coming.

When the Inca learned that the Spaniards were coming, he ordered some Indians placed as watchmen to see when they approached and to tell him because he wanted to see what they looked like from afar on their horses.

When the Spaniards were sighted coming over the plain, the Indians told the Inca they had been sighted and could be seen. When he had been told, he left his rooms to see them come. The Inca's captains ordered the warriors to place themselves in battle order according to their custom, so that the Spaniards would see them and not be given the opportunity to harm them, if that was what they wished.

The Inca saw them come along the road. They were too far away to tell how they looked. They came in wing formation all spread out. The Inca said: "From this distance they resemble huts built on the plain." He remained in that place until they arrived.

The marquis's captain, thinking Ciquinchara was a friendly mediator, sent him ahead. When Ciquinchara reached the Inca and after having completed his formal greeting he went and stood behind him. When the Inca saw him, he ordered him to come before him so that he could question him and find out why the Spaniards had come.

Ciquinchara told him: "Çapa Inca, you should know that one of the *capito*'s captains is coming and he is bringing thirty or forty men. They come on their sheep and these sheep have bells on their necks to scare those who see them.

They are fully armed and carry lances in their hands and their shields hang from those seats they have on their sheep on which they ride seated. They are in a high state of alert, in case you wish to do something here. They are not accustomed to traveling in this manner on the road, since they come to you now in this way. They are people of great understanding.

"They can either sleep or not. But when they want to, they lie down dressed and, at times, naked. They always post guards who at night take turns on watch every four hours. They never sleep in any other way."

The Inca asked him the name of the one who came. The Indian told him that he also was called "*capito*." The Inca also asked what they called the sheep. He said he had heard them call them "cauillos" [*caballos*, horses].

The Inca asked him why they came, and the Indian said they came to visit on behalf of the *capito grande,* who was in Cajamarca. "They brought with them an Indian who knows how to speak their language in order to tell you what they wanted you to know." The Inca asked, "From what land was that interpreter that they were bringing?" He said: "From the *mitimaes* who are in Maycavilca." "Then he is one of mine," said the Inca. The Indian responded, "Yes, unique lord." And the Inca said, "I am greatly pleased by this. This interpreter that they have, how did he learn to speak so rapidly?"

The Indian told him that he had been carried away when he was a child. This was the first time the Spaniards came to Paita. They took him to their land and there he had learned their language. Now they bring him as their interpreter. They also bring another like him, but from the Tallanes, who had also been captured on their first visit.

The Inca was very pleased by this because he intended to find out from these interpreters what kind of people these Spaniards were. While he was occupied in this, the captain arrived with his men. When he arrived, he stopped near a hot stream that goes through the baths. They found the stream was deep and they didn't want to cross. From that point they asked for the Inca. They were told from the other side, on orders of the Inca, that he was there. The Spaniards told them to tell him to come over to where they were. The Indians asked who commanded this group, and the interpreter told them the captain was the son of the creator. When the Inca heard this, he ordered one of his captains, named Unanchullo, to cross over to the other side of the stream to where the Spaniards were and to find out what they wanted.

Unanchullo crossed a small bridge there over the stream and asked the Spaniards what they wanted. He told them to tell him what they wished. They replied that they wanted nothing from him but, rather, from the Inca, who remained on the other side. Unanchullo told them that they should tell him their wishes and he would tell the Inca because the Inca had sent him to do that. They should understand that the Inca did not speak with people like them.

Unanchullo said this because Ciquinchara had told them that these were evil people, thieves and bandits. He again said that they should speak with him because that was why he had come to them on behalf of the Inca. They again replied that they required nothing of him. They wanted to speak to the Inca. Unanchullo went back and told the Inca that those men insisted on speaking with him.

The Inca ordered that the Spaniards be shown the crossing and an *orejon* went and made a hand signal to the Spaniards, telling them that they should follow the stream down until they could cross. The Spaniards did this. They followed the stream down until they reached a junction that the hot stream made with another cold one. The *orejon* told them to cross, that it was a crossing. So the Spaniards crossed. Since the water in the stream was so hot, the horses did not like it.

After leaving the stream, there were some stone steps that led to the lodgings. Since the horses emerged upset from the hot water, their hooves clattered loudly as they ascended the steps. The iron shoes created fiery sparks on the rocks. All of this was noted by the Indians. They were impressed by the sparks.

When they had crossed, they went to where the Inca was. Since the Inca was a serious man, he maintained his demeanor even though they were the first he had seen. The Spaniards told the Inca that their captain, who was a son of the Sun, had sent for him. The Inca told Unanchullo to tell them that at the moment he could not go to Cajamarca because he was taking part in fiestas. He would go and meet the lord who sent them on the morning of the next day.

Unanchullo said this and then the Inca ordered that a large meal of duck, roast lamb, and maize tortillas be prepared. From what he had heard, this was the food that the Spaniards ate and he wanted to see them eat. He wanted to see them dismount and then remount their horses in order to see how they dismounted and remounted. When the food was brought, the Inca told Unanchullo to tell them to dismount and eat. The Spaniards, fearful that the Inca wished to play a trick on them, told the Inca that they had not come there to sit down and eat. They had come under orders from their lord to visit him and have him tell them what he intended to do.

The Inca told Unanchullo to bring out *chicha* in tumblers of fine gold. Since he had been informed that they were fond of gold, he wanted to see if they would carry off the tumblers because they were gold. The *chicha* was brought and given to the Spaniards, who took the golden tumblers in their hands. Some feared that they were given poison in that *chicha* and refused to drink. Some of them drank without any fear. When they finished drinking, they returned the tumblers to the Indians who had given them. Thus they returned all the tumblers that had been given them.

When this was done, one of the horsemen there thought it would be good to leave the Inca a jewel from his hand as a sign of friendship. He approached the Inca on his horse and took the ring from his hand and tried to give it to the Inca. Since the Inca was a grave man, he refused to receive it and did not show he accepted what was offered to him. When the horseman who offered it saw that he did not want to receive it, he insisted that the Inca take it. When the Inca saw this, he ordered Unanchullo to receive it, and he did. The horseman said to Unanchullo that he had given it to the Inca and not to him. The Inca told Unanchullo that he considered it received.

The horseman was not satisfied with this and rode his horse so close to the Inca that the breath and air expelled by the horse's nostrils raised the Inca's *borla* fringe one or two times. He wore this before his eyes as a crown and insignia of his condition as lord, according to their custom. The Inca was very angry and ordered Unanchullo to return the ring and to tell them to leave. They returned the ring. The Inca had not moved a bit from where he was nor given any personal sign that he had received any favor, even though the horse had approached so closely.

Ciquinchara was ordered to rise and tell the Spaniards to leave and that the Inca would go to Cajamarca the next day, as he had said. The Spaniards pranced one horse around in front of the Inca and, paying a kind of respect to the Inca by lowering their heads, they left, saying to the Inca that the next day they awaited him in Cajamarca.

Thus, with their lances in their hands, they left the Inca and when they had crossed the stream and found themselves on the other side in the field, they pranced their horses all together and ran them. This was all seen by the Inca from a window on the other side. When he saw it, he was astounded and said: "Mana unan changa runam cai cuna,"[2] which means, "These are people whom it is impossible to understand."

We must here leave the Inca and speak of how the captain returned to the marquis and what the marquis did when he learned what had happened.

XXII

Wherein the marquis prepares his men and awaits Atahualpa, and how Atahualpa entered into consultation after the Spanish left him, and of the things that Ciquinchara told him in the council.

That captain returned to Cajamarca after meeting with the Inca. He had left the hot baths where the Inca remained after the events took place that you have heard. He arrived in Cajamarca, where he found the marquis, who was awaiting the Inca. When the captain arrived, he told the marquis what had transpired with the Inca and of the great reserve he had shown. He had not wanted to come with him and told him that he would come the next day.

The marquis asked the captain what kind of a man the Inca was and how he looked. The captain told him that he appeared to be a man of thirty years and that he demonstrated great majesty. He was so serious that he had not wished to speak with him except through a third person. What he spoke to them he told one of his captains, even though they were there all together. That captain told it to the interpreter, and the interpreter told them. When he spoke he displayed a very calm countenance and his words were very dignified. It was understood that it was his custom to speak through a third person with whomever he was dealing.

The marquis asked him how many men the Inca had. The captain told him that it seemed to him that there were so many that he had never in his life seen as many Indians together. It appeared that of those present there were more than five hundred Indians for each Spaniard. The marquis told him: "Well, we have God and His blessed Mother on our side."

Next he inspected the position and layout of the town of Cajamarca in order to see where its strongest point would be if there were to be a battle. It seemed to him that the best place was the plaza itself. Therefore, he divided his captains and placed them in some large houses on the square and told them what they were to do and how they should attack the enemies when they entered the gates of that plaza. He gave them a certain signal that they would need; it would be made so that all would attack together.

He exhorted them to display courage, since the divine will must favor such an important and necessary enterprise. Thus he spent that day and the follow-

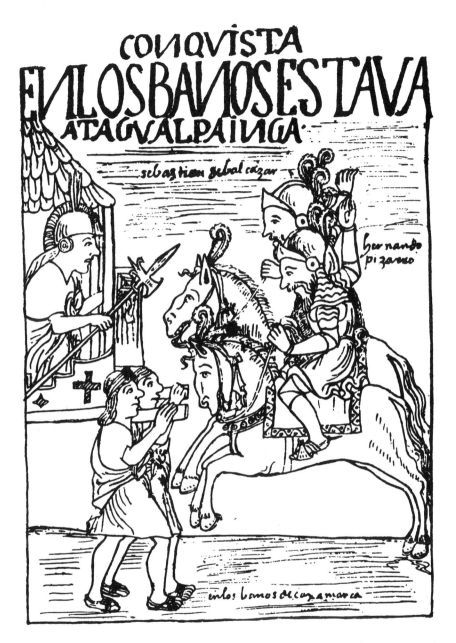

Conquista, En Los Baños Estava Atagualpa. *Sebastian de Benalcazar, Hernado Pizarro, en los baños de Caxamarca. Spanish soldiers visit Atahualpa.*

From the chronicle of Felipe Guaman Poma de Ayala,
Nueva coronica y buen gobierno.

ing night until the next dawn on the alert with many guards and sentinels posted. Here we leave him and will speak of the Inca Atahualpa.

When Atahualpa had seen the Spaniards prance and run their horses and had witnessed the superb horsemanship of all the Spaniards, he was greatly impressed. He ordered that all his captains be gathered in a certain room so that he could talk to them about what should be done. They met and when they were together the Inca ordered that Ciquinchara enter to tell them what he had learned from the Spaniards, since he had come with them from Tangarala and knew them.

Ciquinchara entered the council meeting, and the Inca commanded his captains to ask him what he thought of those men and what had happened to him with them. Had he seen them perform any miracle during his time with them that they might be known as gods? If the Spaniards were gods and the Inca did not accord them the obedience that they, as gods, desired, they could grow angry and do the Inca some evil or harm that would destroy him and result in his reduction and loss.

Ciquinchara was cautioned to advise them carefully about that matter as a man who had come with them and had seen them. In case they decided that the Spaniards were gods, they would obey and serve them. It was possible that when they saw that the Inca gave them obedience and that they had him in their service, they would make him an even more powerful lord than he was.

Ciquinchara heard the interrogation and the question that those nobles had asked him since the Inca had told them to question him. The traitor thought that the strength of the Inca's men was great and that the Spaniards were few and that they would be killed and captured by the great multitude of the Indians. Even though the Inca was impressed by seeing the horses run, the traitor was not because he had seen them run many times on the road when he came with them. He had also learned other things from the Indians and interpreters who had accompanied the Spaniards. He did not think highly of the Spaniards.

He responded to the question that he had been asked and said: "Since I am a vassal of the unique lord I will tell the truth and the words that I say will be true. I have been asked to say what I feel and know of these men because I have come with them.

"What I know of them is that when I first saw them I was truly frightened and felt that they were gods. I did not want to appear before them for some days. I commanded the yungas Indians to serve them and to do what they were ordered. And so they did. After some days, I saw that the Indians dealt and conversed with them and that they did no harm to anyone.

"I then presented myself to them and when they saw me they took me before the *capito*, their lord, whom I adored, thinking that he was Viracocha Pacha-yachachic,", which means the creator god of the world.

"I was asked what was up here, how many people there were, and what those lords were called. To this I replied that there were many people and many leaders, but there was only one lord over them and he was Capac. They asked me his name and I told them it was Çapa Inca Atahualpa.

"When I told them this, I noticed that they were very pleased, and I thought that if they were gods they would not have asked what was up here or if there were many or few people. Nor would they have asked me about the unique lord or his name. Nor would they have asked about things already done and that they would have created.

"They should have reminded me of the facts if I forgot anything and told me that they had created these things. And they should have said that they came for the good of the unique lord and for the good of the people.

"They showed me a piece of gold and silver and asked me if there was much gold and silver up here. I told them there was. They asked me if it was far to Cuzco and whether there was much gold and silver there. They asked me how many months it would take to get from there to Cuzco.

"I told them that there were two roads from there to Cuzco. One went by the seacoast and the other through the mountains. I told them that if the Indians walked from there to Cuzco, they would take three or four months going slowly. If they used the post service, the news of what they wanted to tell the Inca would be received by him in five or six days.

"They asked me if these two roads were well populated and if there was food. They asked me if there were people and towns beyond Cuzco and I told them yes, there were a great many towns.

"I explained the roads, bridges, and passes and what each road of these contained and of the ascent from the plains to the mountains.

"They asked me where the unique lord was and I told them that he was going to Cuzco. At the end of the questioning, he ordered that I be given some *chaquira* beads and combs. When I ate, he gave me what they ate there. All the questions were asked by the *capito* through an interpreter."

Unanchullo asked him: "What took place between you and this interpreter? Did you ever speak to him alone outside?" Ciquinchara said that after the *capito* questioned him as you have heard, together with many other things that in the interest of brevity I do not write here, the interpreter went outside and took him with him. He took him to his lodgings.

He asked him how many people Atahualpa had and was told there were many and in all the land there were many people on his side. Then the interpreter told him that the people they called *viracocha* were not gods. They had taken him as a child from Paita to their land. There he had learned their language. They were not gods but men who died as they did. And the same was true of their horses.

He asked the interpreter where their country was, and the interpreter said: "pachap tiqui cinpillacta yoc xi ñivarga,"[1] which means "at the far ends of the earth." The Inca then commented: "Ticçi viracocha checacon cai cuna,"[2] which means "These must be the gods of the ends of the earth."

Unanchullo asked him how many Spaniards there were. He told him there were very few, no more than two hundred. After Ciquinchara related what he had heard and many other things, they ordered him to leave the council meeting.

When Ciquinchara had left, the Inca asked his captains what they thought they should do. He felt that they should give the Spaniards obedience, since he held the *capito* to be Viracocha. The captains told him to consider the question carefully. They felt that the next day they should leave from there with all their warriors, who should be on alert in case it were necessary. Ciquinchara should leave now and go to Cajamarca and see how the Spaniards were arrayed and what their intentions were.

If he found them to be securely defended, he should send out from Cajamarca one of the interpreters with the Spaniards, who would be able to give information about those men. If he could not send one out, he should observe what the Spaniards were doing. With what he sees he should return to give a report to the Inca. In conformance with what Ciquinchara would tell them of the condition of the Spaniards, they would go and enter Cajamarca.

The Inca thought this a good plan and it should be carried out. He was very tired and wanted to sleep, since it was two hours before dawn. They had entered the council meeting at the hour of vespers the day before. You have heard all their opinions and the things they imagined and the decisions and resolutions that were taken. They left the meeting, and the Inca and the rest of the captains went to sleep after ordering their warriors and the guard to be on the alert and very cautious.

When they left, the Inca told Unanchullo to take Ciquinchara with him to his lodgings and he, with his blessing, should send him out, as had been decided. Ciquinchara should leave immediately in order to arrive in Cajamarca at dawn or before, and he should order him to go as fast as possible. Then the Inca went to sleep, and Unanchullo sent Ciquinchara, as you have heard.

XXIII

Wherein Atahualpa went to Cajamarca and was captured by the marquis, and of the things that occurred during this imprisonment.

Ciquinchara left the baths and reached Cajamarca before dawn. At the entrance to the town, he asked an Indian what the Spaniards were doing and what they had done that night. The Indian told him that they had not slept that night. They had had a bright light and should he enter, he would see it.

Ciquinchara entered and saw that they had their horses saddled and had the reins in their hands and the shields hung from the saddlebows. They were fully armed. When Ciquinchara saw them thus arrayed, he knew that they desired battle, because in all the time he had been with them, he had never seen them like this at night.

Seeing them thus in the morning, he saw that he couldn't speak with any of the interpreters or take them outside. Since he was engaged in mischief, he did not dare enter to speak to them. So he left again and went to a lodging from which he sent out spies to learn what the Spaniards had been doing. When this had been done and he had the information, he sent it to inform the Inca.

Since the Inca had retired late because of the council meeting, he slept until perhaps ten o'clock in the morning. At dawn his captains had ordered the warriors to take up their arms and be prepared to leave for Cajamarca, since the Inca had to go there that day.

When the warriors were prepared and battle ready and with the morning already well advanced to about ten o'clock, the Inca awoke and, since he saw it was late, requested food. After he ate, his captains told him that it was time to leave because they should arrive in Cajamarca while there was still sun. The Inca told them that there was time for everything and that he would tell them when it was time to leave. Then the Inca ordered them to bring him drink. They brought him drink and he drank so much and continued so that he became drunk; thus before he left, he was already under the influence of the drink.

While he was in this condition, an Indian arrived from Cajamarca and told him: "Çapa Inca, you should know that those men have entered the houses of your father and have divided up among themselves all that was in them." The Inca ordered that the warriors set out, and so he left the baths for Cajamarca in search of the marquis.

When he had gone a half a league, another Indian arrived and told him: "Çapa Inca, you should know that those men have entered the houses of the Sun and have distributed among themselves all that was in them." When the Inca had covered half the distance between the baths and Cajamarca, another Indian arrived and told him: "Çapa Inca, you should know that those men have entered your houses and have taken from you all that was there. And they have also forcibly taken your women." The Inca became enraged at this news and ordered that the Indian who had brought him the news be beheaded.

His head was immediately cut off and the Inca ordered another Indian to leave immediately for Cajamarca to alert Ciquinchara to come out to the road before the Inca entered Cajamarca. He ordered his warriors to march.

Ciquinchara soon came out and met the Inca almost half a league from Cajamarca. When Ciquinchara arrived, the Inca ordered his warriors to stop, and the Inca and his captains gathered there on the road and called upon Ciquinchara to sort out what they should do according to the news they had. In that meeting the captains said that they should fight; although the Inca was drunk and knew what the Spaniards had been doing in Cajamarca, he continued to insist that they should not give battle.

Ciquinchara told the Inca that if he did not fight, those people would have no respect for them. Since there were few Spaniards, it would not be any trouble to tear them to pieces and capture them. He told him other ugly things and discredited the Spaniards so much that the captains agreed with what Ciquinchara said. The Inca saw the great determination of the captains and things they did and said based on what Ciquinchara had said and the rest of the things the Indians who had come from there had told them. He told them they would see what the Spaniards did at their entrance in Cajamarca and he would then decide.

When the Inca was but two harquebus shots from Cajamarca, a Spaniard arrived on foot. The marquis had sent him to fetch the Inca. When the Inca saw him, he told Unanchullo to ask that *viracocha* what he had come for and whether his lord and all of them had had enough of stealing and raping women in Cajamarca. Unanchullo told him this, and the Spaniard did not understand what had been said. However, through signs, the Spaniard told them that they had sent him to bring the Inca. Unanchullo told the Spaniard to leave and that the Inca would come.

The Spaniard returned and told the marquis that the Inca was coming and he was bringing a great many soldiers. When the marquis heard this, even though he was on full alert, he went to all the quarters where he had placed his men to give them encouragement. He told them how they should attack and told them that, when certain harquebuses and artillery were fired, they should attack as one. He told the artillerymen to fire their weapons when they saw the signal that he would give them from where he was. With this arranged, he issued a command to all his men that no one was to kill Atahualpa; rather, they were to protect him and capture him alive. This done, he returned to his headquarters.

While the marquis was in his place, the Inca entered. He was very drunk from what he had imbibed in the baths before leaving as well as what he had taken during the many stops on the road. In each of them, he had drunk well. And even there on his litter he requested drink.

When he entered the square of Cajamarca, he asked if his lodgings had been vacated. They should take him directly to them. They told him that those men were staying in them. Then he commanded that they take him to his father, Huayna Capac's, houses. They told him that those men were also occupying them. Then he said that they should take him to the houses of the Sun. He was told that they, too, were occupied by those men.

When he heard this, he said: "There is no place where I can stay. All has been filled." While he was engaged in this conversation, Fray Vicente de Valverde approached him. He brought with him an interpreter. I fully believe, because of what those lords said who were right next to the Inca's litter, that the interpreter did not know how to relate to the Inca what the priest Fray Vicente told him. They said what the interpreter told the Inca when the priest took out a book and opened it. The interpreter said that that priest was the son of the Sun, and that the Sun had sent him to tell the Inca that he should not fight, he should obey the captain who was also the son of the Sun, and that was what was in that book and the painting in the book said that.

Since he said painting, the Inca asked for the book and, taking it in his hands, he opened it. When he saw the lines of letters, he said: "This speaks and says that you are the son of the Sun? I, also, am the son of the Sun." His Indians answered this and said in a loud voice all together: "Thus is Çapa Inca."

The Inca repeated in a loud voice that he also came from where the Sun was. Saying this, he hurled the book away and again all his people answered him: "Yes, he is the only lord."

When Fray Vicente de Valverde saw this, he went to where the marquis was. What he said to the marquis the conquerors who were present will have to say.

When the marquis had heard out Fray Vicente about that turn of events, he made his signal to the artillerymen. When they saw it, they fired their cannon and the harquebuses. Then everybody came out at once and fell upon the Inca's men. The horsemen lanced them and the foot soldiers cut with their swords without the Inca's men putting up any resistance. Given the suddenness of the attack and never having seen a similar thing in all their days, the Indians were

Conquista, Atahualpa Inca held in prison at Cajamarca.

From the chronicle of Felipe Guaman Poma de Ayala,
Nueva coronica y buen gobierno.

so shocked that, without defending themselves and seeing the great slaughter that they were undergoing, they tried to flee. So many men tried to leave by the plaza's gate and the Spanish were so persistent in killing them that a large mass of Indians, as they saw the great massacre they were suffering, pressed against a stretch of the wall that circled the plaza and toppled it under their onslaught. That wall was two feet wide and a little more than one *estado* high. It was poorly constructed and not made of mortar and brick, such that its collapse would cause no one to marvel.

Some horsemen reached the litter where the Inca was and with their swords cut off the arms and hands of the lords and leaders who were carrying the litter on their shoulders in order to bring down the litter and force the Inca to get out. Even though they cut off their hands and arms, the lords and leaders continued to support the litter with the stubs that remained to them until some of them were killed and the litter was partially knocked down.

At this point, one of the horsemen approached and, spurring his horse and thinking the Inca had some protection, he placed the front hooves of the horse on the litter. Since the Inca was drunk and must have seen what was happening, though he saw the horse approach and place its hooves on the litter, he did not move. Next, the horsemen went to another area, where they saw a large group of soldiers, and the Inca was left sitting on his litter. Soon, many of his men charged up and placed themselves in front of the Inca so that they might be killed before the Inca, since the foot soldiers were killing and ravaging them.

While the Inca was in the condition that you have heard, the marquis Francisco Pizarro came through the Indians and the rest of the Spaniards and reached the Inca and took him from the litter and removed him from the multitude of Indians and Spaniards who were coming at him. He carried him to his lodgings. By the time he reached the Inca, many of his troops had reached him, too, and wanted to kill him. In his attempt to defend him, the marquis was wounded in one hand by the swords that were meant for the Inca. Thus he defended him and in this way the Inca Atahualpa was taken prisoner in Cajamarca.

After Atahualpa's capture, the marquis kept him in his lodging and ordered that no one take anything from him. The next morning, the marquis asked Atahualpa if he needed anything, any of his women or an item of his service. Atahualpa told him that he needed a certain service, and the marquis commanded some Spaniards to go with some nobles and look for it and find out who had the items that Atahualpa needed. They were to take them from whoever had them and bring them to Atahualpa and give them to him. The Spaniards went, and gave them to Atahualpa. From that time forward, the marquis attempted to treat Atahualpa well.

Later, the marquis learned of the riches that were in Cuzco and how Huascar was a prisoner of Atahualpa's captains. When he learned this, he ordered three Spaniards to prepare themselves because they were to go to a town that they had told him was called Cuzco, where there was much gold and silver, and they should go see it.

When the Spaniards were ready, the marquis ordered Atahualpa to provide three hammocks with the necessary Indian bearers for each one and to take those three Spaniards to Cuzco because he was sending them there. Atahualpa immediately provided this and ordered them to be taken with all possible speed, changing the Indians bearers in each province. They were to be provided all services and provisions necessary for their sustenance.

So these three Spaniards left Cajamarca for Cuzco. The marquis remained in Cajamarca, where we will leave him and speak of what Cuxi Yupanque did and ordered in Cuzco and of the other captains, Chalcochima and Quizquiz.

XXIV

Wherein we learn how Cuxi Yupanque returned from Cuzco, and how Chalcochima went down from Cuzco to punish those who had not taken part, and how Atahualpa ordered Cuxi Yupanque to return and kill Huascar, and how Huascar died.

Cuxi Yupanque had sent Huascar, his mother, wife, and some of his brothers, such as Guanca Auqui, and other of his captains as prisoners to where Atahualpa was so that Atahualpa could do as he wished with Huascar and the rest. He himself had remained in Cuzco. However, because nothing remained to be done in Cuzco, he suggested that Chalcochima go down and meet with his lord Atahualpa.

As Chalcochima went though the provinces, he should punish those who had not taken part [in the war] and had not come out on his side. He should punish those who were found guilty and had been with Huascar's captains. Chalcochima saw that what Cuxi Yupanque told him to do, punish those he found guilty in the area through which he passed, was something that would result in service to his lord and he left Cuzco, as you have heard.

Cuxi Yupanque told Quizquiz that he should remain in Cuzco and look after it. He should send his men from Quito throughout all the provinces to inspect the lands and coca and maize storehouses and the rest of the services of the provinces until his lord the Inca Atahualpa ordered what should be done.

As soon as Cuxi Yupanque left, Quizquiz should send all the Indians after him who had been ordered to leave and who were to populate Quito. He should make certain that they took their wives and children and personal belongings with them. Quizquiz immediately did what Cuxi Yupanque had ordered.

When this was done, Cuxi Yupanque ordered that Atahualpa's statue, which they called the Inca Guauqui, be placed in a certain house in the city where all would worship and serve it in place of their lord. This was done. When Cuxi Yupanque saw that this had been done and that he had nothing more to do, he left the city and went by the post road to Cajamarca. He entered secretly because he knew that his lord was a prisoner. When he reached him, Cuxi Yupanque explained what he had done and how he had left Huascar on the road with the rest who were coming as prisoners and he had found out that three Christians were going to Cuzco.

Atahualpa drew away from the others and told Cuxi Yupanque that it seemed to him that he should return and kill Huascar and those who accompanied him as prisoners. He thought that if Huascar arrived alive in Cajamarca and those *viracochas* saw him and if Huascar saw that he was a prisoner, Huascar would tell the *viracochas* that he would give them much more gold than Atahualpa would. In this way, they would make him the lord because of the gold that he would promise them. The Spaniards would kill Atahualpa. Cuxi Yupanque said that he wished to return immediately. Atahualpa told him to wait; he wanted to know first how to proceed, since there was a problem.

The next day Atahualpa became very sad. When the marquis saw him so sad, he asked him why he was sad. He should be happy since he was his father and would take care of all his needs. Atahualpa told the marquis, "My lord, you do not wish me to be sad, but I must inform you that the captains who were bringing my brother as a prisoner have killed him on the road without my having ordered it." When Atahualpa told the marquis this, he showed great sadness. When the marquis saw him so saddened, he replied to what he had been told in an attempt to alleviate his condition: "Eat, drink, and relax. If your captains killed him, you are still lord. Do not be saddened by this. I am your father."

Atahualpa did not show any happiness when he heard what the marquis told him. When he returned to his quarters, he called for Cuxi Yupanque and told him to leave immediately, that evening, on the post road in a hammock. When he found Huascar, he should kill him and those who accompanied him.

Cuxi Yupanque left immediately by the post road and found Huascar and those who accompanied him at Antamarca. As soon as he arrived, he killed Huascar and those who had come with him. When this was done, he returned to Cajamarca to where Atahualpa was. Here we leave off speaking of him and we will talk about the three Spaniards and what they did on their journey.

XXV

Wherein we learn how the three Spaniards the marquis had sent from Cajamarca arrived in Cuzco, and of the things that they did there, and how they returned to Cajamarca.

The three Spaniards that the marquis had sent from Cajamarca to view Cuzco and see it traveled on the road that the Indians who bore them wished to take. When they reached a province or *tambo,*[1] they inspected the population and the houses of that town, or *tambo,* or province so as to better inform the marquis of what they had seen on their return. They found Calcochima at Jauja. When Calcochima saw them he did them every service. The Spaniards moved on the next day. Thus they were well provided for on their journey in the provinces through which they passed.

Since they were unknown, the people of the towns they arrived at viewed them as gods. When the old men and women of these towns saw them, they immediately offered their eyelashes and eyebrows and blew them in the air right in front of them. They called them *Ticci viracocha pachayachachic runa yachachic,*[2] which means "gods from the ends of the earth, creators of the world and of the people."

They arrived in Cuzco, and when Quizquiz learned that the Spaniards had arrived, he told Chima, who had charge of the statue they had there in place of Atahualpa, to take that statue and hide it in Jaquijahuana. He also ordered that some of Atahualpa's brothers, who were young boys, hide themselves, and they left. Chima carried the statue to hide it.

When the Spaniards entered Cuzco, they were lodged in some houses that are called Coracora. Quizquiz ordered that they be given food and they ate. After resting, they walked about, looking at the city and its houses and all the gold and silver that it contained. They reached the temple of the Sun and saw that band of gold that went around the room where the idol of the Sun was and they saw this idol and a small terrace covered with sheets of silver and wood covered with the same metal.

They saw the rest of the treasures that these houses of the Sun contained, many pitchers of gold and silver together with pots and large earthen jars and other containers of various types. One of them took a small rock and threw it at one of those golden vessels there in the house of the Sun, and then they left.

Quizquiz noted everything they did. They were in the city of Cuzco for fifteen days. At the end of that time, they left without taking anything from the city. They merely looked at it and admired the great treasures. They left and returned to Cajamarca in their hammocks, as they had come. They reported what they had seen to the marquis.

Quizquiz remained in Cuzco after the Spaniards departed. He paused to consider what he had observed of the Spaniards. He said to those who were with him: "It seems to me that they are not gods because they do not know how to speak our language, or how to eat our food properly, as we do. In the houses of the Sun they threw a rock at a golden pitcher that belongs to the Sun's service. Without a doubt they are not gods. Nor has our lord Atahualpa explained to us who they are. I do not know why he did not send somebody with them to explain to us who they were."

Ten days after the Spaniards had left Cuzco, an Indian sent from Cajamarca by Atahualpa arrived and told Quizquiz that Atahualpa was a prisoner. Those *viracochas*, including one of their nobles called *capito*, had captured him. When Quizquiz learned this, he was greatly saddened and said that the *capito* and his men had done a great wrong. If they had not taken him, they could have negotiated anything they wished with him.

When he learned this, he wanted to go after the three Spaniards who had left there ten days before. Since they told him that they had returned on the post road and regularly changed Indian hammock bearers, he saw that he could not catch them and gave up the idea.

He immediately ordered his warriors to assemble. They were spread out through all the towns and provinces to inspect the coca and maize fields and the rest of the farms. When they were assembled, he commanded that those from Cuzco hide all the gold and silver items that they had, because Atahualpa had sent him word that the Spaniards were fond of gold and silver. Thus a great treasure was hidden.

When the Spaniards came to the city of Cuzco and conquered it from its defender, Quizquiz, they did not find the better part of the gold and silver that the three Spaniards had seen when they went there the first time. Afterward, some of this hidden treasure was found. Even today it continues to be found because some Indians tell their masters, who open the foundations of houses or tear down buildings and sometimes find it and find pits where it was hidden.

We will now leave off speaking of Quizquiz and we will speak of the marquis and what happened with Atahualpa and of the imprisonment of Chalcochima.

XXVI

Wherein we learn how Atahualpa gave the treasure to the marquis in Cajamarca, and how the marquis distributed it among his men, and how, after this, he ordered the death of Atahualpa, and how Atahualpa died, and how Chalcochima was captured.

While Atahualpa was a prisoner in Cajamarca, the marquis held him in his own lodgings, and there Atahualpa slept. The marquis always tried to do everything to please him and bring him pleasure because Atahualpa was a great lord. He saw Atahualpa's power over the entire realm of Peru when he placed it under the rule of the king of Spain. Because of the marquis's character and magnificence and since he had Atahualpa imprisoned, he told him that, if he filled a certain house with gold and silver to a mark that he had made on it, that he would free him. When Atahualpa heard the marquis say that he would free him, he responded by saying that he would fill the house with gold and silver to a point much above that mark. He made another mark much higher than that made by the marquis.

Atahualpa gathered or caused the amassing of all the gold and silver that he had promised and as he gathered it Atahualpa pleaded with the marquis not to allow any of his men to damage or destroy any piece of gold or silver that he placed there or caused to be gathered. Atahualpa's intention must have been to unleash such a war when he was freed that he would once again see his gold and silver items.

When all the gold and silver had been gathered and the house was filled to the mark that had been made, the marquis took the piece which seemed to him appropriate for the captain-general, and then he took the *quinto*, or royal fifth, that belonged to his Majesty and delivered it to his treasurer. This done, he divided the treasure into parts and distributed it among his men, giving to each man there with him the part that belonged to him according to his station and his service. In this way, he distributed this treasure among his men.

When the marquis learned of the treasures that were at a *guaca* called Pachacama, which lies on the coast four leagues from what is now the city of

Los Reyes [Lima], he ordered his brother Hernando Pizarro to go to this shrine and bring back this treasure. Hernando Pizarro left and arrived at the shrine. Although he arrived quickly, the Indians learned of it and removed the majority of the treasure and fled with it. When Hernando Pizarro arrived, he found that they had removed the greater portion of the treasure. He took what remained, and what he could find; from there climbed the mountains and came out at Bonbon. There he learned that Chalcochima was in Jauja punishing those who had just stood by and had not wished to be on his side and those who had opposed Atahualpa.

Pizarro ordered the Indians with him to take him to Chalcochima in the province of Jauja. They took him and the people he had with him to Jauja. He arrived at vespers and found Chalcochima drunk and captured him.

The next day Hernando Pizarro asked Chalcochima where Huascar was and what he had done with his treasure. Chalcochima told him: "I killed him and ended his entire line and that of his followers. You see here his treasure." And he showed him some gold vessels and gave them to him.

Hernando Pizarro then returned from there to Cajamarca, taking Chalcochima with him as a prisoner. So he entered Cajamarca and after the marquis had divided the treasure among his men, he remained in Cajamarca for some time, resting with his men and with Atahualpa. He continued to ask Atahualpa questions. Likewise Atahualpa enjoyed the company of the marquis and that of the rest of the Spaniards in such measure that the Spaniards loved him and he, them.

At that time Atahualpa had some women, among whom was one called Sancta, who was very white and beautiful. This Sancta attracted the attention of an Indian that the marquis had there as an interpreter. Since he liked her, he was alert to when Atahualpa left his quarters. When he left, this Indian interpreter entered Atahualpa's lodgings and raped her. While he was engaged in this treachery, Atahualpa entered and found the interpreter in the manner you have heard with his wife Sancta. When he saw him he told him: "Evil yunga dog, and with my wife. It truly appears that I am a prisoner. If I were not, you know I would exact such a punishment that no knowledge would remain of you and your lineage and all those of your nation."

When this happened to the interpreter, he went outside and hid his wickedness. Atahualpa didn't say anything to anyone. After a few days, it occurred to the interpreter that if he reported that Atahualpa wished to rise up and flee and that he had gathered some warriors near there for this purpose, the Spaniards would kill Atahualpa and he would have Atahualpa's wife, the one he had slept with, for himself.

After the interpreter devised this treachery, he put his plan in motion. To cover his lie about the warriors, since there were none, he sent some of his Indians to a spot two or three leagues from there and ordered them to build many fires and trample the grass and conduct themselves as if warriors were there. When this was done and his Indians had returned, that interpreter went to the marquis and told him that Atahualpa wished to flee and to kill the marquis and all his men and that he had a large group of soldiers some two or three leagues from there.

When the marquis heard this, he asked Atahualpa if it were true and he was told that it was not. Some of the Spaniards said that it was impossible because he was well treated and well guarded. Others said that they should kill him. The marquis did not believe it. A second interpreter the marquis had said that it was a lie and that the first interpreter set it up. The second interpreter told that the first interpreter had made it up.

When the treasurer learned of this, he gave the marquis notice that he would collect the royal fifth of all that treasure the marquis had there from him and from his assets if the treasure were lost because he did not kill Atahualpa. The marquis should either kill him or have him killed. In this way, those riches would not be lost.

Almagro also had bad relations with Atahualpa. Almagro had carried a dagger on his belt since his arrival. The dagger had hanging from it a *borla* tassel. When Atahualpa saw the dagger and they told him that Almagro also was a captain like the marquis, he asked Almagro for that dagger. Almagro told him he did not wish to give it to him. When he saw this, Atahualpa was embarrassed and considered Almagro a miserable man.

Almagro did not get along with Atahualpa, and when he heard what that interpreter had fabricated against Atahualpa, Almagro, together with the treasurer Riquelme, insisted that the marquis kill Atahualpa. When the marquis saw the notice that the treasurer had given him and heard the powerful arguments of Almagro and others for killing Atahualpa, he sentenced Atahualpa to be burned.

One of the marquis's captains, seeing that the marquis was determined to kill Atahualpa, told him that it was all opinion and that he wanted to go and see those warriors and find out where they were and if it were true. They should not kill Atahualpa until he returned. This captain, taking some men to accompany him, left to investigate.

Atahualpa saw that death was approaching and it was because of the false testimony set up by that interpreter whom he caught with his wife. Atahualpa said that he was lord and such a powerful lord that even the birds did not fly in his land without his permission; he had more power over his people, who obeyed him. No one moved without his order. And he had not ordered anything. And since he had not ordered it, nothing was done.

Since the marquis was now determined to kill him, he ordered that the sentence be read and that they take him out to be burned. So they took Atahualpa out to burn him without waiting for the captain who had gone looking for these warriors. When Atahualpa was tied to the stake, Fray Vicente de Valverde asked him if he wished to become a Christian. He said yes and he was baptized and given the name Francisco. Since he was now a Christian, they begged the marquis to permit him to be garroted.

To carry out the sentence, he ordered that some straw be thrown over him and be lighted. Atahualpa was then garroted and they threw straw over him and scorched him. Thus Atahualpa died. When he was dead, Fray Vicente had him removed from the stake and buried him in the church there in Cajamarca. His death was felt and mourned by all of his people.

When Cuxi Yupanque saw that his lord and brother was dead, he went around Cajamarca disguised to see if he could steal away his sister Angelina Yupanque, whom the marquis had with him. When the marquis left Cajamarca, Cuxi Yupanque followed him for several days to see if he could carry off his sister and take her to where she would never more be seen. When he saw that he could not take her because she was well guarded, Cuxi Yupanque returned to Cajamarca and removed Atahualpa's body from the grave where it was and placed it on a litter. In this way, he carried it to Quito.

At that time, one of Atahualpa's captains named Rumiñagui was in Quito. While Cuxi Yupanque was carrying Atahualpa's body, he sent a messenger to this Rumiñagui telling him how he was bringing the body of his lord Atahualpa. When Rumiñagui learned this news and saw that Cuxi Yupanque was coming and that he was a lord and Atahualpa's captain-general and that he brought Atahualpa's body, he knew that Cuxi Yupanque and not he would be lord when he arrived in Quito.

He decided to kill Cuxi Yupanque any way he could and take Atahualpa's body and become lord. To carry this out, he gathered the warriors that he had with him and, pretending he was going to receive Atahualpa's body, went in search of Cuxi Yupanque. When Rumiñagui reached Cuxi Yupangue, he paid his respects to Atahualpa's body and made a sacrifice. Cuxi Yupanque had come crying and dressed in mourning, and Rumiñagui took him aside to some lodgings as if he wanted to speak to him alone. Cuxi Yupanque went with him alone, without taking anyone with him.

When they were alone, some of Rumiñagui's Indian friends, with whom he had plotted his treason, entered. When they had entered, Rumiñagui gave them a signal and they all attacked Cuxi Yupanque and the first thing they grasped was the throat and thus they strangled him. When Cuxi Yupanque was dead, Rumiñagui left and took Atahualpa's body and carried it to Quito. Afterward, the Spanish captured Rumiñagui in Quito and burned him.

Let us return to what happened to Atahualpa's wives. After his death when they saw him dead, all of them hanged themselves. And the Indian woman Sancta was the first. Although that interpreter who had fabricated the testimony against Atahualpa looked for her immediately, she had already hanged herself.

Thus Atahualpa died. The interpreter who had caused it did not avoid punishment. Almagro had him quartered in Chile because he escaped and staged an uprising by the Indians of Chile. Thus he paid.

When Atahualpa died, all the Indians gathered there in Cajamarca returned to their lands, and the roads were full of them as if they were rows of ants.

XXVII

Wherein the marquis named a son of Huayna Capac as Inca and lord after the death of Atahualpa there in Cajamarca; he was called Topa Gualpa; the marquis left Cajamarca and came in search of the city of Cuzco, and of the things that befell him during this time.

After Atahualpa died, it seemed to the marquis that, because there were many leaders and the land was long and large, to have better relations with all them, it was well to name another Inca in Cajamarca. He therefore had all the leaders and noble Indians there in Cajamarca appear before him and in their presence he named as Inca a son of Huayna Capac, called Inca Topa Gualpa, who was in Cajamarca.

Topa Gualpa, with the Indian leaders, held their festivals and rejoicing there. Afterward, he became ill with a disease from which this Topa Gualpa died as he entered Jauja in the company of the marquis.

Since the marquis in Cajamarca had learned of the grandeur and the riches of Cuzco, he decided to send Captain Soto[1] there with some men that he had with him in order to resist if Quizquiz defended the entrance. After Captain Soto had left Cajamarca, Diego de Almagro also left for the city of Cuzco. And after Diego de Almagro, the marquis left. When he arrived in Jauja, he settled a town of Christians. From there he went on to Cuzco and took Chalcochima with him as prisoner.

Captain Soto, since he went earlier, arrived at the *tambo* called Limatambo, which is seven leagues from Cuzco. There he learned that Quizquiz was waiting for him with his warriors half a league from there, at the crest of a hill called Vilcacunga he had to climb.

Captain Soto prepared himself and his men as best he could, and they continued their march, and when they arrived at the top of the hill, Quizquiz emerged with his men and fell upon them. He killed two Christians and forced them to retreat down the hill to a place where there was an Indian market. When they had retreated, some old women who were there told the Spaniards that they should not return for another battle so soon and they should wait there for a while. So they remained and while they were thus stopped, Diego de Almagro arrived and together they defeated Quizquiz and passed the crest and gave chase to Quizquiz, who fled from there to Guacachaca and crossed the bridge and went to Capi. When he saw that the Christians were coming for him, he fled from there to the mountains of the Yanaguaras.

Later the marquis had Spaniards continue after him and warned them to go past Jauja; they followed Quizquiz into Caxas. They captured some spoils and finally Quizquiz reached Quito, where he would die.

The marquis arrived in Jaquijahuana and there the noble lords of Cuzco came out to meet him. They were all crying and they introduced him to Manco Inca, who was at that time fifteen years old. Since the marquis learned there in Jaquijahuana of the great cruelties that Chalcochima had visited upon Cuzco and its citizenry, he had Chalcochima burned there in Jaquijahuana. When this had been done, the marquis left there and went to the city of Cuzco, where he found Captain Soto and Diego de Almagro collecting the gold and silver that was there.

As soon as he arrived, he had all the gold in the towns and provinces from seven leagues around the city of Cuzco brought to him. This included Pacaricatambo, from whence the *orejon* lords say they originated, as you have heard in this account. From there they brought some golden doors that had been at the entrance to this cave and a golden tree that was there. From the town of Urcos, from the shrine of Viracocha, they brought many golden vessels and a gold bench upon which rested the statue of Viracocha.

When all the gold and silver they could find was brought, the marquis took the gold bench as the captain-general's personal treasure. He separated the royal fifth that belonged to his Majesty. The marquis divided and distributed the rest of the treasure among his men, just as he had done in Cajamarca.

When this had been completed, he distributed lots for houses among the Spanish in the city of Cuzco. Then he gathered the nobles and native lords of Cuzco and asked them to whom the leadership and position of the Inca belonged. They should decide among themselves whom he should name as Inca and lord. He wished to appoint him. In a meeting they held there they decided that it should be Manco Capac,[2] and so they came to the marquis and told him what they had decided.

XXVIII

Wherein the marquis names Manco Capac as Inca; during this investiture he was named Manco Inca.

As soon as the lords returned to the marquis to tell him what they had decided, they told him that at that time there was no one in Cuzco who deserved to be named Inca except Manco Capac, who was there present. He was a son of Huayna Capac. Although he was not the son of a mother who was of the ladies of Cuzco, he was the son of an important woman from the town of Anta [Jaquijahuana], which lies three leagues from the city of Cuzco.

The marquis then named him as Inca and the noble lords and leaders there present accepted him as such. As soon as he was named by the marquis, the lords dubbed him Manco Inca and told the marquis that henceforth he would be known as Manco Inca. Then the noble *orejones* of Cuzco took him and held their fiestas and joyous ceremonies, fasts, and sacrifices. When all this was done, Manco Inca and the rest of the nobles felt that he should become Inca and Capac, as his ancestors had been and that the Spaniards should all leave the country and return to Castile.

One day it occurred to the marquis that it would be good to learn what *repartimientos*[1] existed in the lands and to distribute them to the Spaniards who were then with him in order to populate the towns with Spaniards. He called for Manco Inca and ordered him to bring the account and list of all the territorial divisions that had been made. Manco Inca left there and called for the *llacta camayos,*[2] which means the officials of the towns, and for those who were in charge of keeping records in the city of Cuzco. From them he learned of the *repartimientos* that had been made and the Indians who were on each one and he took the report of what he had been asked by the marquis.

The marquis distributed the *repartimientos* among the Spanish citizens who had populated the area. Then he did the same in the rest of the towns populated by Spaniards. When Manco Inca saw this first distribution and what was happening in Cuzco, he and the rest of the lords were saddened. They gave themselves up to the devil when they saw that things were turning out the opposite of what they had intended. They had thought that the Spaniards would return to Castile and leave them as the lords of the land.

One day Manco Inca went to the marquis and begged him, because he had put his people under Spaniards, to order their masters not to treat them badly and, moreover, not to put the noble lords of Cuzco under any Spaniards. The marquis promised him this and left them free.

He told the Inca that, even though he, the marquis, had distributed the Indians, it was he, Manco Inca, who would command them and that if anyone did not wish to do as he ordered, the Inca should come to him and he, the marquis, would personally punish the disobedient one. The Indians would be well treated by their masters.

After leaving everything well and justly ordered in the city of Cuzco, the marquis returned to Jauja. On this trip, he passed through the city he had founded in the valley of Lima. From there the marquis once again climbed to Cuzco in order to send off the *adelantado*,[3] Diego de Almagro, on his journey to Chile.

When he arrived in Cuzco, the marquis saw that Manco Inca went about in the company of one Marticote who watched over him and took care of his affairs. Thus this Marticote went about with the Inca. At that time the marquis had with him a young son of Huayna Capac who served him in his chamber. Since Manco Inca saw that the marquis loved that brother of his, he suspected that his love for him would lead him in the end to name him Inca and to take that office from him [Manco Inca].

He commanded that a way be found to kill his brother, and he told Marticote and his brother Paulo, who at that time was his steward. Paulo and Marticote told Manco Inca to call him and the two of them would kill him.

The Inca thus called him, and when the boy entered the room where his brother Manco Inca was, the other brother, Paulo, and Marticote came out and killed him. When he was dead, Marticote and Paulo hid.

When the marquis learned of this, he was saddened and asked the Inca what had happened. Manco Inca told him that the boy had quarreled with Paulo and at that moment Marticote arrived and the boy also had quarreled with him. Paulo and Marticote had killed him, and he had nothing to do with it. The marquis asked why he had not captured them, and the Inca replied that the incident happened so quickly he did not see it. When he came out, they had already fled. In reality, he had hidden them.

XXIX

Wherein Manco Inca, Vilaoma, and the rest of the lords of Cuzco came to an agreement regarding how to rebel and gave the order for the rebellion.

Manco Inca saw he was lord but the marquis had distributed the land, populated it, and created towns of Spaniards; thus it seemed that he had the title of Inca but was not ruler. Moreover, it seemed to him that there were few Spaniards and that these were scattered out over the land in the towns where they had settled. Since Almagro had gone to Chile, he had taken with him a good quantity of them. Therefore, there remained fewer with whom he would have to battle.

If he rebelled he would kill them all, and it would be easy to do this because he would find them spread out among the towns where they were settled. After considering this, it seemed good to him to come to an agreement about this with the principal leaders of the city of Cuzco. So he ordered them to gather and told them what you have just heard.

In this council the evil Vilaoma[1] took part. He was a principal leader of the city of Cuzco and a man advanced in years. He was in charge of the idol of the Sun and was its custodian. When something arose, he was the first and most important to give an opinion. Sometimes he spoke for himself and sometimes in the place of the Sun as if the Sun were a man and spoke with other men.

When the Spaniards met Vilaoma and became aware of his position, they called him *papa*.[2] Since Vilaoma found himself in this council and was as important as you have heard, he spoke and explained what the Çapa Inca should do in this case: "Paulo should go with Almagro to Chile and should lead him down a path that has no escape. To do this he should go through the barren lands and mountain passes where there is no food. In these passes all will die either of hunger or cold. I will leave here, from Cuzco, with these Spaniards. I will say that I want to go with them to Chile and tell them that there is much gold there. I will tell them that the houses and everything else are made of pure gold. Paulo will say the same thing to Almagro and will quote me. I will agree.

"When the Spaniards see that Paulo and I are accompanying them, they will believe what I have said. Thus both of us will leave the city of Cuzco with the Spaniards. When I see them on the road to Chile, I will flee from them at night. Paulo will go on with them. When they have crossed the passes, those who may escape will be spread out without order. The Indians of Chile and Copayapo will attack them and kill them all. If they do not kill them, we will finish them off when they return.

"So that Paulo, when he returns, will know that we have killed all the Spaniards who stayed here, he will find the Spaniards marked, on foot, and their horses dead on a high mountain. When Paulo sees these figures, he will gather all the people he can and await them. When they emerge from the mountain passes and other unpopulated areas, hunger and thirst will disband them. When they emerge thus disordered, he will kill them all.

"I will have returned after having fled from them. There will be few Spaniards in Cuzco, since the majority will have gone with the Macho Apo,"[33] what they called the marquis, "to Lima and Pachacama. I will come, raising the entire Collao region. When I reach Cuzco the Çapa Inca will come out of Cuzco. Thus we will kill all of them in Cuzco. Afterward, we will descend and kill the Macho Apo and all those who would be with him and the rest of them in the entire country. And so we will have the land."

When Vilaoma finished saying this, it seemed to the Inca and the rest who were present that what Vilaoma had said was what should be done. So they agreed to keep it secret and prepare it the best they could. This done, with many other things that they discussed, they left the council.

XXX

Wherein we learn how Hernando Pizarro returned from Spain, and how the Inca tricked Hernando Pizarro by telling him that if he would let him leave Cuzco he would return and bring a potbellied Indian of solid gold, and how Hernando Pizarro allowed him to leave, and how the Inca left, staged an uprising, and never returned even to this day.[1]

After the marquis had dispatched Almagro to Chile, he left his brother Juan Pizarro in Cuzco as his lieutenant. And he left Manco Inca with him. Vilaoma and Paulo had gone with Almagro. This, then, was the situation in Cuzco.

The marquis went down to Jauja and from Jauja passed through the town he had founded there in the Valley of Lima in order to be closer to the sea and a port. At this time Hernando Pizarro returned from Spain, where he had been sent by the marquis with his Majesty's treasurer. When Hernando Pizarro arrived, the marquis sent him as his lieutenant to the city of Cuzco.

After Manco Inca and his men had made the arrangements for the uprising, Vilaoma, as he had agreed with the Inca, returned. He had been traveling in company with Almagro for almost one hundred leagues. As Vilaoma returned, he came raising a rebellion in all of Collao. Some Indians who lived near a shrine called Hancocagua killed their Spanish master and fortified themselves in the shrine of Hancocagua itself.

When Juan Pizarro learned the news of this trouble in Hancocagua and that they had killed their master, he called for the Inca and he gathered his friends who had Indians in Cuzco. Taking some Spaniards with him, leaving the city in the hands of Gabriel de Rojas, and carefully guarding the Inca, he went to punish those in Hancocagua.

He went to the stronghold of Hancocagua but was unable to gain entry. He laid siege to these Indians for a long time, until the Indians started to run out of water. They were about to give up because of the thirst that assailed them when the night before the day they intended to surrender, it snowed so much on the shrine that the water sustained them.

When Juan Pizarro saw this, he was greatly saddened. Finally he asked some *orejon* lords how, in the past, the Incas had conquered that shrine when they had rebelled, and they told him that they filled the space between the stronghold and the facing hill with many bundles of straw and stone. In this way they filled that space between the shrine and the hill where the Spaniards were then. Juan Pizarro immediately ordered that plan described by the Indians put into effect. So they filled that space and ravine between the stronghold and the hill where they were. When it was filled up level with the shrine, they crossed over to the stronghold and so took it.

Gabriel de Rojas, left by Juan Pizarro in Cuzco, had freed the Inca from the prison in which Juan Pizarro had placed him. At this time, Hernando Pizarro was traveling to the city of Cuzco as a lieutenant of the marquis. When he learned that the Inca was a prisoner, he wrote to Gabriel de Rojas that the Inca should not be freed until he arrived. After Hernando Pizarro found out that the Inca was loose, he wrote again to Rojas from the road to recapture him.

When Hernando Pizarro arrived in Cuzco, he freed the Inca from the prison where he was and accorded him all the good treatment he could. Since Hernando Pizarro treated him well, the Inca gave him a quantity of gold.

In a few days, Vilaoma arrived from Collao, where he had fled from Almagro. He returned to Cuzco to cause the Inca to rebel, as had been agreed among them. When he arrived in Cuzco, to hide his true intentions, he went to where Hernando Pizarro was and gave him some gold vessels. Hernando Pizarro received him well. In a few days Vilaoma told the Inca that it was now time to rebel. Almagro was far away and the Macho Apo was in Lima with few men. At present there were few Spaniards there in Cuzco. If they rebelled they would kill them all quickly. This done, they would go down and fall on the marquis and thus finish them all.

Since Manco Inca agreed with what Vilaoma had told him, he went to Hernando Pizarro and told him that he would give him a statue of gold in the form of an Indian with a pot belly and made like a man of solid gold. He had it in a town some four or five leagues distant. He wished to go there and relax. On his return he would bring the potbellied Indian.

At this time, Manco Inca already had many warriors who agreed that on a certain day they would go with him to that place where he was going. Since Hernando Pizarro saw that the Inca demonstrated his affection for him, he gave him permission to go and enjoy himself and bring him the potbellied Indian.

Since some Indian women and *yanacona* servants belonging to the Spanish residents of Cuzco knew of the uprising, they told their masters and they went to Hernando Pizarro and told him how the Inca was in rebellion.

He laughed and said that what the Indian men and women had told them was a lie. When the Spaniards and the residents of Cuzco heard this, they demanded that Hernando Pizarro arrest the Inca and not let him go. Hernando Pizarro told the Inca what had happened and told him not to fear being made a prisoner and to go and enjoy himself and to bring back the potbellied Indian.

So the Inca left and when he had gone, he began to kill some of the Spaniards that he found in the areas surrounding the city. In this way Hernando Pizarro realized that the Inca was in rebellion. He wrote to the marquis about how the Inca had rebelled and that he should be on alert. Here we leave the Inca in rebellion and we will speak of the marquis.

XXXI

Wherein the marquis went to inspect the towns of Piura and Trujillo, and how he learned of the uprising of the Inca when he returned to Lima, and of what he did about it, and how he sent aid to Hernando Pizarro, and how Manco Inca laid siege to the city of Cuzco and made war on Hernando Pizarro and afterward sent a force to lay siege to the marquis.

After the marquis had sent Hernando Pizarro as his lieutenant to the city of Cuzco, it appeared to him good to go and do an inspection of the towns he had populated earlier, which were San Miguel [de Piura] and Trujillo, to see how the inhabitants lived and how they treated their Indian caciques. Accordingly, he ordered a ship prepared, which was done, and the marquis embarked on the sea. When he arrived at the port of Paita, he disembarked. Since the inhabitants of San Miguel had been alerted that the marquis was coming by sea and had, in fact, landed at Paita, they had everything prepared for his landing. There were plenty of horses and all manner of supplies.

Once the marquis landed at Paita and found everything had been prepared, after resting for a few days, he left for the city of San Miguel. When he arrived and entered it, he did an inspection of the city and its people. He settled the grievances that his lieutenants had caused and learned of the bad treatment given the Indian caciques and he punished his lieutenants.

When this inspection was concluded, he left the city of San Miguel and went to Trujillo. On the journey he was well served and regaled by the caciques of the valleys and *tambos* where he stopped and by their masters. So he arrived at the city of Trujillo and did a thorough inspection, as he had done in San Miguel. When he finished, he left for the city of Los Reyes [Lima], whence he had departed. On the road he was also well served and regaled by the inhabitants.

Two months after he arrived, some Indians from Cuzco arrived with letters from Hernando Pizarro advising the marquis of how the Inca had rebelled and to be on the alert and to send him some men and assistance. When the marquis heard this news, he was saddened and immediately held a council meeting with the most important leaders of the city. It was decided in this meeting that aid be requested from Mexico and Santo Domingo and from the rest of the islands and the mainland. The marquis immediately sent the necessary dispatches and men to the above-mentioned lands and provinces.

As he did this, he alerted the city of Quito and the rest of the towns there, San Miguel and Trujillo and Chachapoyas, to this uprising. He ordered Quito to send him some Cañare Indians to serve as allies in the war. He then sent a captain named Diego Pizarro with fifty men to Cuzco to aid Hernando Pizarro. Since he took with him so few men, he was ambushed by Indian warriors in certain difficult mountain passes. They killed him and all that went with him.

After this he sent another captain, named Gonzalo de Tapia, with eighty men to aid Hernando Pizarro. He, too, was killed in a difficult pass with all those he took with him. After this the marquis sent another captain, named Morgovejo, to assist Hernando Pizarro. They killed this Morgovejo and the majority of his men. Some seven or eight escaped and came to the marquis and told him about their defeat.

After this the marquis sent another captain, named Gaete, with forty men to wait in the province of Jauja until he should send more men in order to continue on to Cuzco. With this Gaete he sent a son of Huayna Capac he had with him named Cuxi Rimachi, who would convince the Indians of the Jauja province to serve Captain Gaete.

When the Indians of Jauja saw Gaete in their land with so few men, they ordered his death. Advised of this, Gaete wrote to the marquis and asked for assistance because he was surrounded by the Indians of Jauja. The marquis sent Francisco de Godoy with some men, who, six leagues from Jauja, met one of Gaete's nephews who was fleeing because he had escaped by the grace of God. He told Godoy how his uncle Gaete was dead with all those he had with him and that he had escaped, as he could see. He was riding a mule and had a broken leg.

Therefore, Godoy returned to the city of Los Reyes and told the marquis what had happened to Gaete and his men. A few days later an *orejon* warrior from Cuzco named Quiço Yupanque arrived and laid siege to Lima. When the marquis saw the siege that the Indians had imposed, he heard the Indian warriors say, "Listen, bearded ones: pack up your belongings and board your ship and go back to your land." He immediately sent the ships to Panama so that none would remain in port. They left and none remained. Quiço Yupanque had the city under siege for seven days. At the end of this time, they killed Quiço Yupanque on a Thursday afternoon.

When the Indians who were laying siege saw that their captain was dead, they placed many large candles and lanterns that night on the hill where they had fortified themselves. At midnight they fled, taking with them the body of Quiço Yupanque.

When the marquis saw that he could not breach the stronghold where the Indians were entrenched the entire time they were there, he ordered a heavy blanket prepared. Under this, some Spaniards would go with him. They would carry a cross to place on top of the hill. They would have to go at night.

On the evening on which the Indians left at midnight, an Indian woman belonging to one of the marquis's black men escaped. She had been captured while the Indians were there. This Indian woman came to where the marquis was preparing to go under his blanket and climb the hill. When the Indian woman arrived and explained what had happened, he ended his plan to go with the blanket. The morning of the next day he saw that the Indians had lifted their siege and he ordered the cross he had prepared taken up to place on the hill. He and the rest of the Spaniards with him carried the cross and placed it on top of the hill. Thus the siege of the city was lifted.

During this time, the marquis had with him one Pedro de Lerma and he promised to send him to the city of Cuzco with five hundred men to assist Hernando Pizarro. And he would be their general. Pedro de Lerma kissed the marquis's hands in gratitude for the favor he had done him.

Within a few days Alonso de Alvarado arrived from the province of Chachapoyas. He brought with him all the Spaniards he had. When the marquis saw him, he was pleased with his arrival and made him the captain-general of the five hundred men and sent him to aid Hernando Pizarro in Cuzco. And Pedro de Lerma, whom he had previously granted the favor, was given the captaincy of some men going with Alonso de Alvarado. Pedro de Lerma felt insulted but, since he had to accept the captaincy in order to continue eating, he accepted it and went with Alonso de Alvarado. Thus Marshal Alonso de Alvarado left Lima for Cuzco.

Four months after the marquis had dispatched Marshal Alonso de Alvarado to Cuzco, he gathered six hundred men and personally left Lima for Cuzco with the intention of leaving no *orejon* Indian alive when he arrived in Cuzco. So he left the city of Lima by the lowland road and arrived in the Valley of Guarco. There he learned that Almagro had returned from Chile and captured Hernando Pizarro and that Alonso de Alvarado had fortified himself at the Abancay bridge, which is twenty leagues from Cuzco, to await further orders.

When the marquis learned this, he ordered forty horsemen to prepare and go to where Alonso de Alvarado was and tell him to wait for him there and not to continue because he was coming with six hundred men. All would go on to Cuzco together. When the forty horsemen were sent, the marquis continued with his men and arrived in the province of Nasca. There he received the forty men he had sent from the Valley of Guarco. They told him the news of how Almagro had routed Alonso de Alvarado and captured him because Pedro de Lerma had turned traitor as a result of the insult done him when he had been relieved of the captaincy.

As soon as the marquis heard this, he sent word to Lima to hide his treasure. He sent licentiate Espinosa and Fuenmayor to Cuzco to speak with Almagro. And the marquis returned to Lima.

Let us not deal further with the Christians' passionate quarrels because the chroniclers have written much on this. Let us leave the marquis and Almagro and speak of Manco Inca's uprising and of the things he did and what happened between the Christians and him until they killed him and he died.

XXXII

Which concerns the siege Manco Inca laid

to the city of Cuzco, and the things that happened

to Manco Inca until he died, and how Timbaya

killed the Spaniards who killed him.

Manco Inca left Cuzco in search of the solid gold potbellied Indian. He went to Mohina, which is four leagues from the city. There he ordered the warriors to attack the city. From Mohina he left for the town of Calca.

When the warriors arrived, they killed all the Christians they found dispersed outside the city. Manco Inca also ordered them to kill all the pigs in all the *repartimientos*.[1]

When Hernando Pizarro learned that the Inca had rebelled, he gathered the Spaniards that he had with him as quickly as possible and prepared them to defend themselves from their enemies. He found that he had two hundred and fifty Christians with him, including priests, monks, young people, children, and the sick. There were but one hundred soldiers among them and these, with the rest, scarcely made up a decent troop.

When Manco Inca had all his warriors assembled with him, he ordered Vilaoma and the rest of the captains to go to Cuzco and kill all the Christians. If possible, they were to capture Hernando Pizarro and bring him back alive because he intended to fill him with gold. Nor were they to kill Gabriel de Rojas or the Spanish women there, or the farrier, barber, or the horses.

Manco Inca thought that his warriors had merely to arrive in Cuzco and, arriving, kill the Spaniards as easily as he had said it. His captains said there would be nothing to it.

Vilaoma and the other captains left and positioned the warriors about the city. They sang their song about how they would kill the Christians. After this the warriors made a surprise attack on the Christians. Since the Christians had seen them coming, they defended themselves. Each captain defended his barracks. The slaughter was so great among the Indians that it seemed that their forces were blessed with divine favor and did not rely solely on their own efforts, because there were more than five hundred Indians for each Christian and each day there were more.

While the Indians and the Christians were fighting, messengers came and went to Manco Inca at the town of Calca, where he was. When the Indians arrived, he would ask them, "Have you now killed them all?" The Indians said they had not but that soon they would finish them all. Thus Manco Inca awaited word that they had killed them all.

When they saw that they could not finish off the Christians, Vilaoma and the rest of Manco's captains burned all the towns around the city and all the supply depots and everything else they could in the city. They did this so thoroughly that the Christians found themselves in such straits that they held only half the plaza and the church, which the Indians had not been able to burn even though it had a straw roof.

They shot flaming arrows at it and were able to ignite a small area of the roof facing the plaza. Then they returned to kill, and the Indians said that, when they came, where the straw had been ignited, a Spanish lady dressed all in white was seated on the roof of the church and she put out the fire with some long, white pieces of cloth she had. All during the time the siege on Cuzco was in place, they always saw this lady seated atop this church.

They say they also saw a man on a white horse fully armed and with a long, white beard preceding the Christians whenever they left the city to do battle. He had on his chest a red cross similar to the habit of Santiago the marquis wore on his chest. This, they say, was the spirit of the marquis leading his men. They saw that he created so much dust with the horse he rode that they were blinded and were unable to fight. And so the Christians defeated them.

When the Indians saw they were unable to do anything with them, they opened the ditches and filled the land and the flats with water where they went out to fight them. They made everything into a muddy bog so that they could not fight on the flats. They destroyed the bridges and dug large holes into which the Spaniards fell with their horses.

A few days later, they displayed some Christian heads belonging to those who had died among the men of the captains the marquis had sent to aid Cuzco. Together with these heads they displayed some *bullas* [letters]. The Christians picked up a few of them. They felt this meant that some captain would come to their aid, and with this captain someone must be bringing them those *bullas*, but the captain and his men had been killed, so they took the *bullas* very sadly. The Christians were besieged and in constant battle with the Indians for thirteen or fourteen months.

At the end of this time, the Indians retreated because Manco Inca learned that Almagro had returned from Chile and was in Arequipa. When Manco Inca heard this, he retreated to Tambo [Ollantaytambo], which is seven leagues from Cuzco. When Almagro came, Manco Inca sent some messengers telling him how he had rebelled because of the bad treatment accorded him by Hernando Pizarro and those in Cuzco.

Manco Inca sent him one of his captains so that when he went to Cuzco that he would give himself up in the company of that captain that he had sent. Almagro also sent him one of his captains named Ruy Diaz.

Manco Inca lied to Almagro and did not come after Almagro had entered Cuzco and been there for a long time. Almagro ordered Orgoñez to go out and defeat him. Orgoñez went out and attacked Manco in such a way that he took him by surprise and captured many women, although Manco Inca, Vilaoma, and most of the leaders escaped.

In this attack made on him, Manco Inca lost a lot of the goods that he had stolen from the marquis's captains who had been sent to relieve Cuzco and whom he had killed. After this battle Orgoñez returned, bringing with him Ruy Diaz and other Christians who were there with Manco Inca.

After the battle of Salinas, Almagro was defeated, captured [and later executed], and Orgoñez was killed. With everything now settled, the marquis sent his brother Gonzalo Pizarro to attack Manco Inca, capture him if he could, and, if possible, eliminate that den of thieves there.

Gonzalo Pizarro took a number of Spaniards and many Indian friends and fell on Manco Inca. He defeated him and captured his principal wife, who was called Cora, and took from him everything that he had stolen. You should know that while the marquis and Almagro were engaged in their quarrels, Manco Inca left the wilds, came to Jauja, and stole everything he could from the Guancas. He got their *guaca* idol and took it with him and returned to Paucarpampa, which is behind Aco.

From there he left for a place called Cocha, which is above Sangaro five or six leagues from Guamanga [Ayacucho]. There he built a town in the image of Cuzco and ordered that it be called Rucquiri. He killed a leader of the province of *Angara*[2] and another man from Aco in this town as well as one of his *orejon* lords. When the caciques who were there with him saw that they were being killed, some of them fled.

Since he had carried off the *guaca* of the Guancas and they knew that it was in that building in the town that he constructed above Sangaro, they gathered men in their province and went to offer him battle. When he learned that the Guancas had come out to fight him, he went out and met them on the road. He found them at Paucarpampa and they fought. Manco Inca was defeated and returned to the town he had built.

Since the Guancas had defeated him, he told the leaders with him that he was no longer their lord and that they should return to their lands and serve the Spaniards. He intended to enter the wilds of the Andes and he asked them for some things they had there. Taking what they could bring him and taking with him some two thousand Indians and many things he had stolen, he entered the wilds. When Gonzalo Pizarro had defeated him, he had taken from him all that he had stolen and had captured his principal wife. Manco Inca had escaped by fleeing through the wilds. Thus Gonzalo Pizarro did not take him and returned with his prey to Cuzco.

When Manco Inca saw that he had lost his wife and had been treated so badly, he wanted to play some trick on the marquis. He sent his messengers to Gonzalo Pizarro and told him that the Inca wanted to come in peace. When Gonzalo Pizarro heard this, he informed the marquis, who was at that time founding the town of Arequipa. When the marquis learned this, he came on the post road to Cuzco and went to the Valley of Yucay.

The marquis had with him there a number of Spaniards and also the wife of Manco Inca. Manco Inca sent him word that the marquis should send those soldiers back to Cuzco because, since there were so many soldiers there, he was afraid they wished to do him some harm. He was afraid since he had no Indians to accompany him and therefore he did not come. He was also indisposed by boils.

When the marquis heard this, he ordered the majority of those with him to return to the city of Cuzco. He sent a message to licentiate de la Gama, his lieutenant-general, not to allow anyone to come to Yucay where he was. He sent a hammock to the Inca in which he might come. With it he sent one of his Spanish servants and a mulatto.

When the Spaniard and the mulatto arrived in Tambo, three leagues away, Manco Inca ordered them killed. When the *yanacona* servants who had accompanied the Spaniard witnessed this, they fled to Yucay and told the marquis what had happened and that Manco Inca was bringing many warriors to attack him.

When the marquis heard this, he ordered that Manco Inca's wife, whom he held there as a prisoner, be brought out and that she be whipped and burned. So they whipped and burned her and threw her into a river below. When this was done, the marquis returned to Cuzco.

When Manco Inca learned of this, he sent many Indians downriver to search for the body of his wife. They searched and found it and took it to him. He mourned over her body and held many ceremonies and sacrifices like those you have heard that they did for their dead.

Manco Inca then returned to his forest retreat. When he learned later that the marquis was dead, he was pleased and sent Diego de Almagro's son, el Mozo, weapons that he had taken from the Christians. After Diego el Mozo was defeated at Chupas, Diego Mendez and others fled from there to the city of Cuzco, where they were captured.

Diego Mendez escaped from his captivity and went to Manco Inca, who received him with great honor and gave him *yanacona* Indians for his service and many stolen goods. He always provided abundantly for him what was needed. After him, another six or seven Spaniards, all from Diego de Almagro's band, came to him. He received them well, as he had done Diego Mendez and provided and arranged to provide all that was necessary for them.

While they were there, the Spaniards played *herron*[3] and went horseback riding and enjoyed themselves with the Inca. While occupied in this, the Inca learned of the arrival of Viceroy Blasco Nuñez Vela and that he was on the side of the Indian leaders. When he learned this, he told Diego Mendez and the rest of the Christians.

When Diego Mendez and the rest heard this, they decided to go out and meet the viceroy. They told this to Manco Inca, who ordered his captains to provide them what was needed and to go out with them. Manco Inca asked Diego Mendez to speak to the viceroy in his behalf. For this purpose, some of his *orejon* lords would go with him to bring back the viceroy's reply resulting from his negotiations with him.

When this had been done, the Inca's men took Diego Mendez and the rest in some hammocks and carried them. When they neared Guamanga, they had news that Gonzalo Pizarro was there and had come with the men of Cuzco to protest the viceroy's ordinances. When Diego Mendez and the others learned of this, they decided to return from there to see how that situation would resolve itself. So they turned back.

When the Inca's captains found themselves turning back, they stole from all those towns they usually stole from and carried off all they could in the way of Indian men and women, sheep, clothing, and all the rest they could find. On their return, Diego Mendez fell ill and returned as a sick man.

Carrying their loot, they reached Manco Inca; he ordered that all they brought from the raid they had conducted be placed in the town square. He ordered the Christians to pick out what they wanted. They did so and the rest he ordered stored in some houses that were set aside for this purpose. He ordered that Diego Mendez be treated and that the rest of the Spaniards be given every service. He was always very careful in this regard.

After Diego Mendez had recovered, Manco Inca gave him two young girls from the Pallas nation. Manco Inca enjoyed the company of Diego Mendez and the rest, and they, his. They played *herron* and other games they liked. While engaged in this activity, a *mestizo* arrived from Cuzco on the pretense that he was fleeing from the Christians in Cuzco in order to serve Manco Inca. He carried a letter from someone in Cuzco, I do not know who, and secretly gave it to Diego Mendez. This letter was intended to tell him what a good thing had happened to the one who sent it to him.

When the Inca saw how the mestizo had come in rags, he ordered that he be given velvet clothing and everything else he needed. And he ordered that he be lodged with Diego Mendez. When the mestizo found himself alone with Diego Mendez he told him what had happened. At this time Diego Mendez had a black women, who overheard what the mestizo told her master and she saw the letter in his hands. Diego Mendez met with Gomez Perez and the rest of the Spaniards and told them what the letter contained and what the mestizo had told him and commanded that the Inca be killed. They ordered that many bread rolls be baked to take with them to eat on the road when they left there.

When the black woman learned this, she went to tell some of the Inca's important leaders. When they heard it, they went to tell the Inca. However, since the Inca was satisfied with the Spaniards and liked them so much and treated them so well, he told those leaders, "Those of you have told me that you covet some things that these Spaniards possess and cannot see how you can take it except by coming to tell me to kill them, saying that you wish me to kill them so that you might take from them what you covet. Leave here and do not tell me this again because I will punish you."

Those leaders left and neither they nor anyone else dared approach the Inca again to warn him of anything.

Once the Christians decided to kill the Inca, they arranged it, thinking that if they killed him, the men there with the Inca would side with them if they saw the Inca dead. They would then leave and return to their lands because the vast majority of those who were there today are forced to be there.

After the Spaniards had agreed on this, they went about looking for the right time to kill him and leave there. The day after the Spaniards had their meeting, the Inca called for the mestizo. He took him aside and told him to tell him what was happening in Cuzco and who was in charge and which Spaniards were there and how many horses they had. The mestizo told him that Toro[4] was in command in Cuzco and that there were but fifty men and they had neither horses nor pack animals because Gonzalo Pizarro had taken them. If any remained, it was because it was a lame horse and had been left because it could not walk. The people in Cuzco did nothing and were off guard.

It seemed to the Inca that the mestizo was telling him the truth. He told the mestizo to go to his room, called for his captains, and told them what the mestizo had told him and that it seemed to him that they had time to go to Cuzco and kill the Spaniards they found there and steal what they could and bring back all the Spanish women they found. The captains told him they would be pleased to go, and the Inca told them to all go on that enterprise and to take Pumasupa as their leader.

So they prepared themselves and left on their undertaking. Ten Indian jungle archers remained with the Inca as his personal guard. These were among those who eat human flesh.

Another fifty Indians, with Timbayci as their captain, remained, as did another two elderly lords who stayed to keep company with the Inca. Also staying were fifty Indians who were *yanacona* servants. Since the Spaniards intended to kill the Inca, it seemed that now was the time because the warriors and captains were gone to attack Cuzco. To carry this business to a successful conclusion, it struck them that they should start a game of *herron*. Perhaps the Inca would wish to play with them at this game, as he usually did. Then, while playing, they could start to quarrel with him and, all together, kill him. When the Indians who were there with them saw he was dead, they would return to their lands and find themselves free of that place.

Just as they intended and arranged it, they put the plan in operation and went to play the game. They took some daggers stuck in their open-toed half boots and carried many bread rolls hidden in their sleeves and in their clothing to eat in the wilderness when they escaped from there.

When they went to play, they asked the Inca to play with them. The Inca said that he didn't want to play. So they asked him to judge the throws. When the Inca would rise to measure the tosses they made, then they could attack him when they saw there were no Indians in the plaza who could come to his aid. So they began their game.

Now, since Pumasupa had gone to attack Cuzco, he passed by the headwaters of the Apurimac. There, he attacked a leader at night and took him in his houses with all his wives. As soon as he captured him, he sent him to the Inca to do with as he wished. When the leader was taken to the Inca and was but one league from where the Inca was, those who brought him that leader sent a messenger to the Inca. They asked him if he wished that leader to enter and give homage that day or the next morning. When this messenger arrived, he found the Inca in the plaza watching how the Spaniards played. At that time, two old lords were with the Inca, one on each side, with the Inca in the center. Behind the Inca was one of his wives.

At this time, no other Indians were in the plaza except those two old lords. The Spaniards intended to kill him that day any way they could. When the messenger reached the Inca, he stood behind him and spoke the message he carried in his ear. The Inca turned his head over his shoulder and told the Indian his pleasure.

When the Spanish saw the Inca thus occupied, they came up and told him that he must judge a toss and settle a dispute. The Inca did not answer them, and they gave him a push on his thigh. The Inca turned his face to Gomez Perez, who had pushed him, and angrily told him to wait until he took care of that messenger. After he finished, he would see what he wanted.

With this, the Inca turned his head to speak with the messenger. This final time that he turned his head all the Spaniards who were there came up and Gomez Perez took out his dagger and plunged it in the Inca's chest. When he received that thrust, the Inca rose and threw the blanket over Gomez's eyes. Gomez Perez gave him another thrust, which was partly successful. The Inca fell and the two lords who were with him rose to their feet and threw their blankets at the Spaniards. The Spaniards jumped them and killed them with their daggers; since the Inca's wife had seen what happened, she screamed.

When the Spaniards had finished this, they told one of them to finish killing the Inca, who was still breathing. They went out running to the armory. While that Spaniard remained to finish killing the Inca and the woman was shouting, the archers and Timbayci, their captain, arrived. When they saw that man killing the Inca, they all went to him and killed him with arrows.

Gomez Perez and Diego Mendez and the rest went to the armory and took swords. They then ran to where there were eight horses that the Inca had there on a hill. Since there was a good distance between the town where they were and the rise, which was uphill, they became tired.

When a leader and the Indians who guarded the horses saw them coming, they thought that these men had killed the Inca. They came and all joined together, some forty Indians, and defended the rise. Timbayci and the rest of the men from the town then arrived and attacked them. One of them, named Cornejo, escaped among the Indians. He climbed up and saddled a horse and rode off and left there. Diego Mendez and Gomez Perez and the rest defended themselves as best they could.

Since they could not withstand the Indian attack, they began to fall back little by little while defending themselves. They returned to the town and entered a large shed and barred the door. The Indians tried to enter and the Spaniards defended themselves in that doorway. Gomez Perez defended his life well and had a large pile of lances and pikes that were deflected at the entrance.

When Timbayci saw that he could not enter and that night was approaching, he ordered that the shed be set on fire from behind. This was done, and when the Spaniards saw the fire overtake them, they went outside and there they were all taken in hand and killed.

I don't know how many Indians had gone after Cornejo, and at the river crossing they killed the horse. He remained in the water and was swept downriver and emerged on a flat area and fled to a forest that was next to a snow-covered mountain. There they caught up with him and killed him. Thus they killed them all.

XXXIII

Wherein Timbayci sent a messenger to Pumasupa

by whom he said that the Inca was dead,

and how Pumasupa returned, and how Pumasupa

and the rest of Manco Inca's captains elected as

Inca one of Manco Inca's sons who they called

Saire Topa Yupanque, and of the things

they did later and what befell them.

After Timbayci had killed the Spaniards, he ordered the Indian warriors to immediately kill Diego Mendez's black woman and all the rest of the Indian male and female servants that the Spaniards had. Thus they killed them all. This done, Timbayci sent two Indians to Pumasupa to tell him to return with all the men because the Inca was dead and that he had already punished those who had killed him. When they had returned, they would decide what should be done.

These messengers found Pumasupa in the hills of Limatambo, which is seven leagues from Cuzco. When these messengers arrived, they approached Pumasupa secretly and, when they were alone, told him what had happened. Pumasupa, telling all his men that the Inca had called for them, returned. Pumasupa said this so that the men would not flee because, if they knew of the death of the Inca, all of them would flee and, possibly, kill him. Thus he returned.

Since the people of Cuzco heard that the Inca's men were coming down on them, they prepared themselves as best they could. They ordered all the friends of the city and the rest of their neighbors in Yucay and the area surrounding Cuzco to form a squadron and go out and defend Cuzco and assist them. So they assembled and went out to Chinchero to await the Inca's forces. When they heard the Inca's forces had left, they returned to the city and from there each one went to his land.

Pumasupa returned to his settlement and to where Manco Inca had been killed. As soon as he arrived with the rest of the captains, they gathered in a council and elected a son of Manco Inca as Inca and lord. He was ten years of age and they called him Saire Topa Yupanque. When this was done, they began

their lamentations and sacrifices for the death of the Inca and performed the
fiesta of Purucaya at the end of the year.

They buried his body and, as the statues of his ancestors had been made,
made up a statue of the nails and hair that he had cut during his life. They
placed it with the statues that he had with him there.

When this was done, they placed guards and garrisons on the roads that left
that place for the city of Cuzco and the town of Guamanga in order to look out
for the Spaniards or other soldiers who might come to conquer them and also
to watch the roads to make sure that nobody appeared who would force them
to go with them.

When licentiate Gasca[1] came to these provinces and defeated and killed
Gonzalo Pizarro, he sent word to Manco Inca's captains and to Saire Topa to
come to Cuzco. He said they should not be afraid for what they had done, since
he would pardon them in the name of his Majesty.

Pumasupa, as the most important captain, asked that Saire Topa be given
his father's possessions and lands and a group of Indians to serve him. He asked
that all of those there be pardoned for their crimes and misdemeanors.

When licentiate Gasca received this reply, he gave Saire Topa a *repartimiento*
of Indians and the lots, houses, and lands that belonged to his father. He sent
a pardon for all their crimes and misdemeanors and asked them to come and
take possession of what had been given them.

They sent Timbayci, that captain who captured the Spaniards who killed
Manco Inca, to Cuzco to take possession of the Indians and lots and lands that
licentiate Gasca gave them. They sent him to tell licentiate Gasca that they
themselves did not come to Cuzco at present because they intended to reap
certain crops they had planted. While they awaited the gathering of their food,
Timbayci would prepare the houses in Cuzco on the lots that were given them
so that when they came to Cuzco they could enter them. They would also bring
enough food to Cuzco so that those Indians who had been given to them, and
Saire Topa, their master, might eat.

Timbayci built the houses and gathered the food, but Pumasupa refused to
come. Neither did Saire Topa dare come because Pumasupa and his men did
not allow him. So they remained hidden in the wilds, where they suffered
greatly from the lack of salt and meat.

The land is so rugged and wild that if it were not because, as men already
knowledgeable about that country, they find places to take their horses along
the roads that go to Cuzco and Guamanga, it would be impossible to enter
there. Even dogs cannot enter some areas and difficult passes; even the Indians
go up arm in arm on ropes and tree roots and vines and are thus able to cross.

They spend their time where they are in the celebration of sacrifices and fasts and in pagan worship of their *guacas* and idols and in celebrating all the rest of the fiestas according to what was done in Cuzco in the time of the ancient Incas and according to what had been ordained by the Inca Yupanque.

Here ends the history of the past Inca Capas who, from antiquity, were the lords of the provinces of Peru and the city of Cuzco until Marquis Francisco Pizarro, of glorious memory, conquered them in the name of his Majesty and placed them under the royal dominion and crown of Spain and of our Castile.

XXXIV

Wherein, after many years had passed since the departure of licentiate Pedro de la Gasca from this kingdom of Peru and while Hurtado de Mendoza[1] was the viceroy of this kingdom for his Majesty, the author, Juan de Betanzos, a resident of the city of Cuzco, went, by order of the viceroy, out in the wilds where Saire Topa was, with orders and royal provisions, to persuade him to come out peacefully, and what happened to him on that mission.

After the passage of much time and while Hurtado de Mendoza, the marquis of Cañete, was viceroy of these lands, Juan de Betanzos, living in the city of Cuzco, learned that the aforementioned marquis was in Lima, the city of Los Reyes. He knew of the poor results of the mission that licentiate Gasca had sent to Saire Topa and felt that he would be able to do better, since he, better than any other, knew how to explain to the Incas who were in the wilds what his Majesty wanted them to do. Beyond this, he would be doing a service to his Majesty.

He descended from the city of Cuzco to the city of Los Reyes and, after having kissed his Excellency's hands, he explained to him why he had come. He inquired if his Excellency would be well served if he went on his mission to the rebellious Indians who were in the wilds. His Excellency answered that he would be very grateful and pleased by this. In addition, this would be a great service to God, our Lord, and his Majesty. And he would compensate him for it in the name of his Majesty.

So he gave him the messages and the royal dispensations, which contained a general pardon. With these documents his Majesty pardoned Saire Topa and his brothers and the rest of the lords and captains for all the crimes of murdering and robbing Christians that they had committed since the day Manco Inca, his father, had rebelled until these dispensations were delivered, provided they came out in peace and pledged obedience to his Majesty. If they came out and gave obedience to his majesty, he would do the Inca and his people great favors. If he did not, war would be visited upon them.

Juan de Betanzos asked his Excellency for a gift from his Majesty to give to the Inca. His Excellency did so, and the gift was pieces of dyed silk and richly worked shirts embroidered with gold and pearls and some gold-plated silver tumblers for the Inca to drink from together with other gems of quality and value. All of this cost more than four hundred silver pesos, assayed and marked. And so Juan de Betanzos left for the wilds where the rebellious Incas were.[2]

NOTES

INTRODUCTION
Juan de Betanzos and Inca Traditions

1. In Pt. II, chap. 34, Betanzos tells about his trip to Lima, where he planned to meet with Viceroy Andres Hurtado de Mendoza, Marquis of Cañete, in 1557. Scholars had Betanzos's account dated earlier because he dedicated it to Viceroy Antonio de Mendoza in 1551, and in Pt. I, at the end of chap. XIV, he gives the date as 1551. The whole second part, including the chapter about his trip to Lima, was missing. See below for more details about the two manuscripts of the Betanzos account.

2. Father Bernabe Cobo, a learned Jesuit priest, wrote extensively on the Incas in *Historia del nuevo mundo*, finished in 1653 but not published in Spanish until 1892–1893. A translation by Roland Hamilton has been published by the University of Texas Press in two volumes: *History of the Inca Empire* (1979) and *Inca Religion and Customs* (1990).

3. Pedro Pizarro was a first cousin of Francisco Pizarro, whom he accompanied to Peru in 1532 as a page and later served as a cavalryman. Pedro Pizarro finished a remarkable account of the discovery and conquest of Peru in 1571. The first Spanish edition did not come out until 1844. The best English translation available, by P.H. Means, appeared in 1921.

4. Father Joseph de Acosta, a scholarly Jesuit priest, published his masterful study *Historia natural y moral de las Indias* in Seville in 1590. The *Doctrina christiana y catecismo* has not been translated, and the only English translation of the *Historia* was done in 1604.

5. See ahead in the Betanzos *Narrative*, Pt. I, chap. 47, where Huayna Capac says, "That is my mother and I want her for myself." This appears to be the Inca's expression of endearment for his newborn niece. He later arranges her marriage to his son Atahualpa.

6. See *Royal Commentaries of the Incas* (Austin: University of Texas, 1970), pt. I, p. 621, pt. II, p. 1436.

7. See n. 1.

8. Father Gregorio Garcia (1575–1612) published *Origen de los indios de el Nuevo Mundo* (Valencia, 1607), in which he discusses various theories of the origin of the inhabitants of the New World. In Book V, chap. 7, Garcia quotes two full chapters from the Betanzos *Narrative*, Pt. I, chaps. I and II, on the creation at Tiahuanaco and the spread of people throughout Peru. Garcia's work has not been translated into English.

9. William Prescott, *History of the Conquest of Peru* (Boston, 1847), 2 vols. See vol. I, p. 17, n. 21, where Prescott cites *Narr. de los Yngas*, manuscript, chap. 12 of

Betanzos to corroborate comments on the fortress of Cuzco. However, Betanzos does not mention the fortress in the chap. cited. See also vol. I, p. 127, n. 13, where Prescott correctly cites the Betanzos manuscript, chap. XVI, on the calendar.

10. The manuscript held in El Escorial, Spain, has the following abbreviated title: *Suma y narracion de los yngas* . . . , including Pt. I, chaps. I–XVII and parts of chap. XVIII.

11. This complete manuscript has the same title as in n. 9, but includes Pt. I, chaps. I–XLVIII and Pt. II, chaps. I–XXXIV.

12. See *Suma y narración de los Incas*, Atlas edition, p. 132.

13. See ibid., p. 107.

14. For a discussion of modern theories of Inca expansion, See Brian S. Bauer, *The Development of the Inca State* (Austin: University of Texas Press, 1992), pp. 1–9.

15. See Garcilaso de la Vega, *Royal Commentaries of the Incas*, trans. with an intro. by Harold Livermore (Austin: University of Texas Press, , 1966, 2 vols.).

16. See *Handbook of South American Indians*, vol. II, esp. pp. 201–209.

17. See *Inca Architecture*, pp. 234–255.

PREFACE

1. The Quechua term *capac* means lord or king; the suffix *cuna* can mean either plural or member of a class. The Quechua word *Inca* also means king or a member of the royal nobility. Following the usage of most Spanish writers of his day, Betanzos spelled this word *Ynga* in the manuscript.

PROLOGUE

1. Antonio de Mendoza (1490–1552), first viceroy of New Spain, served as viceroy of Peru in 1551 for about one year just before his death.

2. The manuscripts for this book have been lost, but it may have been used by Father Joseph de Acosta in compiling the first book published in Peru, *Doctrina christiana y catecismo* (Los Reyes, 1584).

3. This list contains almost the same names in the same order as provided by other reliable chronicles such as Bernabe Cobo's *History of the Inca Empire* (Austin: University of Texas Press, 1979). The main difference lies in the fact that Cobo and most other chronicles omit Yamque Yupanque. See Pt. I, chap. XXV, n. 1.

Part One

I

1. Viracocha refers to the supreme being and creator. Contiti Viracocha means something like "fundamental god." He had a number of assistant gods called *viracochas*. Betanzos was the only sixteenth-century author to use the names *Contiti* together. He states that he got the name from the Cana Indians. See below. This god also had the additional title Pacha-yachachic.

2. Peru is a place name of uncertain origin made up during the conquest period. Here it refers to the Inca empire, roughly from modern Chile to Ecuador.

3. Collasuyo or Collao was used as a general term for the Lake Titicaca region. Collasuyo eventually extended to Chile.

II

1. Condesuyo, part of the empire to the southwest of Cuzco.

2. Andesuyo, part of the empire roughly east and north of Cuzco and including the tropical forest.

3. Guaca, shrine or object worshiped as a deity; includes idols, shrines, temples, burial places, stones, and springs.

4. For *vara*, see Measurements.

5. *Orejon*, Spanish, "big ears." The Spaniards used the word to describe Inca nobles because of their large earplugs.

III

1. Commander of a military order; Francisco's half brother.

2. See Measurements for Spanish league.

IV

1. Agi. Taino, *Capsicum*, pepper, a condiment like chile.

V

1. Cacique, Taino, "native chief."

VIII

1. MS f12r, 22: Aco çapa ynga aucay quita atixu llacxaimoctiangui cuna punchaupi, Quechua, "Let us go, one and only king; we will overpower your enemy [ies]; they will gaze at you in panic as you sit."

IX

1. The Palma manuscript reads at f15v, 1–8, "le avia muerto . . . un herno suyo en la emboscada/avia muerto." A missing passage that completes the meaning appears in the Escorial manuscript, at f26v, 1–19, "emboscada/el señor le dijo que lloraua por un hermano suyo que en la emboscada/avia muerto."

X

1. Inca noblemen wore a headband woven of wool. The Inca emperor wore a fringe called *borla* in Spanish; it was sewn to the band so as to hang in the middle of the forehead and reach down to the eyebrows. This fringe symbolized the office of the emperor as a crown.

2. *Chicha*, uncertain origin, probably from an Indian language of Panama; an alcoholic beverage made by fermenting maize, other seeds, or fruits.

3. Coca, Quechua; leaves from a plant similar to a rosebush, which were chewed for their mild narcotic effect.

XI

1. *Yanacona*, Quechua; retainers who were exempt from the usual labor service; *yana* means "retainer," the suffix *cona* indicates either the plural or a member of a class.

2. *Mamaconas*, Quechua; cloistered women dedicated to the service of the Inca gods. The word *mama* means "mother," and the suffix *cona* or *cuna* indicates either the plural or a member of a class.

3. For *estado*, see Measurements.

XII

1. *Quipo*, Quechua; a device used to record numbers; it was made of strands of cord or wool strings. From the main cord, smaller strings hung like fingers. Knots tied in the smaller strings indicated the numbers in a decimal system. Usually spelled *quipu* in English.

2. *Choclo*; Quechua; maize cob.

3. *Chuño*; Quechua; freeze-dried potatoes.

4. *Quinoa* or *Quinua*; Quechua; a plant cultivated in the higher altitudes of the Andes for its seeds. Usually spelled *quinoa* in English.

XIII

1. *Cabuya*; Taino; fiber of the agave or maguey.

XIV

1. The Palma manuscript reads at f27v, 1–10, "cierta fiesta/vuiese memoria." A missing passage appears in the Escorial manuscript, at f48, 1–9, "cierta fiesta/la cual fiesta queria que se hiziese cada año al sol por la victoria que le abia dado y hecho señor y porque desta feast/vuiese. . . ."

2. Betanzos quotes Inca Yupanque here and in the following passages.

3. This first month falls in December. See Raime in Glossary.

XV

1. *Pacha unan changa* or *pacha unan cha* (see n. 3, this chap.). Quechua; *pacha*, "time," and *unancha*, any marker or indicator.

2. *Pucoi quilla raime quis*, December. The Inca calendar derives from lunar months. The Quechua word for both month and moon is *quilla*.

3. See n. 1, this chap. The reference here is to pillars or markers placed on the hills near Cuzco over which the sun rises and over which it sets. From the main square one could determine the months by the movement of the sun along the pillars.

XVI

1. See chap. XI, where this same quarry is mentioned. The Escorial manuscript f55v reads "saluoma."

2. *Esparto*, Spanish; a word used in English for two kinds of long, coarse grass used to make cordage, baskets, etc.

3. The alder tree of the birch family, *aliso* in Spanish, grows in the Andes highlands, as well as elsewhere, and was the major source of Inca building poles.

4. *Haguacolla quisca* or *hahuan collay quisca*, Quechua; a large treelike cactus.

5. *Guacchaconcha*, from Quechua *huaccha*, meaning "orphan," and concha, "nephew."

6. *Piuiguarme*, from Quechua *piui*, "wife," "daughter," or "son"; *guarmi*, "wife."

7. *Mamanguarme*, from Quechua *mama*, "mother"; *guarmi*, "wife."

8. *Paxxa yndi Usus çapaicoya guacchacoyac*, Quechua; "full moon"; "daughter of the sun"; "one and only queen"; "friend of the poor."

9. See n. 10. Only two of the last Inca kings, Topa Inca and Huayna Capa, probably married their sisters.

10. *Piuichuri*, Quechua; *piui*, "son" or "daughter"; *churi*, used by a father to refer to his son or daughter. The succession really did not follow such a strict rule. See the case of Inca Yupanque, chaps. VIII, XVII, and that of Topa Inca, chap. XX.

XVII

1. Inca Yupanque or his predecessors thought of Cuzco as a puma whose head was the fortress of Sacsahuaman, whose body fell between the Huatanay and Tullumayo rivers, and whose tail started where the rivers came together at Pumachupa, "puma's tail." See map 1.

2. *Pachacuti*; Quechua; "cataclysm," "an upheaval that causes great changes."

3. These narrative poems probably served as the basis for the information Juan de Betanzos collected for this chronicle. This would explain why he got so little about the first Incas and so much more detail about Pachacuti and his successors.

4. *Oron*; Spanish; a type of large storage basket.

XVIII

1. *Achigua* or *achihua*, Quechua for "parasol."

2. Since the Castillian foot measured 11 inches, this equals the *estado*, or 5 feet 6 inches.

XIX

1. Ynga yupangue yndi n yoca sola y malca chinbo lei sola y malca axco ley haguaya guaya haguaya guaya. On the basis of the gloss by Betanzos this means "Inca Yupanque, child of the Sun, put the *borla* fringe on the Soras, defeated the Soras, tra-la-la." In the following analysis, expressions are identified as Quechua (Q), Aymara (A), or origin questionable (O). After the word from the manuscript, a traditional Spanish-based spelling and an English translation, if possible, have been used.

Ynga, Inca, (Q), king; *yupangue* (Q), Yupanque, name of the Inca ruler; *yndi*, (Q), Inti, Sun; *n yoca* (O); *sola*, (Q), Sora, tribe and province west of Cuzco; *y* (O); *malca* (A), *marca*, tribe; *chinbo* (A), *chimpu*, headband used by certain tribes; *lei* (O); *axco* (O); *haguaya*, etc. (O). For more information on the Quechua used in Betanzos, see "Un texto en el idoma olvidado," by Jan Szeminskii in *Histórica* XIV, no. 2 (December 1990): 379–389.

2. *Çanga guaçi*, from Quechua *zanca* (?) *huasi*, "house."

3. *Llaxa guaçi*, from Quechua *llaclla* (?), "coward," *huasi*, "house."

XX

1. *Çaramama*, Quechua; *çara* or *zara*, "maize," and *mama*, "mother."

2. *Çapa apo yndi chori*, Quechua; *zapa*, "unique," *apo*, "lord"; *yndi* or *inti*, "sun"; *chori* or *churi*, applied by a father to his son.

3. Cay pacha tu coptin atarixunxi llapan chic runa caoçarispa aichantin ymanamcuna canchic; Quechua; "When this world ends, we will rise up, all of us humans coming back to life, in the flesh, as we are now."

4. *Tocorrico*, Quechua; *tucuy*, "all"; *ricuc*, "look at." The two words together mean "inspector."

XXI

1. *Repartimiento*; Spanish; distribution of Indians for labor service.

2. *Çapçi churi*; Quechua; *sapsi*, "the people," "community"; *churi*, applied by a father to his son.

3. *Aillo* or *ayllo*, Quechua; a weapon made of two or three cords with balls on the end (*bolas* in Spanish and English). It was used in hunting and war. This word and the word meaning "lineage" are homonyms.

4. *Cozcoy naca cuna*; Quechua; *cozco* or *Cuzco ñaca*, "matron"; *cuna*, suffix that indicates the plural or a member of a class.

5. *Virqui*; Quechua; a large pitcher with a wide mouth.

6. *Apo Ynga randi rimaric*, Quechua; *apo*, "lord"; *ynga* or *inca*, "king"; *randi* or *ranti*, "deputy"; *rimaric*, "represent or speak for someone."

7. *Cuxipata cato*, Quechua; *cuxi* or *cussi*, "fortunate or happy"; *pata*, "square"; *cato*, "marketplace." See maps on pp. xxii and xxiii.

XXII

1. *Tambo*; Quechua; *tampu*, a station with shelter or lodging and storehouses and located at convenient intervals along Inca roads.

2. *Xuco guaman*; Quechua; *xuco* or *soco*, "flight" (?); *guaman* or *huaman*, "hawk."

3. *Parcialidad*; Spanish; social unit of several extended families.

4. *Llacta camayo*, Quechua; *llacta*, "town"; *camayo*, "official."

XXIV

1. *Yungas*; Quechua; *yunca*, "hot, humid lowlands." This word applies here to the people of the tropical valleys. It is used as an adjective, "los [indios] yungas," meaning the *yungas*, or lowland Indians.

2. *Mitimaes*; Quechua; Hispanicized plural of the word *mitmac* or *mitima*; any Inca subject ordered to live in a place other than his or her place of ethnic origin. See Pt. I, chaps. XXVI and XLIII for a brief definition.

XXV

1. Topa is usually spelled Tupa or Tupac now. Topa Inca became the tenth Inca king, as this account tells in Pt. I, chap. XXVII and at the end of chap. XXXII. Though Yamque appears on the list at the end of the prologue as the tenth Inca, this account makes it clear he did not become Inca but simply the designated heir.

XXVI

1. In the Palma manuscript f63r, lines 12–14, there is a garbled phrase after "Yaguarcocha": "Quito que es de la ciudad del Cuzco."

2. *Topo*; Quechua; measure of distance about 4 1/2 miles or 1 1/2 leagues. This word and the word for a woman's pin are homonyms.

XXVII

1. Cañocap randi canga. Caiñoap randi cachun; Quechua; "This one will be in my place. Let him be in my place."

2. The Inca kings had a number of titles. Two are mentioned here: *çapa* or *sapa*, "unique"; *capac*, "emperor" or "king"; *cuna* is the suffix to indicate plural or a member of a class.

XXVIII

1. *Yuca*; Taino; manioc or cassava root, dietary staple of the tropical forest Indians; used to make bread.

2. *Perico ligero*; Spanish; the sloth, a slow-moving tree-dwelling mammal.

3. *Amaro*; Quechua; serpent.

XXX

1. *Capa cocha*; Quechua; *capa*, "royal"; *cocha*, "sea" or "large lake."

XXXI

1. *Purucaya*; Quechua; *puru*, "feathers"; *caya* or *cayo*, a special dance (?).

2. Paulo or Paullu, son of Huayna Capac, died in 1548 at about thirty years of age.

3. See chap. 21, n.3.

4. At this point Betanzos starts quoting the Inca Yupanque.

XXXII

1. Doña Angelina Yupanque, born around 1522, relative of Huayna Capac. Her Inca name was Cuxirimay Ocllo. In 1532 she married Atahualpa (see Pt. I, chap. 47). Subsequently, Francisco Pizarro took her as his mistress. Finally, after Pizarro's death in 1541, she married Betanzos and provided much information for his account of the Incas.

2. *Capacaillo Ynga Yupangue haguaynin*; Quechua; lineage of King Inca Yupanque, his grandchildren.

XXXIV

1. *Uturungo*; Quechua; *uturungo* or *uturuncu*, "jaguar," or *tigre* in Spanish.

XXXV

1. Río de la Plata refers to what is now called the Paraná River and one of its Andean tributaries.

XXXVI

1. *Xagüey* or *jagüey*; Taino; a hole artificially made to catch or collect water.
2. *Paco*; Quechua; reddish brown.

XXXVII

1. Xacxaguaman or Sacsahuaman, commonly referred to as the fortress of Cuzco in the sixteenth- and seventeenth-century chronicles.

XXXIX

1. *Chumbe*; Quechua; *chumpi*, "sash."

XLV

1. See Pt. I, chap. XIV.
2. See Pt. I, chap. II.
3. The ruins of this temple can be seen today near the town of San Pedro de Cacha, or Racchi, on the road from Cuzco to Lake Titicaca. Recent measurements coincide with those of Betanzos. See Introduction, n. 17.

XLVII

1. See Pt. I, chap. XVI, nn. 9 and 10.
2. Cuxirimay, from Quechua; *cuxi* or *cussi*, "venture" or "good fortune"; *rimani*, "speak."

XLVIII

1. *Ganbo*; Quechua; *huanpu*, "boat."
2. *Chaquira*; uncertain origin; beads made from red seashells.

Part Two

II

1. Hanan and Hurin, Quechua; upper and lower Cuzco. Most Inca towns had two sections, Hanan, upper, and Hurin, lower. The first five Inca kings belonged to Hurin Cuzco, the rest, including Huayna Capac, to Hanan Cuzco. See, Pt. I, chap. XVI.

III

1. See Pt. I, chap. XLVI.

VI

1. See, Pt. I, chap. XV, nn. 10, 11.
2. *Guanquin* or *huauque*; Quechua; "brother"; used by a man to refer to his brother.
3. *Caccha*; Quechua; a brave man.

VII

1. *Auca*; Quechua; "soldier," "warrior," "enemy," "traitor."

VIII

1. Tambo de Janja refers to the same town; there were lodgings there. See also Tambo de Urcas, Tambo de Vilcas.

IX

1. Since the Inca nobles used large earplugs, the lobe of the ear was pierced and greatly stretched. Atahualpa's earlobe was torn, a sign of bad luck.
2. Collana Chacara; Quechua; *collana*, "excellent"; *chacara*, "cultivated field."

X

1. See, Pt. I, chap. XXIV, n. 1.

XII

1. *Ñaca*; Quechua; "mature woman," "matron."

XIV

1. *Macana*; Taino; a sword-shaped double-edged war club made of hardwood.

XVI

1. Cuxi Yupanque's sister, Doña Angelina, Cusirimai, Atahualpa's wife.

XVII

1. Yungas Tallanes, a coastal tribe near present town of Piura. See also Pt. I, chap. XXIV, n. 1.
2. See Pt. I, chap. 1, n. 1. *Viracocha*, creator god or one of his assistants; *cuna*, suffix to indicate the plural or a member of a class.
3. The informants here refer to the northern coast of Peru, where Pizarro arrived and from which Viracocha left, according to their traditions. See Pt. I, chap. II.
4. *Chuco*; Quechua; "cap" or "hat."
5. See Pt. II, chap. XIV, n. 1. Since the word *macana* comes from the Taino language of the West Indies, Betanzos uses it here as Spanish.

6. *Runa quiçachac*; Quechua; *runa*, "people"; *quiçachac* or *que za chac*, "one who damages or destroys."

7. *Allichac*; Quechua; "one who does good."

XIX

1. *Chacnac*; Quechua; from *chac nac*, "torture by whipping."

2. *Chanbi*, Quechua; *champi*, "war club" or "mace."

XX

1. *Quitas pumarangra*; Quechua; *quitas*, "wild," "fugitive"; *pumaranra*, "robber," "holdup man."

2. *Supai cuna*; Quechua; *supai*, "devil," *cuna*, suffix that indicates the plural or a member of a class.

XXI

1. Pizarro had picked up two young Indians on his second visit to Peru in 1528. He took them to Spain, taught them some Spanish, and used them as interpreters.

2. Mana unan changa runam cai cuna; Quechua; "They are people beyond understanding, these."

XXII

1. Pachap tiqui cinpillacta yoc xi ñivarga; Quechua; "He told me he is from a land at the extreme end of the world."

2. Ticçi viracocha checacon cai cuna; Quechua; "Gods of far away, these" (?).

XXV

1. *Tambo*, as explained in the glossary, means a station with lodging. Since many *tambos* were located at major towns, the word also means a town with lodgings, Tambo de Vilcas.

2. Ticci viracocha pachayachachic runa yachachic (see Pt. I, chap. 1, n. 1), Quechua; *ticci*, "lord"; *viracocha*, creator; *pacha*, "world," "land"; *yachachic*, "instructor"; *runa*, "people." Thus, Lord creator, instructor of the world and of the people.

XXVII

1. Hernando de Soto, the conquistador who later explored North America.

2. Manco Inca (1516–1545), younger son of Huayna Capac. See Pt. II, chap. XXVIII.

XXVIII

1. *Repartimiento*; Spanish; here it refers to territorial divisions for Inca tax collected in labor. See Pt. II, chap. XXXII, n. 1.

2. *Llacta camayo*; Quechua; *llacta*, "town"; *camayo*, "official."

3. *Adelantado*; Spanish; an official authorized by the king to conquer a certain territory.

XXIX

1. Vilaoma; Quechua; *villac*, "he who speaks"; *oma* or *umu*, "diviner." *Villacumu* means "high priest."
2. *Papa*, an Aztec or Nahuatl word for "priest."
3. Macho Apo; Quechua; *machu*, "old man"; *apo*, "lord."

XXX

1. Probably 1551, when Betanzos worked on this account. He seems to have finished up to Pt. II, chap. XXXIII in that year; however, he wrote chap. XXXIV in 1557. See Pt. II, chap. XXXIV, n. 2.

XXXII

1. *Repartimiento* was the distribution of Indians for labor service. Here it refers to settlements in which Indians leaders were required to provide workers to a Spaniard in charge.
2. This tribe and province, Angara, south of Jauja and northwest of Cuzco, included the area to the east known as Aco.
3. *Herrón*, a game in which the players pitch metal rings at a stake, as in horseshoes. The object is to make a ringer or come as close as possible.
4. Alonso de Toro, one of the Spanish soldiers at Cajamarca with Francisco Pizarro. He became a prominent citizen of Cuzco.

XXXIII

1. Pedro de la Gasca, a priest and lawyer, was selected by the king of Spain to restore order in the Viceroyalty of Peru after the forces of Gonzalo Pizarro killed the first viceroy, Blasco Nuñez Vela, in 1545. Gasca arrived in 1547, defeated and executed Gonzalo Pizarro in 1548, and returned to Spain in 1550.

XXXIV

1. Andres Hurtado de Mendoza, Marquis of Cañete, second viceroy of Peru, 1555 to 1561.
2. This embassy left in 1557 and, after long months of negotiating, Saire Topa came to Lima in January of 1558. The viceroy received Saire cordially. Later Saire settled in Cuzco with ample grants and properties. He died in 1560. Since Betanzos's account ends as the embassy to Saire Topa was leaving, he finished his *Narrative of the Incas* in 1557.

GLOSSARY

Loan Words from American Indian Language
Key: Q, Quechua; T, Taino; N, Nahuatl; A, Aymara.

Achigua. Q. Parasol.

Acclaguaci. Q. House of chosen women.

Aclla. Q. Chosen women. *Acllas* were selected at about eight or nine years of age.

Agi. T. Aji, Capsicum pepper. A condiment like chile.

Allapo Coi quis. Q. February.

Allichac. Q. One who does good.

Amaro. Q. Snake or serpent. Also used in names such as Topa Amaro.

Anacu. Q. Women's dress. It extended from the neck to the feet and was fastened with pins.

Apo. Q. Lord, a person of great power and authority.

Arpa. Q. Arpay, blood sacrifice.

Auca. Q. Soldier, enemy, traitor.

Auqui. Q. Nobleman.

Ayllo or *Ayllu. Q.* An extended family or lineage believed to have a common ancestor; a weapon made of cords with stone or copper weights attached at the ends. It was used in war at fairly close range to entangle the enemy's feet. It was also used in hunting. *Ayllos,* meaning weapon, and *ayllo,* meaning lineage, are homonyms. The Spanish word for the weapon is *bolas* or *boleadoras.*

Ayriguay quis. Q. April.

Buhio. T. House. Used in Spanish to designate an Indian hut with a thatched roof.

Cabuya. T. Fiber of the agave or maguey cactus, used for making coarse blankets or cordage.

Caccha. Q. A brave man. Also the name of a war god.

Cacique. T. A native chief.

Cagua quis. Q. July.

Caliz. Probably *Q.* Used for a certain jug of *chicha.* See place name Calizpuquio, Part I, chap. XIV.

Camayo or *Camayu. Q.* Official.

Canipo. Q. Metal disk used as a chest or head ornament by soldiers.

Canoe. T. Native boat made from a hollowed-out tree trunk or from three boards. The Hispanicized term used in the manuscript is *canoa.*

Cantarai quis. Q. November.

Capa. Q. Rich or royal, as in *capa huayna,* rich young man.

Capa cocha. Q. Refers to a royal (*capa*) sacrifice made by drowning the victims in a lake (*cocha*) or by burying them alive.

Capac. Q. Lord, king, as in *capac cuna,* lords.

Carpai quis. Q. August.

Cato. Q. *Catu,* marketplace.

Çanga guaçi. Q. *Çanga* (?), and *guaçi,* house.

Çapa. Q. Unique, as in *çapa Inca,* unique king.

Çapçi churi. Q. *Sapsi,* the people; *churi,* term used by a father to refer to his son. Together the terms mean "son of the community."

Chacara. Q. A piece of ground or field under cultivation.

Chacnac. Q. Torture by whipping.

Chambi. Q. Champi. One of the Inca's royal insignias. A mace with which the Inca fought in the wars.

Chaquira. Uncertain origin, but probably from the Indians of Panama. Thin beads usually made from seashells.

Charqui. Q. Dried llama meat.

Chasque. Q. Runner or messenger who carried the Inca's orders to the empire's governors and caciques. These runners were stationed at intervals of one-quarter of a Spanish league (slightly less than a mile), and they used a relay system.

Chayachaya. Q. After them, after them.

Chicha. Uncertain origin, but probably from an Indian language of Panama. Any of various alcoholic beverages made by fermenting maize, other seeds, or fruits.

Choclo. Q. Maize cob.

Chuco. Q. A knitted cap. Called *chullo* in Spanish today.

Chumbi or *Chumbe.* Q. *Chumpi.* Sash worn around the waist by women.

Chuño. Q. Freeze-dried potatoes.

Coca. Q. *Erythroxylon coca,* a plant similar to a rosebush or the leaves of the *coca* plant, which contain a mildly stimulating narcotic. The Andean Indians chew these leaves. The word *coca* is used in both Spanish and English.

Collana. Q. Excellent.

Collca. Q. Large storehouse; *collcas* were located in all of the provinces of the Inca Empire. Goods collected as tribute were stored in them.

Coricancha. Q. Golden House; the most sacred Inca shrine; located in Cuzco.

Coya. Q. Queen or principal wife of the Inca.

Cuna. Q. Suffix added to nouns to indicate the plural or to indicate a member of a class.

Curaca. Q. Title given to the higher-ranking officials in the Inca government; they were in charge of one hundred or more taxpayers. The *curaca* with the highest rank was the superior of ten thousand taxpayers.

Duho. T. A low stool or bench that was a symbol of high public office.

Galpón. Uncertain origin, but probably from a South American Indian language. A large storehouse or shed with only one room.

Ganbo. Q. *Huanpu,* boat. See *guambo.*

Guaca. Q. Any object, place, or person worshiped as a deity. The Incas had numerous such shrines or sacred things, including temples, burial places, idols, stones, and springs. Also spelled *huaca.*

Guacchaconcha. Q. Huaccha, poor person or orphan; *concha,* nephew.

Guacchaycoya. Q. Huaccha, poor people; *cuya,* compassion.

Guaci. Q. Huaci, house.

Guaman. Q. Huaman, hawk. A nickname for a boy.

Guambo. Q. Huanpu, boat.

Guambracuna. Q. Boys. *Guambra* or *huarma,* boy; the suffix *cuna* indicates the plural.

Guanaco. Q. Lama guanicoe, the larger wild species of llama.

Guaraca. Q. Sling. One of the major long-range weapons used by the Incas.

Guarachicuy. Q. Maturity rite held for boys. See *Raime.*

Guasca. Q. Huasca, rope.

Guauqui. Q. Huauque, brother, term used among brothers. Also a statue taken by the Inca emperors as their personal guardian.

Guazavara or *Guazabara. T.* Battle or skirmish.

Haguacolla quisca. Q. Hahuan collay quisca, a large treelike cactus.

Hammock. T. A hanging bed. The Hispanicized equivalent is *hamaca.*

Hanan. Q. Upper moiety or subdivision of most Inca towns and provinces. See also *hurin* and Pt. I, chap. XVI.

Hatun pocoi quis. Q. January.

Hatun quosqui quilla. Q. June.

Haucai quosqui quilla. Q. May.

Hicho. Q. Stipa. Puna grass. Coarse bunch grass common in the Andean highlands.

Hochaymi. Q. Huchallini, to sin, take blame.

Huancar. Q. Drum.

Huarmi. Q. Married woman.

Huata. Q. Year.

Huminta. Q. Small cakes made of maize flour.

Hurin. Q. Lower moiety or subdivision of most Inca towns and provinces.

Inca. Q. King or emperor. A member of the royal *ayllos* or nobility. Spelled *Ynga* in the manuscript.

Inti. Q. Sun, a major deity.

Llacta. Q. Town.

Llacta camayo. Q. Town official.

Llama. Q. Lama glama. The well-known domestic animal of South America, used as a beast of burden and a source of wool. It was also important for sacrifice in religious ceremonies. Betanzos uses the Spanish word *oveja,* sheep, for the llama.

Llauto. Q. A woolen headband worn by the Indians of Cuzco and all those of Inca lineage. It was not a symbol of royalty but was used to support the royal fringe, which was called *maxcapaycha* in Quechua. Betanzos uses the Spanish word *borla* for the royal fringe.

Llaxa guaçi. Q. Llaxa (?), and *guaçi,* house.

Locro. Q. A stew of meat, potatoes, vegetables, and lots of capsicum peppers.

Macana. T. A sword-shaped double-edged war club made of hardwood.

Macho. Q. Machu, old man.

Maguey. T. Agave, especially the century plant.

Maize. T. Zea mays, the native name for the corn of America. The Spanish equivalent used in the manuscript is *maiz.*

Mamacona. Q. Cloistered women dedicated to the service of the Inca gods. These women also trained the newly chosen girls, the *aclla,* in household occupations such as spinning, weaving, and cooking. The word *mama* means mother, and the suffix *cona* can indicate either the plural or a member of a class.

Mamanguarme. Q. mama, mother, and *huarme,* woman, wife, principal wife.

Mara. Q. Year.

Mita. Q. Labor service, performed by taxpayers who worked by turns that lasted up to several months. This labor service supplied soldiers, laborers for public works, servants for the nobles, and workmen for other official jobs.

Mitayo. Q. Laborer or workman in the service of the *mita.*

Mitimaes. Q. Settlers or newcomers who were brought into a recently conquered province to propagate Inca culture. In exchange, an equal number of newly conquered people were sent to take the place of the settlers. The term *mitimaes* was also applied to these new vassals who were moved from their native lands. The word *mitimaes* and its singular form, *mitima,* are Hispanicized forms of the word *mitma.*

Ñaca. Q. Mature woman, matron.

Oca. Q. Oxalis crenata, a plant cultivated for its edible roots.

Ojota. Q. Sandal or shoe.

Omarime quis. Q. October.

Pachacuti. Q. Cataclysm; an upheaval that causes great changes. Title given to the ninth Inca emperor.

Pacha pocoi quis. Q. March.

Pacha unan changa or *chac. Q. Pacha,* time; *unancha,* marker or indicator. Markers or pillars on the hills near Cuzco marked the beginning of summer and winter as the sun rose and set by them as seen from the central plaza.

Pacha-yachachic. Q. A name of the creator. See *Viracocha.*

Paco. Q. Reddish brown.

Palla. Q. A woman of the Inca nobility.

Papa. N. Priest.

Petaca. N. Case or chest.

Pillaca-llauto. Q. Many-colored headband. The *llauto,* or wool headband, was worn by the men of Cuzco and those of Inca lineage. The many-colored one was given to the young men as they became warriors.

Piñas. Q. Indian captured in a war. See manuscript f49v, line 20.

Piñi (*piña* in the manuscript). *Q*. Beads of shell or bone worn by women on a necklace.

Piuichuri. *Q*. *Piui*, eldest daughter or son, and, *churi*, used by the father to refer to his his son or daughter. Refers to the son or daughter of the Inca's principal wife.

Piuiguarme. *Q*. *Piui*, eldest daughter or son; *huarmi*, woman, wife. Inca's principal wife who, among the later emperors, was his sister or first cousin.

Poray Upia. *Q*. A feast held in September.

Pucoi quilla raime quis. *Q*. December.

Puma or *poma*. *Q*. Mountain lion. A nickname for a boy. This term is also used in the Cuzco district name; *pumachupa*, the lion's tail.

Puna. *Q*. The highest lands of the Andes. The word is used in both Spanish and English.

Puquiu. *Q*. A spring or fountain.

Quiçachac. *Q*. *Que zacha*, one who damages or destroys.

Quilla. *Q*. Month. This word also means moon; the months were counted by moons. In addition, it is used to mean iron.

Quinua. *Q*. *Chenopodiium quinoa*. A plant cultivated for its seeds in the higher altitudes of the Andes, where it replaces *maize*. Usually spelled *quinoa* in English.

Quipo. *Q*. A device used to record numbers; it was made of strands of cord or thin wool strings. From the main cord, smaller strings hung like fingers. Knots tied in the smaller strings indicated the numbers in a decimal system. Usually spelled *quipu* in English.

Quitas pumarangra. *Q*. *Quitas*, wild, fugitive; *pumaranra*, robber.

Raime or *Raymi*. *Q*. A December festival. At this time a maturity rite was held for boys about 14 years old in which they became warriors. Very elaborate ceremonies were held in Cuzco for boys of Inca families.

Runa. *Q*. People. This word came to mean Indian after the Spaniards arrived. See also *Viracocha*.

Rutuchico. *Q*. An elaborate ceremony in which a child was named; it was celebrated after the child was weaned and it involved, among other things, cutting the child's hair. The word also means hair cutting.

Sipas. *Q*. Marriageable woman.

Situai quis. *Q*. September.

Supay. *Q*. The devil.

Suyo. *Q*. *Suyu*, a section or division of land assigned to one man and his family for their share of agricultural labor. This same word is used in the toponyms Chinchasuyo, Condesuyo, Collasuyo, and Andesuyo for the four main provinces of the Inca empire.

Tambo. *Q*. *Tampu*, a station with shelter or lodging and storehouses. *Tambos* were located at convenient intervals along the Inca roads. Since many *tambos* were at major towns, the word also means town in some contexts.

Tianguez. *N*. Marketplace.

Ticciviracocha. *Q*. A name of the creator. See *Viracocha*.

Tocorrico. *Q*. *Tucuy*, all; and *ricuc*, look at; the two words together mean inspector.

Topo. Q. Large pins of copper, silver, or gold used by women to fasten their clothing. Homonym of *tupu.*

Tupu. Q. Measure of distance, 4 1/2 miles or 1 1/2 leagues. Homonym of *topo.*

Tuna. T. A type of cactus pear.

Uncu. Q. Tunic worn as a sleeveless shirt by men.

Uta. A. House.

Uturungo. Q. *Uturuncu,* jaguar.

Vicuña. Q. *Lama vicugna.* The smaller wild species of llama. See also *guanaco.*

Vilaoma. Q. High priest; *villac,* he who speaks; and *umu,* diviner.

Viracocha. Q. Creator of the world. He was the Inca's major deity, and he was also known as Viracocha Yachachic, Viracocha the Creator, or Virachocha Pacha-yachachic, Creator of the World. He had a number of assistant gods, also called *viracocha.* After the arrival of the Spaniards, the name *viracoccha* was applied to the Europeans in contrast to the Indians, who were known as runa, person.

Virqui. Q. Large drinking tumblers made of gold or silver.

Xaguey. T. *Jaguey,* a hole made in the ground to catch and collect water.

Yaguar guaca. Q. *Yahuar,* blood, and *guaca,* shrine or sacred object.

Yaguayracha aymoray. Q. A feast held in May and June.

Yanacona. Q. Retainers. As officials of the Inca government, they were exempt from the *mita* labor service. *Yana* means retainer; the suffix *cona* can indicate either the plural or a member of a class.

Yndichuri. Q. *Yndi* or *inti,* sun; *churi,* applied to a son by his father.

Yuca. T. *Manihot.* The many varieties of this manioc root were grouped in use as poisonous and nonpoisonous. Cassava bread was made from the poisonous kind after the poisonous juice was squeezed out.

Yunga. Q. Hot, humid lowlands. Used as an adjective for lowland Indians.

INDEX

adobe, description of, 70. *See also* Chile
adultery, penalty for, 105
agi (capsicum pepper): purchased for fiesta of
   Purucaya, 171; stored in Tambos, 108
Aguapante (Huascar's captain), escapes following defeat and capture, 198, 206
aillos (slings): boys taught to use, 103; description of, 135–136; Mama Guaco kills with,
   16
Alcavicça: death of, 17; origin of, 11
Almagro, Diego de: defeat and capture of, 291;
   insists on Atahualpa's death, 273; sent to
   Chile, 279
amaro (snake), description of, 88, 127
Anaguarque (shrine), *orejon* ceremony at, 61
Andahuaylas (province), Huascar's army at,
   210–211
Andesuyo (eastern province): cannibalism of
   inhabitants, 125; conquered by Topa Inca,
   124–127; location of, 9
Angelina: birth and naming, 180–181; birth of
   sons by Pizarro, 181; marriage to
   Atahualpa, 204; mistress to Pizarro, 181;
   taken to Atahualpa, 198; tells Pizarro location of Inca Yupanque's statue, 139. *See
   also* Cuxirimay Ocllo
Angoyaco (bridge), destroyed, 209
Apo Gualpaya, named governor by Topa Inca,
   161
Apomayta, 21; settles in Hurin Cuzco, 71;
   watches over Inca Yupanque, 34
Apo Ynga randi rimaric, Inca's spokesman,
   106
Apurimac (bridge), cut by Guanca Auqui, 218
Arpa, sacrifice to idol of the Sun, 48
Atahualpa (Inca) *[subentries arranged in chronological order]:* born in Cuzco, 204; lineage of, 178; resemblance to Topa Inca,
   177; names Huascar as Inca, 184; conducts
   funeral for father, 191; named successor to
   Huayna Capac, 177–179; raises army in
   Quito, 197–199; defeats Pastos, 203–204;
   marries Cuxirimay Ocllo [later named
   Angelina], 204; investiture as Inca, 204;
   names Cuxitopa Yupanque governor of
   Quito, 205; defeated at Yaguarcocha, 182–
   183; defeats and punishes Cañares, 198,

200–203, 213; atrocities against Cañares
   denied, 212; arrives in Tomebamba, 212;
   story of the torn ear, 212; receives *borla*
   fringe, 204; treads on Huascar's emblems,
   252; intends to build new Cuzco in Quito,
   233; destroys guaca at Guamachuco, 231–
   234; orders death of enemies in Cuzco, 233;
   orders Chalcochima's arrest, 215–216; cel-
   ebrates *Raime,* 250; learns of Pizarro's arrival, 235–239; described to Pizarro, 256;
   drunk at Cajamarca, 261; speaks to Fray
   Vicente de Valverde, 274; captured by
   Pizarro, 265; orders Huascar's death, 268;
   death of, 272–275; body carried to Quito,
   274
Atecayqui (Huascar's captain), 210
Atoc (Huascar's commander), imprisoned and
   killed by Atahualpa, 201–202
auca (enemy), 232, 239; definition of, 207
auqui, definition of, 62
Ayar Auca, origin of, 13
Ayar Cache: emergence of, 13; great strength,
   14; imprisoned, 14
Ayar Manco (Manco Capac), origin of, 13
Ayar Oche, origin of, 13
Ayavire (Collasuyo town): 171; Huayna Capac
   hunts at, 174

Betanzos, Juan de: other works by, 3; sent to
   Saire Topa, 300–301; spends time with
   elders of Cuzco, 212; visits shrine of
   Viracocha at Cacha, 10; witnessed mourning for Paulo in Cuzco, 135
bolas (weapon), description of, 135–136. See
   also *aillos*
borla fringe (Inca royal emblem), description of,
   42, 74–80, 87
braza (measurement), 68, 88, 136; length of
   sword, 235
bridges: construction, 83–85; maintained and
   guarded, 111. *See also* Angoyaco, Apurimac

Caacha (idol; god of battles), 83, 205; borne by
   Cuxi Yupanque, 195
cabuya: blankets of, 56; cords for bridges, 84;
   footwear made of, 99, 105; given to newly
   married, 58

orejon ceremony, 63; to recall deeds of Inca emperors, 79, 166–167

Soras: defeated by Inca Yupanque, 85–88; forced to sing of their defeat, 87; ordered to serve Inca Yupanque's statue, 167

Spaniards: attitude toward natives, 3; as devils, 249; Indians' description of, 235; regarded as gods, 269

storehouses: description of, 51–52; for garments, 55; instituted by Inca Yupanque, 99; placed every forty leagues from Cuzco, 108

tambo: conquering general to build, 107–108

Temple of the Sun: ordered built in the provinces, 110

Tiaguanaco (town): creation of the world at, 7; Paulo, son of Huayna Capac, born at, 176

time: measurement of, 65–68

Tomebamba (town): Cañares prepared to fight at, 197; Huayna Capac stops at, 182; Yamque Yupanque arrives in, 119

Topa Cuxigualpa (Huascar): receives name, 189. *See also* Huascar

Topa Inca Yupanque *[subentries arranged in chronological order]*: birth of, 93; conquers Andesuyo, 124–127; enters Cuzco with Yamque Yupanque, 116–117; governs with brother, 140; leads expedition to Chile, 147–149; puts down rebellion in Collasuyo, 143–146; puts down rebellion in Andes, 140–142; investiture as Inca and receives principal wife, 119; returns to Cuzco from Andesuyo, 127; shows great generosity, 154; death of, 162

topo (measurement): defined, 120

topo (pin): definition of, 14

Unanchullo (Atahualpa captain): meets with Spaniards, 253–254; named general by Atahualpa, 197; placed in charge of construction at Carangue, 200

Uscovilca (Chanca ruler): prepares to attack Cuzco, 19–26; Viracocha Inca submits to, 20–21; defeated, captured, and killed, 27–30

Valverde, Fray Vicente de, confronts Atahualpa, 264–265

victory ceremony: description of, 87–89

Vilaoma (priest): plots rebellion against Spaniards, 280–283

Viracocha Inca *[subentries arranged in chronological order]*: origin of name, 18; submits to Uscovilca, 19–21; abandons Cuzco, 21; refuses to return to Cuzco, 24–25; attempts to kill Inca Yupanque, 33; establishes town of Caquea Xaquixahuana, 37; rejects royal fringe, 43; returns to Cuzco, 76–80; gives *borla* to Inca Yupanque, 76–80; death of, 79

Viracocha Pacha-yachachic (creator god): description of, 44; Pizarro as, 259; shrine at Cacha, 175; speaks to Inca Yupanque, 29; speaks to Viracocha Inca, 18

viracochas: benefactors of the people, 237–238; description of, 72; duties of, 9–11; as gods, 235; as soldiers, 39

war: bodies of dead returned to Cuzco, 94; discipline of soldiers, 108–109; punishment of defeated, 41–42; treatment of prisoners, 32; victory ceremony, 87–88; war cry, 226

Yamque Yupanque *[subentries arranged in chronological order]*: birth of, 93; Inca Yupanque's favorite, 115; asks Inca Yupanque to give *borla* to another, 121; gives up the *borla*, 124; conquers Chinchasuyo, 115; conquests of, 119–121; gives sister to brother as wife, 119; governs with brother, 140; receives *borla* from Inca Yupanque, 117; dies in Cuzco, 152–153; funeral for, 153–154

yanacona (perpetual servant): origin of, 104; taken in war, 20; in the temple of the Sun, 46, 78, 165

Yucay (Valley of): farmland created in, 170; inspected by Huayna Capac, 169; populated by *mitimaes,* 170; river realigned in, 170

Yungas: description of, 115; rebellion of, 215–216

Yupanque. *See* Pachacuti Inca